American Library Resources

A Bibliographical Guide · Supplement 1961-1970

Robert B. Downs

**Assisted by Elizabeth C. Downs
and John W. Heussman**

American Library Association

Chicago 1972

International Standard Book Number 0-8389-0116-6 (1972)
Library of Congress Catalog Card Number 51-11156

Printed in the United States of America

Contents

Preface

The present volume—*American Library Resources: A Bibliographical Guide, Supplement, 1961-70*—is the second supplement to *American Library Resources: A Bibliographical Guide,* published by the American Library Association in 1951.

The plan and scope of the two supplements are essentially the same as for the basic work: the listing of printed library catalogs, union lists of books and periodicals, descriptions of special collections, surveys of library holdings, calendars of archives and manuscripts, and catalogs of exhibitions. Also included are a number of unpublished bibliographies, chiefly theses and dissertations, since these are usually available in some form of reproduction. The body of the work is classified broadly by the Dewey Decimal System, followed by a detailed index of authors, editors, compilers, libraries and other organizations, subjects, types of material, and occasional titles. Each entry is numbered and intended to be recorded only once, though a few titles may have been repeated inadvertently under different headings. The period covered is 1961-70; however, several 1960 items missed in the first supplement and others issued in early 1971 are included.

It is of interest to note that the number of items listed for the 1961-70 decade, a total of 3,421, is substantially higher than the 1950-61 figure of 2,818, and nearly two thirds as large as the total of 5,578 recorded in the original volume, which covered a 75-year period, from 1875 to 1950.

Grateful acknowledgment is made to the librarians who supplied data on publications relating to the resources of their own institutions. In the case of the larger and more active libraries, especially, a considerable expenditure of time and effort was required to compile a comprehensive listing.

Indispensable editorial assistance in discovering elusive references and in verifying an infinite number of bibliographical details was provided by the two associates listed on the title page, Elizabeth C. Downs and John W. Heussman. The former also carried a major share of responsibility for assembling the extensive index.

The arduous task of preparing the manuscript for publication was in the highly competent hands of Clarabelle Gunning, ably assisted by Deloris Holiman.

Finally, I wish to express warm appreciation to the Council on Library Resources, Inc., whose financial aid made the undertaking possible.

Robert B. Downs

Introduction

Great strides were made during the 1961-70 decade toward increasing the availability of the research resources of American libraries. The fact that the present compilation contains 600 more references than its 1951-60 counterpart is indicative of the accelerated growth of library collections in the United States, increased recognition of the importance of making information on these resources accessible to the scholarly world, and a prevailing spirit of cooperation among research libraries.

Not only did the number of references descriptive of library holdings expand substantially in the course of the 10-year period, but the size, scope, and quality of the published data are equally impressive. Note, for example, the beginning of the reproduction of the *National Union Catalog: Pre-1956 Imprints,* to be completed in 610 volumes; Gale's *Library of Congress and National Union Catalog Author Lists, 1942-1962;* publication of the third edition of the *Union List of Serials in the United States and Canada;* the *National Union Catalog of Manuscript Collections;* scores of local, state, and regional union lists of serials, production of which was facilitated by computer techniques; issuance in book form of the University of California's general library catalogs at Berkeley and Los Angeles; monumental reproductions of general and specialized library catalogs by G. K. Hall and Greenwood; the Harvard shelflist series; and hundreds of similar, but smaller, enterprises.

One of the chief media for publicizing current acquisitions, as well as older collections, is the periodicals issued by a number of individual libraries. Noteworthy are the Library of Congress's *Quarterly Journal of the Library of Congress* and *Information Bulletin, Bulletin of the New York Public Library, Harvard Library Bulletin, Princeton University Library Chronicle, Yale University Library Gazette, Texas Library Chronicle, Pennsylvania Library Chronicle, Rochester Library Bulletin,* Duke University's *Library Notes, Books at Brown, Books and Libraries at Kansas, Columbia Library Columns, Colby Library Quarterly, Indiana Bookman, Books at Iowa,* and *Rutgers Library Journal.* Certain more comprehensive journals also are full of bibliographical data relating to library collections, notably the *Papers of the Bibliographical Society of America; American Archivist* (especially its annual "Writings on Archives, Current Records, and Historical Manuscripts"); the *American Historical Review* (especially its periodical compilations of "Recently Published Articles"); and the Association of Research Libraries's *Foreign Acquisitions Newsletter.* Also useful is H. W. Wilson's *Library Literature.*

As in the past, certain libraries were far more prolific than others in publications relating to their resources. The Library of Congress was well in the lead, both in number of titles and in the variety and volume of its holdings. An examination of the index reveals that other extraordinarily active institutions were the National Archives, New York Public Library, Harvard, Yale, Princeton, UCLA, Texas, and Stanford (Hoover Institution and the Libraries). Also productive were Cornell, Dartmouth, Duke, Huntington, Illinois, Indiana's Lilly Library, Iowa, Newberry, North Carolina, Ohio State, Pennsylvania State, Syracuse, Virginia, National Agricultural Library, and National Medical Library. Other major libraries are somewhat scantily represented, e.g., Berkeley, Chicago, Michigan, Minnesota, Northwestern, Pennsylvania, and Wisconsin.

The picture of American library resources presented here is necessarily uneven, since it does not reflect the strength of libraries from which publications were lacking. In particular, important collections newly acquired may not yet have been covered by catalogs, guides, or other descriptive material.

Significant changes in library collecting interests are apparent from a review of bibliographical publishing during the past decade. Most striking are the global concerns of American research libraries—a fairly recent phenomenon stimulated by Public Law 480, the Farmington Plan, the National Program for Acquisitions and

Cataloging, and the Latin American Cooperative Acquisition Project. The present national goal is to acquire for university and other research-type libraries in the United States all publications of potential value emanating from every corner of the world: Europe, Asia, Africa, Australia, North and South America, and lesser geographical units. If the undertaking is as successful as anticipated, the world's publishing output will come to the United States promptly after production, be cataloged at home or abroad, and be ready for immediate use.

Social problems afflicting our society also emerge in the present record. Note, for example, items 817 to 851 on Negroes, a considerable increase over the previous decade and evidence of an acute awareness of racial tensions; and items 1700 to 1705, the beginning of a lively concern with problems of pollution and environmental control.

A prime influence on bibliographical activities and research library development since 1956 has been the Council on Library Resources. Its support has made possible such projects of basic importance to the research world as the third edition of the *Union List of Serials in the United States and Canada,* the *National Union Catalog of Manuscript Collections,* the *International Inventory of Musical Sources,* the *National Register of Microform Masters,* and numerous smaller undertakings, including the present work.

General

GENERAL BIBLIOGRAPHY AND REFERENCE BOOKS

1. Bako, Elemer. "Finnish and Hungarian reference works." Library of Congress quarterly journal of current acquisitions, 20 (1963), 101-10.
   Report on acquisitions, Library of Congress.

2. Balys, John P. "Baltic encyclopedias and biographical directories." Quarterly journal of the Library of Congress, 22 (1965), 270-73.
   Report on acquisitions, Library of Congress.

3. Emory University Library. Selected indexing and abstracting services in the Emory University Library. Atlanta, Ga., 1969. 43p.
   Detailed descriptions of 39 services, excluding those most commonly known; covers all major fields.

4. Gropp, Arthur E. Bibliography of Latin American bibliographies, 3d ed. N.Y.: Scarecrow, 1968. 515p.
   Copies located in institutions other than the Columbus Memorial Library and Library of Congress. Contains 7,210 references.

5. Harvard University Library. Bibliography and bibliography periodicals: classification schedule, classified listing by call number, alphabetical listing by author or title, chronological listing. Cambridge, Mass., 1966. 1,066p. (Widener Library shelflist, no.7)
   Lists 19,586 titles.

6. ———. Reference collections. Cambridge, Mass., 1970. 130p. (Widener Library shelflist, no.33)
   Lists about 5,000 titles.

7. ———. Reference collections shelved in the Reading Room and Acquisitions Dept. Cambridge, Mass.: Harvard Univ. Pr., 1966. 187p. (Widener Library shelflist, no.8)
   Classified listing by call numbers, alphabetical listing by author and title.

8. Hoskins, Janina W. "Bibliographic activities in Poland." Quarterly journal of the Library of Congress, 21 (1964), 225-27.
   Report on acquisitions, Library of Congress.

9. New England Board of Higher Education. Joint list of the major microfilm holdings of the New England state university libraries and the Vermont Council of Academic Libraries. Wellesley, Mass., 1970. 90p.
   A project of the New England Library Information Network.

10. Newberry Library. The circle of knowledge; encyclopedias past and present, comp. by James M. Wells. Chicago, 1968. 56p.
   Catalog of an exhibition to commemorate the 200th anniversary of the Encyclopaedia Britannica; includes items dating from 1472 to 1968.

11. Philadelphia Bibliographical Center and Union Library Catalogue. Union list of microfilms; cumulation 1949-1959. Ann Arbor, Mich.: J. W. Edwards, 1961. 2v.
   Lists more than 52,000 microfilms reported by 200 U.S. and Canadian libraries.

12. Price, Arnold H. "Germany: recent bibliographies and reference works." Library of Congress quarterly journal of current acquisitions, 29 (1962), 21-29.
   Report on acquisitions, Library of Congress.

13. Special Libraries Association, Translations Center. Translations register index, June 15, 1967- , v.1- . Chicago, 1967- . Semimonthly.
   Housed in John Crerar Library, Chicago.

14. Stanford University, Hoover Institution. Guide to Russian reference books, by Karol Maichel. Stanford, Calif., 1962-67. 3v. (In progress) (Bibliographical series, no.10, 18, 32).

v.1, general bibliographies and reference books; v.2, history, ethnography, and geography; v.5, science, technology, and medicine.

15. Tilton, Eva Maude. A union list of publications in opaque microforms, 2d ed. N.Y.: Scarecrow, 1964. 744p.

16. U.S. Library of Congress. National register of microfilm masters. Wash., 1966. 251p.

Listing of master negatives, with library locations; includes books, pamphlets, serials, newspapers, and foreign dissertations.

17. ———. General Reference and Bibliography Division. Current national bibliographies, comp. by Helen F. Conover. Westport, Conn.: Greenwood, 1968. 132p.

18. West Virginia University Library. The development of a bibliographic center in the West Virginia region; final report, 1966. Morgantown, 1966. 23p.

GOVERNMENT PUBLICATIONS

General

19. Henderson, James W. "The acquisition and preservation of foreign official gazettes." Farmington Plan newsletter, no. 31 (May 1970), 1-24.

p.6, "Official gazettes microfilmed in New Delhi and available on positive microfilm from the Library of Congress"; p.7-21, "Gazettes available on microfilm from the New York Public Library collection."

20. ———. "Supplemental list of foreign official gazettes." Foreign acquisitions newsletter, Association of Research Libraries, 32 (Oct. 1970), 23-24.

Lists gazettes in New York Public Library.

21. United Nations, Dag Hammarskjöld Library. Annotated list of official gazettes. N.Y., 1962. 70p.

22. ———, Secretariat. List of libraries and information centres receiving United Nations material. N.Y., 1965. 61, 3, 3, 3p.

23. University Microfilms. Latin American serial documents: a holdings list, by Rosa Q. Mesa. Ann Arbor, Mich., 1968. 4v.

v.1, Colombia; v.2, Brazil; v.3, Cuba; v.4, Mexico—the first of a projected series of 19v. Record of holdings of Latin American official documents in major U.S. depositories.

United States

24. Alaska State Library. State publications received. Juneau, 1965- . Annual.

25. Arizona Dept. of Library and Archives. Annual checklist of publications of the state of Arizona received by the Dept. of Library and Archives during the fiscal year. Phoenix, 1956-57- .

26. Arkansas, University, Library. Checklist of Arkansas state publications received by the University of Arkansas Library. Fayetteville, 1943- , no.1- . Semiannual.

27. California State Library. California state publications, Sacramento, 1947- , v.1- . Monthly with annual cumulations.

28. Colorado Division of State Archives and Public Records. Checklist, Colorado publications. Denver, Jan. 1956- , v.1- . Quarterly.

29. Connecticut State Library. Checklist of publications of Connecticut state agencies received by the Connecticut State Library. Hartford, 1962- . Frequency varies.

30. Downs, Robert B. "Government publications in American libraries." Library trends, 15 (1966), 178-94.

Listing of principal repositories of federal, state, and local documents in U.S. libraries.

31. Florida Atlantic University Library. A keyword-in-context index to Florida public documents in the Florida Atlantic University, ed. by Walter L. Newsome. Tallahassee: Fla. State Library, 1969. 127p.

32. Florida State Library. Florida public documents. Tallahassee, Feb. 1968- . Monthly, with annual cumulations.

List of publications of Florida official agencies received by Florida State Library, Tallahassee.

33. Florida, University, Libraries, Documents Dept. Short-title checklist of official Florida publications received. Gainesville, 1942-68, no.1-162.

Superseded by Florida State Library's Florida public documents.

34. Georgia State Library. Checklist of official publications of the state of Georgia. Atlanta, Jan. 1948- . Quarterly.

35. Hawaii Library Association, Hawaiiana Section. Official publications of the Territory of Hawaii, 1900-1959. Honolulu: Public Archives, Dept. of Accounting and General Services, 1962. 250p.

Based on holdings of Hawaiian libraries and state agencies.

36. Hawaii State Library. Hawaii documents. Honolulu, Jan. 1967- , v.1- . Bimonthly, with annual cumulation.

37. Idaho State Library. The Idaho librarian. Pocatello, Idaho, 1945- , v.1- . Quarterly.

"Partial checklist of Idaho state publications," included annually since 1964, is "compiled chiefly from holdings of the Idaho State Library, the University of Idaho, Idaho State University, and the Idaho State Historical Society."

38. Illinois, Secretary of State. Publications of the state of Illinois. Springfield, Jan. 1959- . Semiannual.

Based on Illinois State Library's holdings.

39. Indiana State Library. Library occurrent. Indianapolis, April 1906- , v.1- . Quarterly.

Records Indiana state publications received by State Library.

40. Iowa, University, Library. Iowa documents. Iowa City, Jan. 1956- , no.1- . Quarterly.

41. Kansas State Library, State Documents Division. Checklist of official publications of the state of Kansas received by the State Library. Topeka, May 1953- , v.1- . 4 nos. a year.

42. Kansas, University, Governmental Research Center. Bibliography of the official publications of Kansas, 1854-1958, by Bessie E. Wilder. Lawrence, 1965. 318p.

Locates copies of 20,000 printed items in 7 Kansas depository libraries.

43. Kentucky State Archives and Records Service. Checklist of Kentucky state publications. Frankfort, 1962- . Annual.

44. Louisiana, Dept. of State. Public documents of Louisiana distributed to depository libraries. Baton Rouge, March 1949- . Monthly.

Contains list of depository libraries.

45. Maine State Library. Checklist of state of Maine publications received. Augusta, 1941- . Quarterly.

46. Massachusetts State Library. Commonwealth of Massachusetts publications received at Massachusetts State Library. Boston, 1962- . Monthly.

Annual cumulative listing.

47. ———. Massachusetts executive department publications, 1962-1966: cumulative listing of publications of Massachusetts executive agencies (with some selected publications of the General Court) received at Massachusetts State Library during 1962-1966, with index. Boston, 1968. 77p.

48. Michigan State Library. Michigan documents. Lansing, July 1952- . Frequency varies.

49. Minnesota Historical Society Library. Minnesota state documents received in the Minnesota Historical Society Library. St. Paul, Jan. 1970- , v.1- . Quarterly.

50. Minnesota State Library. Official publications. St. Paul, 1946- . Irregular.

51. Mississippi, Secretary of State. Public documents of the state of Mississippi. Jackson, July 1966- . Semiannual.

Contains list of Mississippi depository libraries.

52. Missouri State Library. Checklist of official publications of state of Missouri. Jefferson City, 1951- . Monthly, with biennial cumulations since 1959.

53. Nevada State Library. Nevada official publications. Carson City, March 1953- . Irregular, with annual cumulation.

54. New Hampshire State Library. Checklist of New Hampshire state departments' publications. Concord, 1942- . Frequency varies.

55. New Jersey State Library. Checklist of official New Jersey publications. Trenton, July 1965- , v.1- . Bimonthly.

Lists only items received by State Library.

56. New York State Library. Annotated list of selected United States government publications available to depository libraries, prep. by Sylvia Mechanic. Albany, 1968. 286p.

57. ———. Checklist of official publications of the state of New York. Albany, 1947- . Monthly.

Cumulations for v.1-15 (1947-62), 16-21 (1962-67), 22 (1968), and 23 (1969) have been published.

58. North Carolina, University, Library. North Carolina publications; a checklist of official state publications. Chapel Hill, August 1952- , no.1- . Bimonthly.

Issued in cooperation with North Carolina State Library.

59. North Dakota State Library Commission. North Dakota state publications. Bismarck, 1965- , no.1- . Semiannual.

60. Ohio Library Foundation. Checklist publications of the state of Ohio, 1803-1952. Columbus, 1964. 131p.

Union list of publications on file in Ohio State Library, Ohio State University Library, and 3 other Ohio libraries.

61. Ohio State Library. Selected publications of the state of Ohio. Columbus, Dec. 1945- , no.1- . Quarterly.

62. Oregon State Library. Checklist of official Oregon publications. Salem, Jan. 1951- , no.1- . Quarterly.

63. Pennsylvania State Library. Checklist of official Pennsylvania publications. Harrisburg, Sept. 1963- , v.1- . Monthly.

64. Rhode Island State Library. Checklist of publications of state agencies. Providence, 1956- .

Each issue covers one or more years.

65. South Carolina, Dept. of Archives and History. A checklist of South Carolina state publications. Columbia, 1950- , no.1- . Annual.

66. Stanford University Libraries. United States government publications at Stanford; a selective list, comp. by Ann W. Latta and Judy Fair. Stanford, Calif., 1969. 10p.

67. Tennessee State Library and Archives. A list of Tennessee state publications. Nashville, 1954- , no.1- . Annual.

68. Texas State Library, Documents Division. Checklist for official state publications. Austin, 1921-67. Superseded by Library's Texas state documents, Jan. 1968- . Monthly.

69. U.S. Library of Congress, Card Division. Non-GPO imprints received in the Library of Congress, July 1967 through December 1969; a selective checklist. Wash.: The Library, 1970. 73p.

Lists serials, important monographs, and pamphlets.

70. ---, Processing Dept. Monthly checklist of state publications. Wash.: Govt. Print. Off., 1910- .

A record of state documents currently received by the Library of Congress.

71. ---, Serial Division. Popular names of U.S. government reports; a catalog, comp. by Donald F. Wisdom and William P. Kilroy. Wash.: Govt. Print. Off., 1966. 32p.

Lists 479 reports, published during past 75 years, identified with individuals. All held by Library of Congress.

72. Utah State Library Commission. Official publications of the state of Utah. Salt Lake City, July 1970- , v.1- .

73. Utah, University, Libraries. Public serials list, 1970-71. Salt Lake City, 1970. 528p.

74. Virginia State Library. Checklist of Virginia state publications. Richmond, 1926- . Annual.

75. ---. Virginia state publications in print. Richmond, 1965- . Annual.

76. Washington State Library. Washington state publications. Olympia, April 1952- , v.1- . Quarterly.

77. West Virginia, Archives and History Dept. Short-title checklist of West Virginia state publications. Charleston, 1947- . Annual.

78. Wisconsin State Historical Society. Wisconsin public documents. Madison, 1917- , v.1- . Frequency varies.

LIBRARY SCIENCE

79. Columbia University, School of Library Service Library. Dictionary catalog. Boston: G. K. Hall, 1962 7v.

Lists 34,000 titles in 72,400 volumes.

80. Kentucky, University, Libraries. Librarians and archivists on postage stamps; a guide to an exhibit in the University of Kentucky Library, by John Henry Richter. Lexington, 1962. 34p. (Occasional contribution, no.117)

81. Lowenhaupt, Warren H. "The Andrews memorial

bookplate collection of Irene D. Andrews Pace." Yale University Library gazette, 37 (1963), 178-81.

Describes collection of 150,000 bookplates of all periods and countries, received by Yale Library.

82. Missouri, University, Library. Library science periodicals; a title listing of periodicals relating to library work and library service in the University of Missouri Library. Columbia, 1970. 39p.

83. Special Libraries Association. Guide to the SLA loan collection of classification schemes and subject heading lists on deposit at Western Reserve University, comp. by Bertha R. Barden and Barbara Denison, 5th ed. N.Y., 1961. 97p.

Lists 788 classification schemes and other systems for organization of special collections.

84. U.S. Library of Congress, African Section. African libraries, book production, and archives; a list of references, comp. by Helen F. Conover. Wash.: The Library, 1962. 64p.

85. ---, Slavic and Central European Division. West German library developments since 1945, with special emphasis on rebuilding of research libraries, by Gisela von Busse. Wash.: The Library, 1962. 82p.

Includes a bibliography.

GENERAL SURVEYS OF LIBRARIES

86. American library directory, 1970-1971, 27th ed. N.Y.: Bowker, 1970. 1,174p.

Includes number of volumes and listing of special collections and special subjects under individual libraries.

87. Ash, Lee, and Lorenz, Denis. Subject collections; a guide to special book collections and subject emphases as reported by university, college, public, and special libraries in the United States and Canada, 3d ed. N.Y.: Bowker, 1967. 1,221p. 2d ed., 1961.

References to about 40,000 collections.

88. Benton, Mildred, and Ottersen, Signe. Roster of federal libraries. Wash.: George Washington Univ. Medical Center, Dept. of Medical and Public Affairs, Biological Sciences Communication Project, 1970. 282p.

Directory of federal libraries, wherever located, in three parts: agency, geographic location, subject.

89. Bowker annual of library and book trade information. N.Y.: Bowker, 1956- . Annual.

Includes statistics of various types of libraries.

90. Connecticut State Library. Directory of subject strengths in Connecticut libraries, ed. by Charles E. Funk, Jr. Hartford, 1968. 1v. (Various pagings) Supplement. Hartford, 1968.

91. Council of Higher Educational Institutions in New York City. A directory of resources of cooperating libraries in metropolitan New York, 3d ed. N.Y., 1965. Unpaged.

Describes collections and services of academic, special, and public libraries, with subject guide.

92. Downs, Robert B. Resources of Missouri libraries. Jefferson City: Mo. State Library, 1966. 190p.

"Special collections in Missouri libraries," alphabetically arranged by subjects, p.135-56.

93. ---. Resources of North Carolina libraries. Raleigh, N.C.: Governor's Commission on Library Resources, 1965. 236p.

"Special collections in North Carolina libraries," p.177-90; "Archive and manuscript collections in North Carolina," p.197-212.

94. ---. University library statistics. Wash.: Assoc. of Research Libraries, 1969. 129p.

Comprehensive statistics on library resources and other aspects of 50 major libraries.

95. English, Thomas H. Roads to research; distinguished library collections of the Southeast. Athens: Univ. of Ga. Pr., 1968. 116p.

Descriptions of special collections in history and literature held by 28 member libraries of the Association of Southeastern Research Libraries.

96. Garrison, Guy G., and Slanker, Barbara O. Library resources in the North Country area of New York State. Urbana: Library Research Center, Graduate School of Library Science, Univ. of Ill., 1966. 104p.

97. Hendricks, Donald D. "Special collections in larger college libraries" [in Illinois]. Illinois libraries, 47 (1965), 819-75.

98. ---. "Special collections in smaller college libraries" [in Illinois]. Illinois libraries, 47 (1965), 542-94.

99. Holley, Edward G., and Hendricks, Donald D. Resources of Texas libraries. Austin: Coordinating Board, Tex. College and Univ. System, 1968. 125p.

Chapter X, "Subject Strength in Texas Libraries," describes special collections, in alphabetical order.

100. International library directory, 1st ed. London: A. P. Wales Organization, 1963. 1,083p.

Lists libraries around world, including number of volumes and subject specializations.

101. Jackson, William V. A handbook of American library resources, 2d ed. Champaign, Ill.: Illini Union Bookstore, 1962. 88p.

Includes statistics of American scholarly and research libraries.

102. ———. Resources of research libraries; a selected bibliography. Pittsburgh: Univ. Book Center, 1969. 65p.

Listing of works describing and evaluating library resources, cooperative agreements among libraries, union catalogs, and related topics.

103. Joint Venture. Library and reference facilities in the area of the District of Columbia, 8th ed., ed. by Mildred Benton. Wash., 1971. 217p.

Lists 426 libraries, with data on hours, regulations, and resources.

104. Kansas State Library. Survey of public library facilities and book resources in Kansas, by Claire Vincent. Topeka, 1969. 39p.

105. Kruzas, Anthony T. Directory of special libraries and information centers, 2d ed. Detroit: Gale, 1968. 2v.

Describes resources and services of 11,577 libraries; alphabetically arranged with subject, geographic, and personnel indexes.

106. ———. Special libraries and information centers: a statistical report on special library resources in the United States. Detroit: Gale, 1965. 42p.

107. Liles, Annette. "Library acquisitions, 1962-1963." South Atlantic bulletin, 29 (May 1964), 6-8.

Describes special collections in humanities and types of research publications acquired by certain libraries in South Atlantic states.

108. Linton, Howard P. Survey of the research library resources on Asia, Africa, Russia and East Europe, and Latin America in New York State. Albany: Univ. of the State of N.Y., 1964. 37p.

109. Long, Marie Ann. Directory of library resources in Wisconsin. Urbana: Library Research Center and Madison: Wis. Library Assoc., 1964. 1v. Unpaged.

Describes resources and services of 155 libraries.

110. McComb, Ralph W. Guide to the resources of the regional library resource centers of Pennsylvania. Harrisburg: Dept. of Public Instruction, 1967. 57p.

111. Maine State Library. Special subject resources in Maine, 1967, comp. by Louise Hazelton. Augusta, 1967. 52p.

"A directory of special subject resources in Maine."

112. Moore, John H. Research materials in South Carolina; a guide. Columbia: Univ. of S.C. Pr., 1967. 346p.

Lists specialized library resources and special collections, and locates newspaper and periodical files. Emphasizes unpublished materials and serial publications.

113. National Library Week, Missouri State Committee. A catalogue of the specialized libraries and library collections of the state of Missouri. Columbia?, 1963? 34p.

114. New York State Library, Division of Library Development. The 3 R's: reference and research library resources. Albany, 1969. 17p.

115. Pacific Northwest Library Association. College, university and special libraries of the Pacific Northwest. Seattle: Univ. of Wash. Pr., 1961. 310p.

Part II, p.107-270, discusses law and medical libraries, their collections and services.

116. Pennsylvania Dept. of Public Instruction. Library resources and facilities at Pennsylvania institutions of higher education, 1966-67. Harrisburg, 1967. 29p.

117. Reichmann, Felix, and others. Library resources in the Mid-Hudson Valley. Poughkeepsie, N.Y.: Mid-Hudson Libraries and Ramapo-Catskill Library System, 1965. 511p.

118. Research Centers Directory, 3d ed. Detroit: Gale, 1968. 884p.

Lists some libraries.

119. Robertson, Giles B. "Directory of Illinois special collections." Illinois libraries, 49 (1967), 960-70.

120. Skau, Dorothy B., and others. "Directory of special libraries and special collections in Louisiana." Louisiana Library Association bulletin, 29 (Fall 1966), 97-103.

121. Southeastern Library Association, Reference Ser-

vices Division. A guide to union catalogs in the Southeastern United States. Ann Arbor, Mich.: Cushing-Malloy, 1965. 26p.

Describes 7 union catalogs, with lists of libraries included.

122. Special Libraries Association. Special Libraries Association directory 1969-70. N.Y., 1969. 219p.

Directory of members; alphabetical, geographical, and subject area lists.

123. ———, Boston Chapter. Directory of special libraries, Boston, vicinity and member libraries in New England, 6th ed. Boston, 1961. Unpaged.

Describes resources and services of 244 libraries.

124. ———, Colorado Chapter. Specialized library resources of Colorado, 1966, ed. by Lawrence E. and Carolyn M. Leonard. Denver, 1966. 72p.

Information on 169 special libraries and specialized collections.

125. ——— ———. Specialized library resources of Colorado, 2d ed., ed. by Allen Wynne. Denver, 1970. 103p.

126. ———, New York Chapter. Special libraries of Greater New York, 11th ed. N.Y., 1967. Unpaged.

Describes resources and services of 8,232 libraries.

127. ———, Southern California Chapter. Directory of special libraries of Southern California, 3d ed. Los Angeles, 1968. 125p.

Describes resources of 439 special libraries in area.

128. ———, Upstate New York Chapter. A directory of special libraries and research resources in New York State. Rochester, 1966. 37p.

Notes subject emphases and special collections in 343 libraries.

129. Special Libraries Council of Philadelphia and Vicinity. Directory of libraries and information sources in the Philadelphia area, 12th ed. Philadelphia, 1968. 189p.

Describes collections and services of 431 libraries within 200-mile radius of Philadelphia.

130. Stevenson, Noel C. Search and research, the researcher's handbook; a guide to official records and library sources for investigators, historians, genealogists, lawyers, and librarians, rev. ed. Salt Lake City: Deseret Book Co., 1964. 364p.

Lists libraries, historical societies and archives, etc.

131. Thompson, Donald E., and Rothacker, J. Michael. Directory of special and subject collections in Indiana. Bloomington, Ind., 1970. 94p. (Ind. library studies, report no. 12)

Arranged by subjects.

132. U.S. Dept. of Health, Education, and Welfare, Office of Education, Bureau of Research. A study of resources and major subject holdings available in U.S. federal libraries maintaining extensive or unique collections of research materials. Wash., 1970. 670p.

Guide to research resources of 188 federal libraries, including books, periodicals, maps, manuscripts, etc.; covers all fields. "List of special collections," p.545-56.

133. White, William Chapman. "Some special collections in New York State libraries." Bookmark, New York State Library, 22 (1963), 223-26.

134. Williams, Edwin E. Farmington Plan handbook, rev. ed. Ithaca, N.Y.: Assoc. of Research Libraries, 1961. 141p.

Lists subject and area assignments to individual libraries for collecting foreign research materials.

135. World guide to libraries, 3d ed. N.Y.: Bowker, 1970. 4v.

Covers 25,000 special, university, and public libraries in 157 countries; contains subject index to collections.

SURVEYS OF INDIVIDUAL LIBRARIES

136. Brigham Young University Library. A survey of the library of Brigham Young University, by Robert B. Downs. Provo, Utah, 1969. 165p.

Analysis of library's special collections and other resources, p.88-115.

137. California, University, Library. A guide to research materials for graduate students, by Ardis Lodge. Los Angeles, 1964. 29p.

138. California, University, Libraries. Libraries of the University of California, by Russell H. Fitzgibbon. Berkeley: President's Office, Univ. of Calif., 1964. 93p.

Describes collections on all 9 campuses of University of California.

139. Center for Research Libraries. Handbook, the Center for Research Libraries. Chicago, 1969. Unpaged.

Inventory and description of collections in Center for Research Libraries.

140. ———. Library materials available for research. Chicago, 1970. 13p.

Descriptions, by subject or type of material, of collections in Center for Research Libraries.

141. Emory University, Robert W. Woodruff Library for Advanced Studies. Special collections. Atlanta, Ga., 1970. Unpaged.

Descriptions of special collections in Emory University Library.

142. Florida, University, Libraries. A guide to the special collections at the University of Florida Libraries. Gainesville, 1967. 27p.

143. Hodges, John I. H. "Special collections in the University of the South Library." Tennessee librarian, 16 (Spring 1964), 80-81.

144. Idaho, University, Library. Special collections of the University of Idaho Library. Moscow, 1969. Unpaged.

145. Kansas, University, Libraries. A guide to the collections, by Alexandra Mason. Lawrence, 1969. 31p.

A guide to special collections in University of Kansas Libraries.

146. McCoy, Ralph E. "Morris Library and Lovejoy Library, Southern Illinois University." Illinois libraries, 47 (1965), 854-60.

Brief description of the libraries' special collections of books and manuscripts.

147. Mann, Charles. "The Williamscote Library." Library history, 2, no.1 (1970), 11-12.

Eighteenth-century gentleman's library from England preserved as a special collection in Pennsylvania State University Library.

148. New York Public Library. Search and research; the collections and uses of the New York Public Library, by William K. Zinsser. N.Y., 1961. 46p.

149. New York State Library. For the government and people of this state; a history of the New York State Library, by Cecil R. Roseberry. Albany, 1970. 126p.

Describes some of New York State Library's major collections.

150. Newberry Library. An uncommon collection of uncommon collections: the Newberry Library, by Lawrence W. Towner. Chicago, 1970. 36p.

Describes outstanding special collections in Newberry Library.

151. Ohio State University Libraries. Directory of specialized information centers, services, and libraries of the Ohio State University, by Howard W. Dillon. Columbus, 1965. 13p.

152. Olson, Richard D., and Panofsky, Hans E. "Charles Deering Library, Northwestern University." Illinois libraries, 47 (1965), 845-53.

Describes rare book holdings and special collections, such as Africana.

153. Pierpont Morgan Library. An introduction to the Pierpont Morgan Library, by Frederick B. Adams, Jr. N.Y., 1964. 32p.

History of collection and guide to library's holdings.

154. Pomfret, John E. "The Huntington Library: fifteen years' growth, 1951-1966." California Historical Society quarterly, 45 (Sept. 1966), 241-57.

A general account of growth of collections.

155. Rosenthal, Robert. "Harper Library, University of Chicago." Illinois libraries, 47 (Nov. 1965), 821-29.

Describes special collections in University of Chicago Library.

156. Stanford University, Hoover Institution. Hoover Institution on War, Revolution and Peace; report 1966-1969. Stanford, Calif., 1969. 90p.

Includes description of Hoover Library's resources.

157. Texas, University, Humanities Research Center. A creative century; collections at the University of Texas. Austin, 1964. 72p.

Descriptions of special collections.

158. Tucker, Louis L. "Collections and exhibits; the Historical and Philosophical Society of Ohio: its resources." Ohio history, 71 (Oct. 1962), 254-61.

159. Virginia, University, Library. The Tracy W. McGregor Library; three decades of development 1939-1969; a selection of books, documents, maps and manuscripts acquired since 1939. Charlottesville, 1970. 34p.

160. Wells, James M. "The Newberry Library holdings." Restoration and 18th century theatre research, 3 (May 1964), 11-14.

161. Wisconsin, University, Library. Renaissance, Reformation, and seventeenth century in the Library of the University of Wisconsin: a description of special collections, by Louis Kaplan and others. Madison, 1966. 14p.

162. Wright, Louis B. The Folger Library; two decades of growth: an informal account. Charlottesville: Univ. Pr. of Va., 1968. 300p.

Discusses resources.

GENERAL LIBRARY CATALOGS

163. American Antiquarian Society, Worcester, Mass. Dictionary catalog of the holdings through 1821. Westport, Conn.: Greenwood, 1970. 20v.

Records Society's valuable collection of pre-1821 American imprints, genealogy, and literary first editions.

164. Boston Athenaeum Library. Catalogue of the Library of the Boston Athenaeum, 1807-1871. Boston: G. K. Hall, 1969. 5v.

Reprint of famous 19th-century catalog.

165. Boston University Library. Index to the classed catalog of the Boston University Libraries; a relative index based on the Library of Congress classification, 2d ed., comp. by Mary Darrah Herrick. Boston: G. K. Hall, 1964. 2v.

166. California, University, Library. Author-title catalog, University of California Library (Berkeley). Boston: G. K. Hall, 1963. 115v.

Catalog of approximately 2,800,000 volumes at Berkeley.

167. ———. Dictionary catalog, University of California Library (Los Angeles). Boston: G. K. Hall, 1963. 129v.

Reproduction of 2,703,000 cards representing all divisions of UCLA Library.

168. Center for Research Libraries, Chicago. Center for Research Libraries catalogue. London, 1969-70. 6v.

v.1-5, monographs; v.6, newspapers; v.7 (to be published in 1971), serials. Includes only cataloged holdings of Center.

169. Columbia University, Teachers College Library. Dictionary catalog of the Teachers College Library, Columbia University. Boston: G. K. Hall, 1970. 36v.

170. Evans, Marjorie D. Descriptive and subject catalog of the Library Company books in the Alexandria Room of the Alexandria, Virginia library, pt.1, with a historical introduction. Wash., 1967. 130*l.* (Master's thesis, School of Library Science, Catholic Univ. of America)

171. Florida Atlantic University Library. Catalog. Sept. 1964. Boca Raton, 1964. 9v. Authors, 463p., Supplements 1-2; titles, 471p., Supplements 1-2; Subjects, 568p., Supplements 1-2.

172. Folger Shakespeare Library. Catalog of printed books of the Folger Shakespeare Library (Washington, D.C.). Boston: G. K. Hall, 1970. 28v.

173. Frazee, Helen D. Catalog of books, pamphlets, articles, and periodicals shelved in the library of the New Almaden Museum. Los Altos, Calif.; The author, 1970. 194p.

Museum devoted to history, Indians, archeology, mineralogy, etc.; catalog of supporting library.

174. Herrick, Mary Darrah. "The classified catalog at Boston University, 1948-1964." Library resources and technical services, 8 (1964), 289-300.

Describes growth and subject coverage.

175. John Crerar Library, Chicago. Author-title catalog. Boston: G. K. Hall, 1967. 35v.

Reproduction of catalog of 563,000 cards.

176. ———. Classified subject catalog. Boston: G. K. Hall, 1967. 42v.

177. ———. Subject index to the classified subject catalog. Boston: G. K. Hall, 1967. 610p.

178. Peabody Institute Library. Catalogue of the Library of the Peabody Institute, 1883-1905 (Baltimore). Boston: G. K. Hall, 1962. 13v.

Reissue of a famous catalog.

179. Princeton University Library. The Julian Street Library; a preliminary list of titles, comp. by Warren B. Kuhn. N.Y.: Bowker, 1966. 789p.

Catalog of undergraduate library collection at Princeton; 8,400 titles listed.

180. Southern Illinois University Library. Catalog of Morris Library: author-title. Carbondale, 1965. 39v. Supplement 1. Carbondale, 1968. 5v. Supplement 2. Carbondale, 1970. 6v.

181. Stanford University, Hoover Institution. The li-

brary catalogs of the Hoover Institution on War, Revolution and Peace, Stanford University. Boston: G. K. Hall, 1969. 88v.

Contents: Western-language collections, 63v.; Western-language serials and newspapers, 3v.; Chinese collection, 13v.; Japanese collection, 7v.; Arabic collection, 1v.; Turkish and Persian collections, 1v.

182. Stanford University Libraries. Undergraduate Library catalog, 4th ed. Stanford, Calif.: 1967-70. 12v.

Lists 56,000 titles; subject catalog, 4v.; author-title catalog, 5v.; audio catalog, 3v.

183. Tennessee State Library and Archives. Adult book catalog of the Tennessee Regional Library System. Nashville, 1968. 3v.

184. U.S. Dept. of the Interior. Dictionary catalog of the Department Library, Boston: G. K. Hall, 1967. 37v. First supplement. 1968. 4v.

185. U.S. Library of Congress. Library of Congress catalog. Books: subjects; a cumulative list of works represented by Library of Congress printed cards, 1960-1964. Ann Arbor, Mich.: J. W. Edwards, 1965. 25v. 1965- ; Wash.: Library of Congress, 1966- . Quarterly with annual cumulations.

186. ———. National union catalog, 1952-1955 imprints; an author list representing Library of Congress printed cards and titles reported by other American libraries. Ann Arbor, Mich.: J. W. Edwards, 1961. 30v.

187. ———. National union catalog, pre-1956 imprints; a cumulative author list representing Library of Congress printed cards and titles reported by other American libraries. London: Mansell, 1968- . v.1- .

A monumental work, to be completed over a 10-year period in 610 volumes, which will contain 10,000,000 entries and indicate locations in more than 700 libraries.

188. ———. National union catalog; a cumulative author list representing Library of Congress printed cards and titles reported by other American libraries, 1958-1962. N.Y.: Rowman and Littlefield, 1963. 54v.

Includes 1956-57 imprints.

189. ———. Library of Congress and National union catalog author lists, 1942-1962: a master cumulation. Detroit: Gale, 1969- , v.1- . (In progress)

Cumulation of 4 supplements to basic set entitled Catalog of books represented by Library of Congress printed cards, issued to July 31, 1942.

190. ———. National union catalog. Register of additional locations, 1963-1967. Ann Arbor, Mich.: J. W. Edwards, 1969. 8v. (v. 60-67 of National union catalog, 1963-1967). Supplements: 1968-69. Wash., 1969-70. 2v.

Books for Blind and Physically Handicapped

191. American Foundation for the Blind. Dictionary catalog of the M. C. Migel Memorial Library (New York City). Boston: G. K. Hall, 1966. 2v.

192. Auburn University Library. Holdings in speech and hearing sciences, comp. by Curtis R. Smith. Auburn, Ala.: Speech and Hearing Clinic, Auburn Univ., 1969. 41p.

193. Bray, Robert S. "Books for the blind." D C libraries, 32 (July 1961), 40-44.

Discussion of Library of Congress collection.

194. Gallaudet College Library. Dictionary catalog on deafness and the deaf, Gallaudet College Library (Washington, D.C.). Boston: G. K. Hall, 1970. 2v.

195. U.S. Library of Congress, Division for the Blind and Physically Handicapped. Books on magnetic tape. Wash., 1968. 48p.

Books on taped recordings for blind and physically handicapped.

196. ———, Division for the Blind. Reading for profit; an annotated list of selected press braille books, talking books, and books on magnetic tape. Wash., 1963. 29p.

197. ———, Division for the Blind and Physically Handicapped. Talking books–adult. Wash., 1967-68. 2v.

Covers acquisitions for 1964-67.

198. ——— ———. Talking books–for younger readers; braille and talking books. Wash., 1967-68. 2v.

Acquisitions for 1964-67.

199. ———, Division for the Blind. Talking books provided by the Library of Congress, 1955-1961. Wash., 1962. 185p. Supplement, 1962-63. 1964. 94p.; Index, 1965. 16p.

200. Washington State Library. Dimension: selected bibliographies on blindness. Olympia, 1967. 10p.

Based on collections in Seattle Public Library's Division for the Blind and Physically Handicapped and the Washington State Library's Institutional Library Services Division.

PERIODICALS, NEWSPAPERS, AND JOURNALISM

General

201. A.C.C.K. union list of serials, 1968. McPherson, Kans.: Associated Colleges of Central Kans., 1968. 107p.
Lists holdings of 6 colleges: Bethany, Bethel, Kansas Wesleyan, McPherson, Sterling, and Tabor.

202. Alaska Library Association, Southeast Chapter. Periodical holdings in Southeast Alaska libraries. Juneau, 1969. 69p.
Records holdings of 12 libraries.

203. Alaska, University, Library. Periodicals and serials, 1970, 2d ed. College, Alaska, 1970. 306p.
Lists over 8,000 titles held by library.

204. Area College Library Cooperative Program. Union list of serials. Shippensburg, Pa.: Shippensburg State College Library, 1969. 170*l.*
Lists 7,510 titles, including current and noncurrent holdings of 13 central Pennsylvania college and university libraries.

205. Arkansas Foundation of Associated Colleges. Periodical holdings in the Arkansas Foundation of Associated Colleges. Arkadelphia: Ouachita Baptist College, 1963. 111p.

206. Arndt, Karl J. R., and Olson, May E. German-American newspapers and periodicals, 1732-1955; history and bibliography. Heidelberg: Quelle and Meyer, 1961. 794p. 2d ed. N.Y.: John Reprint Corp., 1965. 810p.
Lists about 5,000 serials with locations in more than 300 U.S. libraries and historical societies and 50 European libraries.

207. California, University, Libraries. Current serials in the libraries of the University of California, Davis. Davis: Univ. of Calif. Library, 1970. 636p.

208. ———. Current serials titles list. Los Angeles, 1970. 2v.

209. Catholic Library Association, College Section, Illinois Unit. Periodical holdings in eleven college libraries in the Chicago area, comp. by Sister Mary Clara. 1962. Unpaged.

210. Central New York Reference and Resources Council. Central New York union list of serials. Canastota, 1970. 500p.
Lists more than 8,000 periodical titles in Council libraries.

211. City University of New York Libraries. The union list of periodicals in the libraries of the City University of New York, ed. by Margaret K. Rowell. N.Y., 1969. 1,044p.
Entries for over 8,500 titles in 18 libraries.

212. Colorado, University, Libraries. Catalog of serials, 2d ed. Boulder, 1970. 651p.
Lists 35,000 titles; updates 1967 list.

213. Connecticut State Library. A check list of current periodicals in central Connecticut libraries, 3d ed., comp. by George Adams, Hartford, 1961. 95p.

214. Cornell University Libraries. Serials currently received. Ithaca, N.Y.: Cornell Univ. Pr., 1962. 418p. Supplement. 1965. 260p.

215. Dertien, James L. South Dakota union list of serials. Vermillion: Univ. of S. Dak., 1970. 640p.
Lists holdings of 14 college and university, 3 public, and 2 special libraries.

216. Dikewood Corporation. The southwestern union list of serials; a regional union list of serial holdings as reported by 30 participating libraries, 2d ed. Albuquerque, N.M., 1969. 876p.
Entries for about 25,000 titles, held by 28 libraries in New Mexico and 2 in Texas.

217. Duke University Library. Periodicals and other serials in the libraries of Duke University, Durham, N.C., 1971. 2v.
Contains over 50,000 entries for titles held by Duke; excludes Medical Center Library.

218. Eastern Regional Public Library System. Union list of serial holdings in ninety-four libraries. Boston, 1970. 193p.
System, with headquarters in Boston Public Library, serves 210 libraries. Serial holdings of Boston Public Library not included.

219. Eastern Washington State College, Library Dept. Union list of periodicals in libraries of the Spokane, Washington area. Cheney, 1968. 129*l.*
Entries for about 3,000 titles, with holdings located in 19 libraries.

220. Fort Wayne and Allen County Public Library. Union list of periodicals of Fort Wayne area libraries, comp. by Wesley Avins. Fort Wayne, Ind., 1967. 148p.
Includes holdings of 30 libraries.

221. Goldwater, Walter. Radical periodicals in America, 1890-1950; a bibliography with brief notes. New Haven, Conn.: Yale Univ. Library, 1966. 51p.
No locations, but lists 12 libraries which "have substantial collections of radical periodicals."

222. Harper, J. Russell. Historical directory of New Brunswick newspapers and periodicals. Fredericton: Univ. of N.B., 1961. 121p.
Lists 461 titles with locations of files, including 11 U.S. libraries.

223. Harvard University Library. Periodical classes; classified listing by call number, alphabetical listing by title. Cambridge, Mass., 1968. 758p. (Widener Library shelflist, no.15)
Lists nearly 26,000 titles.

224. Hawaii Library Association. Union list of serials in libraries of Honolulu, 3d ed., ed. by Geraldine K. Maurer. Honolulu, 1965. 624p.
Holdings of 21 reference and special libraries for more than 10,000 titles.

225. Illinois, University, Library. Current periodical holdings list, University of Illinois Library, Urbana, with a supplement: current serial holdings of the Library of Medical Sciences, Chicago. Urbana, 1966. 339, 30p.

226. ———. Current serial holdings list of the University of Illinois Library at Urbana-Champaign. Urbana, 1968. 2v. Supplement, 1969. 333p.
Entries for 46,428 titles; supplement adds 13,117 titles.

227. Intermountain union list of serials, ed. by Donald W. Johnson and Larry Larason. Tempe: Ariz. State Library Assoc., 1969. 793p. 2d ed., 1970. 1623p.
Entries for 13,000 titles, with holdings of 13 Arizona and 2 Nevada libraries.

228. International Young Men's Christian Association College. Union list of periodicals in the college and special libraries of greater Springfield. Springfield, Mass., 1964. 136p.
Lists 2,000 titles with holdings in 18 libraries.

229. Iowa, University, Libraries. Serials currently received in the University of Iowa Libraries. Iowa City, 1968. 235p.

230. Kansas, University, Libraries. Kansas union list of serials, ed. by Anne Bruce and Anna R. Condit. Lawrence: Univ. of Kans. Libraries for the Kans. Library Council, 1965. 357p.
Lists holdings of 8 Kansas academic libraries for about 22,000 titles.

231. Kent State University Library. A complete listing of periodicals and newspapers as of January 1, 1964. Kent, Ohio, 1964. 99*l.*

232. Long Island University, Brooklyn Center Library. Periodicals: holdings of the Brooklyn College Library, Long Island University. Brooklyn, 1971. 112p.

233. Maine, University, Library. List of abstracting journals, periodicals and newspapers currently received by the University of Maine Library, comp. by Jane M. Holmes. Orono, 1962. 32p.

234. Massachusetts, University, Library. Four college libraries; union list of journal and serial holdings, 4th ed. Amherst: Hampshire Inter-Library Center, Univ. of Mass., 1969. 306p.
Complete holdings of University of Massachusetts, Smith, Mount Holyoke, and Amherst Libraries, and Hampshire Inter-Library Center.

235. ———. Journal and serial holdings as of July 1, 1966. Amherst, 1966. 113p.

236. ———. Periodicals currently received as of December 31, 1969. Boston, 1970. 83p.

237. Mecklenburg Library Association. Union list of periodical holdings in Mecklenburg County, ed. by Ellen D. Moreland. Charlotte, N.C.: Public Library, 1966. 59p.
Locates periodical holdings of 19 libraries in Mecklenburg County, N.C.

238. Memphis Librarians' Committee. Memphis area union list of serials, ed. by Diane Cofer. Houston, Tex.: Phil Wilson, 1966. 272p.
Includes holdings of 26 public, special, and university libraries.

239. Michigan State University Libraries. Serial holdings list. East Lansing, 1969. 784p.
Record of holdings of periodicals and serials, with locations, as of June 1, 1969.

240. Mid-Appalachia College Council. Union list of the periodicals in the libraries of the Mid-Appalachia College Council, Inc. Bristol, Tenn., 1970. 136p.

Shows extent of holdings in 11 libraries in Tennessee, Kentucky, and Virginia.

241. Missouri State Library. Union list of serials in libraries and state offices in Jefferson City. Jefferson City, 1961. 80p.

242. New York Public Library. Periodicals in the Mid-Manhattan Library. N.Y., 1970. 208p.

Listing of 2,836 titles held by New York Public Library's new central branch.

243. New York State Library. New York state union list of serials. N.Y.: CCM Information Corp., 1970. 2v.

Records serial holdings of American Museum of Natural History, Columbia Teachers College, Engineering Societies Library, New York Public Library, New York State Library, Syracuse University, Union Theological Seminary, and major divisions of the State University of New York; entries for 46,000 titles.

244. New York, State University, at Buffalo, Libraries. Union list of serials. Buffalo, 1970. 720p.

245. New York University Libraries. UNISEC; union list of serials computerized. N.Y., 1970. 422p.

246. North Carolina, University, Library. Periodicals and other serials held by the libraries of the University of North Carolina at Chapel Hill. Chapel Hill, 1967. 600p. Supplement, 1969. 2v.

Original list recorded about 34,500 titles.

247. Ohio State University Libraries. Periodicals and newspapers currently received in the Ohio State University Libraries. Columbus, 1969. 181p.

Alphabetical list of more than 8,000 titles, with locations.

248. Oklahoma, University, Library. Periodicals received currently in the libraries of Oklahoma State University and the University of Oklahoma. Norman, 1967. 118p.

249. ———. The University of Oklahoma Libraries serial holdings. Norman, 1968. 308p.

250. Oregon State Library. Periodicals currently received, title and subject lists. Salem, 1961. 126p. Supplement, 1963. 28p.

251. Pennsylvania State University Libraries. Serial holdings. University Park, 1969. 2v.

252. Pollak, Felix. "Little magazine collection of the University of Wisconsin." Wisconsin library bulletin, 58 (Jan. 1962), 5-8.

253. Queens College Library. Periodicals available in the Queens College Library, December 1969. Flushing, N.Y., 1969. Unpaged.

Alphabetical list with holdings.

254. Rhode Island, University, Library. Periodical holdings. Kingston, 1969. 106p.

255. Richmond Area University Center. A union list of periodicals and selected continuations in Richmond area libraries, rev. ed., ed. by Sarah Wood Matthews. Richmond, Va., 1961. 320p.

256. Riffe, Nancy L. "Contributions to a finding list of eighteenth-century British periodicals." New York Public Library bulletin, 67 (1963), 431-34.

Lists 25 journals published before 1789, with locations in 7 U.S. libraries.

257. Rochester area union list of periodical holdings. Rochester, N.Y., 1965. 73p.

Lists about 3,000 business, scientific, and technical periodicals held by 14 special libraries.

258. Rochester Regional Research Library Council. A union list of serials, comp. by Maryanne Clark and others. Rochester, N.Y., 1970. 554p.

Represents holdings of 30 academic and special libraries in Rochester area.

259. Rochester, University, Library. Union list of serials—education, science, medicine—in the libraries of the University of Rochester as of October 15, 1968. Rochester, N.Y., 1968. 2v. in 1.

260. Sizemore, W. Christian. Serial holdings of South Georgia academic libraries. Douglas: South Ga. Academic Libraries, 1967. 116p.

Lists holdings of more than 1,200 titles of 7 member libraries of organization.

261. South Dakota Library Association. South Dakota union list of serials. Sioux Falls, 1968? 512p.

Lists holdings of 15 college and university libraries.

262. Southern Illinois University Library. Current peri-

odicals list. Carbondale: Central Publications, Southern Ill. Univ., 1971. 112p.

Lists about 7,200 periodicals and newspapers.

263. Special Libraries Association, Heart of America Chapter. A union list of serials for Mid-America in libraries of Greater Kansas City and sections of Missouri, Oklahoma, and Kansas, 2d ed., comp. by Idris Smith, Kansas City, Mo., 1964. 2v.

Includes holdings of 37 libraries.

264. ———, Minnesota Chapter. Union list of serials. Minneapolis, 1963. 130p. 2d ed., 1965. 126p.

Lists 3,500 titles with holdings in 25 libraries.

265. ———, New Jersey Chapter. Union list of serials in New Jersey, 3d ed. Bound Brook: Lit. Serv., 1963. Unpaged.

Reports holdings of 61 libraries.

266. ———, Rio Grande Chapter. The Southwestern union list of serials; a regional union list of serial holdings as reported by the 24 participating libraries on October 1, 1964. Albuquerque, N.M.: Sandia Corp., 1965. 585p.

Entries for about 18,000 titles, with holdings for 21 New Mexico and 3 Texas libraries.

267. ———, San Francisco Bay Region Chapter. Union list of periodicals: science-technology-economics. Palo Alto, Calif., 1966. 235p.

Lists holdings of about 4,000 titles in 73 special libraries in San Francisco area.

268. ———, Southern California Chapter. Union list of periodicals in libraries in Southern California, 5th ed. Santa Ana: Professional Library Service, 1968. 458p.

Records holdings of 127 libraries for 33,000 titles.

269. Suburban Washington union periodical list. Fairfax, Va.: Fairfax County Library, 1967. 66p.

Records holdings of periodicals and newspapers in 7 Virginia and Maryland suburban libraries.

270. Texas A&M University Library. Serials holdings list. College Station, 1969? 953p.

Entries for 14,514 titles.

271. Texas, University, Library. Location list of serials and continuations. Austin, 1964. 218*l.*

272. Union list of periodicals . . . expanded to include holdings of TLA District III libraries, 7th ed. Abilene, Tex.: Abilene Christian College Library, 1967. 105, 8*l.*

273. Union list of periodicals for the top 26 counties of Texas. Amarillo, Tex.: Mary E. Bivins Memorial Library, 1967. 73*l.* Second edition, 1969. 101*l.*

274. Union list of periodicals in libraries of the Kalamazoo area, 3d ed. Kalamazoo, Mich.: Upjohn, 1962. 184p.

Represents holdings of 13 libraries.

275. Union list of serials, 2d ed. Wash.: Consortium of Universities of the Washington Metropolitan Area, 1970. Unpaged.

Records holdings of American, Catholic, George Washington, Georgetown, and Howard universities; includes 23,787 titles.

276. Union list of serials currently received in St. Louis area libraries. St. Louis, 1969. 1,037 cols.

Holdings not indicated.

277. Union list of serials in Connecticut, 1966. Bound Brook, N.J.: Lit. Serv., 1967? 1v. Loose-leaf.

Records holdings of 75 libraries.

278. Union list of serials in libraries of the United States and Canada, 3d ed. N.Y.: Wilson, 1965. 5v.

Locates files of 157,000 journals in 956 U.S. and Canadian libraries.

279. Union list of serials in Maine, New Hampshire, and Vermont, ed. by Anne E. Gremling. Bound Brook, N.J.: Lit. Serv., 1965? 1v. Loose-leaf.

Lists holdings of 70 libraries.

280. Union list of serials in Maryland. Bound Brook, N.J.: Lit. Serv., 1962. Unpaged.

Records holdings of 108 libraries.

281. Union list of serials in Maryland and Delaware, 2d ed., ed. by Anne E. Gremling. Bound Brook, N.J.: Lit. Serv., 1965? 1v. Loose-leaf.

Lists holdings of 125 libraries.

282. Union list of serials in Massachusetts, ed. by Anne E. Gremling. Bound Brook, N.J.: Lit. Serv., 1965. 1v. Loose-leaf.

Holdings shown for 70 libraries.

283. Union list of serials in New Jersey, 4th ed., 1966-68. Bound Brook, N.J.: Lit. Serv., 1967? 1v. Loose-leaf.

Holdings shown for more than 80 libraries.

284. Union list of serials in Pennsylvania and Delaware, 2d ed., ed. by Anne E. Gremling. Bound Brook, N.J.: Lit. Serv., 1969? 1v. Loose-leaf.

285. Union list of serials in the libraries in the Miami Valley (Ohio), 2d ed. Dayton, Ohio: Wright State Univ. Library, 1969. 472p.

Records about 9,700 titles with holdings. Supplement, 1970, 135p., lists 754 new titles.

286. Union list of serials in the libraries of the Consortium of Universities of the Metropolitan Washington area. Wash.: Catholic Univ. of America Pr., 1967. 370p.

Lists 20,000 serials in the libraries of American, Catholic, Georgetown, and Howard universities and Wesley Theological Seminary.

287. Union list of serials in the libraries of the State University of New York, 2d ed., comp. by Valerie Feinman and Carol Salverson. Syracuse: State Univ. of N.Y. Upstate Medical Center, 1967. 1,038p.

Lists holdings of 82 libraries in State University of New York.

288. Union list of serials in the libraries of the State University of New York, 3d ed., ed. by Sandy Frazier. Syracuse, 1969. 777p.

Entries for 15,241 titles, showing holdings in 54 libraries.

289. U.S. Argonne National Laboratory, Library Services Dept. Argonne journal holdings. Lemont, Ill., 1962. 150p.

Lists holdings of 9 departmental libraries.

290. U.S. Library of Congress. New serial titles. 1950-60. Wash., 1961. 2v.; 1961-65. N.Y.: Bowker Co. and Arno Publishing Co., 1966. 3v.; 1966-68. Wash., 1969. 2v.

Supplemented by monthly, quarterly, and annual issues.

291. ———, General Reference and Bibliography Division. Union lists of serials; a bibliography, comp. by Ruth S. Freitag. Wash.: Govt. Print. Off., 1964. 150p.

International list; locates copies in U.S. libraries.

292. Washington State University Library. Union list of serials of the libraries of Washington State University and University of Idaho. Pullman, 1963. 2v.

Entries for about 15,000 titles in 1 Washington and 3 Idaho libraries.

293. Wayne State University Libraries. Union list of serials in the Wayne State University Libraries incorporating the Selected list of biomedical serials in Metropolitan Detroit, 2d ed. Detroit, 1968. 484p. Cumulative supplement, 1969. Unpaged.

Records holdings for 38 libraries.

294. Wepsiec, Jan. Polish American serial publications, 1842-1966; an annotated bibliography. Chicago, 1968. 191p.

Entries for 1,201 titles; holdings shown for 173 U.S. and Canadian and 13 Polish libraries.

295. West Virginia University Library. West Virginia union list of serials. Morgantown, 1966- . Annual.

Includes all libraries of any substantial size in West Virginia.

296. Western New York Library Resources Council. Western New York union list of serials, ed. by Nina Cohen and others. Buffalo, 1970. 323p.

297. Willocks, R. Max. Periodical holdings of the South Carolina private college libraries. Greenville: Planning Center, S.C. Private Colleges, 1969. 183p.

298. Zalewski, Caroline. Serials in language, literature, psychology, sociology, and social work; a union list of serials in selected libraries in Western New York, comp. by Caroline Zalewski and Manuel D. Lopez. Buffalo: State Univ. of N.Y., 1965. 117p.

Holdings shown for 11 libraries.

Newspapers

299. Arizona Dept. of Library and Archives. A union list of Arizona newspapers in Arizona libraries. Phoenix, 1965. 24*l.*

Records 442 entries with holdings for 11 libraries.

300. Bibliographical Center for Research, Rocky Mountain Region. Guide to Colorado newspapers, 1859-1963, comp. by Donald E. Oehlerts. Denver, 1964. 184p.

Locates holdings of 2,844 titles in 38 libraries in Colorado and elsewhere.

301. Boston Public Library. Newspapers currently received. Boston, 1967. 11p.

Lists more than 300 titles. Revised and enlarged edition scheduled for 1971 publication.

302. Brigham, Clarence S. History and bibliography of American newspapers, 1690-1820. Worcester, Mass.:

American Antiquarian Society, 1947. 2v. Reprinted, with additions and corrections, Hampden, Conn.: Archon, 1962. 2v.

303. ———. History and bibliography of American newspapers, 1690-1820. Additions and corrections. Worcester, Mass.: American Antiquarian Society, 1961. 50p. (Reprinted from Proceedings of the American Antiquarian Society, April 1961)

Original work, 1947. Supplement adds new holdings and new items.

304. Center for Research Libraries. Catalogue: newspapers. Chicago, 1969. 176p.

Detailed holdings of American and foreign newspapers in Center.

305. Cleveland Public Library. A list of local and out-of-town newspapers. Cleveland, Ohio, 1969. 13p.

Newspapers available in Cleveland Public Library.

306. Columbia University, International Affairs Library. List of newspapers currently received, N.Y., 1970. 6p.

Arranged alphabetically by country of origin.

307. Consortium of Western Universities and Colleges. Union list of newspapers currently received by the member libraries, December 1968. Stanford, Calif.: Hoover Institution, 1969, 41*l.*

Lists holdings of 12 university and college libraries in Western United States for 987 titles.

308. Dartmouth College Library. "Newspapers in Baker." Dartmouth College Library bulletin, n.s. 10 (1969), 28-39.

Reports Dartmouth's American newspaper holdings up to 20th century; includes also abolitionist, religious, and political papers.

309. Delaware, University, Library. Union list of newspapers in microform. Newark, 1964. 11*l.*

Holdings of more than 100 titles shown for 5 Delaware libraries.

310. Ellen, John C., Jr. "Political newspapers of the South Carolina up country, 1850-1859." South Carolina historical magazine, 63 (April-July 1962), 86-92, 158-63.

Locates files.

311. Emory University Library. Newspaper files in the Emory University Library, rev. ed. Atlanta, Ga., 1964. 72*l.*

312. Folkes, John G. Nevada's newspapers; a bibliography; a compilation of Nevada history, 1854-1964. Reno: Univ. of Nev. Press, 1964. 197p. (Nevada studies in history and political science, no.6)

Entries for more than 400 papers, with locations of files.

313. Ham, F. Gerald. "Central Kentucky broadsides and newspapers, 1793-1846, in the John M. McCalla papers, West Virginia University Library." Register of Kentucky Historical Society, 59 (Jan. 1961), 47-78. (Continued from October 1960 Register)

314. Harbin, Dorothy. List of newspapers currently received in seven major Atlanta-Athens libraries. Atlanta: Ga. Union Catalogue of the Atlanta-Athens Area, 1968. 22*l.*

315. Hoole, William S. Foreign newspapers in Southeastern libraries. University: Univ. of Ala. Pr., 1963. 64*l.*

Entries geographically arranged; holdings of 37 libraries in 10 states reported.

316. Houston, University, Libraries. Newspaper resources of District V, Texas Library Association; a union list, comp. by Virginia B. Murphy. Houston, 1968. 46p.

Reports holdings of U.S. and foreign newspapers in 50 libraries.

317. Illinois State Historical Library. "Newspapers in the Illinois State Historical Library," ed. by William E. Keller. Illinois libraries, 52 (1970), 489-602.

In two sections: Illinois newspapers, arranged by place of publication, and "out-of-state papers," arranged by state and country. Lists exact holdings. Revision of lists in Illinois libraries, 46 (June 1964), 447-560, and in Illinois libraries, 49 (June 1967), 439-543.

318. Iowa State Historical Society. Newspaper collection of the State Historical Society of Iowa, comp. by L. O. Cheever. Iowa City, 1969. 118p.

319. Kent State University Libraries. Newspapers in Kent State University Libraries. Kent, Ohio, 1969. 33p.

Lists 1,163 titles, including 209 Negro newspapers.

320. Lingenfelter, Richard E. Newspapers of Nevada, 1858-1958; a history and bibliography. San Francisco: J. Howell, 1964. 228p.

Lists about 500 titles, with locations, when known, in 49 U.S. libraries. Supplementary list of "Border papers" (Arizona, California, Idaho, Oregon, and Utah) reports on files in 37 libraries.

321. Louisiana State Archives and Records Commission. Index to microfilmed newspapers deposited in the Lake Charles Public Library, Lake Charles, Louisiana, 1889-1951. Baton Rouge, 1962. 80p.

322. Louisiana State University Library. Louisiana newspapers, 1794-1961: a union list of Louisiana newspaper files available in public, college and university libraries in Louisiana, ed. by T. N. McMullan. Baton Rouge, 1965. 281p.

Lists holdings of 16 libraries.

323. ———. Newspaper files in Louisiana State University Library. Baton Rouge, 1961. 211*l.*

pt.1, Louisiana; pt.2, out-of-state; pt.3, foreign newspapers; exact holdings shown.

324. Michigan Dept. of Education, Bureau of Library Services. Michigan newspapers on microfilm. Lansing, 1969. Unpaged.

Locations reported in 7 Michigan libraries.

325. Minnesota Historical Society. Newspapers on the Minnesota frontier, 1849-1860, by George S. Hage. St. Paul, 1967. 176p.

Locates files in Society's collections.

326. Minnesota, University, Library. Newspapers in the University of Minnesota Library: a complete list of holdings. Minneapolis, 1964. 52p. Rev. ed., 1969. 65p.

327. Missouri State Historical Society. Missouri newspapers: when and where, 1808-1963, comp. by William H. Taft. Columbia, 1964. 205p.

Lists holdings for about 6,000 titles in more than 50 libraries, in Missouri and elsewhere.

328. Nebraska State Historical Society. A guide to the newspaper collection of the State Archives. Lincoln, 1969. 88p. (Bulletin, no.4)

329. North Carolina State Dept. of Archives and History. North Carolina newspapers on microfilm; a checklist of early North Carolina newspapers available on microfilm from the State Department of Archives and History, 3d ed., ed. by H. G. Jones and Julius H. Avant. Raleigh, 1965. 96p.

List of more than 700 titles.

330. ———. Union list of North Carolina newspapers, 1751-1900, ed. by H. G. Jones and Julius H. Avant. Raleigh, 1963. 152*l.*

Records holdings of public and private libraries in North Carolina and elsewhere.

331. Northwestern University Library. Guide to underground newspapers in the Special Collections Department, by Roxanna Siefer and John Simmons. Evanston, Ill., undated. 50p.

332. Oregon State Library. Oregon newspapers; holdings of Library Association of Portland, Oregon Historical Society Library, Oregon State Library, and University of Oregon Library. Salem, 1963. 70p.

333. Oregon, University, Library. Newspapers on microfilm, comp. by Elizabeth Findly. Eugene, 1963. 17p. (Univ. of Oreg. Library occasional paper, no.2)

University of Oregon Library's holdings, largely of Oregon papers.

334. Pennsylvania Library Association. Pennsylvania newspapers: a bibliography and union list, ed. by Ruth Salisbury. Pittsburgh, 1969. 179p.

Holdings recorded for 228 Pennsylvania libraries.

335. Pittsburgh, University, Libraries. Newspapers in the University of Pittsburgh Libraries. Pittsburgh, Pa.: Univ. Book Center, 1970. 152p. (Bibliographic series, no.6)

Includes Pennsylvania, out-of-state, and foreign newspapers.

336. Stanford University, Hoover Institution. Current newspapers received by the Hoover Institution, Stanford University, July 1, 1970. Stanford, Calif., 1970. 17*l.*

Arranged by countries.

337. Stratton, Porter A. The territorial press of New Mexico, 1834-1912. Albuquerque: Univ. of N.M. Pr., 1969. 306p.

Holdings shown for 732 newspaper titles in 10 libraries and various county courthouses in New Mexico.

338. Tennessee State Library and Archives. Tennessee newspapers: a cumulative list of microfilmed Tennessee newspapers in the Tennessee State Library and Archives, July 1966, progress report. Nashville, 1966. 109*l.*

339. U.S. Library of Congress, Serial Division. Newspapers currently received and permanently retained in Library of Congress, rev. ed. Wash.: The Library, 1970. 20p.

340. ———, Union Catalog Division. Newspapers on microfilm, 6th ed., comp. under the direction of George A. Schwegmann, Jr. Wash.: The Library, 1967. 487p.

Contains about 21,700 entries, representing 4,640

foreign and 17,100 domestic newspapers. 4th ed. 1961; 5th ed. 1963.

341. Wallace, John M. Gaceta to gazette: a check list of Texas newspapers, 1813-1846. Austin: Dept. of Journalism Development Program, Univ. of Tex., 1966. 89p.
Entries for 59 papers with holdings shown in 3 collections.

342. Washington State Library. Washington newspapers and historical materials on microfilm in the Washington State Library. Olympia, 1966. 27p.

343. Wayne State University Libraries. Newspaper resources of metropolitan Detroit libraries; a union list, comp. by Howard A. Sullivan and Thelma Freides. Detroit, 1965. 46p.

344. West Virginia University Library. Index to the press of the Kanawha Valley, 1855-1865, by Robert F. Munn. Morgantown, 1963. 115p.
Microfilm copy of all material indexed is in West Virginia University Library.

345. ———. Newspapers in the West Virginia University Library, comp. by Lorise C. Boger. Morgantown, 1964. 129p.

346. Wrone, David R. "Newspapers of DeWitt County [Illinois], 1854-1960, a bibliography and checklist." Illinois libraries, 46 (1964), 367-92.
Files of 62 papers located in 4 libraries and 4 publishers' offices.

Foreign Periodicals and Newspapers

347. Association for Asian Studies, Committee on American Library Resources on the Far East. Chinese periodicals: international holdings, 1949-1960. Ann Arbor, Mich., 1961. 85*l.* (Preliminary data paper, no.2) Indexes and supplement. Ann Arbor, 1961. 107*l.* (Preliminary data paper, no.3)
Holdings shown for 23 U.S. libraries.

348. California, University, East Asiatic Library. Index to learned Chinese periodicals, comp. by Richard C. Howard. Boston: G. K. Hall, 1962. 215p.

349. ———, Library. Slavic studies: a checklist of periodicals and serials in the University Library at UCLA. Los Angeles: Univ. Research Library and East European Studies Center, 1965. 74p.
Limited to social sciences and humanities. Excludes newspapers.

350. Charno, Steven M. Latin American newspapers in the United States; a union list. Austin: Univ. of Tex. Pr., 1968. 619p.
Lists 5,500 titles for 20 Latin American countries and Puerto Rico, to be found in 70 U.S. libraries.

351. Chicago, University, Far Eastern Library. List of Chinese periodicals as of March 1, 1961. Chicago, 1961. 18p.

352. ——— ———. List of periodicals in Japanese. Chicago, 1968. 42p.

353. Columbia University, East Asian Library. Index to learned Chinese periodicals, comp. by Richard C. Howard. Boston: G. K. Hall, 1962. 215p.
Based on Columbia's holdings.

354. Cornell University, Dept. of Asian Studies. A guide to Indonesian serials, 1945-1965, in the Cornell University Library, by Yvonne Thung and John M. Echols. Ithaca, N.Y.: Modern Indonesia Project, Southeast Asia Program, Dept. of Asian Studies, 1966. 151p.

355. Cornell University Libraries. Cornell University Library holdings of pre-1949 Chinese mainland periodicals, comp. by Irene W. Hurlbert. Ithaca, N.Y., 1966. 105*l.*
In English and Chinese.

356. ———. Post-1949 Chinese mainland periodicals (scientific and technical), comp. by Irene Woo. Ithaca, N.Y., 1963. 10*l.*

357. ———. Russian serials currently received. Ithaca, N.Y., 1965. 54p.

358. El Hadi, Mohamed M. Union list of Arabic serials in the United States. Urbana: Univ. of Ill. Graduate School of Library Science, 1965. 61p. (Occasional papers, no.75)
Records holdings of 17 libraries for more than 400 titles; Arabic titles are transliterated.

359. Fernández, Oscar. A preliminary listing of foreign periodical holdings in the United States and Canada which give coverage to Portuguese and Brazilian language and literature. Iowa City: Univ. of Iowa Pr., 1968. 28*l.*
Locates files in more than 100 libraries.

360. Harvard University, East Asian Research Center. A research guide to China-Coast newspapers, 1822-1911, by Frank H. H. King and Prescott Clarke. Cambridge, Mass., 1965. 235p.

Surviving files of more than 100 papers located in libraries around the world, including 17 in U.S.

361. Harvard University Library. Latin America and Latin American periodicals. Cambridge, Mass., 1966. 2v. (Widener Library shelflist, no.5-6)

Contains 27,292 titles arranged by classification numbers, author and title, and chronologically.

362. Hawaii, University, East-West Library. Philippine newspapers in selected American libraries, a union list, comp. by Shiro Saito. Honolulu, 1967. 46p. (East-West Center Library's Occasional paper, no.6)

List of 120 titles in 28 U.S. libraries.

363. Illwitzer, R. P. Union list of Russian serials in English translation available in Washington area libraries. Silver Spring, Md.: Johns Hopkins University Applied Physics Laboratory, 1961. 16p.

About 100 titles; holdings shown for 32 libraries.

364. Indiana University Libraries. Handlist of selected periodicals and other serials for African studies in the Indiana University Libraries, comp. by D. Michael Warren. Bloomington: Ind. Univ. African Studies Program, 1967. 28*l.*

365. Kase, Karel A. Czechoslovak periodicals in 1959-1960; an annotated bibliography. Wash., 1964. 186*l.* (Master's thesis, Dept. of Library Science, Catholic Univ. of America)

Entries for 834 titles, locating files in 194 U.S. and 19 Canadian libraries.

366. Lauritsen, Frederick M. "Rare nineteenth-century Latin American periodicals." Books at Iowa, 11 (Nov. 1969), 3-18.

Annotated bibliography of 74 titles held by University of Iowa Libraries.

367. Linda Hall Library. Japanese, Chinese & Russian serial holdings in the Linda Hall Library. Kansas City, Mo., 1970. 96p.

368. ———. Oriental and East European serial titles currently being received, Sept. 1963. Kansas City, Mo., 1963. 18p. (Bulletin, no.10)

369. Marino, Samuel J. The French-refugee newspapers and periodicals in the United States, 1789-1825. Wash., 1962. 394p. (Ph.D. thesis, Dept. of Library Science, Univ. of Mich.)

Lists 61 titles with locations of files in libraries.

370. Massachusetts, University, Library. African newspapers held by the University of Massachusetts Library; a list of newspapers currently received and a copy of the catalog cards of African newspapers on microfilm in the University of Massachusetts Library, comp. by Carol Jopling. Amherst, 1968. 58*l.*

371. Michigan State University Library. Current periodicals; a select bibliography in the area of Latin American studies at Michigan State University, by Tamara Brunnschweiler. East Lansing, 1968. 100p. (Mich. State Univ., Latin American Studies Center, Monograph series, no.3)

Lists 740 titles, with holdings.

372. Michigan, University, Library. Holdings of Chinese journals of the Asia Library, University Library, University of Michigan. Ann Arbor, 1961. 41*l.*

373. New York State Library. South Asian serials; list of serials published in Ceylon, India, Nepal, and Pakistan held by the New York State Library, comp. by Henry Ferguson. Albany: Univ. of the State of N.Y., State Education Dept., 1965. 34p.

374. North Carolina, University, Library. List of Chinese books and periodicals in the Far Eastern collection of the University of North Carolina, comp. by Regina S. Ro. Chapel Hill, 1965-66. 2v. in 3.

375. Nunn, G. Raymond. Chinese periodicals, international holdings, 1949-1960. Ann Arbor, Mich.: Association for Asian Studies, Committee on American Library Resources on the Far East, 1961. 85*l.* Index and supplement, 1961. 107*l.*

A union list.

376. Pan American Union, Columbus Memorial Library. Index to Latin American periodical literature, 1929-1960. Boston: G. K. Hall, 1962. 8v. First supplement, 1961-65. 2v. Annual cumulation, v. 1-2, 1961-62.

Compiled in the Pan American Union Library, Washington, D.C.

377. Pittsburgh, University, East Asian Library. Periodicals and serials of the East Asian Library. Pittsburgh, 1968. 60*l.*

378. Shih, Bernadette P. N., and Snyder, Richard L. International union list of Communist Chinese serials; scientific, technical and medical with selected social science titles. Cambridge: Mass. Inst. of Technology, 1963. Unpaged.

Lists 874 items in 19 U.S. libraries.

379. Special Libraries Association, Western New York Chapter. Russian journals in translation; holdings list, 2d ed., comp. by Jasmine H. Mulcahey. n.p., 1961. 22p.

380. Stanford University, Hoover Institution. A checklist of serials for African studies, based on the libraries of the Hoover Institution and Stanford University, by Peter Duignan and Kenneth M. Glazier. Stanford, Calif., 1963. 104p.

Lists about 1,400 serial publications with holdings.

381. ——— ———. Soviet and Russian newspapers at the Hoover Institution, a catalog, comp. by Karol Maichel. Stanford, Calif., 1966. 235p. (Bibliographical series, no.24)

Lists 1,108 titles; includes holdings of Library of Congress and Columbia University Library.

382. Stanford University Libraries. German periodical publications; a checklist of German language serials and series currently received in the Stanford University Libraries, prep. by Gabor Erdelyi and Agnes F. Peterson. Stanford, Calif.: Hoover Institution, 1967. 175p. (Hoover Institution bibliographical series, no.27)

Lists 2,000 titles in 30 collections.

383. Syracuse University Library. Current subscriptions to Southeast Asian periodicals, by Donn V. Hart. Syracuse, N.Y., 1966. 6*l.*

384. ———. Serials and newspapers for African studies: a checklist. Syracuse, N.Y., 1970. 36p.

385. ———. Serials and newspapers for Slavic studies: a checklist, comp. by Roger Beasley. Syracuse, N.Y., 1970. 216p.

386. Union Library Catalogue of the Philadelphia Metropolitan Area. Union list of English translations of Russian journals, April 15, 1961. Philadelphia, 1961. 8p.

387. U.S. Library of Congress, African Section. Serials for African studies, comp. by Helen F. Conover. Wash.: The Library, 1961. 163p.

Lists more than 2,000 titles with locations in Library of Congress or 42 other American libraries.

388. ———, American Libraries Book Procurement Center, Karachi. Annual list of serials. Karachi, Dacca: American Libraries Book Procurement Centers, 1966- .

Materials acquired under Public Law 480 program.

389. ———, Hispanic Foundation. Holdings of selected newspapers from Spain in United States libraries, by Donald F. Wisdom. Wash.: The Library, 1966. 10*l.*

A preliminary inventory listing holdings for 14 newspapers in 21 libraries.

390. ———, Reference Dept. Half a century of Soviet serials, 1917-1968; a bibliography and union list of serials published in the USSR, comp. by Rudolf Smits. Wash.: The Library, 1968. 2v.

Lists about 30,000 titles. Symbols indicate titles held in U.S. and Canadian libraries.

391. ——— ———. Serial publications of the Soviet Union, 1939-1961; a preliminary checklist, comp. by Rudolf Smits. Wash.: Govt. Print. Off., 1961. 316p.

A national union list.

392. ———, Serial Division. African newspapers in selected American libraries, a union list, 3d ed., comp. by Rozanne M. Barry. Wash.: Govt. Print. Off., 1965. 135p.

Includes holdings of 33 U.S. libraries; lists 708 titles. 2d ed., Wash., 1962, 68p., lists issues in 20 American libraries.

393. ——— ———. Latin American newspapers in United States Libraries: a union list, comp. by Stephen M. Charno. Austin: Univ. of Tex. Pr., 1968. 619p.

Reports holdings of 5,500 titles in 70 U.S. libraries.

394. ———, Slavic and Central European Division. Newspapers of East Central and Southeastern Europe in the Library of Congress, ed. by Robert G. Carlton. Wash.: The Library, 1965. 204p.

Lists 787 titles, 1918-65.

395. ——— ———. Newspapers of the Soviet Union in the Library of Congress (Slavic, 1954-1960; non-Slavic, 1917-1960), prep. by Paul L. Horecky and others. Wash.: Govt. Print. Off., 1962. 73p.

396. ——— ———. The USSR and Eastern European periodicals in Western languages, 3d ed., comp. by Paul L. Horecky and Robert G. Carlton. Wash.: The Library, 1967. 89p.

Previous edition 1964. Covers 708 current periodicals from Albania, Baltic countries, Bulgaria, Czechoslovakia, Hungary, Poland, Rumania, Soviet Union, and Yugoslavia.

397. Virginia, University, Library. A list of foreign newspapers in the University of Virginia Library; including World War II newspapers collected and microfilmed

by the U.S. Interdepartmental Committee for the Acquisition of Foreign Publications. Charlottesville, 1965. 1v. Unpaged.

398. Washington University Libraries. Chinese and Japanese periodicals held in the Washington University Library, St. Louis, Missouri, October 1968. St. Louis, 1968. 37, 14, 5*l.*

399. ———. A guide to Chinese periodicals, comp. by David Y. Hu. St. Louis, 1966. 30*l.* (East Asian collection bibliographical series, no.1)

400. ———. Research sources for Ibero-American studies; a union list of serials in the fields of the humanities and social sciences held by Washington University Libraries, comp. by David S. Zubatsky. St. Louis, 1969. 202p. (Washington University Library studies, no.5)

401. Yale University Library. Chinese periodicals; a guide to indexes of periodicals relating to China. New Haven, Conn.: Yale Univ. Library, East Asian collection, 1965. 10*l.*

402. ———. A partial listing of the periodical holdings of the Sterling Memorial Library, Yale University, relevant to the study of Africa. New Haven, Conn., 1962? 52*l.*

403. ———, Southeast Asia Collection. The checklist of Southeast Asian serials. Boston: G. K. Hall, 1968. 320p.

Lists more than 2,800 serials in all languages for Burma, Thailand, Laos, Vietnam, Cambodia, Malaysia, Singapore, Philippines, Indonesia, etc., held by Yale Libraries.

Journalism

404. Cornell University, Dept. of Communication Arts. A bibliography of journalism. Ithaca, N.Y., 1965. 44*l.*

"Comprehensive view of the library resources at Mann Library," Cornell University.

405. Hiebert, Ray E. "Ivy Lee: father of modern public relations." Princeton University Library chronicle, 27 (1966), 113-20.

Description of Lee papers in Princeton Library.

406. Wisconsin, State Historical Society, Mass Communications History Center. The collections of the Mass Communications History Center. Madison, 1965? 38*l.*

MANUSCRIPTS

General

407. Burnette, O. Lawrence. "Manuscript collections at the national level." In Beneath the footnote. Madison: State Historical Society of Wis., 1969, p.130-66.

History of Library of Congress' Manuscript Division, including discussion of presidential papers.

408. Bush, Alfred L. "William E. Gates, 1863-1940." Manuscripts, 15 (Spring 1963), 42-46.

A portion of Gates collection of Aztec and Mayan manuscripts is now in Princeton University Library.

409. Folger Shakespeare Library. Catalog of manuscripts of the Folger Shakespeare Library (Washington, D.C.). Boston: G. K. Hall, 1970. 3v.

410. Hamer, Philip M. A guide to archives and manuscripts in the United States. New Haven, Conn.: Yale Univ. Pr., 1961. 775p.

Lists thousands of collections by individuals, organizations, subjects, and origins.

411. Hirsch, Rudolf. "Catalogue of manuscripts in the libraries of the University of Pennsylvania to 1800, supplement A." University of Pennsylvania Library chronicle, 35 (1969), 3-32; 36 (1970), 3-36.

412. Indiana University, Lilly Library. Manuscripts ancient-modern; an exhibition. Bloomington, 1964? 19p.

Catalog of medieval, Latin American, American, Lincoln, English literary, maps, and other manuscripts.

413. Kentucky, University, Libraries. Index to the Alexander collection of letters and autographs on microfilm in the University of Kentucky Library. Lexington, 1963. 29p. (Occasional contribution, no.143)

Miscellaneous collection of letters and autographs of American and European authors, statesmen, religious leaders, etc.

414. ———. The Samuel P. Gilmore collection. Lexington, 1962. 5p. (Occasional contribution, no.133)

Collection of miscellaneous letters and autographs of literary and political figures, mainly 19th century.

415. Manuscripts for research; five associated university libraries: Binghamton, Buffalo, Cornell, Rochester, Syracuse. Syracuse, N.Y.: Ronald F. Miller, 1969. 36p.

Listing by subject, inclusive dates, linear feet, and location of manuscript collections in 5 university libraries.

416. New York Public Library. Dictionary catalog of the Manuscript Division. Boston: G. K. Hall, 1967. 2v.

417. Pennsylvania, University, Library. Catalogue of manuscripts in the libraries of the University of Pennsylvania to 1800, comp. by Norman P. Zacour and Rudolf Hirsch. Philadelphia: Univ. of Pa. Pr., 1965. 279p.

Describes 1,150 manuscripts, dated 1000-1800.

418. Pittsburgh, University, Libraries. A descriptive checklist of its manuscript collections in the Darlington Memorial Library. Pittsburgh: Univ. Book Center, 1969. 10*l.*

419. Russell, Mattie. "Manuscript collections in the Duke University Library." North Carolina libraries, 19 (Winter 1961), 21-27.

420. ———. "The manuscript department in the Duke University Library." American archivist, 28 (1965), 437-44.

History and description of collections included.

421. Stocking, Robert E. "Manuscripts in Virginia." University of Virginia newsletter, 41 (Dec. 15, 1964), 13-16.

Survey of historical manuscript collecting in Virginia.

422. U.S. Library of Congress. The National union catalog of manuscript collections, 1959-1961, based on reports from American repositories of manuscripts. Ann Arbor, Mich.: J. W. Edwards, 1962. 1,061p.; Index, 1959-1962. Hamden, Conn.: Shoe String, 1964. 732p.; 1962. Hamden, Conn.: Shoe String, 1964. 532p.; 1963-1968. Wash.: Library of Congress, 1965-69. 5v.

423. ———, Manuscript Division. "Manuscripts." Library of Congress quarterly journal of current acquisitions, 18 (1961), 129-45; 19 (1962), 133-45; 20 (1963), 177-92; 21 (1964), 181-201; 22 (1965), 319-35; 23 (1966), 274-89; 24 (1967), 260-85; 25 (1968), 328-61; 26 (1969), 234-69.

Annual reports on Library's current acquisitions.

424. ——— ———. "Recent acquisitions of the Manuscript Division: private papers of public men." Quarterly journal of the Library of Congress, 27 (1970), 332-75.

425. ———, Processing Dept. British manuscripts project; a checklist of the microfilms prepared in England and Wales for the American Council of Learned Societies, 1941-1945, comp. by Lester K. Born. Westport, Conn.: Greenwood, 1968. 179p.

426. U.S. National Park Service, Morristown National Historical Park. A guide to the manuscript collection, ed. by Bruce W. Stewart and Joan Reilly. Morristown, N.J., 1967. 142p.

427. Washington, University, Libraries. The manuscript collection of the University of Washington Libraries. Seattle, 1967. 33p.

Medieval and Renaissance

428. Chicago, University, Library. A provisional list of the catalogues and other inventories of medieval and renaissance manuscripts, principally Latin and Greek, in the University of Chicago Libraries, prep. by Maxine F. Neidinger and Blanche B. Boyer. Chicago, 1965. 72*l.*

429. Gilfillan, Ellen. A study of illustrated medieval manuscripts in the rare book collection of the Boston Public Library. 1965. 129p. (Thesis, University of North Carolina)

430. Huntington Library. Ten centuries of manuscripts in the Huntington Library, by Herbert C. Schulz and others. San Marino, Calif., 1962. 87p.

431. Indiana University, Lilly Library. Medieval manuscripts; an exhibition of selections from the notable collection formed by C. Lindsay Ricketts. Bloomington, 1962. 4p.

432. Küp, Karl. "The Christmas story in medieval and Renaissance manuscripts from the Spencer collection." Bulletin of the New York Public Library, 73 (1969), 625-746. Reprinted. 121p. and 55 facsimiles.

Detailed descriptions and illustrations of 55 manuscripts.

433. Newberry Library. French and Flemish illuminated manuscripts from Chicago collections. Chicago: Division of the Humanities of the University of Chicago and the Newberry Library, 1969. [55] p.

Exhibition catalog, illustrated; 24 examples drawn mainly from Newberry and University of Chicago collections.

434. Pierpont Morgan Library. The Glazier collection

of illuminated manuscripts, comp. by John Plummer. N.Y., 1968. 50p.

Illustrated catalog of Western illuminated manuscripts.

435. Princeton University Library. Mirrors of the mediaeval world; illuminated manuscripts from the Princeton collections; an exhibition. Princeton, N.J., 1966. 4p.

436. Ricci, Seymour de. Census of medieval and Renaissance manuscripts in the United States and Canada. Supplement, ed. by C. U. Faye and W. H. Bond. N.Y.: Bibliographical Society of America, 1962. 626p.

Corrects and supplements original edition (N.Y.: Wilson, 1935-40. 3v. Reprinted, N.Y.: Kraus, 1961).

437. Rice, Howard C., Jr. "Mirrors of the mediaeval world; illuminated manuscripts from the Princeton collections." Princeton University Library chronicle, 27 (1966), 182-90.

General description, followed by checklist, of 74 miniatures shown in "Mirrors of the mediaeval world" exhibition, comp. by Rosalie B. Green.

438. Szabo, György. Fourteenth century manuscripts in the United States, a bibliography. N.Y., 1961. 9p.

Oriental

439. Freer Gallery of Art. Armenian manuscripts in the Freer Gallery of Art, by Sirarpie Der Nersessian. Wash., 1963. 146p., 108 plates. (Freer Gallery of Art, Oriental studies, no.6)

440. Michigan, University, Library. Manuscripts and papyri; an exhibition. Ann Arbor, 1967. 21p.

Descriptions of 80 items from the library's collection of 10,000 ancient and medieval manuscripts of Oriental interest.

441. Oates, John F. Yale papyri in the Beinecke Rare Book and Manuscript Library, by John F. Oates and others. New Haven, Conn.: American Society of Papyrologists, 1967. 288p.

442. U.S. Library of Congress, Near East Section. Arabic manuscripts at the Library of Congress, by Salah al-Munajjid. Beirut, Lebanon: New Book Publishing House, 1969. 70p.

Descriptive list of 99 manuscripts in Arabic.

RARE BOOKS

443. American Antiquarian Society. A society's chief joys; an exhibition from the collections of the American Antiquarian Society. Worcester, Mass., 1969. 137p.

Rare books in the Society's library relating to American history, literature, art and music, pastimes, medicine, transportation, book trades, and practical arts.

444. Baer, Elizabeth. "Evergreen House: the John Work Garrett Library of the Johns Hopkins University." Maryland libraries, 32 (Spring 1966), 17-19.

Describes collection of about 30,000 volumes, covering wide range of interests, now rare-book division of Johns Hopkins University Library.

445. Barton, Mary N. "Rare books and other bibliographical resources in Baltimore libraries." Papers of the Bibliographical Society of America, 55 (1st quarter 1961), 1-16.

446. California, University, Library. Magisteri terrarum; a selection of old and rare books from the library of the University of California, Davis, California, ed. by Hilton Landry. Davis, 1962. 55p.

447. ———, William Andrews Clark Memorial Library. Report of the third decade, 1956-1966. Los Angeles, 1966. 75p.

Covers holdings in literature, 1640-1750; music and musical literature; early sciences; Wilde, Yeats, and the 1890s; Eric Gill; and fine printing.

448. Chicago, University, Library. A catalogue to an exhibition of notable books and manuscripts from the collections of the University of Chicago Library. Chicago, 1970. 95p.

Describes in detail 109 rare books and manuscripts selected from library's collections.

449. Coleman, Earle E. "The Department of Rare Books and Special Collections at Princeton." Princeton University Library chronicle, 32 (1970), 34-54.

450. Dartmouth College Library. A brief guide to the principal collections of the Rare Book Department, prep. by Elizabeth M. Sherrard. Hanover, N.H., 1966. 43p.

451. Fingerson, Ronald L. "Treasures of the University Libraries." The Iowan, 16 (Spring 1968), 2-6, 51.

Books and manuscripts in University of Iowa Libraries.

452. Harvard University, Houghton Library. The Houghton Library, 1942-1967; a selection of books and manuscripts in Harvard collections. Cambridge: Harvard College Library, 1967. 255p.

Includes medieval manuscripts, incunabula, early maps, Reformation, Erasmus, etc.

453. Huntington Library. Great books in great editions, rev. ed., by Roland Baughman and Robert O. Schad. San Marino, Calif., 1965. 65p.

454. ———. "The only copies known": an exhibition. San Marino, Calif., 1970. 15p.

455. Indiana University, Lilly Library. Printing and the mind of man; an exhibition of the world's most influential books. Bloomington, 1964. 6p.

456. Krader, Barbara. "The Glagolitic missal of 1483." Library of Congress quarterly journal of current acquisitions, 20 (1963), 93-98.

Copy of earliest known Croatian printed book, acquired by Library of Congress.

457. Minnesota, University, Libraries. Guide to collections in the Rare Book Division, University of Minnesota Libraries. Minneapolis, 1970. 15p.

Brief descriptions of principal special collections.

458. New York Public Library. "Sixty-four treasures: an exhibition for World's Fair visitors." Bulletin of the New York Public Library, 68 (1964), 209-24. Reprinted, 1964. 20p.

Annotated list of some of New York Public Library's most famous books.

459. Newberry Library. A catalogue of an exhibition of books and manuscripts selected from the Louis H. Silver collection. Chicago, 1965. 17p.

Rare book collection acquired by Newberry Library.

460. ———. Henry Raup Wagner, 1862-1957, an exhibition of rare books honoring the centenary of his birth. Chicago, 1962. 17p.

461. ———. A selection of books and manuscripts from the Louis H. Silver collection now in the Newberry Library; a handlist. Chicago, 1964. 29p.

An exhibition catalog.

462. ———. Treasures of the Newberry Library, an exhibition, ed. by James M. Wells. Chicago, 1962. 24p.

463. Ohio State University Libraries. The shoulders of giants; an exhibition of the world's most influential books in the Ohio State University Libraries. Columbus: 1965. 24p.

464. Pierpont Morgan Library. Books and manuscripts from the Heineman collection. N.Y., 1963. 96p.

Illustrated exhibition catalog of musical manuscripts, French and German literary and historical manuscripts, letters, French 18th-century illustrated books, fine bindings, and illuminated manuscripts.

465. ———. A review of acquisitions. N.Y., 1969. 186p. and 49 plates.

Short-title catalog of acquisitions of Morgan Library during period 1949-68.

466. Ringling Museum of Art Library. Rare books of the 16th, 17th, and 18th centuries from the library of the Ringling Museum of Art, Sarasota, Florida; an exhibition prep. by Valentine L. Schmidt. Sarasota, Fla., 1969. 32p.

467. Robinson, Stewart M. "Notes on the Witherspoon pamphlets." Princeton University Library chronicle, 27 (1965), 53-59.

Portion of John Witherspoon library preserved in Princeton University Library; Witherspoon was president of the College of New Jersey at Princeton and delegate to the Continental Congress.

468. Shaffer, Ellen. "The rare book department, Free Library of Philadelphia." Papers of the Bibliographical Society of America, 64 (1970), 1-11.

General description of library's several major collections.

469. South Carolina, University, Library. Rare book collection in the McKissick Memorial Library, the University of South Carolina, by Davy-Jo Stribling Ridge. Columbia, 1966. 396p.

470. Southern Methodist University, Bridwell Library. From Homer to Erasmus, an exhibit of printed books. Dallas, Tex., 1967. 4p. (Bridwell broadside, no.6)

471. Syracuse University Libraries. The George Arents Research Library at Syracuse University. Syracuse, N.Y., 1970. 36p.

Description of collections of rare books, manuscripts, archives, and records at Syracuse.

472. U.S. Library of Congress, Rare Book Division. The Rare Book Division: a guide to its collections and services, rev. ed. Wash.: Govt. Print. Off., 1965. 51p.

473. ——— ———. "Rare books." Library of Congress quarterly journal of current acquisitions, 18 (1961), 146-52; 19 (1962), 146-51; 20 (1963), 193-99; 21 (1964), 234-43; 22 (1965), 209-15; 23 (1966), 219-29; 24 (1967), 201-12; 25 (1968), 230-41; 26 (1969), 149-69; 27 (1970), 295-315.

Annual reports on Library's current acquisitions.

474. Watkinson Library. David Watkinson's Library, by Marian G. M. Clarke. Hartford, Conn.: Trinity College Pr., 1966. 177p.

History of notable collection of rare books, Americana, etc., housed on Trinity College campus.

475. Westlake, Neda M., and Riley, Lyman W. "Rare book collection." University of Pennsylvania Library chronicle, 33 (1967), 54-60.

Survey of areas of major strength in University of Pennsylvania Library collection.

476. Wofford College Library. Seventeenth century imprints, comp. by Alan B. Johns. Spartanburg, S.C.: Wofford Library Pr., 1971. 22*l.*

Lists 43 titles, English and continental, with full bibliographical descriptions, in Wofford College Library.

PRINTING HISTORY

General

477. Newberry Library. Dictionary catalogue of the history of printing from the John M. Wing Foundation, the Newberry Library (Chicago). Boston: G. K. Hall, 1961. 6v.

Records collection of 20,000 volumes on history of printing.

478. ———. The scholar printers: two exhibitions at the Newberry Library . . . I. Printers, publishers, and scholars: books mainly from the John M. Wing Foundation on the history of printing. II. The learned presses. Chicago: Univ. of Chicago Pr., 1964. 59p.

Annotated, illustrated catalog of 59 examples, 14th century to 1935.

479. U.S. Library of Congress. Papermaking: art and craft; an account derived from the exhibition presented in the Library of Congress. Wash., 1968. 96p.

480. Williams College, Chapin Library. An exhibition of alphabets from clay tablet to photo-composition through 30 April 1969. Williamstown, Mass., 1969. Unpaged.

Selected examples from the Chapin Library to illustrate history of alphabets and writing.

Incunabula

481. Brandeis University Library. A descriptive catalogue of the incunabula of the Brandeis University Library, by David S. Berkowitz. Waltham, Mass.: Brandeis Univ., 1963. 69p.

Describes in detail 22 15th-century works in Brandeis Library.

482. California, University, Library. Catalogue of the incunabula in the Elmer Belt Library of Vinciana, by Frances L. Finger. Los Angeles: Friends of the UCLA Library, 1970. 80p.

Housed in UCLA's Art Library.

483. Corré, Alan D. "Two rare incunabula in Milwaukee." Wis. Academy of Sciences, Arts and Letters, Transactions, 54 (1965), 185-86.

484. Dartmouth College Library. A checklist of incunabula in the special collections of the Dartmouth College Library. Hanover, N.H., 1970. 16*l.*

Lists 120 titles, including 8 works from the Erhart Ratdolt press.

485. Goff, Frederick R. "Five undescribed French incunabula in the Library of Congress." Gutenberg-Jahrbuch (1967), 88-93.

486. ———. "Four undescribed German broadsides of the XVth century in the Library of Congress." Beiträge zu Inkunabelkunde, 3d ser., 3 (1967), 165-67.

487. ———. Incunabula in American libraries: a third census of fifteenth-century books recorded in North American collections. N.Y.: Bibliographical Society of America, 1964. 798p.

Locates copies of 47,181 incunabula owned in America, by hundreds of institutions and private individuals.

488. ———. Some undescribed ephemera of the 15th century in the Library of Congress. Berlin: Akademie-Verlag, 1965. Sonderdruck aus Beiträge zur Inkunabelkunde, dritte Folge, I, p.100-2.

489. Indiana University, Lilly Library. The first twenty-five years of printing, 1455-1480; an exhibition, comp. by Josiah Q. Bennett and W. Gordon Wheeler. Bloomington, 1967. 58p. (Lilly Library publication, no.5)

490. Manhattan College Library. A descriptive catalogue of incunabula in the Cardinal Hayes Library. N.Y.: Manhattan College, 1967. 67p.

Bibliographical and content descriptions of 91 incunabula in the Manhattan College Library.

491. Southern Methodist University, Bridwell Library. The Bridwell-DeBellis collection of fifteenth century printing. Dallas, Tex., 1962. 38p.

Lists about 300 incunabula.

492. ——— ———. Bridwell Library's 300th incunable. Dallas, Tex., 1966. 4p. (Bridwell broadside, no.3)

Great Britain

493. Frye, Roland Mushat. "The new Xerox library of British Renaissance books at the University of Pennsylvania." University of Pennsylvania Library chronicle, 34 (1968), 3-6.

Collection of xerographic reproductions of titles listed in Pollard and Redgrave's Short title catalogue.

494. Kovacs, Suzanne. Holdings of the Miriam Lutcher Stark Library, the University of Texas at Austin, of titles in the Short title catalogue of English books, 1475-1640. Austin, 1969. 213p. (Master's report, Graduate School of Library Science, Univ. of Tex.)

United States

General

495. Bristol, Roger P. Index of printers, publishers, and booksellers indicated by Charles Evans in his American bibliography. Charlottesville: Bibliographical Society of the Univ. of Va., 1961. 172p.

496. ———. Supplement to Charles Evans' American bibliography. Charlottesville: Univ. Pr. of Va., 1970. 636p.

Adds 11,262 citations of books, pamphlets, newspapers, journals, broadsides, and other published material to the 39,162 listed by Evans. Locations reported for all titles found.

497. Greely, Georgiana Mathews. Early American imprints in the American Antiquarian Society; bibliographic problems in the revision of Evans' American bibliography. Wash., 1966. 59p. (Master's thesis, Dept. of Library Science, Catholic Univ. of America)

498. Madison, Charles A. "Gleanings from the Henry Holt files." Princeton University Library chronicle, 27 (1966), 86-106.

Describes selected items from publisher's archives in Princeton Library.

499. Michigan State University Library. The Douglas C. McMurtrie manuscripts collection at the Michigan State University Library. East Lansing, 1963. 9*l.*

Relates to history of U.S. printing.

500. Ohio State University Libraries. A catalog of the exhibition of selected private presses in the United States, comp. by Mary P. Key. Columbus, 1965. 23p.

501. Princeton University Library. "Archives of Charles Scribner's Sons." Princeton University Library chronicle, 28 (1967), 187-89.

Description of publisher's archives received by Princeton.

502. Shaw, Ralph R., and Shoemaker, Richard H. American bibliography: a preliminary checklist. N.Y.: Scarecrow, 1958-65. 19v.

Covers period 1801-19, one volume each year; locations of copies noted, if known.

503. ——— ———. American bibliography: a preliminary checklist 1801 to 1819—corrections, author index. N.Y.: Scarecrow, 1966. 189p.

504. ——— ———. American bibliography, a preliminary checklist 1801-1819: addenda, list of sources, library symbols. N.Y.: Scarecrow, 1965. 256p.

505. ——— ———. American bibliography, a preliminary checklist 1801 to 1819: title index. N.Y.: Scarecrow, 1965. 517p.

506. Shipton, Clifford K., and Mooney, James E. National index of American imprints through 1800, the short-title Evans. [Worcester, Mass.]: American Antiquarian Society, 1969. 2v.

Alphabetical index to Evans' American bibliography, with corrections and additions; locates copies.

507. Shoemaker, Richard H. Checklist of American imprints, 1820-1827. N.Y.: Scarecrow, 1964-70. 8v.

Locates copies.

508. Trienens, Roger J. "The Library's earliest colonial imprints." Library of Congress quarterly journal of current acquisitions, 24 (1967), 186-200.

Description of imprints, 1640-1763, under individual colonies, in Library of Congress collection.

509. Virginia State Library. Southeastern broadsides before 1877; a bibliography, ed. by Ray O. Hummel, Jr. Richmond, 1971. 501p. (Va. State Library publications, no.33)

Locates copies in numerous Southern libraries.

California

510. Conlan, Eileen M. A checklist of California imprints for the year 1870, with a historical introduction. Wash., 1967. 150p. (Master's thesis, Dept. of Library Science, Catholic Univ. of America)

Locates copies.

511. Drury, Clifford M. California imprints, 1846-1876. Glendale, Calif.: A. H. Clark, 1970. 220p.

Books, pamphlets, broadsides, periodicals, newspapers, and manuscripts, each described, annotated, and located.

512. Greenwood, Robert. California imprints, 1833-1862; a bibliography, comp. by Seiko June Suzuki and Marjorie Pulliam. Los Gatos, Calif.: Talisman, 1961. 524p.

Locates copies in numerous libraries.

513. Groves, Esther P. A checklist of California imprints from 1863 and 1864, with a historical introduction. Wash., 1961. 147p. (Master's thesis, Dept. of Library Science, Catholic Univ. of America)

Locates copies.

514. Kidd, Deborah Dove. A checklist of California non-official imprints for the year 1872, with a historical introduction. Wash., 1967. 172p. (Master's thesis, Dept. of Library Science, Catholic Univ. of America)

Locates copies.

515. McCarvel, Mary Kay. A checklist of California imprints for the year 1874, with a historical introduction. Wash., 1967. 115p. (Master's thesis, Dept. of Library Science, Catholic Univ. of America)

Locates copies.

516. Martinez, Patrick. A checklist of California imprints for the year 1869-1870, with a historical introduction. Wash., 1966. 117p. (Master's thesis, Dept. of Library Science, Catholic Univ. of America)

Locates copies.

517. Pryor, Lewis A. "The Kemble collections on American printing and publishing." California librarian, 30 (1969), 244-49.

Comprehensive collection, with special strength in California material, assembled by California Historical Society Library, San Francisco.

518. Sacconaghi, Charles D. Checklist of California imprints for the years 1865-1868 with a historical introduction. Wash., 1963. 219p. (Master's thesis, Dept. of Library Science, Catholic Univ. of America)

Locates copies.

Connecticut

519. Balas, Leslie. A checklist of New Haven, Connecticut, imprints for the years 1835-1837. Wash., 1965. 87p. (Master's thesis, Dept. of Library Science, Catholic Univ. of America)

Locates copies.

520. Bengston, Betty Grimes. A checklist of Hartford, Connecticut, imprints for the years 1832-1833 with a historical introduction. Wash., 1967. 103p. (Master's thesis, Dept. of Library Science, Catholic Univ. of America)

Locates copies.

521. Bonneau, Fr. Ward. A checklist of New Haven, Connecticut, imprints for the years 1865-1867, with a historical introduction. Wash., 1964. 70p. (Master's thesis, Dept. of Library Science, Catholic Univ. of America)

Locates copies.

522. Cale, William E. A checklist of Hartford, Connecticut, imprints from 1826-1828, with a historical introduction. Wash., 1966. 127p. (Master's thesis, Dept. of Library Science, Catholic Univ. of America)

Locates copies.

523. Dion, Dora E. A checklist of Hartford, Connecticut, imprints from 1828-1829, with a historical introduction. Wash., 1966. 86p. (Master's thesis, Dept. of Library Science, Catholic Univ. of America)

Locates copies.

524. Draper, Greta H. Balfour. A checklist of New Haven, Connecticut, imprints for the years 1832-33,

with a historical introduction. Wash., 1961. 83p. (Master's thesis, Dept. of Library Science, Catholic Univ. of America)

Locates copies.

525. Goldenbaum, Mary Bacon. A checklist of New Haven, Connecticut, imprints for the years 1871 and 1872. Wash., 1965. 115p. (Master's thesis, Dept. of Library Science, Catholic Univ. of America)

Locates copies.

526. Hall, Ruth Louise. A checklist of Hartford, Connecticut, imprints from 1806-07, with a historical introduction. Wash., 1963. 74p. (Master's thesis, Dept. of Library Science, Catholic Univ. of America)

Locates copies.

527. Larouche, Leo O. A checklist of New Haven, Connecticut, imprints for the years 1870, 1875 and 1876 with a historical introduction. Wash., 1968. 86p. (Master's thesis, Dept. of Library Science, Catholic Univ. of America)

Locates copies.

528. Lewis, Ida M. Checklist of New Haven, Connecticut, imprints for the years 1843-1844, with a historical introduction. Wash., 1964. 76p. (Master's thesis, Dept. of Library Science, Catholic Univ. of America)

Locates copies.

529. Pablo, Winifred O'Connor. A checklist of New Haven, Connecticut, imprints for the years 1830-1831. Wash., 1961. 45p. (Master's thesis, Dept. of Library Science, Catholic Univ. of America)

Locates copies.

530. Ratra, Paramjit K. A checklist of New Haven, Connecticut, imprints for the years 1873-74, with a historical introduction. Wash., 1965. 76p. (Master's thesis, Dept. of Library Science, Catholic Univ. of America)

Locates copies.

531. Rier, Nadine S. A checklist of New Haven, Connecticut, imprints for the years 1861-62, with a historical introduction. Wash., 1966. 98p. (Master's thesis, Dept. of Library Science, Catholic Univ. of America)

Locates copies.

532. Robinowitz, Grace. A checklist of New Haven, Connecticut, imprints from 1823 through 1825 with a historical introduction. Wash., 1961. 60p. (Master's thesis, Dept. of Library Science, Catholic Univ. of America)

Locates copies.

533. Shih, Walter D. A checklist of New Haven, Connecticut, imprints for the years 1820-22, with a historical introduction. Wash., 1962. 75p. (Master's thesis, Dept. of Library Science, Catholic Univ. of America)

Locates copies.

534. Zakrzewski, Esteban A. Checklist of New Haven, Connecticut, imprints for the years 1841 and 1842, with a historical introduction. Wash., 1964. 100p. (Master's thesis, Dept. of Library Science, Catholic Univ. of America)

Locates copies.

Delaware

535. Rink, Ewald. Printing in Delaware 1761-1800; a checklist. Wilmington, Del.: Eleutherian Mills Historical Library, 1969. 214p.

Lists 566 books and pamphlets, with locations in 79 libraries.

536. Schalau, Robert D. A checklist of Delaware imprints for the years 1870-76, with a historical introduction. Wash., 1962. 80p. (Master's thesis, Dept. of Library Science, Catholic Univ. of America)

Locates copies.

District of Columbia

537. Franco, Diane Marion. A checklist of non-official imprints of the District of Columbia for the year 1840, with a historical introduction. Wash., 1965. 125*l.* (Master's thesis, Dept. of Library Science, Catholic Univ. of America)

Locates copies.

538. Slaughter, Peggy Ann. A checklist of Washington, D.C., imprints from 1838-39, with a historical introduction. Wash., 1965. 111p. (Master's thesis, Dept. of Library Science, Catholic Univ. of America)

Locates copies.

Georgia

539. Kress, Virginia E. A checklist of Savannah, Georgia, imprints, 1838-1853, with a historical introduction. Wash., 1965. 69p. (Master's thesis, Dept. of Library Science, Catholic Univ. of America)

Locates copies.

540. Scott, Edith S. A checklist of Augusta, Georgia, imprints for 1806 to 1860, with a historical introduction. Wash., 1968. 73*l.* (Master's thesis, Dept. of Library Science, Catholic Univ. of America)

Locates copies.

541. Sheffield, Joanne Wagner. A checklist of Savannah, Georgia, imprints for the years 1854-1864, with a historical introduction. Wash., 1967. 67p. (Master's thesis, Dept. of Library Science, Catholic Univ. of America)

Locates copies.

542. Sullivan, Joan Theresa. A checklist of Savannah, Georgia, imprints for the years 1865-1876, with a historical introduction. Wash., 1966. 83p. (Master's thesis, Dept. of Library Science, Catholic Univ. of America)

Locates copies.

Illinois

543. Byrd, Cecil K. A bibliography of Illinois imprints, 1814-1858. Chicago: Univ. of Chicago Pr., 1966. 601p.

Chronological arrangement; library locations for 3,089 books, pamphlets, broadsides, and maps.

Indiana

544. Bartlett, Mary Ellen. A checklist of Indiana imprints, non-official, for the years 1864-1866, with a historical introduction. Wash., 1967. 107p. (Master's thesis, Dept. of Library Science, Catholic Univ. of America)

Locates copies.

Iowa

545. Carpenter, Zoe Irene. A checklist of Des Moines, Iowa, imprints from 1861 through 1864, with a historical introduction. Wash., 1961. 64p. (Master's thesis, Dept. of Library Science, Catholic Univ. of America)

Locates copies.

546. Cheever, Lawrence O. "The Prairie Press: a thirty-year record." Books at Iowa, 3 (Nov. 1965), 15-20, 25-30.

Checklist of publications of a private press; nearly all titles in University of Iowa Library.

547. Rickman, Marilee S. A checklist of Des Moines, Iowa, imprints from 1866 through 1867, with a historical introduction. Wash., 1968. 49p. (Master's thesis, Dept. of Library Science, Catholic Univ. of America)

Locates copies.

Maine

548. Eckman, Florence. Checklist of Portland, Maine, imprints for the years 1856-1858, with a historical introduction. Wash., 1968. 143p. (Master's thesis, Dept. of Library Science, Catholic Univ. of America)

Locates copies.

549. Fischmeister, Marie Antonie. Checklist of Portland, Maine, imprints for the years 1851-1858, with a historical introduction. Wash., 1966. 116p. (Master's thesis, Dept. of Library Science, Catholic Univ. of America)

Locates copies.

550. Flynn, Jane M. A checklist of Bangor, Maine, imprints for the years 1861-1876, with a historical introduction. Wash., 1967. 78p. (Master's thesis, Dept. of Library Science, Catholic Univ. of America)

Locates copies.

551. Frawley, Margaret Lenora. A checklist of Augusta, Maine, imprints from 1848 through 1876, with a historical introduction. Wash., 1963. 134p. (Master's thesis, Dept. of Library Science, Catholic Univ. of America)

Locates copies.

552. Martin, Abbott Waite. A checklist of Portland, Maine, imprints for the years 1859-1862, with a historical introduction. Wash., 1966. 72p. (Master's thesis, Dept. of Library Science, Catholic Univ. of America)

Locates copies.

553. Muller, Violette K. A checklist of Bangor [Maine] imprints for the years 1847-60, with a historical introduction. Wash., 1962. 82p. (Master's thesis, Dept. of Library Science, Catholic Univ. of America)

Locates copies.

554. Theiss, Kay Thomas. A checklist of Portland, Maine, imprints for the years 1854-1855, with a historical introduction. Wash., 1967. 57p. (Master's thesis, Dept. of Library Science, Catholic Univ. of America)

Locates copies.

555. Vandergrift, Barbara P. A checklist of Portland, Maine, imprints for the years 1875-1876, with a histori-

cal introduction. Wash., 1967. 104p. (Master's thesis, Dept. of Library Science, Catholic Univ. of America)
Locates copies.

556. Young, Patricia Miller. Checklist of Portland, Maine, imprints for the years 1871-1874, with a historical introduction. Wash., 1968. 103p. (Master's thesis, Dept. of Library Science, Catholic Univ. of America)
Locates copies.

Maryland

557. Chin, Elisabeth May. A checklist of Maryland imprints from 1864 through 1866, with a historical introduction. Wash., 1963. 253p. (Master's thesis, Dept. of Library Science, Catholic Univ. of America)
Locates copies.

558. Gildea, Matthew Edward. A checklist of Maryland imprints for the year 1859. Wash., 1965. 116p. (Master's thesis, Dept. of Library Science, Catholic Univ. of America)
Locates copies.

559. Lambert, Robert A. A checklist of Maryland imprints for the year 1862, with a historical introduction. Wash., 1963. 84p. (Master's thesis, Dept. of Library Science, Catholic Univ. of America)
Locates copies.

560. Neavill, Helen Aldena. A checklist of Maryland imprints for the year 1861, with a historical introduction. Wash., 1962. 106p. (Master's thesis, Dept. of Library Science, Catholic Univ. of America)
Locates copies.

561. O'Neill, Maureen. A checklist of Maryland imprints for the year 1860, with a historical introduction. Wash., 1963. 135p. (Master's thesis, Dept. of Library Science, Catholic Univ. of America)
Locates copies.

562. Rosenthal, Elaine P. A checklist of Maryland imprints for the year 1863, with a historical introduction. Wash., 1962. 88p. (Master's thesis, Dept. of Library Science, Catholic Univ. of America)
Locates copies.

563. Titus, Thomas R. A checklist of Maryland imprints for the year 1839, with a historical introduction. Wash., 1963. 86p. (Master's thesis, Dept. of Library Science, Catholic Univ. of America)
Locates copies.

Massachusetts

564. Bell, Matthew J. A checklist of Worcester, Massachusetts, imprints from 1826-1833, with a historical introduction. Wash., 1966. 89p. (Master's thesis, Dept. of Library Science, Catholic Univ. of America)
Locates copies.

565. Burnett, Charlene R. A checklist of New Bedford, Massachusetts, imprints from 1866 to 1876, with a historical introduction. Wash., 1964. 108p. (Master's thesis, Dept. of Library Science, Catholic Univ. of America)
Locates copies.

566. Gatley, Flora McKenzie. Checklist of Salem, Massachusetts, imprints from 1866-1870, with a historical introduction. Wash., 1968. 94p. (Master's thesis, Dept. of Library Science, Catholic Univ. of America)
Locates copies.

567. Houchin, Margaret Y. Checklist of Salem, Massachusetts, imprints, 1871-1873, with a historical introduction. Wash., 1968. 71p. (Master's thesis, Dept. of Library Science, Catholic Univ. of America)
Locates copies.

568. Kanick, Mary Joanne. A checklist of Salem, Massachusetts, imprints from 1874 to 1876, with a historical introduction. Wash., 1966. 95p. (Master's thesis, Dept. of Library Science, Catholic Univ. of America)
Locates copies.

569. Kudravetz, Barbara F. A checklist of Worcester, Massachusetts, imprints from 1846-1849, with a historical introduction. Wash., 1968. 86p. (Master's thesis, Dept. of Library Science, Catholic Univ. of America)
Locates copies.

570. Relleve, Rosalie. Checklist of Worcester, Massachusetts, imprints for the years 1834 to 1840, with a historical introduction. Wash., 1965. 85p. (Master's thesis, Dept. of Library Science, Catholic Univ. of America)
Locates copies.

571. Slattery, William J. A checklist of Worcester, Massachusetts, imprints for the years 1840 to 1845, with a historical introduction. Wash., 1967. 95p. (Master's thesis, Dept. of Library Science, Catholic Univ. of America)
Locates copies.

572. Tierney, Sr. M. Jeanne. A checklist of Worcester, Massachusetts, imprints for the years 1850-1853, with a historical introduction. Wash., 1967. 100p. (Master's thesis, Dept. of Library Science, Catholic Univ. of America)

Locates copies.

Michigan

573. Collins, Sara Dobie. A checklist of non-official Michigan imprints for the years 1859-1860, with a historical introduction. Wash., 1966. 105p. Master's thesis, Dept. of Library Science, Catholic Univ. of America)

Locates copies.

574. Sammons, Vivian O. A checklist of Michigan imprints for the years 1856-1858, with a historical introduction. Wash., 1967. 83p. (Master's thesis, Dept. of Library Science, Catholic Univ. of America)

Locates copies.

Minnesota

575. Bergstrom, Doris M. A checklist of Minnesota imprints, 1866-68, with a historical introduction. Wash., 1964. 75p. (Master's thesis, Dept. of Library Science, Catholic Univ. of America)

Locates copies.

576. Bertrand, Marcella M. Checklist of St. Paul, Minnesota, imprints for the years 1869-1871, with a historical introduction. Wash., 1966. 81p. (Master's thesis, Dept. of Library Science, Catholic Univ. of America)

Locates copies.

577. Goldbeck, Gwendolyn Owens. A checklist of St. Paul, Minnesota, imprints for the years 1872-1874, with a historical introduction. Wash., 1968. 101p. (Master's thesis, Dept. of Library Science, Catholic Univ. of America)

Locates copies.

578. Radyx, Sylvia G. Checklist of St. Paul, Minnesota, imprints for the years 1875-1876, with a historical introduction. Wash., 1968. 83p. (Master's thesis, Dept. of Library Science, Catholic Univ. of America)

Locates copies.

Mississippi

579. Chambers, Moreau B. C. A checklist of Mississippi imprints, 1865-1870, with a historical introduction. Wash., 1968. 121p. (Master's thesis, Dept. of Library Science, Catholic Univ. of America)

Locates copies.

Missouri

580. Perotti, Viola Andersen. Important firsts in Missouri imprints 1808-1858. Kansas City, Mo.: R. F. Perotti, 1967. 51p.

Based on Snyder collection in University of Missouri Library at Kansas City; also locates copies in other libraries.

New Hampshire

581. Kavanagh, Mary Whitney. A checklist of Dover, New Hampshire, imprints for the years 1848-1865. Wash., 1968. 68*l.* (Master's thesis, Dept. of Library Science, Catholic Univ. of America)

Locates copies.

582. Slyfield, Donna Christensen. A checklist of Hanover, New Hampshire, imprints from 1801 to 1848, with a historical introduction. Wash., 1963. 117p. (Master's thesis, Dept. of Library Science, Catholic Univ. of America)

Locates copies.

583. Stockton, Patricia. A checklist of Hanover, New Hampshire, imprints from 1850 to 1876, with a historical introduction. Wash., 1966. 113p. (Master's thesis, Dept. of Library Science, Catholic Univ. of America)

Locates copies.

584. Tapley, Priscilla M. A checklist of Dover, New Hampshire, imprints from 1826 to 1847, with a historical introduction. Wash., 1968. 94p. (Master's thesis, Dept. of Library Science, Catholic Univ. of America)

Locates copies.

New Jersey

585. Bishop, David F. A preliminary checklist of Trenton, New Jersey, imprints for the years 1843-1851. Wash., 1965. 72p. (Master's thesis, Dept. of Library Science, Catholic Univ. of America)

Locates copies.

586. Harman, Eleanor Randall. A checklist of Trenton, New Jersey, imprints 1867-1870, with a historical introduction. Wash., 1967. 57p. (Master's thesis, Dept. of Library Science, Catholic Univ. of America)

Locates copies.

587. Nekritz, Leah K. A checklist of Trenton imprints from 1826-1842, with a historical introduction. Wash., 1963. 89p. (Master's thesis, Dept. of Library Science, Catholic Univ. of America)
Locates copies.

588. Rockefeller, George C. "The first New Jersey imprint." Journal of the Rutgers University Library, 31 (1967), 11-13.
A 1723 William Bradford imprint acquired by Rutgers Library.

589. Soponis, Leocadia Ann. A checklist of Morristown, New Jersey, imprints for the years 1821-1876, with a historical introduction. Wash., 1967. 51p. (Master's thesis, Dept. of Library Science, Catholic Univ. of America)
Locates copies.

590. Wentz, Loretta Ann. A checklist of Trenton, New Jersey, imprints from 1862-1866, with a historical introduction. Wash., 1965. 75p. (Master's thesis, Dept. of Library Science, Catholic Univ. of America)
Locates copies.

591. Whitelock, Margaret M. A checklist of Princeton, New Jersey, imprints for the years 1826-1845, with a historical introduction. Wash., 1967. 75p. (Master's thesis, Dept. of Library Science, Catholic Univ. of America)
Locates copies.

New York

592. Bird, Sr. Dorothy Margaret. A checklist of Syracuse, New York, imprints from 1870 through 1872, with a historical introduction. Wash., 1968. 57p. (Master's thesis, Catholic Univ. of America, Dept. of Library Science)
Locates copies.

593. Goldberg, Merle. A checklist of Syracuse, New York, imprints from 1871-1872, with a historical introduction. Wash., 1962. 71p. (Master's thesis, Dept. of Library Science, Catholic Univ. of America)
Locates copies.

594. Healy, Sr. Frances. A checklist of Rochester, New York, imprints for the years 1855-1858, with a historical introduction. Wash., 1966. 82p. (Master's thesis, Dept. of Library Science, Catholic Univ. of America)
Locates copies.

595. Healy, Mary Agnes. A checklist of Rochester, New York, imprints for the years 1863-1865, with a historical introduction. Wash., 1968. 61p. (Master's thesis, Dept. of Library Science, Catholic Univ. of America)
Locates copies.

596. Hogan, Jane S. A checklist of Buffalo imprints from 1853-1855, with a historical introduction. Wash., 1966. 81p. (Master's thesis, Dept. of Library Science, Catholic Univ. of America)
Locates copies.

597. Hurley, Maryjane E. A checklist of Buffalo, New York, imprints, 1871-1873. Wash., 1967. 82p. (Master's thesis, Dept. of Library Science, Catholic Univ. of America)
Locates copies.

598. Kabelac, Karl Sanford. Book publishing in Auburn, New York, 1851-1876; an introduction and an imprints bibliography. Auburn, N.Y., 1969. 136*l.* (Thesis, State University College, Oneonta, N.Y.)
Locates copies.

599. Kelly, William M. Checklist of Buffalo imprints for the years 1868-1870, with a historical introduction. Wash., 1968. 65p. (Master's thesis, Dept. of Library Science, Catholic Univ. of America)
Locates copies.

600. Mack, Wilmetta S. A checklist of Buffalo imprints from 1865-1866-1867, with a historical introduction. Wash., 1967. 77p. (Master's thesis, Dept. of Library Science, Catholic Univ. of America)
Locates copies.

601. McKay, Alice A. A checklist of Rochester, New York, imprints for the years 1851-1854, with a historical introduction. Wash., 1965. 71p. (Master's thesis, Dept. of Library Science, Catholic Univ. of America)
Locates copies.

602. Marcinowski, Constance. A checklist of Buffalo imprints from 1851-1852, with a historical introduction. Wash., 1961. 71p. (Master's thesis, Dept. of Library Science, Catholic Univ. of America)
Locates copies.

603. Mounteer, Sr. Honor. A checklist of Buffalo imprints from 1857-1860, with a historical introduction. Wash., 1969. 126*l.* (Master's thesis, Dept. of Library Science, Catholic Univ. of America)
Locates copies.

604. Murphy, Margaret A. A checklist of Buffalo, New York, imprints for the years 1861-1863, with a historical introduction. Wash., 1967. 63p. (Master's thesis, Dept. of Library Science, Catholic Univ. of America)

Locates copies.

605. Pierpont Morgan Library. The Spiral Press through four decades; an exhibition of books and ephemera. N.Y., 1966. 100p.

Illustrated exhibition catalog of New York press.

606. Pietropaoli, Frank A. A checklist of Fulton and Herkimer Counties, New York, imprints from the introduction of printing through 1876, with a historical introduction. Wash., 1961. 115p. (Master's thesis, Dept. of Library Science, Catholic Univ. of America)

Locates copies.

607. Smyth, Sheila A. A checklist of Rochester, New York, imprints for the years 1859-1862, with a historical introduction. Wash., 1966. 75p. (Master's thesis, Dept. of Library Science, Catholic Univ. of America)

Locates copies.

Ohio

608. Redmond, John Oliver. A checklist of Columbus, Ohio, imprints for the years 1833-1841, with a historical introduction. Wash., 1966. 109p. (Master's thesis, Dept. of Library Science, Catholic Univ. of America)

Locates copies.

609. Stoddard, Roger E., and Litchfield, Hope P. "A. D. Ames, first dramatic publisher in the West." Books at Brown, 21 (1966), 95-156.

Listing, with locations, of 491 plays published at Clyde, Ohio, from about 1873 to 1917.

610. Swider, Veronica. A checklist of Cleveland, Ohio, imprints from 1866 through 1868, with a historical introduction. Wash., 1962. 86p. (Master's thesis, Dept. of Library Science, Catholic Univ. of America)

Locates copies.

611. Woolridge, Geraldine. A checklist of Cleveland, Ohio, imprints from 1875 through 1876, with a historical introduction. Wash., 1968. 82*l.* (Master's thesis, Dept. of Library Science, Catholic Univ. of America)

Locates copies.

Oregon

612. Belknap, George N. "McMurtrie's Oregon imprints: a fourth supplement." Oregon historical quarterly, 64 (June 1963), 137-82.

Locates copies.

613. ———. Oregon imprints, 1845-1870. Eugene: Univ. of Oreg. Books, 1968. 305p.

Lists and describes more than 1,500 imprints, chronologically, with locations in academic, special, and research libraries; includes books, pamphlets, folders, broadsides, and newspaper extras.

Pennsylvania

614. Altheide, Dorothy P. Checklist of Harrisburg, Pennsylvania, imprints for the years 1826-30, with a historical introduction. Wash., 1963. 67p. (Master's thesis, Dept. of Library Science, Catholic Univ. of America)

Locates copies.

615. Baxtresser, Betty B. A preliminary checklist of imprints, Harrisburg, Pennsylvania, 1841-48, with a historical introduction. Wash., 1964. 72p. (Master's thesis, Dept. of Library Science, Catholic Univ. of America)

Locates copies.

616. Brennan, Minnie Elizabeth. A checklist of Pittsburgh, Pennsylvania, imprints for the years 1801-1818. Wash., 1966. 87p. (Master's thesis, Dept. of Library Science, Catholic Univ. of America)

Locates copies.

617. Costabile, Salvatore L. A checklist of Pittsburgh imprints from 1841 to 1851, with a historical introduction. Wash., 1963. 70p. (Master's thesis, Dept of Library Science, Catholic Univ. of America)

Locates copies.

618. Fletcher, Joseph J. A checklist of Pittsburgh imprints from 1852 through 1856, with a historical introduction. Wash., 1961. 93p. (Master's thesis, Dept. of Library Science, Catholic Univ. of America)

Locates copies.

619. Goode, Paul Killian. A checklist of Chambersburg, Pennsylvania, imprints 1846-76. Wash., 1961. 70p. (Master's thesis, Dept. of Library Science, Catholic Univ. of America)

Locates copies.

620. Halpern, Kathryn D. A preliminary checklist of Allentown and Bethlehem, Pennsylvania, imprints,

1813-76, with a historical introduction. Wash., 1964. 89p. (Master's thesis, Dept. of Library Science, Catholic Univ. of America)

Locates copies.

621. Johnson, Marjorie J. A checklist of Pittsburgh, Pennsylvania, imprints for the years 1862, 1874, 1875-1876, with a historical introduction. Wash., 1961. 153p. (Master's thesis, Dept. of Library Science, Catholic Univ. of America)

Locates copies.

622. Moran, Robert F. A checklist of Pittsburgh imprints from 1870 through 1873, with a historical introduction. Wash., 1965. 90p. (Master's thesis, Dept. of Library Science, Catholic Univ. of America)

Locates copies.

623. Schmidt, Thomas V. A checklist of Pittsburgh imprints from 1867-1869, with a historical introduction. Wash., 1967. 85p. (Master's thesis, Dept. of Library Science, Catholic Univ. of America)

Locates copies.

Rhode Island

624. Bachmann, George T. A checklist of Rhode Island imprints from 1854 to 1856, with a historical introduction. Wash., 1961. 113*l.* (Master's thesis, Dept. of Library Science, Catholic Univ. of America)

Locates copies.

625. Cutting, Helen Francis. A checklist of Providence, Rhode Island, imprints from 1848-1850, with historical introduction. Wash., 1961. 93p. (Master's thesis, Dept. of Library Science, Catholic Univ. of America)

Locates copies.

626. Dupont, Julie Andree. A checklist of Providence, Rhode Island, imprints for the years 1858 and 1859, with a historical introduction. Wash., 1965. 115p. (Master's thesis, Dept. of Library Science, Catholic Univ. of America)

Locates copies.

627. Farkas, Cathrine Ann. A checklist of Rhode Island imprints from 1860-1861, with a historical introduction. Wash., 1965. 79p. (Master's thesis, Dept. of Library Science, Catholic Univ. of America)

Locates copies.

628. Schekorra, Eva W. A checklist of Rhode Island imprints for 1863 and 1864, with historical introduction. Wash., 1965. 80p. (Master's thesis, Dept. of Library Science, Catholic Univ. of America)

Locates copies.

629. Snuggs, Myrtle Ann. A checklist of Providence, Rhode Island, imprints for 1865, with a historical introduction. Wash., 1967. 73p. (Master's thesis, Dept. of Library Science, Catholic Univ. of America)

Locates copies.

South Carolina

630. Brown, Julie K. A checklist of South Carolina imprints for the years 1873, 1874, 1875, and 1876, with a historical introduction. Wash., 1967. 65*l.* (Master's thesis, Dept. of Library Science, Catholic Univ. of America)

Locates copies.

631. Dunn, Barbara Butts. A checklist of Charleston, S.C., imprints for the years 1826-1830, with a historical introduction. Wash., 1967. 127p. (Master's thesis, Dept. of Library Science, Catholic Univ. of America)

Locates copies.

632. Eastham, Lucy Beale. A preliminary checklist of imprints, Charleston, South Carolina, 1800-1810, with a historical introduction. Wash., 1961. 89p. (Master's thesis, Dept. of Library Science, Catholic Univ. of America)

Locates copies.

633. Meacham, Miriam D. A checklist of South Carolina imprints for the years 1811-18. Wash., 1962. 83p. (Master's thesis, Dept. of Library Science, Catholic Univ. of America)

Locates copies.

634. Ragsdale, Betty McFarland. Checklist of Columbia, South Carolina, imprints for the years 1866-1870, with a historical introduction. Wash., 1967. 63p. (Master's thesis, Dept. of Library Science, Catholic Univ. of America)

Locates copies.

Texas

635. Friend, Llerena. "Additional items for the Winkler checklist of Texas imprints, 1846-1860." Southwestern historical quarterly, 65 (July 1961), 101-7.

636. Winkler, Ernest W., and Friend, Llerena. Checklist of Texas imprints 1861-1876. Austin: Texas State Historical Assoc., 1963. 734p.

Locations in numerous libraries.

Utah

637. Conner, Helen West. A checklist of Utah imprints for the years 1862-1882. Wash., 1962. 105p. (Master's thesis, Dept. of Library Science, Catholic Univ. of America)
Locates copies.

Vermont

638. American Antiquarian Society. Additions and corrections to Vermont imprints, by Marcus Allen McCorison. Worcester, Mass., 1968. 33p.

639. Levant, Muriel Roberta. A checklist of Vermont imprints for the years 1863-1865, with a historical introduction. Wash., 1964. 96p. (Master's thesis, Dept. of Library Science, Catholic Univ. of America)
Locates copies.

640. McCorison, Marcus A. Vermont imprints, 1778-1820. Worcester, Mass.: American Antiquarian Society, 1963. 597p.
Identifies–and usually locates–2,273 books, pamphlets, and broadsides, in 143 public and private collections, nearly all in U.S.

641. Maki, Suiko. A checklist of Vermont imprints for the years 1851-1856, with a historical introduction. Wash., 1964. 126p. (Master's thesis, Dept. of Library Science, Catholic Univ. of America)
Locates copies.

642. Wright, Lottie M. A checklist of Vermont imprints from 1873 through 1876, with a historical introduction. Wash., 1961. 79p. (Master's thesis, Dept. of Library Science, Catholic Univ. of America)
Locates copies.

Virginia

643. Bulley, Joan Sumner. A checklist of Richmond, Virginia, imprints from 1831 through 1834, with a historical introduction. Wash. 1967. 109p. (Master's thesis, Dept. of Library Science, Catholic Univ. of America)
Locates copies.

644. Horst, Irvin B. "Singers Glen, Virginia, imprints, 1847-1878; a checklist." EMC [Eastern Mennonite College] bulletin, 44 (Feb. 1965), 6-14.
List of 99 imprints with locations of copies.

645. McGrath, Mary Kathryn. A checklist of Richmond, Virginia, imprints for the year 1876, with a historical introduction. Wash., 1966. 66p. (Master's thesis, Dept. of Library Science, Catholic Univ. of America)
Locates copies.

646. Preston, Katherine Emily. A checklist of Richmond, Virginia, imprints for the years 1871-1875, with a historical introduction. Wash., 1963. 119p. (Master's thesis, Dept. of Library Science, Catholic Univ. of America)
Locates copies.

Other Countries

647. Harvard University Library, Dept. of Printing and Graphic Arts. Catalogue of books and manuscripts, comp. by Ruth Mortimer. Cambridge, Mass.: Belknap Pr. of Harvard Univ. Pr., 1964. 2v.
Catalog of French 16th-century books; lists 557 titles.

648. Hoskins, Janina W. "Printing in Poland's golden age." Quarterly journal of the Library of Congress, 23 (1966), 204-18.
Library of Congress' holdings indicated.

649. Rodriguez, Antonio. "First printing of South America in the Harvard Library." Harvard Library bulletin, 16 (1968), 38-48.
Description of four 16th-century Peruvian imprints with illustrations in Harvard Library.

650. Short-title catalog of books printed in Italy and of books in Italian printed abroad, 1501-1600, held in selected North American libraries. Boston: G. K. Hall, 1970. 3v.
Holdings of about 35 libraries listed.

Illustrated Books

651. Dartmouth College Library. A checklist of the class of 1926 memorial collection; illustrated books published in New England 1769-1870. Hanover, N.H., 1971. 37p.
Lists alphabetically by author about 1,000 books relevant to New England book illustration during Dartmouth's first century.

652. ———. Sampler from the class of 1926 memorial collection of illustrated books published in New England 1769-1869. Hanover, N.H., [1970]. 36p.

Representative selections from Dartmouth Library collection of New England illustrated books.

653. Harvard University, Houghton Library. The turn of a century, 1885-1910; art nouveau-Jugendstil books, catalogue by Eleanor M. Garvey and others. Cambridge, Mass.: Harvard Univ. Dept. of Printing and Graphic Arts, 1970. 124p.

Exhibition of illustrated books held at Houghton Library.

654. New York Public Library. Catalogue of Japanese illustrated books and manuscripts in the Spencer collection of the New York Public Library. Tokyo, 1968. 130p.

In Japanese; only short-title listing in English. Illustrated.

655. Princeton University Library. Early American book illustrators and wood engravers, 1670-1870, by Sinclair Hamilton. Princeton. N.J.: Princeton Univ. Pr., 1968. 2v.

Catalog of important collection in Princeton University Library.

656. Roylance, Dale R. "A collection of modern French illustrated books." Yale University Library gazette, 42 (1967), 1-7.

Describes special collection of 20th-century works in Yale Library.

657. Yale University Library. The arts of the French book, 1900-1965; illustrated books of the School of Paris, by Eleanor M. Garvey and Peter A. Wiek, Dallas, Tex.: Southern Methodist Univ. Pr., 1967. 119p.

Catalog of an exhibition.

Typography and Book Design

658. Bennett, Paul A. Some notes on the engaging by-paths and enduring pleasures of fine bookmaking. San Francisco: Grabhorn, 1963. 54p.

Based on exhibition, "The book, its art and history," in Stanford University Library.

659. California, University, Library, Santa Barbara. "Collections of the University Library." Soundings, 2:1 (May 1970), 1-40.

Articles on William Edwin Rudge, Bruce Rogers, and other private press imprints in library.

660. Columbia University Libraries. Frederic William Goudy, 1865-1947: a commemorative exhibition arranged and described by Roland Baughman, Columbia University Libraries. N.Y., 1966. 21p.

Exhibition based mainly on Columbia Libraries' Goudy collection.

661. Dartmouth College Library. Canadian books—Livres Canadiens; current design and production on exhibit 1 March-1 May 1967. Lunenburg, Vt.: Stinehour, 1967. 20p.

662. Dickinson, Lenore M. "The Rosamond B. Loring collection of decorated papers." Guild of Book Workers journal, 6 (Winter 1967-68), 3-12.

In Harvard University Library.

663. Kleist, Herbert. "The book jacket collection of the Fine Arts Library." Fine Arts Library newsletter (March 1970), 1-4.

At Harvard University.

664. Marvin, H. M. "Bruce Rogers and his work." Yale University Library gazette, 36 (1961), 13-23.

Description of extensive collection of works designed by Rogers, acquired by Yale Library.

665. New York Public Library. Cuts, borders, and ornaments selected from the Robinson-Pforzheimer typographical collection in the New York Public Library. N.Y., 1962. 44p.

666. Purdue University Libraries. Books by BR; an exhibition of selected books from the Rogers collection in the Purdue University Libraries, comp. by Robert A. Tibbetts. Lafayette, Ind., 1964. 32p.

667. Roylance, Dale R. "The arts of the French book, 1838-1967." Yale University Library gazette, 44 (1969), 47-105.

Describes collection relating to the arts of modern French bookmaking in Yale Library; accompanied by checklist compiled by Donald Gallup, of 306 books issued from 1838 to 1967.

668. Sanborn, Herbert J. "The Cleland papers." Library of Congress quarterly journal of current acquisitions, 20 (1963), 163-73.

Papers of Thomas Maitland Cleland, printer, typographer, type designer, artist, and illustrator, in Library of Congress.

669. [Stanford University Libraries. Ashendene Press collection] College & research libraries news, no.4 (April 1970), 97.

Extensive collection of Ashendene Press books and ephemera presented to Stanford.

670. Texas, University, Humanities Research Center. An exhibition of books designed by Merle Armitage. Austin, 1963. 36p.

671. Webb, Allie Bayne, "Bruce Rogers and the LSU Library." Louisiana State University, New books in the library, 19 (Aug. 16, 1966), 1-3.

Description of Bruce Rogers typography collection in Louisiana State University Library.

672. Williams College, Chapin Library. The English art of the book, exhibition. Williamstown, Mass., 1970. 10p.

Exhibition catalog, arranged by date, 1478-1969, and briefly annotated, of imprints held by Chapin Library.

673. ——— ———. French art of the book; exhibition. Williamstown, Mass., 1968. Unpaged.

Handlist of 77 titles, 15th to 20th centuries.

674. Yale University Library. Altschul collection: the arts of the French book, 1838-1967; with checklist. Yale University Library gazette, 44 (1969), 45-102.

Book Bindings

675. California, University, Library. A checklist of trade bindings, designed by Margaret Armstrong, by Charles B. Gullans and John J. Espey. Los Angeles, 1968. 37p. (UCLA Library occasional papers, no.16)

Based upon materials in UCLA Library.

676. Forman, Sidney. "Simplicity and utility: examples of early American bindings." Columbia Library columns, 12 (Feb. 1963), 23-31.

Illustrated article describing about 25 American book bindings, 1728-1836, in Columbia University Library.

677. French, Hannah D. "John Roulstone's Harvard bindings." Harvard Library bulletin, 18 (1970), 171-82.

Descriptions with illustrations of early 19th-century examples of Roulstone's bindings done at Harvard.

678. Pierpont Morgan Library. Bookbindings by T. J. Cobden-Sanderson, 1884-1893, by Frederick B. Adams, Jr. N.Y., 1969. 48p.

Illustrated catalog of an exhibition of 34 book bindings from American private and public collections.

679. Trienens, Roger J. "Hans Breitmann's bindings." Quarterly journal of the Library of Congress, 23 (1966), 3-8.

In Library of Congress collections.

680. Washington, University, Libraries. Bookbinding at the University of Washington, by Kenneth S. Allen. Seattle, 1962. 14p.

Philosophy and Psychology

GENERAL

681. California, University, Library. Sidney Hook, a bibliography. Santa Barbara, 1966. 34p.
Modern American philosopher.

682. Columbia University Libraries. The Spinoza bibliography; published under the auspices of the Columbia University Libraries, comp. by Adolph S. Oko. Boston: G. K. Hall, 1964. 602p.

683. Southern California, University, Library. Catalog of the Hoose Library of Philosophy, University of Southern California (Los Angeles). Boston: G. K. Hall, 1968. 6v.

684. [Southern Illinois University Library, Carbondale. Philosophy collection] College & research libraries news, no.3 (March 1969), 71.
Archives of Paul Carus and Open Court Publishing Company, LaSalle, Illinois, 60,000 pages, relating to modern philosophy, received by S.I.U. Library.

685. Syracuse University Libraries. Pschology serials in Syracuse University Libraries, comp. by Janet Graham. Syracuse, N.Y., 1970. 26p.
Alphabetical list with holdings.

686. Texas, University, Humanities Research Center. David Hume, 1711-1776; program and exhibition commemorating the 250th anniversary of his birth. Austin, 1961. 12p.

Religion

GENERAL

687. Farris, Donn Michael. "Duke Divinity School Library." North Carolina libraries, 25 (Summer 1967), 82-84.
A general survey.

688. Harvard University, Andover-Harvard Theological Library. Periodicals currently received by the Andover-Harvard Theological Library, Harvard Divinity School. Cambridge, Mass., 1968. 45p.

689. Idaho State Library. World of religion, selected from the holdings of the Idaho State Library, by Mildred Selby. Boise, 1968. 21p.

690. Kansas State University Library. A descriptive catalogue of seventeenth-century English religious literature in the Kansas State University Library, by William P. Williams. Manhattan, 1966. 26p. (Bibliography series, no.3)

691. Morris, Raymond P. "The Yale University Divinity Library." Yale University Library gazette, 43 (1968), 33-38.
Summary of resources relating to religion held by Yale Libraries.

692. Rodda, Dorothy J., and Harvey, John. Directory of church libraries. Philadelphia: Drexel, 1967. 83p.
Lists Protestant, Catholic, and Jewish libraries in all 50 states.

693. Society of American Archivists, Church Archives Committee. A preliminary guide to church records repositories, comp. by August R. Suelflow. St. Louis, 1969. 108p.
Records 500 depositories, with brief statements on holdings and services available.

694. ———, Church Records Committee. Directory of religious archival and historical depositories in America, comp. by Aug. R. Suelflow. n.p. 1963. 38*l.*

695. Syracuse University Library. Religion serials in Syracuse University libraries, comp. by Janet Graham. Syracuse, N.Y., 1970. 29p.
Alphabetical list with holdings.

696. Union Theological Seminary Library, New York. Alphabetical arrangement of main entries from the shelflist. Boston: G. K. Hall, 1965. 10v.

697. ———. Shelflist of the Union Theological Seminary Library. Boston: G. K. Hall, 1961. 10v.
Arranged by class order.

BIBLE

698. Cathedral Rare Book Library. In the beginning was the word: opening exhibition of written and printed Biblical and liturgical texts from the eighth century to the present. Wash., 1965. 71p.

699. Clark, Kenneth W. "Greek and Biblical resources for research at Duke." Library notes, a bulletin issued for the Friends of Duke University Library, 39 (April 1965), 1-9.
Describes three groups of works held by Duke University Library: Greek manuscripts, editions of Greek New Testament, and early English Bibles.

700. Herbert, Arthur S. Historical catalogue of printed editions of the English Bible: 1525-1961. N.Y: American Bible Society, 1968. 549p.
Locations in American and British libraries.

701. Hills, Margaret T. The English Bible in America: a

bibliography of editions of the Bible and the New Testament published in America, 1777-1957. N.Y.: American Bible Society and N.Y. Public Library, 1961. 477p.

Locates copies of 2,500 separate editions. Based primarily on American Bible Society's holdings.

702. Houston, University, Library. University of Houston exhibition of Bibles and related materials. Houston, Tex., 1970. Unpaged.

Exhibition catalog, illustrated, describing 46 examples of early and rare Bibles and related works.

703. Huntington Library. European drawings from the Kitto Bible: an exhibition, by Marcel Roethlisberger. San Marino, Calif., 1969. 41p.

704. ---. An exhibition of great Bibles. San Marino, Calif., 1961. 8p.

705. Princeton University Library. Book of Books, the English Bible and its antecedents; an exhibition. Princeton, N.J., 1963. 7p.

706. Rumball-Petre, Edwin A. R. Rare Bibles: an introduction for collectors and a descriptive checklist, 2d ed. N.Y.: Philip C. Duschnes, 1963. 60p.

Locates limited number of items described.

707. Southern Methodist University, Bridwell Library. The English Bible before the King James. Dallas, Tex., 1964. 44p.

Describes library's holdings.

708. Stark, Lewis M., and Cole, Maud D. "Bibles in many languages 1455-1966." Bulletin of the New York Public Library, 70 (1966), 495-504.

Catalog of an exhibition in New York Public Library.

709. Texas, University, Humanities Research Center. The Holy Bible at the University of Texas, rev. ed., comp. by David R. Farmer, Austin, 1967. 71p.

710. Williams, Jeane M. A checklist of the Bizzell Bible collection in the University of Oklahoma Library, prefaced by a discussion of certain items outstanding for their importance and contribution to Biblical scholarship. 1963. 103p. (Master's thesis, School of Library Science, Univ. of Okla.)

711. Wright, Dora L. E. "Bibles in National Archives." National Genealogical Society quarterly, 55 (1967), 149-51.

List of 82 family Bibles among Revolutionary War pension applications.

MISSIONS

712. Anderson, Gerald H. "Research libraries in New York City specializing in Christian missions." Journal of Asian studies, 25 (1966), 733-36.

713. Bellamy, V. Nelle. "The Liberia papers: library and archives of the Church Historical Society." Historical magazine of the Protestant Episcopal Church, 37 (March 1968), 77-82.

In the library and archives of the Church Historical Society.

714. Center for Research Libraries. Church Missionary Society archives relating to Africa and Palestine, 1799-1923; index to records on microfilm at the Center for Research Libraries. Chicago, 1968. 6*l.*

715. Missionary Research Library. Cumulative list of doctoral dissertations and master's theses in foreign missions and related subjects as reported by the Missionary Research Library in the Occasional bulletin, 1950 to 1960, comp. by Laura Person. N.Y., 1961. 46p.

Locations in institutions where theses were written.

716. ---. Current periodicals in the Missionary Research Library; alphabetical list and indexes, 2d ed., comp. by John T. Ma. N.Y., 1961. 38*l.*

717. ---. Dictionary catalog. Boston, G. K. Hall, 1967. 17v.

Contains about 273,000 entries by author, title, and subject.

718. Virginia, University, Library. Guide to the microfilm edition of the Letter book, 1688-1761, of the Company for Propagation of the Gospel in New England, ed. by Vesta Lee Gordon. Charlottesville, 1969. 9p. (Microfilm publications, no.8)

CHRISTIAN CHURCHES AND SECTS

General

719. Deutrich, Mabel E. "American church archives; an overview." American archivist, 24 (1961), 387-402.

Identifies important depositories of records of major denominations in United States.

720. Luesing, Lois L. "Church historical collections in liberal arts colleges." College & research libraries, 27 (1966), 291-303, 317.

Baptist

721. Boyer, Calvin James. Library resources and services at San Marcos Baptist Academy: a survey. Austin, 1964. 77p. (Master's thesis, Graduate School of Library Science, Univ. of Tex.)

722. Starr, Edward C. A Baptist bibliography, being a register of printed material by and about Baptists, including works written against the Baptists. Rochester, N.Y.: American Baptist Historical Society, 1947- . v.1- . (In progress)

Locates copies.

Disciples of Christ

723. College of the Bible Library. The Disciples of Christ in Kentucky: a finding list of the histories of local congregations of Christian churches, by Roscoe M. Pierson. Lexington, Ky., 1962. 63p.

Lists about 700 items.

Lutheran

724. Concordia Historical Institute. Microfilm index and bibliography of the Concordia Historical Institute, the Department of Archives and History, Lutheran Church–Missouri Synod, St. Louis, Missouri, 1954-1963. St. Louis: Concordia Pr., 1966. 182p.

Indexes 100,000 feet of film in Institute's microfilm collection on American Lutheranism.

Mennonite

725. Schmidt, John F. "Bethel College historical library: storehouse of Anabaptistica–Mennonitica." Mountain Plains library quarterly, 9 (Fall 1964), 13-15.

Collection at Bethel College, Newton, Kansas.

Methodist

726. Baker, Frank. "The Frank Baker collection; an autobiographical analysis." Library notes, a bulletin issued for the Friends of Duke University Library, no.36 (Dec. 1962), 1-9.

Description of collection of Wesleyana Methodism in Duke Library.

727. ———. "The Frank Baker collection of Wesleyana and British Methodism." Gnomon (1970), 52-62 (special number of Duke University Library's Library notes)

Describes collection in Duke Library.

728. ———. A union catalogue of the publications of John and Charles Wesley. Durham, N.C.: Divinity School, Duke University, 1966. 230p.

729. DePauw University. Indiana Methodism; a bibliography of printed and archival holdings in the archives of DePauw University and Indiana Methodism, comp. by Eleanore Cammack. Greencastle, Ind., 1964. 64p.

730. Lind, William E. "Methodist archives in the United States." American archivist, 24 (1961), 435-40.

Description of principal collections of Methodist archives throughout United States.

731. Methodist union catalog of history, biography, disciplines, and hymnals, ed. by Brooks B. Little. Lake Junaluska, N.C.: Assoc. of Methodist Historical Societies, 1967. 478p.

Lists holdings of 16 libraries, chiefly in Methodist seminaries.

732. Union list of Methodist serials, 2d ed., comp. by John Batsel. Evanston, Ill.: Commission on Archives and History of the United Methodist Church, 1969. 156p.

Revision of 1963 edition.

Moravian

733. Hamilton, Kenneth G. "The Moravian Archives at Bethlehem, Pennsylvania." American archivist, 24 (1961), 415-23.

General discussion of collection for Moravian history.

Mormon

734. Southern Illinois University Library. Sources of Mormon history in Illinois, 1839-48: an annotated catalog of the microfilm collection at Southern Illinois University, 2d ed., comp. by Stanley B. Kimball. Carbondale, 1966. 104p. (Bibliographic contributions, no.1)

Includes copies of documents, theses, and indexes to contemporary newspaper items.

Presbyterian

735. Albaugh, Gaylord P. "American Presbyterian periodicals and newspapers, 1752-1830, with library loca-

tions." Journal of Presbyterian history, 41 (1963), 165-87, 243-62; 42 (1964), 54-67, 124-44.

Alphabetical listing with holdings in various U.S. libraries and British Museum.

736. Presbyterian Historical Society. Special collections in the Presbyterian Historical Society. Philadelphia, 1961? 9p.

737. Trinterud, Leonard J. A bibliography of American Presbyterianism during the colonial period. Philadelphia: Presbyterian Historical Society, 1969. Unpaged.

Records 1,129 items identified by Evans numbers or, if not in Evans, by specific locations.

Protestant Episcopal

738. Kinney, John Mark. A guide to the archives of the General Convention of the Episcopal Church, 1785-1958. Austin, 1958. 82p. (Master's report, Graduate School of Library Science, Univ. of Tex.)

739. ———. "Inventory of archives of the General Convention: library and archives of the Church Historical Society." Historical magazine of the Protestant Episcopal Church, 38 (Sept. 1969), 291-326.

740. Winfrey, Dorman H. "Protestant Episcopal Church archives." American archivist, 24 (1961), 431-33.

Description and list of major holdings in the archives of the Protestant Episcopal Church, U.S., in the Episcopal Seminary of the Southwest Library, Austin, Texas.

Puritanism

741. Benton, Robert M. "An annotated checklist of Puritan sermons published in America before 1700." Bulletin of the New York Public Library, 74 (1970), 286-337.

Evans numbers cited, from which copies may be located.

Quaker (Friends)

742. Adams, Thomas R. "A list of eighteenth-century manuscript maps of New England yearly meetings." Quaker history, 52 (Spring 1963), 6-9.

Cites locations.

743. Capon, Ross B. "Good and bad moments in Quaker history." Friends journal, 15 (1969), 724-25.

Describes notable editions, anti-Quaker literature, special collections, and exhibits in Friends Historical Library, Swarthmore College.

744. Heiss, Willard C. "Guide to research in Quaker records in the Midwest." Indiana history bulletin, 39 (March-April 1962), 51-68, 71-82.

Lists major repositories, but does not locate individual items.

745. Maryland Hall of Records. Quaker records in Maryland, by Phebe R. Jacobsen. Annapolis, 1966. 154p.

746. Poole, Herbert. "A Quaker library." North Carolina libraries, 25 (Winter 1967), 9-12.

Describes collection in Guilford College Library.

747. Swarthmore College. Friends Historical Library. Friends Historical Library of Swarthmore College, by Frederick B. Tolles. Swarthmore, Pa., 1969. 8p.

Describes library's holdings of books, manuscripts, maps, pictures, and archives on Quakerism, peace, and related subjects.

Roman Catholic

748. Bryson, Thomas A. "The Walter George Smith papers in the archives of the American Catholic Historical Society." Records of the American Catholic Historical Society of Philadelphia, 80 (1969), 203-9.

749. Kapsner, Oliver L. A Benedictine bibliography: an author-subject union list, 2d ed. Collegeville, Minn.: St. John's Abbey Press, 1962. 2v.

Locates copies in about 100 libraries. Serials listed in v.1, p.643-64.

750. Lane, Sr. M. Claude. Catholic archives of Texas; history and preliminary inventory. Houston: Sacred Heart Dominican College, 1961. 114p. (Master's thesis, Graduate School of Library Science, Univ. of Tex.)

751. McAvoy, Thomas T. "Catholic archives and manuscript collections." American archivist, 24 (1961), 409-14.

Discussion of principal Catholic archival collections in the United States.

752. Notre Dame, University, Archives. Guide to the microfilm edition of the records of the Diocese of Louisiana and the Floridas 1576-1803, ed. by Lawrence J. Bradley. Notre Dame, Ind., 1967. 45p.

753. St. Louis University Libraries. "A checklist of Vatican manuscript codices available for consultàtion at the Knights of Columbus Vatican Film Library." Manuscripta 1 (1957), 27-44, 104-16, 139-74; 2 (1958), 41-49, 84-99, 167-81; 3 (1959), 38-46, 89-99; 12 (1968), 176-78.

In St. Louis University Library.

754. Santos, Richard. "A preliminary survey of the San Fernando archives." Texas libraries, 28 (1966-67), 152-72.

Records at San Fernando Cathedral, San Antonio, Texas.

755. Verret, Mary Camilla. A preliminary survey of Roman Catholic hymnals published in the United States of America. Wash.: Catholic Univ. of America Pr., 1964. 165p.

Copies located in numerous libraries.

756. Willging, Eugene P., and Hatzfeld, Herta. Catholic serials of the nineteenth century in the United States; a descriptive bibliography and union list, 2d series. Wash.: Catholic Univ. of America Pr., 1959-68, pts. 1-15.

Grouped by states.

NON-CHRISTIAN RELIGIONS

Judaism

757. Adan, Adrienne Hinds. A survey of the resources in Judaica and Hebraica held by the University of Texas at Austin. Austin, 1968. 47p. (Master's report, Graduate School of Library Science, Univ. of Tex.)

758. American Jewish Archives. "Acquisitions." American Jewish archives, 13 (April 1961), 113-28.

Includes records of congregations, societies, institutions, and private individuals; in American Jewish Archives, Jewish Institute of Religion, Hebrew Union College, Cincinnati, Ohio.

759. American Jewish Historical Society. The Lee Max Friedman collection of American Jewish colonial correspondence: letters of the Franks family (1733-1748), ed. by Leo M. Hershkowitz. Waltham, Mass., 1969. 171p. (Studies in American Jewish history, no.5)

760. American Jewish Historical Society Library. A preliminary survey of the manuscript collections found in the American Jewish Historical Society, part 1. N.Y., 1967. 30p. Supplement, 1969. 27p.

Describes 68 collections acquired by society between 1892-1967, now located on Brandeis University campus.

761. Berger, Abraham. "The Jewish Division of the New York Public Library." Jewish book annual, 23 (1965-66), 42-47.

History and description of Division.

762. Berlin, Charles. "The Judaica collection at Harvard." Jewish book annual, 26 (1968-69), 58-63.

763. Brisman, Shimeon. "The Jewish studies collection at UCLA." Jewish book annual, 1969-70, 27 (1969), 42-47.

764. California State Library, Sutro Branch, San Francisco. Sutro Library Hebraica: a handlist, by William M. Brinner. Sacramento, 1966. 82p.

Description of 167 important manuscripts which survived the fire and earthquake of 1906.

765. California, University, Library. Hebraica & Judaica, the Theodore E. Cummings collection; an exhibit at the UCLA Library. Los Angeles, 1963. 12p.

Collection comprises about 35,000 volumes.

766. ———. Jewish Studies Collection. List of periodicals. Los Angeles, 1970- . Published in parts.

767. ———. Jewish Studies Collection. New additions, June-July 1963- . No. 1- . Los Angeles, 1963- . Quarterly since Jan. 1964.

768. Chicago, University, Library. Hebraica at the University of Chicago. Chicago, 1965. 23p.

769. [Denver, University, Library. Judaica collections] College & research libraries news, no.3 (March 1970), 73.

Describes 10,000-volume collection of Judaica, representing all periods and various subjects, received by Denver.

770. [Duquesne University Library. Hebraica and Judaica collection] College & research libraries news, no.9 (Oct. 1969), 336-37.

Collection of 2,687 titles of Hebraica and Judaica acquired by Duquesne Library.

771. Egnal, Freda. "An annotated critical bibliography of materials relating to the history of the Jews in Rhode Island located in Rhode Island depositories (1678-

1966)." Rhode Island Jewish historical notes, 4 (1966), 305-527.

772. Fraenkel, Josef. Exhibition of the Jewish press in Great Britain, 1823-1963. London: Narod Pr., 1963. 63p.

Locates files in 9 libraries, including 3 in U.S., of 483 items.

773. Freimann, Aaron. Union catalog of Hebrew manuscripts and their location. N.Y.: American Academy for Jewish Research, 1964. 462p.

774. Harvard University Library. Catalogue of Hebrew books. Cambridge, Mass., 1968. 6v.

Record of Harvard's Judaica collection, approximately 100,000 volumes in Hebrew, Yiddish, etc.; reproduces 75,800 cards.

775. Hebrew Union College. Jewish Institute of Religion Library. Dictionary catalog of the Klau Library (Cincinnati). Boston: G. K. Hall, 1964. 32v.

Collection contains 200,000 volumes of Judaica and Hebraica.

776. [Hebrew Union College Library. Bookplate collection] College & research libraries news, no.5 (May 1969), 166.

Describes collection of over 7,000 bookplates of Jewish interest received by Hebrew Union College Library.

777. Jewish Theological Seminary of America Library. Illuminated Hebrew manuscripts from the Library of the Jewish Theological Seminary of America . . . catalogue by Tom L. Freudenheim and others. N.Y., 1965. 32p.

778. Ohio State University Libraries. Books of the people of the Book; an exhibit of Hebraica and Judaica at the Ohio State University Libraries. Columbus, 1968. 22p.

Description of rarest items in libraries' collection of Hebraica and Judaica.

779. Schoyer, George P. "Anti-semitica at Ohio State University." College & research libraries, 24 (1963), 335-36.

Collection of 251 items acquired by Ohio State University Library, chiefly relating to anti-Semitism in France, dating from 1841 to the present.

780. U.S. Library of Congress, Hispanic Foundation. Ladino books in the Library of Congress, a bibliography, comp. by Henry V. Besso. Wash.: Govt. Print. Off., 1963. 44p.

Books in Ladino, a form of Spanish printed in Hebrew characters; contains 289 entries.

781. [Utah, University, Libraries. Yiddish collection] College & research libraries news, no.5 (May 1969), 166.

Describes 4,000-volume collection, covering entire span of Yiddish culture, acquired by Utah.

782. Wisconsin, University, Dept. of Hebrew Studies. Catalogue of pamphlets in the Joseph L. Baron Judaica library pamphlet collection at the University of Wisconsin–Milwaukee Library. Milwaukee, n.d. 19*l.*

783. Wolfson, Harry A. Hebrew books in Harvard. Cambridge, Mass., 1968. 12p.

Social Sciences

GENERAL

784. Colorado State University Libraries. Information sources in the social sciences, comp. by Donald E. Oehlerts. Fort Collins, 1966. 170p.

785. Idaho, University, Library. Evaluation of the holdings in social science in the University of Idaho Library, by Charles A. Webbert. Moscow, 1962. 18p. (Bookmark, v.14, no.3, supplement)

786. New York University Libraries. The Tamiment library, by Daniel Bell. N.Y., 1969. 27p. (NYU Libraries bibliographical series, no.6)

Deals with Communism, Jews, labor and labor unions, and Socialism.

787. Purdue University Libraries. Union list of periodicals and periodic serials in the social sciences and humanities at Purdue University, comp. by Jane Ganfield and Margaret Stearns. Lafayette, Ind., 1962. 289p.

Records 14,700 titles with holdings in about 40 departmental collections.

788. Special Libraries Association, New York Chapter, Social Science Group. Social science serials in special libraries in the New York area; a selected list, ed. by Philip Rappaport and others. N.Y., 1961. 82p.

Lists about 1,200 titles with holdings and locations for 131 libraries.

789. Stevens, Rolland E. Reference books in the social sciences and humanities, 2d ed. Champaign, Ill.: Illini Union Bookstore, 1968. 181p.

Comprehensive guide, based primarily on University of Illinois Library collections.

790. U.S. Bureau of the Census. Bibliography of social science periodicals and monograph series: Hungary, 1947-62. Wash., 1964. 137p.

Notes Library of Congress holdings.

791. U.S. Dept. of Commerce, Bureau of the Census. Bibliography of social science periodicals and monograph series: mainland China, 1949-1960. Wash.: Govt. Print. Off., 1961. 32p.

Library of Congress call numbers included.

792. U.S. Dept. of Health, Education, and Welfare Library. Author-title catalog of the Department Library. Boston: G. K. Hall, 1965. 29v.

Collection of more than 500,000 volumes, particularly strong in education and the social sciences.

793. ———. Subject catalog of the Department Library. Boston: G. K. Hall, 1965. 20v.

Records 500,000-volume collection, with particular strength in education and other social sciences.

794. U.S. Library of Congress, National Referral Center for Science and Technology. A directory of information resources in the United States: social sciences. Wash.: Govt. Print. Off., 1965. 218p.

About 700 entries for organizations "having a substantial amount of unpublished material, or having a uniquely comprehensive or specialized collection of published information."

SOCIOLOGY

795. Allen, Robert V. "Recent Soviet literature in sociology and cultural anthropology." Quarterly journal of the Library of Congress, 22 (1965), 246-58.

Report on acquisitions, Library of Congress.

STATISTICS

796. Stanford University, Hoover Institution. Foreign statistical documents; a bibliography of general, international, trade, and agricultural statistics, including holdings of the Stanford University Libraries, ed. by Joyce Ball and comp. by Robert Gardella. Stanford, Calif., 1967. 173p. (Bibliographical series, no.28)

Demography-Population

797. Michigan Historical Commission, Division of Archives. Finding aid for the records of the United States census for Michigan, 1820-1880, comp. by Geneva Kebler. Lansing, 1962. 4p. (Finding aid, no.2)

798. North Carolina State Dept. of Archives and History. North Carolina census records, 1787-1890, by Ellen Z. McGrew. Raleigh, 1967. 15p. (Archives information circular, no.2)

799. Sanchez, Irene. "Index to census and manuscript microfilm materials in Texas State Archives." Texas libraries, 23 (May-June 1961), 60-71.

800. U.S. National Archives. Preliminary inventory of the records of the Bureau of the Census, comp. by Katherine H. Davidson and Charlotte M. Ashby. Wash., 1964. 141p. (Preliminary inventories, no.161)

POLITICAL SCIENCE

General

801. Harvard University Library. Government. Cambridge, Mass., 1969. 263p. (Widener Library shelflist, no.22)

Lists 6,800 titles of general nature on history and theory of political science.

802. Minnesota Historical Society. Guide to the public affairs collection of the Minnesota Historical Society, comp. by Lucile M. Kane. St. Paul, 1968. 46p.

Describes 158 groups of papers dealing with politics and government, mainly associated with Minnesota.

803. North Carolina, University, Library. A guide to library resources for political science students at the University of North Carolina, by Clifton Brock. Chapel Hill, 1965. 69p.

Lists and reviews periodical guides, government publications, bibliographies, and other reference sources.

804. Pittsburgh, University, Libraries, Archives of Industrial Society. Allegheny City, Pennsylvania voting records, 1926-69; a guide, comp. by Frank Zabrosky. Pittsburgh, 1970. 65p.

805. U.S. Library of Congress, General Reference and Bibliography Division. Presidential inaugurations; a selected list of references, 3d ed., comp. by Ruth S. Freitag. Wash., 1969. 230p.

Locates copies in Library of Congress and 4 other libraries.

806. U.S. National Archives. Papers of the United States Senate relating to Presidential nominations, 1789-1901, comp. by George P. Perros and others. Wash., 1964. 111p. (Special list, no.20)

807. ———. Preliminary inventory of the records of the 1961 Inaugural Committee, comp. by Marion M. Johnson. Wash., 1964. 18p. (Preliminary inventories, no.162)

Political Parties

808. Gray, Virginia R. "Radical thought—a coat of many colors." Gnomon (1970), 63-70. (Special number of Duke University Library's Library notes)

Describes Duke Library's holdings on radical organizations, parties, etc.

809. Kantor, Harry. Latin American political parties: a bibliography. Gainesville: Reference and Bibliography Dept., Univ. of Fla. Libraries, 1968. 113p. (Bibliographic series, no.6)

Listing by countries with subdivisions by parties.

810. Minnesota Historical Society. Guide to a microfilm edition of the National Nonpartisan League papers, by Deborah K. Neubeck. St. Paul, 1970. 22p.

811. Nebraska State Historical Society. Nebraska Farmers' Alliance papers, 1887-1901, ed. by Douglas A. Bakken. Lincoln, 1966. 9p.

812. Wisconsin, State Historical Society. Records of the Socialist Labor Party of America, guide to a microfilm edition, ed. by F. Gerald Ham. Madison, 1970. 30p.

Relates particularly to last quarter of 19th century.

Socialism and Collectivism

813. Stanford University, Hoover Institution. The Communist International and its front organizations; a research guide and checklist of holdings in American and European libraries, by Witold S. Sworakowski. Stanford, Calif., 1965. 493p. (Bibliographical series, no.21)

About 2,200 entries located in 36 American and 4 European libraries.

814. U.S. Senate, Committee on the Judiciary. World Communism, a selected annotated bibliography, by Joseph G. Whelan. Wash.: Govt. Print. Off., 1964. 394p.
Prepared by Legislative Reference Service, Library of Congress.

Utopias

815. Duke University Library. Utopia collection of the Duke University Library, comp. by Glenn R. Negley. Durham, N.C., 1965. 83p. Supplement. 1967. 9*l.*
Records more than 500 titles.

816. Pennsylvania State University Library. Checklist of Utopian literature. University Park, 1968. 58p.

Negroes

817. "Availability of Negro source material in Philadelphia." Negro history bulletin, 32 (March 1969), 17.

818. California State College Library, Long Beach. Black bibliography, a selected list of books on Africa, Africans, and Afro-Americans. Long Beach, 1969. 88p.

819. California, University, Library. Black sojourn: a bibliography, by Sherri Kirk and Glenda Peace. Davis, 1969. 95p.
Selective bibliography on Afro-Americans, based on holdings of University of California Library, Davis.

820. Durden, Robert F. "Primary sources for the study of Afro-American history." Gnomon (1970), 39-42. (Special number of the Duke University Library's Library notes)
Describes Duke Library's holdings.

821. Fisk University, Amistad Research Center. American Missionary Association Archives. Westport, Conn.: Greenwood, 1970. 3v.
Composed of 300,000 letters and other materials relating to evangelistic abolitionism and other aspects of Negro and Civil War history.

822. Fisk University Library. Special collections in the Erastus Milo Cravath Memorial Library, Fisk University. Nashville, Tenn., 1967. Unpaged. (Fisk University Library publication, no.5)
Describes Negro, Fiskiana, American Missionary Association, George Gershwin, and other collections.

823. Fresno State College Library. Afro and Mexican-Americana. Fresno, Calif., 1969. 109p.
Bibliography of holdings, arranged by subjects.

824. Friends of Florida State University Library. Catalog of the Negro collections in the Florida Agricultural and Mechanical University Library and the Florida State University Library. Tallahassee, 1969. 1v. Unpaged.

825. Howard University Library. The American Negro: a selected checklist of books, by Ethel M. Vaughan Ellis. Wash.: Negro Collection, Howard Univ. Library, 1968. 46*l.*

826. ———. Dictionary catalog of the Arthur B. Spingarn collection of Negro authors, Howard University Libraries (Washington, D.C.). Boston: G. K. Hall, 1970. 2v.
Catalog of about 8,000 volumes, including many rare works.

827. ———. Dictionary catalog of the Jesse E. Moorland collection of Negro life and history, Howard University Libraries (Washington, D.C.). Boston: G. K. Hall, 1970. 9v.
One of largest collections in its field, containing more than 100,000 volumes and other materials.

828. Illinois, University, Library. The black community and Champaign-Urbana; a preliminary subject list, comp. by Margo Trumpeter and Kathryn Scarich. Urbana: Library Research Center, 1970. 37*l.*
Listing under subjects, with locations in University of Illinois Library, of materials significant for race relations.

829. Johnson, Clifton H. "Some archival sources on Negro history in Tennessee." Tennessee librarian, 22 (1970), 80-94. (Also appeared in Tennessee historical quarterly, Winter 1969)
Analysis of resources of various Tennessee libraries and other repositories.

830. McDonough, John J. "Manuscript resources for the study of Negro life and history." Library of Congress quarterly journal of current acquisitions, 26 (1969), 126-48.
Survey of Library of Congress collections.

831. Michigan State University Library. A partial bibliography on the American Negro; books and their call numbers in the Library of Michigan State University, by J. F. Thaden and Walter E. Freeman. East Lansing, 1962. 12*l.*

832. Michigan, University, Library, Reference Dept. A bibliography of bibliographies on Blacks contained in

libraries of the University of Michigan: a tentative list, comp. by Agnes N. Tysse. Ann Arbor, 1970. 21p.

833. Michigan, University, William L. Clements Library. Education of Negroes in ante-bellum America; a guide to an exhibition in the William L. Clements Library. Ann Arbor, 1969. 18p. (Bulletin, no.76)

834. New Jersey Library Association, Bibliography Committee. New Jersey and the Negro: a bibliography, 1715-1966, ed. by Donald A. Sinclair. Trenton, 1967. 196p.

Union list of holdings of a number of libraries; about 60 percent of items listed are in Rutgers University Library.

835. New York Public Library. Dictionary catalog of the Schomburg collection of Negro literature and history. Boston: G. K. Hall, 1962. 9v. Supplement. Boston: G. K. Hall, 1967. 2v.

Reproduction of card catalog; includes more than 36,000 volumes.

836. North Carolina State University Library. Black literature; a classified bibliography of newspapers, periodicals, and books by and about the Negro in the D. H. Hill Library, N.C. State University at Raleigh, comp. by W. Robert Pollard. Raleigh, 1969. 77*l*.

837. Oberlin College Library. Anti-slavery propaganda in the Oberlin College Library. Louisville, Ky.: Lost Cause, 1968. 101p.

Includes annual reports, slave narratives, newspapers and periodicals, poetry and songs.

838. Ohio State University Libraries. Afro-Americana: a comprehensive bibliography of resource materials in the Ohio State University Libraries by and about black Americans, by Mary D. Walters. Columbus, 1969. 220p.

839. ———. Black history holdings of the Ohio State University Libraries, by Mary D. Walters. Columbus, 1969. 36p.

840. Peavy, Charles D. "Black journals at the University of Houston." Aldus, 8 (April 1970). Unpaged.

Review of collection of journals originating with black cultural revolution in U.S.

841. Pendergrass, Margaret E., and Roth, Catherine E. "Selected list of books by and about the Negro." Illinois libraries, 51 (1969), 62-82.

Books for general readers in Illinois State Library.

842. Pennsylvania State Library. The contemporary Negro; a selected bibliography of recent material in the Pennsylvania State Library, 4th ed., comp. by Mirjana Tolmachev. Harrisburg, 1970. 24p.

843. Pennsylvania State University Libraries. Negroes in the United States; a bibliography of materials for schools . . . with a supplement of recent materials on other American minority peoples, by Mildred L. Treworgy and Paul B. Foreman. University Park, 1967. 93p.

844. Rochester, University, Libraries. A guide to Afro-American resources in University of Rochester Libraries, by Barbara Taylor and Margaret Mattern. Rochester, N.Y., 1971. 34p.

"An introduction to reference sources for Afro-American studies" at Rochester.

845. Rutgers University Library. The Negro and New Jersey; a checklist of books, pamphlets, official publications, broadsides, and dissertations, 1754-1964, in the Rutgers University Library, comp. by Donald A. Sinclair. New Brunswick, N.J., 1965. 56p.

846. ———. Slavery in America: manuscripts and other items, 1660-1865, selected from the collection of Philip D. and Elsie O. Sang, prep. by Anthony S. Nicolosi. New Brunswick, N.J., 1963. 16p.

847. U.S. Library of Congress. The Negro in the United States: a selected bibliography, comp. by Dorothy B. Porter. Wash., 1970. 313p.

Lists 1,781 items in Library of Congress and 12 other American libraries.

848. Washington State Library. The Negro in the State of Washington, 1788-1967; a bibliography of published works and of unpublished source materials on the life and achievements of the Negro in the Evergreen State. Olympia, 1968. 14p.

849. Wayne State University Library. Selective guide to materials on black studies. Detroit, 1971. 5*l*.

Descriptive guide to library resources on black studies available at the Wayne State University Library.

850. Yale University Library. Black biographical sources: an annotated bibliography, by Barbara L. Bell. New Haven, Conn., 1970. 20p.

851. ———. A selected list of periodicals relating to Negroes, with holdings in the Libraries of Yale Univer-

sity, by Joyce B. Schneider. New Haven, Conn., 1970. 26p.

ECONOMICS

852. Barringer, G. Martyn. "Novotný collection of economics." Syracuse University Libraries bulletin, no.13 (April 29, 1970), 3-4.

More than 1,600 titles relating to the history of economics; strong for German, French, Czech, and early English works, in Syracuse University Libraries.

853. Fisher, Irving Norton. "The Irving Fisher collection." Yale University Library gazette, 36 (1961), 45-56.

Collection relating to American economist, held by Yale Library.

854. Harvard University, Graduate School of Business Administration, Baker Library, Kress Library of Business and Economics. An exploration of bibliographies of economics, by Kenneth E. Carpenter. Boston: Baker Library, 1970. 10p. (Bulletin, no.6)

855. Harvard University, Graduate School of Business Administration, Baker Library. Resources for the study of economic history; a preliminary guide to pre-twentieth century printed material in collections located in certain American and British libraries, comp. by Dorothea D. Reeves. Boston, 1961. 62p.

Describes 36 libraries or special collections.

856. Harvard University Library. Archives of André Marty. [Inventaire] Cambridge, Mass., 1961. 76*l.*

Marty, 1886-1956, was a French writer on economics, communism, labor, and social problems.

857. ———. Economics. Cambridge, Mass., 1970. 2v. (Widener Library shelflist, no.23-24)

Includes 79,580 titles in all major branches of economics.

858. Pittsburgh, University, Libraries. Catalog of the Library of the Center for Regional Economic Studies of the University of Pittsburgh. Pittsburgh, Pa.: Univ. Book Center, 1969. 1v. Unpaged.

859. Rosovsky, Henry. Quantitative Japanese economic history; an annotated bibliography and a survey of U.S. holdings. Berkeley: Center for Japanese Studies of the Institute of International Studies, Univ. of Calif., 1961. 173p.

Classified list of Japanese-language materials since 1868. Locations in 7 U.S. libraries.

860. U.S. National Archives. Preliminary inventory of the records of the Temporary National Economic Committee. Wash., 1966. 8p. (Revision of Preliminary checklist, no.16)

861. Yale University Library. A bibliography of the writings of Irving Fisher, comp. by Irving Norton Fisher. New Haven, Conn., 1961. 543p.

Location guide for Fisher collection in Yale Library.

Land Economics

862. Heard, John P. "Resource for historians: records of the Bureau of Land Management in California and Nevada." Forest history, 12 (July 1968), 20-26.

Describes collections and files in Bureau of Land Management and other Federal depositories.

863. Louisiana State Archives and Records Commission. Guide to the records of the Louisiana Conservation Department. Baton Rouge, 1962. 28p.

864. Michigan, University, Michigan Historical Collections. A bibliography of manuscript resources relating to natural resources and conservation in the Michigan Historical Collections of the University of Michigan, comp. by J. Fraser Cocks III. Ann Arbor, 1970. 14p.

865. Ohio State University Libraries. Natural resources bibliography. Columbus, 1970. 242p.

866. U.S. Dept. of the Interior Library. Natural resources in foreign countries; a contribution toward a bibliography of bibliographies, by Mary Anglemyer. Wash., 1968. 113p. (U.S. Dept. of the Interior Library, Bibliography, no.9)

867. U.S. Federal Records Center, Los Angeles. Preliminary inventory of the records of the Bureau of Land Management, comp. by Gilbert Dorame. Los Angeles, 1966. 83*l.*

868. U.S. National Archives. List of cartographic records of the General Land Office, comp. by Laura E. Kelsey. Wash., 1964. 202p. (Special list, no.19)

Covers materials relating to public lands, 1790-1946.

BUSINESS AND COMMERCE

General

869. California State Library. What's new in accounting? Sacramento, Jan. 1952- . Monthly.

Annotated list of periodical articles, books, and pamphlets received by library.

870. ———. What's new in management? Sacramento, Jan. 1952- . Monthly.

Annotated list of periodical articles, books, and pamphlets received by library.

871. ———. What's new in personnel? Sacramento, Jan. 1952- . Monthly.

Annotated list of books, pamphlets, and periodical articles received by library.

872. California, University, Business Administration Library. Foreign information guides. Los Angeles: Univ. of Calif., Graduate School of Business Administration, 1969- .

Brief guides to foreign materials in the Business Administration Library.

873. ——— ———. Reference guides. Los Angeles: Univ. of Calif., Graduate School of Business Administration, 1968- .

Brief guides to various aspects of the Business Administration Library's resources.

874. ———, Graduate School of Business Administration. The arts and the art of administration: a bibliography, by Charlotte Georgi. Los Angeles, 1970. 51p.

Based on UCLA libraries' holdings.

875. ——— ———. The Robert E. Gross collection of rare books in business and economics, by Charlotte Georgi. Los Angeles, 1965. 4p.

Housed in UCLA's Business Administration Library.

876. ——— ———. Serials bibliographies. Los Angeles: Univ. of Calif., Graduate School of Business Administration, 1969. 10p.

Brief subject guide to serials in the library.

877. Cleveland Public Library. Business and technology sources; bulletin of the Business and Technology Department. Cleveland, Ohio, 1930- . Quarterly.

Classified listing of books and other materials available in library.

878. Harvard University, Graduate School of Business Administration, Baker Library. Business forecasting for the 1970's; a selected, annotated bibliography, comp. by Lorna M. Daniells. Boston, 1970. 48p. (Reference lists, no.26)

879. ——— ———. Business literature: an annotated list for students and businessmen, ed. by Lorna M. Daniells. Boston, 1968. 139p. (Reference lists, no.25)

In Baker Library.

880. ——— ———. Corporate and business finance; a classified bibliography of recent literature, comp. by Gordon Donaldson and Carolyn Stubbs. Boston, 1964. 85p. (Reference lists, no.22)

881. ——— ———. List of business manuscripts in Baker Library, 3d ed., comp. by Robert W. Lovett and Eleanor C. Bishop. Boston, 1969. 334p.

Manuscripts dated from 1200 to 20th century.

882. ——— ———. Power & morality; a list of books selected by Benjamin M. Selekman for the Baker Library. Boston, 1963. 40p.

883. ——— ———. Printed catalog of current journals, 2d ed. Cambridge, Mass., 1966. 64p.

Periodicals and newspapers in Baker Library.

884. ——— ———. Selected business reference sources, comp. by Lorna M. Daniells. Boston, 1965. 72p. (Reference list, no.24)

Selective guide to Baker Library's resources.

885. ——— ———. Selected reference sources: a guide for Harvard Business School students, comp. by Lorna M. Daniells. Boston, 1963. 46p. (Reference lists, no.21)

886. ——— ———. Statistical and review issues of trade and business periodicals, 3d ed., comp. by Reece Alfriend. Boston, 1964. 20p. (Reference lists, no.23)

887. ——— ———. Subject list of current journals, 2d ed. Boston: 1966. 72p.

888. ———, Law School Library. Doing business abroad, a selected and annotated bibliography of books and pamphlets in English, by Vaclav Mostecky. Cambridge, Mass., 1962. 88p.

889. Hoffman, Morris. A union list of serials for public utility libraries. Omaha, 1965. 245*l.*

Lists holdings of 20 libraries belonging to the Public Utility Section, Science-Technology Division, Special Libraries Association.

890. Illinois, University, Library. A catalogue of the business records and other manuscripts in the University of Illinois Library, by Icko Iben. Urbana, 1968. 34p.

891. John Crerar Library. Selected references on industrial development. Wash.: Technical Aids Branch, Office of Industrial Resources, International Cooperation Administration, 1961. 140p.

Prepared by the John Crerar Library.

892. McDonough, John J. "Manuscript materials on finance and banking." Banking, 56 (1963), 199-200.

Materials in Library of Congress collections.

893. Nebraska, University, Libraries. Business and economics periodical holdings in the University of Nebraska Libraries: a bibliography, comp. by Mohamed Hussein El-Zehery. Lincoln: College of Business Administration, 1970. 121p.

894. Ohio State University Libraries. Investment sources in the Commerce Library. Columbus, 1970. 8p.

895. Phelps, Ralph H. "Service to industry by professional and trade association libraries." Library trends, 14 (1966), 273-87.

Description of holdings and services of 8 leading professional and trade association libraries.

896. Special Libraries Association, New York Chapter. Serials: advertising, business, finance, marketing, social science, in libraries in the New York area. N.Y., 1965. 146p.

Entries for about 1,900 titles show holdings for 192 libraries.

897. Stanford University, Graduate School of Business Library. Jackson Library periodicals. Stanford, Calif., 1969. 2v.

Record of holdings, alphabetical by title, with indexes by subject, language, and country of origin.

898. U.S. National Archives. Preliminary inventory of the records of the Bureau of Foreign and Domestic Commerce, comp. by Forrest R. Holdcamper. Wash., 1963. 11p.

Business History

899. Alaska, University, Library. Alaska Commercial Company records: 1868-1911, by Wendell H. Oswalt. College, 1967. 30p.

In University of Alaska Library.

900. Fishbein, Meyer H. "Business history resources in the National Archives." Business history review, 38 (1964), 232-57.

901. Gold, Neil Newton. "The Olcott papers, a new source on New York State banking history." Columbia Library columns, 11 (Nov. 1961), 19-24.

Collection in Columbia University Library of business, financial, and legal papers of Thomas Worth Olcott (1795-1880), prominent figure in Jacksonian politics and finance.

902. Hancock, Harold B. "Materials for company history in the National Archives." American archivist, 29 (1966), 23-32.

903. Harvard University, Graduate School of Business Administration, Baker Library. The Kress Library of Business and Economics, catalogue supplement, 1473-1848, giving data also upon cognate items in other Harvard libraries. Boston, 1967. 453p.

Lists 6,902 items.

904. Harvard University, Graduate School of Business Administration, Baker Library. The Kress Library of Business and Economics. Catalogue 1818-1848, giving data also upon cognate items in other Harvard libraries. Boston, 1964. 397p.

Lists 7,642 items.

905. Harvard University, Graduate School of Business Administration, Baker Library. The South Sea Company: an historical essay and bibliographical finding list, by John G. Sperling. Boston, 1962. 92p.

906. Michigan Historical Commission, Division of Archives. Finding aid for the records of the Michigan Department of Economic Development, 1934-1959, comp. by Geneva Kebler. Lansing, 1963. 13p. (Finding aid, no.13)

907. ——— ———. Finding aid for the records of the Michigan State Planning Commission, 1934-1946, comp. by Geneva Kebler. Lansing, 1962. 13p. (Finding aid, no.4)

908. Minnesota, University, Libraries. The James Ford Bell collection, a list of additions, 1955-59. Minneapolis: Univ of Minn. Pr., 1961. 217p.

Lists additions to collection concerned mainly with expansion of European commerce from 15th century to 1800.

909. ———. The James Ford Bell collection, a list of additions, 1960-64. Minneapolis: Univ. of Minn. Pr., 1967. 207p.

910. ———. The James Ford Bell collection, a list of

additions, 1965-69. Minneapolis: Univ. of Minn. Pr., 1970. 102p.

911. ———. The merchant explorer; occasional papers of the James Ford Bell Library. Minneapolis, April 1961- .

Annual publication listing additions to Bell Library with commentary on selected items.

912. Nicholes, Eleanor L., and Reeves, Dorothea D. "The Kress Library of Business and Economics and some of its treasures." Business history review, 40 (1966), 237-49.

913. Oklahoma, University, Library. The Harry W. Bass collection in business history: a short title catalog, 3d ed. Norman, 1969. Unpaged.

914. Pennsylvania Historical and Museum Commission. Guide to the microfilm of the Baynton, Wharton, and Morgan papers in the Pennsylvania State Archives. Harrisburg, 1967. 29p.

Records of famous trading firm of colonial Philadelphia, 1757-87.

915. Pittsburgh, University, Libraries. Guide to the collections in the Archives of Industrial Society, comp. by Frank Zabrosky. Pittsburgh, 1969. 2v.

916. Porter, Patrick G. "Advertising in the early cigarette industry: W. Duke, Sons & Company of Durham." North Carolina historical review, 48 (Jan. 1971), 31-43.

Based on collection of advertising premiums at Duke University.

917. Washington, University, Libraries. Callbreath, Grant and Cook, merchants, letterpress copy books. Seattle, 1965. 4p.

In University of Washington Libraries.

918. ———. Oregon Improvement Company records, 1880-1896. Seattle, 1965. 18p.

In University of Washington Libraries.

919. Washington, University, Libraries. Washington Mill Company records, 1857-1888. 4p.

In University of Washington Libraries.

Transportation

920. American Railroad Association, Economics and Finance Department Library, Washington, D.C. Dictionary catalog. Westport, Conn.: Greenwood, 1970. 75v.

921. Harvard University, Graduate School of Business Administration, Baker Library. Inland waterways transportation; a collection of Baker. Boston, 1963. 10p.

922. ——— ———. Periodicals in the area of transportation currently in the transportation collection of Baker Library. Boston, 1962. 20p.

923. Kolbet, Richard M. "The Levi O. Leonard railroad collection." Books at Iowa, 8 (April 1968), 3-10.

Collection of correspondence, ledgers, etc., assembled by historian of Union Pacific and Rock Island railroads; in University of Iowa Library.

924. Marine Historical Association Library. Inventory of the Lawrence & Co. papers; 1822-1904, comp. by Charles R. Schultz. Mystic, Conn.: Marine Historical Assoc., 1966. 31p. (Mystic Seaport manuscripts inventory, no.5)

925. ———. Inventory of the Mallory family papers, 1808-1958, comp. by Charles R. Schultz. Mystic, Conn., 1964. 24*l.* (Mystic Seaport manuscripts inventory, no.2)

926. Marine Historical Association, Mystic Seaport Library. Mystic Seaport manuscripts inventory, no.1-5, 1964-66. Mystic, Conn., 1964-66.

Records materials relating to American maritime history in Mystic Seaport Library.

927. Mariners' Museum. Catalog of maps, ships' papers, and logbooks. Boston: G. K. Hall, 1964. 505p.

Collection dating back to 17th century, in Newport News, Virginia.

928. ———. Catalog of marine photographs, the Mariners' Museum Library (Newport News, Va.). Boston: G. K. Hall, 1964. 5v.

Records more than 100,000 photographs of maritime subjects; international in scope.

929. ———. Catalog of marine prints and paintings, the Mariners' Museum Library (Newport News, Va.). Boston: G. K. Hall, 1964. 3v.

930. ———. Dictionary catalog of the Library, the Mariners' Museum (Newport News, Va.). Boston: G. K. Hall, 1964. 9v.

Extensive collection relating to maritime history.

931. Michigan Historical Commission, Division of Archives. Finding aid for the records of the Michigan State Highway Department, 1916-1953, comp. by Geneva Kebler. Lansing, 1962. 21p. (Finding aid, no.8)

932. ——— ———. Finding aid for the records of the Michigan Turnpike Authority, 1953-1958, comp. by Geneva Kebler. Lansing, 1962. 13p. (Finding aid, no.5)

933. Northwestern University, Transportation Center Library. Current literature in traffic and transportation. Evanston, Ill., Jan. 1960- . Monthly.

Records material received by library.

934. Oregon, University, Library. Transportation materials in University of Oregon Library. Eugene? 1961. 1v. (Various pagings)

935. Port of New York Authority, Library Services Section. A selected bibliography of the Port of New York Authority, 1921-1962. N.Y., 1965. 118p.

936. Purdue University Libraries. A bibliography of railroads and railroad related publications in the Purdue University Libraries, by Richard D. Daubert. Lafayette, Ind.: Krannert Graduate School of Industrial Administration Library, 1970. 99p.

937. "Steamboat round the bend." The Tulanian, 40 (Feb. 1967), 15-23.

Description of Donald T. Wright collection of steamboat memorabilia in Tulane University Library.

938. Syracuse University Libraries. Delaware, Lackawanna and Western Railroad Company; a register of the corporate records, ed. by Howard L. Applegate and Lyall Squair. Syracuse, N.Y., 1964. 32p. (Manuscript register series, no.6)

939. ———. Erie Railroad Company; a short tentative inventory of corporate records of the Erie Railroad Company placed in Syracuse University Library in May 1964, comp. by Lyall D. Squair. Syracuse, N.Y., 1964. 11p.

940. U.S. Bureau of Public Roads Library. Highways; current literature. Wash., 1927- . Weekly.

Issued under various titles, indexing contents of new periodicals in U.S. Bureau of Public Roads Library.

941. U.S. Dept. of Housing and Urban Development Library. Urban public transportation, selected references. Wash.: Govt. Print. Off., 1966. 20p.

Includes HUD Library call numbers.

942. U.S. National Archives. Preliminary inventory of the records of the Bureau of Public Roads, comp. by Truman R. Strobridge. Wash., 1962. 34p. (Preliminary inventories, no.134)

943. ———. Preliminary inventory of the records of the Bureau of Ships, comp. by Elizabeth Bethel and others. Wash., 1961. 241p. (Preliminary inventory, no.133)

944. ———. Preliminary inventory of the records of the Commissioner of Railroads, comp. by Marion M. Johnson. Wash., 1964. 18p. (Preliminary inventories, no.158)

945. ———. Preliminary inventory of the records of the Presidential Railroad Commission, comp. by Marion M. Johnson. Wash., 1965. 4p.

946. ———. Preliminary inventory of the records of the U.S. Maritime Commission, comp. by Forrest R. Holdcamper. Wash., 1962. 15p.

947. ———. Preliminary inventory of the records of the U.S. Railroad Administration, 1917-1945, comp. by Charles Zaid. Wash., 1962. 31p.

948. ———. Preliminary inventory of the records of the United States Shipping Board, comp. by Forrest R. Holdcamper. Wash., 1966. 157p. (Revision of Preliminary inventory, no.97)

949. ———. Selected list of titles in the Bureau of Public Roads Highway Transport File (prints), comp. by Susan Kay Parker and Sadie S. Mittman. Wash., 1965. 21p.

950. ———. Supplement to Preliminary inventory No. 10, records of the Bureau of Yards and Docks, comp. by Harry Schwartz. Wash., 1965. 3p.

951. ———. Supplement to Preliminary inventory No. 133, records of the Bureau of Ships, comp. by Harry Schwartz. Wash., 1965. 7p.

LABOR

952. Blum, Albert A. "Local union archives in Michigan." Labor history, 3 (1962), 335-40.

953. Brickett, Margaret F. "Labor history resources in the U.S. Department of Labor Library." Labor history, 2 (1961), 236-40.

954. Cornell University, New York State School of Industrial and Labor Relations. Guide to the records. Ithaca, N.Y., 1963. 62p.

955. Cornell University, New York State School of Industrial and Labor Relations Library. Library catalog. Boston: G. K. Hall, 1967. 12v. Supplements 1-4. Boston: G. K. Hall, 1967-70. 4v.

Collection of 78,000 volumes and bound periodicals and 80,000 pamphlets.

956. [Cornell University, New York State School of Industrial and Labor Relations. Railroad collection] College & research libraries news, no.8 (Sept. 1969), 274.

"The largest collection of materials on railroad labor history in the United States," the files of the United Transportation Union, deposited at Cornell.

957. DiRoma, Edward. "The industrial relations collection, its scope and organization." Bulletin of the New York Public Library, 65 (1961), 177-84.

Analysis of New York Public Library's collection.

958. ———. "Notes on resources for research in labor history in the Reference Department of the New York Public Library." Labor history, 4 (Winter 1963), 93-99.

959. Eberlein, Alfred. Die Presse der Arbeiterklasse und der sozialen Bewegungen. Berlin: Akademie-Verlag, 1968-69. 4v.

Contains 22,875 entries, recording holdings in 957 libraries, including 87 in United States, of publications from 1830s to 1967 of German, Austrian, and Swiss worker organizations, trade unions, and occupational groups.

960. Fishbein, Meyer H. "Labor history resources in the National Archives." Labor history, 8 (1967), 330-51.

961. Ham, F. Gerald. "Labor manuscripts in the State Historical Society of Wisconsin." Labor history, 7 (1966), 313-42.

962. Harvey, O. L. "Inventory of [U.S.] Department of Labor archives." Labor history, 4 (1963), 196-98.

963. Heffron, Paul T. "Manuscript sources in the Library of Congress for a study of labor history." Labor history, 10 (1969), 630-38.

964. Illinois, University, Institute of Labor and Industrial Relations. Industrial relations bibliographies; a check-list, comp. by George F. Mundle. Champaign, Ill., 1965. 54*l.*

"Nearly all items are found in the University of Illinois Library."

965. Lewinson, Paul, and Rieger, Morris. "Labor union records in the United States." American archivist, 25 (Jan. 1962), 39-57.

966. Lovett, Robert W. "Labor history materials in the Harvard University Library." Labor history, 4 (1963), 273-79.

967. Mason, Philip P. "Labor history archives at Wayne State University." Labor history, 5 (Winter 1964), 67-78.

968. Pflug, Warner W. "The Labor History Archives, Wayne State University." Internationale wissenschaftliche korrespondenz zur geschichte der deutschen arbeitenbewegung, 8 (1969), 20-23.

969. Thompson, Glenn E. "AFL papers and other manuscript accessions; State Historical Society of Wisconsin." Business history review, 35 (1961), 574-76.

In Wisconsin State Historical Society.

970. U.S. Bureau of Labor Statistics. A bibliography on labor in Ghana, comp. by Lester N. Trachtman. Wash., 1962. 9p.

Locates items listed.

971. U.S. Dept. of Labor Library. List of American trade union journals and labor papers currently received by the Department of Labor Library. Wash., 1938- . Irregular.

972. U.S. National Archives. Preliminary inventory of the records of the Bureau of Labor Standards, comp. by William J. Lescure. Wash., 1965. 7p.

973. ———. Preliminary inventory of the records of the Committee on Fair Employment Practice, comp. by Charles Zaid. Wash., 1962. 50p. (Preliminary inventories, no.147)

974. U.S. National Archives. Preliminary inventory of the records of the Federal Mediation and Conciliation Service, comp. by Norwood N. Biggs. Wash., 1965. 7p.

975. ———. Preliminary inventory of the records of the President's Organization on Unemployment Relief, comp. by Leo Pascal. Wash., 1962. 26p. (Preliminary inventories, no.137)

976. ———. Preliminary inventory of the records of the Wage and Hour and Public Contracts Division, comp. by Herbert J. Horwitz. Wash., 1964. 8p.

977. U.S. Veterans Administration, Medical and General Reference Library. We hold these truths, comp. by Rosemary D. Reid. Wash.: Govt. Print. Off., 1969. 31p.

Bibliography relating to fair employment practices and other minority problems.

978. Utah, University, Libraries. Western Americana Dept. Register of the records of Utah State Federation of Labor and the Utah State Industrial Union Council and their affiliates. Salt Lake City, 1971. 72p. (Register 3, Manuscript collection)

Inventory of collection held by University of Utah.

979. Wisconsin, State Historical Society. Labor manuscripts in the State Historical Society of Wisconsin, comp. by F. Gerald Ham. Madison, 1967. 48p. (First published in Labor history, 7 [Fall 1966], no.3)

Describes 177 collections relating to the American labor movement.

980. ———. Labor papers on microfilm: a combined list, 2d ed., prep. by Benton H. Wilcox. Madison, 1966. 66p.

Union list, with locations in many libraries, of trade union newspapers and periodicals.

981. ———. The Morris Hillquit papers, guide to a microfilm edition, ed. by F. Gerald Ham and Carole Sue Warmbrodt. Madison, 1969. 116p.

Papers of a leader of American trade unionism and socialism, 1890-1933.

982. ———, John R. Commons Labor Reference Center. Labor sources in the Libraries. Madison: Wis. State Historical Society and Univ. of Wis., 1965-67. (List no.1-17)

983. ——— ———. The Textile Workers Union of America papers; a descriptive guide, comp. by Esther Thelen. Madison, 1966. 28p. (Library bulletin, no.1)

Includes inventory and detailed description of primary divisions.

LAW

General

984. American Association of Law Libraries. Directory of law libraries, 1968 edition, 14th ed. N.Y.: Commerce Clearing House, 1968. 117p.

Geographical arrangement, with number of volumes in each library; lists law libraries with more than 5,000 volumes each in U.S. and Canada.

985. California State Library, Law Library. Administrative law. Sacramento, 1964. 28p. (Law Library paper, no.12)

986. ——— ———. Annotated bibliography on freedom of information: the right to know, comp. by Carleton W. Kenyon. Sacramento, 1965. 13p.

987. ——— ———. Bibliography on commitment of mentally irresponsible persons, prep. by Marija M. Hughes. Sacramento, 1969. 8p.

988. ——— ———. Bibliography on gun legislation, prep. by Marija M. Hughes. Sacramento, 1969. 10p.

989. ——— ———. Capital punishment—a selective bibliography. Sacramento, 1965. 10p.

990. ——— ———. Comparative negligence; annotated bibliography of material in the Law Library. Sacramento, 1961. 11p.

991. ——— ———. Computers in law practice; a bibliography. Sacramento, 1966. 11p.

992. ——— ———. Contested election cases. Sacramento, 1964. 6p. (Law Library paper, no.8)

993. ——— ———. Military service and the law, a bibliography, prep. by Betty Anne McCarthy. Sacramento, 1969. 5p.

994. ——— ———. The ombudsman, a bibliography, comp. by Carleton W. Kenyon. Sacramento, 1966. 7p.

995. ——— ———. Public employee labor relations, a bibliography, prep. by Carleton W. Kenyon. Sacramento, 1966. 8*l.*

996. ——— ———. Reapportionment; a selective bibliography. Sacramento, 1966. 22p.

997. ——— ———. Recent material on debtor's rights and problems: a selective bibliography. Sacramento, 1967. 9p.

998. ——— ———. Riots and demonstrations: a selected bibliography, prep. by Betty Anne McCarthy. Sacramento, 1969. 5p.

999. ——— ———. A selected bibliography on population control; abortion, birth control, euthanasia, and sterilization, comp. by Carleton Kenyon. Sacramento, 1966. 17p.

1000. California, University, School of Law Library. Admiralty, maritime law, ships and shipping, and related subjects; a bibliography of the holdings of the U.C.L.A. Law Library, comp. by Robert Faris. Los Angeles, 1964. 40*l.* Supplement. 1965. 23*l.*

1001. ——— ———. Holdings in copyright law. Los Angeles, 1963. 33*l.*

1002. ——— ———. Holdings in legal aspects of the entertainment industry and peripheral materials. Los Angeles, 1963. 28*l.*

1003. ——— ———. Holdings in patents and trademarks law. Los Angeles, 1963. 47*l.*

1004. ——— ———. Oil and gas; books in the U.C.L.A. School of Law Library. Los Angeles, 1961. 25*l.*

1005. ——— ———. Water, irrigation and related subjects; a bibliography of the holdings of the U.C.L.A. Law Library, comp. by Robert Faris. Los Angeles, 1965. 78*l.*

1006. Carp, Robert A. "The public and private papers of Judge William F. Riley." Books at Iowa, 11 (Nov. 1969), 19-24, 29.

Papers of Federal district judge for southern district of Iowa; in University of Iowa Library.

1007. Chicago, University, Law School Library. The Karl Nickerson Llewellyn papers, by William L. Twining. Chicago: Univ. of Chicago Law School, 1968. 113p.

Llewellyn, 1893-1962, was legal author and educator.

1008. ——— ———. The Karl Llewellyn papers, a guide to the collection, by Raymond M. Ellingwood and William L. Twining. Chicago, 1970. 93p. (University of Chicago Law School Library publications, bibliographies and guides to research, no.1)

American legal educator and author, 1893-1962.

1009. ——— ———. Max Rheinstein's writings, a bibliography published by the University of Chicago Law School, by Adolf Sprudz. Chicago, 1968. 29p. (University of Chicago Law School Library publications, bibliographies and guides to research, no.4)

Papers of legal educator and author.

1010. ——— ———. Selected list of recent publications added to the Library. Chicago, March 1947- . Frequency varies.

1011. Columbia University, Law Library. Dictionary catalog of the Columbia University Law Library. Boston: G. K. Hall, 1968. 28v.

1012. ——— ———. New books and pamphlets. N.Y., 1950-68. 15v.

1013. ——— ———. Pollard and Redgrave's short title catalogue; list by item number of Columbia Law Library holdings, comp. by Gersten Rappaport. N.Y., 1964. 14*l.*

1014. Harvard University, Law School Library. Annual legal bibliography. Cambridge, Mass., 1961- .

Lists monographs and articles received in Harvard Law School Library; a cumulation of Current legal bibliography, Cambridge, 1960- .

1015. New York State Law Library. Condominiums; a selected bibliography of the historical, common law, Federal and State legislation aspects of unit ownership, horizontal property and airspace ownership in real property, comp. by Ernest Henry Breuer. Albany: New York State Library, 1962. 17p.

1016. ———. Learned Hand, January 27, 1872-August 8, 1961: bibliography by Ernest Henry Breuer. Albany: New York State Library, 1964. 18p.

Collection relating to American jurist, in New York State Law Library.

1017. Northwestern University, School of Law Library. The rare book collection. Chicago, 1961. 8p.

1018. Philadelphia Free Library. Catalog of the Hampton L. Carson collection illustrative of the growth of the common law, in the Free Library of Philadelphia. Boston: G. K. Hall, 1962. 2v.

1019. Pennsylvania, University, Law School Library. Bibliography of materials in the Berger space law collection of the Biddle Law Library, comp. by Nancy I. Arnold. Philadelphia, 1970. 50*l.*

1020. Rutgers University, Law Library. Bibliography of bibliographies of legal material, by Margaret A. Howell. Woodbridge: N.J. Appellate Print. Co., 1969. 2v.

1021. U.S. Federal Records Center. Preliminary inventory of the records of the United States District Court for the Atlantic and Newnan Divisions of the Northern District of Georgia and Confederate States of America District Court for the Northern District of Georgia, comp. by Mary C. Frost and others. East Point, Ga.: 1967. 17p.

1022. ———. Preliminary inventory of the records of the United States District Court for the District of Oregon, comp. by Hubert E. Comer. Seattle, Wash., 1967. 7p.

1023. ———. Preliminary inventory of the records of the United States District Court for the Eastern District of Missouri, comp. by Don White. Kansas City, Mo., 1968. 20p.

1024. ———. Preliminary inventory of the records of the United States District Court for the Southern District of Georgia and Confederate States of America District Court for the Southern District of Georgia, comp. by Mary C. Frost and John E. Martin. East Point, Ga., 1967. 18p.

1025. ———. Preliminary inventory, records of the United States Courts for the District of Indiana, comp. by Warren B. Griffin. Chicago, 1967. 32p.

1026. ———. Preliminary inventory, records of the United States Courts for the District of Wisconsin, comp. by Roger Hilgenbrink. Chicago, 1968. 25p.

1027. ———. Preliminary inventory, records of the United States District Court for the District of Nebraska, comp. by Fred W. Ilons and Delbert A. Bishop. Kansas City, Mo., 1967. 26p.

1028. ———. Preliminary inventory, records of the United States District Court for the District of New Mexico, comp. by E. Stuart Howard. Denver, 1968. 19p.

1029. U.S. Library of Congress, Law Library. "Law." Library of Congress quarterly journal of current acquisitions, 18 (1961), 218-60; 19 (1962), 192-222; 20 (1963), 235-66; 21 (1964), 285-344; 22 (1965), 336-96.

Annual reports on Library's acquisitions.

1030. U.S. National Archives. Index to the manuscript and revised printed opinions of the Supreme Court of the United States in the National Archives, 1808-73, comp. by Marion M. Johnson and others. Wash., 1965. 58p. (Special list, no.21)

1031. ———. Preliminary inventory of the records of the National Commission on Law Observance and Enforcement, comp. by Marion M. Johnson. Wash., 1965. 9p.

1032. ———. Preliminary inventory of the records of the Supreme Court of the United States, comp. by Marion M. Johnson. Wash., 1962. 20p. (Preliminary inventories, no.139)

1033. ———. Preliminary inventory of the records of the Supreme Court of the United States, supplementary to National Archives preliminary inventory no. 139, comp. by Marion M. Johnson. Wash., 1964. 5p.

1034. ———. Preliminary inventory of the records of the United States Commerce Court, comp. by Hardee Allen and Janet Weinert. Wash., 1962. 4p.

1035. ———. Preliminary inventory of the records of the United States District Courts for the District of Columbia, comp. by Janet Weinert. Wash., 1962. 15p.

1036. ———. Preliminary inventory of the records of the United States District Court for the Western District of Virginia, comp. by Marion M. Johnson and Elaine Everly. Wash., 1963. 9p.

1037. ———. Preliminary inventory of United States Government documents having general legal effect, comp. by Ralph E. Huss. Wash., 1964. 16p. (Preliminary inventories, no.159)

Periodicals

1038. Alabama, University, School of Law Library. Guide to law reviews and other related periodicals in the University of Alabama, School of Law Library, comp. by Igor I. Kavass and Kathleen Price. University, 1970. 147p.

1039. American Association of Law Libraries, Southwest Chapter. Union list of foreign legal periodicals of the Southwest Chapter, comp. by Guido F. Olivera. Austin: Univ. of Tex. Law Library, 1970. 76*l.*

1040. California State Library, Law Library. Periodicals currently received by the Law Library. Sacramento, 1965. 84*l.*

1041. Law Librarians' Society of Washington, D.C. Union list of legal periodicals, District of Columbia area, 2d ed. Vienna, Va.: Coiner Publications, 1969. 87p.

Records holdings of 45 libraries for about 1,900 titles; excludes Library of Congress Law Library.

1042. Michigan, University, Law School Library. List of current foreign legal periodicals received at the University of Michigan Law Library, 2d ed. Ann Arbor, 1968. 34, 35*l.*

1043. New York University, School of Law Library. Guide to the serials collection currently received by the Library of the School of Law. N.Y., 1968. 134p. Supplement, 1968-69. N.Y., 1969.

1044. Schwerin, Kurt. "Foreign legal periodicals in American law libraries–a new union list." Law library journal 59 (1966), 177-204.

Entries for 305 titles; files located in 29 libraries.

1045. Stern, William B. "Soviet Russian legal periodicals: current or presumed to be current holdings of selected American libraries." Law library journal, 62 (Feb. 1969), 40-46.

Entries for 121 titles with locations in 5 libraries.

Foreign Law

1046. California, University, School of Law Library. Books on Latin American law, politics and economics published in English since 1959; a bibliography, comp. by Robert Faris. Los Angeles, 1964. 21*l.*

1047. Chicago, University, Law School Library. Legal aspects of Yugoslav foreign trade, a selected bibliography, by Adolf Sprudz. Chicago, 1968. 27p. (University of Chicago Law School Library publications, bibliographies and guides to research, no.3)

1048. ——— ———. Soviet codes and statutes in German and French, a bibliography, by Heidrun Nökel. Chicago, 1970. 23p. (University of Chicago Law School Library publications, bibliographies and guides to research, no.7)

1049. Crouch, William H. "And be it enacted . . . some early laws for Van Diemen's Land" [Tasmania] Quarterly journal of the Library of Congress, 25 (1968), 299-305.

Bountiana collection, acquired by Library of Congress.

1050. Dawson, John P. "The Harvard collections of foreign law: changing dimensions of legal study." Harvard Library bulletin, 16 (1968), 101-10.

1051. Harvard University, Law School Library. Preliminary union list of materials on Chinese law; with a list of Chinese studies and translations of foreign law. Cambridge, Mass., 1967. 919p. (Studies in Chinese law, no.6)

Inventory of 21 major library collections of Chinese legal materials.

1052. ——— ———. Soviet legal bibliography, ed. by Vaclav Mostecky and William E. Butler. Cambridge, Mass., 1965. 288p.

Books and serial publications issued in Soviet Union since 1917, to be found in Harvard Law School Library.

1053. ——— ———. Writings on Soviet law and Soviet international law; a bibliography of books and articles published since 1917 in languages other than East European, comp. by William E. Butler. Cambridge, Mass., 1966. 165p.

1054. Hsia, Tao-tai, and Murray, Deborah. "Communist Chinese legal development reflected in the country's legal publications." Quarterly journal of the Library of Congress, 25 (1968), 290-98.

Report on acquisitions, Library of Congress.

1055. Jwaideh, Zuhair E. "African law collections in the Library of Congress." Quarterly journal of the Library of Congress, 27 (1970), 213-22.

1056. U.S. Library of Congress, Far Eastern Law Division. Guide to selected legal sources of mainland China, listing of laws and regulations and periodical legal literature with brief survey of administration of justice, by Tao-tai Hsia. Wash., 1967. 357p.

1057. ———, Law Library. Index to Latin American legislation, 1950 through 1960. Boston: G. K. Hall, 1961. 2v. First supplement. 1970.

Index maintained in Library of Congress Law Library.

International Law and Relations

1058. Columbia University, International Affairs Library. List of periodicals currently received. N.Y., 1970. 43p.

Excludes newspapers, annuals, and monographic series.

1059. Council on Foreign Relations Library. Catalog of the Foreign Relations Library, the Council on Foreign Relations, Inc. (New York City). Boston: G. K. Hall, 1969. 9v.

1060. Harvard University, Law School Library. Catalog of international law and relations, ed. by Margaret Moody. Cambridge, Mass., 1965-67. 20v.

Reproduction of 350,000 catalog cards representing about 150,000 titles.

1061. ——— ———. Index to multilateral treaties; a

chronological list of multi-party international agreements from the sixteenth century through 1963, ed. by Vaclav Mostecky and Francis R. Doyle. Cambridge, Mass., 1965. 301p.

Lists 3,859 items; based on Harvard Law Library's holdings.

1062. U.S. Library of Congress. French consuls in the United States: a calendar of their correspondence in the Archives Nationales, by Abraham P. Nasatir and Gary Elwyn Monell. Wash., 1967. 605p.

Describes some Library of Congress holdings of photoreproductions of French diplomatic material.

1063. U.S. National Archives. List of Foreign Service post records in the National Archives, comp. by Mark G. Eckhoff and Alexander P. Mavro. Wash., 1967. 35p. (Special list, no.9)

1064. ———. Preliminary inventory of the general records of the Department of State, comp. by Daniel T. Goggin and H. Stephen Helton. Wash., 1963. 311p. (Preliminary inventories, no.157)

In two parts: I, diplomatic, consular, and miscellaneous correspondence; II, other materials not part of central files.

1065. ———. Preliminary inventory of records relating to international boundaries, comp. by Daniel T. Goggin. Wash., 1968. 98p. (Preliminary inventories, no.170)

Records listed from 1794 to recent times.

1066. ———. Preliminary inventory of the records of the Foreign Funds Control, comp. by Lyle J. Holverstott and Fred L. Miller. Wash., 1962. 10p.

1067. ———. Preliminary inventory of the records of the International Cooperation Administration, comp. by J. Eric Maddox. Wash., 1965. 3p.

1068. ———. Preliminary inventory of the records of the United States participation in international conferences, commissions, and expositions, comp. by Marion M. Johnson and Mabel D. Brock. Wash., 1965. 22p. (Supplementary to National Archives, Preliminary inventory, no.76)

Constitutional Law and History

1069. Illinois State Library. The Constitution of Illinois; a selective bibliography, comp. by Charlotte B. Stillwell and Stanley E. Adams. Springfield, 1970. 171p.

1070. Michigan Historical Commission. Records of the Michigan Constitutional Convention, 1961-62. Lansing, 1966. 32p. (Finding aid, no.14)

1071. [Southern Illinois University Library. Schroeder papers] College & research libraries news, no.6 (June 1970), 178, 182.

Papers and correspondence of Theodore A. Schroeder, constitutional lawyer and a founder of the Free Speech League, forerunner of the American Civil Liberties Union, acquired by S.I.U. Library.

PUBLIC ADMINISTRATION

1072. Michigan Historical Commission. Records of the Executive Office, Harry F. Kelly, Governor, 1943-1946. Lansing, 1966. 57p. (Finding aid, no.19)

1073. U.S. Civil Service Commission Library. Bibliography of bibliographies in personnel administration. Wash.: U.S. Civil Service Commission, 1963. 62p. (Personnel bibliography series, no.9)

1074. ———. The National Civil Service League collection: a preliminary list of holdings, 1880-1964. Wash., undated. 127p.

1075. ———. The Pendleton Room: a preliminary list of holdings. Wash., 1965. 22p.

1076. U.S. Dept. of the Army Library. The Executive: philosophy, problems, and practices, a bibliographic survey. Wash.: Govt. Print. Off., 1966. 76p. (DA pamphlet 600-10)

Lists about 500 titles, mostly available in the Army Library.

1077. ———. Planning and evaluation of personnel management programs. Wash., 1969. 319p. (DA pamphlet 600-9)

1078. U.S. Federal Records Center. Guide to the records in the Federal Records Center . . . Kansas City, Missouri, comp. by Harry L. Weingart. Kansas City, 1966. 46p.

1079. U.S. National Archives. Index to appropriation ledgers in the records of the office of the Secretary of the Interior, Division of Finance, 1853-1923. Wash., 1964. 202p.

1080. ———. Preliminary inventory of audio-visual records made by the National Archives or for it by Federal agencies, comp. by J. Eric Maddox. Wash., 1965. 5p.

1081. ———. Preliminary inventory of gift still pictures in the National Archives, comp. by J. Eric Maddox. Wash., 1965. 11p.

1082. ———. Preliminary inventory of the general records of the Department of Health, Education and Welfare, comp. by Forrest R. Holdcamper. Wash., 1965. 5p.

1083. ———. Preliminary inventory of the general records of the Federal Works Agency, comp. by William E. Lind. Wash., 1962. 21p.

1084. ———. Preliminary inventory of the general records of the General Services Administration, comp. by William J. Lescure. Wash., 1965. 3p.

1085. ———. Preliminary inventory of the records of interdepartmental and intradepartmental committees (State Department), comp. by Forrest R. Holdcamper. Wash., 1967. 8p.

1086. ———. Preliminary inventory of the records of interservice agencies, comp. by Olive K. Liebman and others. Wash., 1963. 37p.

1087. ———. Preliminary inventory of the records of the Bituminous Coal Division, comp. by Norman D. Moore. Wash., 1967. 18p.

1088. ———. Preliminary inventory of the records of the Bureau of Accounts (Treasury), comp. by Donald L. King. Wash., 1963. 46p.

1089. ———. Preliminary inventory of the records of the Bureau of Customs, comp. by Forrest R. Holdcamper. Wash., 1968. 215p.

1090. ———. Preliminary inventory of the records of the Bureau of the Mint, comp. by Forrest R. Holdcamper. Wash., 1968. 62p.

1091. ———. Preliminary inventory of the records of the Bureau of the Public Debt, rev. by Forrest R. Holdcamper. Wash., 1965. 127p.

1092. ———. Preliminary inventory of the records of the Capital Issues Committee, comp. by Norwood N. Biggs and William F. Sherman. Wash., 1964. 6p.

1093. ———. Preliminary inventory of the records of the Central Intelligence Agency, comp. by Harry Schwartz. Wash., 1964. 4p.

1094. ———. Preliminary inventory of the records of the Commission on Intergovernmental Relations, comp. by Kathryn M. Murphy. Wash., 1965. 11p.

1095. ———. Preliminary inventory of the records of the Commission on Organization of the Executive Branch of the Government (1947-49), comp. by Kathryn M. Murphy. Wash., 1965. 9p.

1096. ———. Preliminary inventory of the records of the Commission on Organization of the Executive Branch of the Government (1953-1955), comp. by Kathryn M. Murphy. Wash., 1965. 18p.

1097. ———. Preliminary inventory of the records of the Committee on Conservation and Administration of the Public Domain, comp. by Helena Higgins, and others. Wash., 1965. 9p.

1098. ———. Preliminary inventory of the records of the Commodity Credit Corporation, comp. by Norman D. Moore. Wash., 1965. 6p.

1099. ———. Preliminary inventory of the records of the Defense Electric Power Administration, comp. by Evans Walker. Wash., 1963. 9p.

1100. ———. Preliminary inventory of the records of the Federal Bureau of Investigation, comp. by Marion M. Johnson. Wash., 1964. 5p.

1101. ———. Preliminary inventory of the records of the Federal Communications Commission, comp. by Forrest R. Holdcamper. Wash., 1965. 7p. (Supplement to Preliminary inventory, no.93)

1102. ———. Preliminary inventory to the records of the Federal Extension Service; supplementary to National Archives, Preliminary inventory No. 83, comp. by James E. Primas and Virgil E. Baugh. Wash., 1965. 9p.

1103. ———. Preliminary inventory of the records of the Federal Fuel Distributor, rev. by Genevieve S. O'Brien. Wash., 1965. 9p. (Revision of Preliminary inventory, no.13)

1104. ———. Preliminary inventory of the records of the Federal Home Loan Bank System, comp. by Forrest R. Holdcamper. Wash., 1965. 4p.

1105. ———. Preliminary inventory of the records of the Federal Inter-Agency River Basin Committee, comp. by Roland C. Rieder. Wash., 1962. 4p.

1106. ———. Preliminary inventory of the records of the Federal Power Commission, comp. by Herbert J. Horwitz and Charlotte M. Ashby. Wash., 1965. 79p.

1107. ———. Preliminary inventory of the records of the Federal Reserve System, comp. by James E. Primas. Wash., 1965. 3p.

1108. ———. Preliminary inventory of the records of the Federal Supply Service, comp. by Edward E. Hill. Wash., 1965. 13p.

1109. ———. Preliminary inventory of the records of the Internal Revenue Service, comp. by Forrest R. Holdcamper. Wash., 1968. 45p.

1110. ———. Preliminary inventory of the records of the National Bituminous Coal Commission, 1935-36, comp. by Wallace B. Goebel. Wash., 1963. 25p. (Preliminary inventories, no.156)

1111. ———. Preliminary inventory of the records of the National Bureau of Standards, comp. by William J. Lescure. Wash., 1964. 29p.

1112. ———. Preliminary inventory of the records of the National Park Service, comp. by Edward E. Hill. Wash., 1966. 52p. (Preliminary inventories, no.166)

1113. ———. Preliminary inventory of the records of the National Security Resources Board, comp. by Elaine C. Everly and Patricia Andrews. Wash., 1966. 49p.

1114. ———. Preliminary inventory of the records of the Office of Contract Settlement, comp. by Kenneth F. Bartlett. Wash., 1964. 24p.

1115. ———. Preliminary inventory of the records of the Office of Personnel of the Office of Price Administration, comp. by Walter W. Weinstein. Wash., 1963. 35p.

1116. ———. Preliminary inventory of the records of the Office of Territories, comp. by Richard S. Maxwell and Evans Walker. Wash., 1963. 117p. (Preliminary inventories, no.154)

1117. ———. Preliminary inventory of the records of the Office of the Chief of Chaplains, comp. by Garry D. Ryan. Wash., 1965. 3p.

1118. ———. Preliminary inventory of the records of the Office of the Commissary General of Prisoners, comp. by Patricia Andrews. Wash., 1966. 81p.

1119. ———. Preliminary inventory of the records of the Office of the Special Adviser to the President on Foreign Trade, comp. by Robert R. Nicolosi. Wash., 1966. 12p.

1120. ———. Preliminary inventory of the records of the Petroleum Administration Board, comp. by Herbert J. Horwitz. Wash., 1964. 7p.

1121. ———. Preliminary inventory of the records of the Post Office Department, rev. by Forrest R. Holdcamper. Wash., 1967. 54p. (Preliminary inventories, no.168)

1122. ———. Preliminary inventory of the records of the President's Advisory Committee on Government Organization, comp. by Kathryn M. Murphy. Wash., 1965. 16p.

1123. ———. Preliminary inventory of the records of the President's Advisory Commission on Presidential Office Space, comp. by Kathryn M. Murphy. Wash., 1964. 8p.

1124. ———. Preliminary inventory of the records of the President's Materials Policy Commission, comp. by Henry T. Ulasek and José D. Lizardo. Wash., 1962. 16p.

1125. ———. Preliminary inventory of the records of the Prison Industries Reorganization Administration, rev. by William Lescure and Kathleen E. Riley. Wash., 1966. 10p.

1126. ———. Preliminary inventory of the records of the Rent Commission of the District of Columbia, comp. by Buford Rowland. Wash., 1965. 3p.

1127. ———. Preliminary inventory of the records of the Securities and Exchange Commission, comp. by Herbert J. Horwitz. Wash., 1964. 3p.

1128. ———. Preliminary inventory of the records of the Smithsonian Institution, comp. by Charlotte M. Ashby and others. Wash., 1965. 5p.

1129. ———. Preliminary inventory of the records of the Social Security Administration, comp. by Herbert J. Horwitz. Wash., 1965. 7p.

1130. ———. Preliminary inventory of the records of the Solicitor of the Treasury, comp. by George S. Ulibarri. Wash., 1968. 35p. (Preliminary inventories, no.171)

1131. ———. Preliminary inventory of the records of the Surplus Marketing Administration, comp. by Forrest R. Holdcamper. Wash., 1965. 14p.

1132. ———. Preliminary inventory of the records of the Tennessee Valley Authority, comp. by J. Eric Maddox and Charlotte M. Ashby. Wash., 1965. 7p.

1133. ———. Preliminary inventory of the records of the United States Coal Commission, comp. by Robert R. Nicolosi. Wash., 1965. 24p.

1134. ———. Preliminary inventory of the records of the United States Fuel Administration, comp. by Harold W. Ryan and Thomas J. Stallans. Wash., 1964. 15p.

1135. ———. Preliminary inventory of the records of the United States Secret Service, comp. by Lyle J. Holverstott and Forrest R. Holdcamper. Wash., 1965. 16p. (Revision of Preliminary inventory, no.16)

1136. ———. Preliminary inventory of the records of the United States Soldiers' Home, comp. by Patricia Andrews. Wash., 1965. 7p.

1137. ———. Supplement to Preliminary checklist 44, insurance records of the Bureau of War Risk Insurance and of the Insurance Division of the Veterans' Bureau, comp. by Evelyn Wade. Wash., 1965. 3p.

1138. ———. Supplement to Preliminary inventory No. 39, records of the Hydrographic Office, comp. by Harry Schwartz. Wash., 1965. 4p.

1139. U.S. Senate Library. Cumulative index of Congressional Committee hearings . . . second quadrennial supplement, from eighty-eighth Congress (January 3, 1963) through eighty-ninth Congress (January 3, 1967), together with selected Committee prints in the United States Senate Library. Wash.: U.S. Govt. Print. Off., 1967. 664p.

1140. ———. Quadrennial supplement to cumulative index of Congressional Committee hearings . . . from eighty-sixth Congress (January 7, 1959), through eighty-seventh Congress (January 3, 1963), together with selected Committee prints in the United States Senate Library, comp. by Mary F. Sterrett. Wash.: U.S. Govt. Print. Off., 1963. 762p.

MILITARY SCIENCE

General

1141. Day, James M. "Sources for military history in the Texas State Archives." Texas military history, 2 (May 1962), 113-25.

1142. Dornbusch, Charles E. Histories, personal narratives, United States Army; a checklist. Cornwallville, N.Y.: Hope Farm, 1967. 402p.

Lists 2,742 entries with locations.

1143. Glazier, Kenneth M. "Recent acquisitions of important military papers at the Hoover Institution on War, Revolution and Peace, Stanford University." Military affairs, 33 (1969), 397-99.

1144. Holt, Daniel D. "Citadel archives and Mark Clark manuscript collection." South Carolina librarian, 11 (Oct. 1966), 6-9.

1145. Johnson, Robert K. "Resources of selected American military libraries." Library quarterly, 32 (1962), 40-50.

Description, with statistics on holdings, of types of material in 18 military libraries.

1146. Michigan Historical Commission, Division of Archives. Finding aid for the records of the Michigan military establishment, 1838-1941, comp. by Geneva Kebler. Lansing, 1962. 27p. (Finding aid, no.1)

1147. Stanford University, Hoover Institution. An English bibliography of Soviet armed forces, 1950-1967, by Michael Parrish. Stanford, Calif., 1970. 128p. (Bibliographical series, no.48)

1148. ——— ———. The Russian Imperial Army; a bibliography of regimental histories and related works, comp. by M. Lyons. Stanford, Calif., 1968. 188p. (Bibliographical series, no.35)

Contains 1,239 titles.

1149. ——— ———. The Soviet armed forces: books in English, 1950-1967, comp. by Michael Parrish. Stanford, Calif., 1970. 128p. (Bibliographical series, no.48)

Lists 2,146 titles.

1150. ——— ———. Soviet disarmament policy 1917-1963; an annotated bibliography of Soviet and Western sources, comp. by Walter C. Clemens, Jr. Stanford, Calif., 1965. 151p. (Bibliographical series, no.22)

Lists 820 titles.

1151. U.S. Army Military History Research Collection, Carlisle Barracks, Pennsylvania. Catalog. Westport, Conn.: Greenwood, 1970. 4v.

1152. U.S. Dept. of the Army Library. Checklist of periodicals currently received in the Army Library. Wash., 1963. 67p. (Special list 1963-2)

1153. ———. Civilian in peace, soldier in war; a bibliographic survey of the Army and Air National Guard. Wash.: Govt. Print. Off., 1967. 192p. (DA pamphlet 130-2)

Prepared by the Army Library.

1154. ———. The college graduate and national security: utilization of manpower by the U.S. Armed Services, a bibliographic survey, comp. by Harry Moskowitz and Jack Roberts. Wash.: Govt. Print. Off., 1968. 74p.

Most materials listed are in Army Library or found through location symbols.

1155. ———. Military manpower policy; a bibliographic survey. Wash.: Govt. Print. Off., 1965. 142p.

More than 700 references, principally in Army Library in Pentagon; other locations indicated.

1156. ———, Army Library. Nuclear warfare and NATO. Wash.: Govt. Print. Off., 1970. 450p. (DA pamphlet 50-1)

1157. ——— ———. Nuclear weapons and the Atlantic Alliance. Wash., 1965. 193p. (DA pamphlet 20-66)

1158. ——— ———. Strength in reserve, a bibliographic survey of the United States Army Reserve. Wash.: Govt. Print. Off., 1968. 119p. (DA pamphlet 140-3)

Material listed principally in Army Library.

1159. ——— ———. Theses and dissertations in the holdings of the Army Library, a list of titles, 3d ed. Wash., 1966. 101p. (Special bibliography, no.20)

Contains 836 items.

1160. ——— ———. U.S. national security and the Communist challenge–the spectrum of east-west conflict. Wash., 1961. 93p. (DA pamphlet 20-60)

Materials mainly for 1958-60; "almost all are available in the holdings of the Army Library."

1161. ——— ———. U.S. overseas bases present status and future prospects. Wash., 1963. 133p. (DA pamphlet 20-63)

1162. ——— ———. U.S. security, arms control, and disarmament, 1960-1961. Wash., 1961. 144p.

1163. ——— ———. U.S. security, arms control, and disarmament, 1961-1965. Wash., 1965. 140p.

1164. ———, Office of Civil Defense. Civil Defense: 1960-67, a bibliographic survey. Wash.: Govt. Print. Off., 1967. 124p. (DA pamphlet 500-3)

Prepared by the Army Library; more than 500 references selected from the Army Library and from various divisions of the Office of Civil Defense.

1165. U.S. Library of Congress, Arms Control and Disarmament Bibliography Section. Arms control and disarmament; a quarterly bibliography with abstracts and annotations, 1964 to date. v.1- . Wash.: The Library, 1964- .

Locates copies in Library of Congress.

1166. U.S. Military Academy Library. Preliminary guide to the manuscript collection of the U.S. Military Academy Library, comp. by J. Thomas Russell. West Point, N.Y., 1968. 260p. (USMA Library bulletin, no.5)

Descriptions of groups of manuscripts, alphabetically arranged under personal names.

1167. ———. Subject catalog, with selected author and added entries of the military art and science collection and a preliminary guide to the manuscript collection. Westport, Conn.: Greenwood, 1970. 4v.

1168. U.S. National Archives. Guide to records of Italian armed forces. Wash., 1967. 3v.

1169. ———. Preliminary inventory of private papers given to the National Archives that are in the care of Military Archives, comp. by Evelyn Wade. Wash., 1962. 10p.

1170. ———. Preliminary inventory of the records of Allied Operational and Occupation Headquarters, World War II, comp. by Kathleen E. Riley and others. Wash., 1962. 2pts.

Part I: Records of Supreme Headquarters Allied Expeditionary Forces (SHAEF); Combined Administrative Liquidating Agency; Combined Civil Affairs Liquidating Agency. Part II: Records of General Headquarters, Supreme Commander for the Allied Powers (SCAP).

1171. ———. Preliminary inventory of the records of Headquarters Army Ground Forces, comp. by Olive K. Liebman. Wash., 1962. 11p.

1172. ———. Preliminary inventory of the records of international military agencies, comp. by Mabel P. Milstead. Wash., 1962. 3p.

1173. ———. Preliminary inventory of the records of

Joint Army and Navy Boards and Committees, comp. by Harry W. John. Wash., 1965. 10p.

1174. ———. Preliminary inventory of the records of Joint Commands, comp. by Mary Joe Head and Jessie T. Midkiff. Wash., 1962. 12p.

1175. ———. Preliminary inventory of the records of the Army staff, 1939, comp. by Helene L. Bowen and others. Wash., 1962. 42p.

1176. ———. Preliminary inventory of the records of the Board of War Communications, comp. by Leo Pascal and Robert E. Webb. Wash., 1965. 16p.

1177. ———. Preliminary inventory of the records of the Chiefs of Arms, comp. by John E. Taylor and Patricia Andrews. Wash., 1962. 19p.

1178. ———. Preliminary inventory of the records of the Defense Materials Service, comp. by J. Eric Maddox. Wash., 1965. 3p.

1179. ———. Preliminary inventory of the records of the Office of the Chief of Finance (Army), comp. by Richard W. Giroux. Wash., 1962. 17p. (Preliminary inventories, no.142)

1180. ———. Preliminary inventory of the records of the Office of the Secretary of the Army, comp. by Helene L. Bowen and Mary Joe Head. Wash., 1962. 13p.

1181. ———. Preliminary inventory of the records of the Office of War Information, by Forrest R. Holdcamper. Wash., 1967. 164p. (Revision of Preliminary inventory, no.56)

1182. ———. Preliminary inventory of the records of the President's Committee to Study the United States Military Assistance Program ("Draper Committee"), comp. by Marion M. Johnson. Wash., 1965. 3p.

1183. ———. Preliminary inventory of the records of the Smaller War Plants Corporation, comp. by Katherine H. Davidson. Wash., 1964. 85p. (Preliminary inventories, no.160)

1184. ———. Preliminary inventory of the records of the United States Joint Chiefs of Staff, comp. by Garry D. Ryan. Wash., 1964. 4p.

1185. ———. Preliminary inventory of the records of the War Minerals Relief Commission, rev. by Kathleen E. Riley. Wash., 1965. 7p.

1186. ———. Preliminary inventory of the records of United States Army Commands, 1784-1821, comp. by Maizie Johnson and Sarah Powell. Wash., 1966. 76p.

1187. ———. Preliminary inventory of the seized enemy records in the Office of Military Archives, comp. by Cleveland E. Collier and others. Wash., 1965. 27p.

1188. ———. Preliminary inventory of the textual records of the American Battle Monuments Commission, comp. by Garry D. Ryan. Wash., 1965. 4p.

1189. ———. Preliminary inventory of the textual records of the American Expeditionary Forces (World War I), 1917-23, Part I, comp. by Aloha Broadwater and others. Wash., 1968. 164p.

1190. ———. Preliminary inventory of the textual records of the American Expeditionary Forces (World War I), 1917-23, Part II, comp. by Aloha Broadwater and others. Wash., 1968. 176p.

1191. ———. Preliminary inventory of the textual records of the Combined Raw Materials Board and the Combined Production and Resources Board, comp. by Sarah D. Powell. Wash., 1967. 38p.

1192. ———. Preliminary inventory of the textual records of the International Military Tribunal for the Far East (IMTFE), comp. by Charles V. Kirchman. Wash., 1965. 5p.

1193. ———. Preliminary inventory of the textual records of the Office of Strategic Services, comp. by Harry W. John. Wash., 1965. 13p.

1194. ———. Preliminary inventory of the textual records of the Office of the Chief of Ordnance. Part II, Records of Ordnance Field Installations. Wash., 1965. 79p.

1195. ———. Preliminary inventory of the textual records of the Office of the Quartermaster General, Part I, comp. by Maizie H. Johnson. Wash., 1967. 234p.

1196. ———. Preliminary inventory of the textual records of the Office of the Quartermaster General, Part II, comp. by Maizie H. Johnson. Wash., 1967. 38p.

1197. ———. Preliminary inventory of the textual records of the War Department General and Special Staffs, comp. by Harry W. John and Olive K. Liebman. Wash., 1967. 62p.

1198. ———. Preliminary inventory of the textual records of United States Army Coast Artillery Districts and Defenses, 1901-42, comp. by Sarah D. Powell. Wash., 1967. 33p.

1199. ———. Preliminary inventory of the textual records of United States Army Continental Commands, 1920-42, comp. by Sarah D. Powell. Wash., 1967. 60p.

1200. ———. Records of Headquarters of Army, National Archives inventory record group 108, comp. by Aloha South. Wash., 1970. 32p. (National Archives inventory series, no.1)

1201. ———. Records of the Chemical Warfare Service; supplement to Preliminary inventory No. 8, comp. by Garry D. Ryan. Wash., 1964. 6p.

1202. ———. Records of the National Guard Bureau and its predecessors; supplement to Preliminary checklist 33, comp. by Patricia Andrews. Wash., 1964. 3p.

1203. ———. Records of the Office of the Inspector General; supplement to Preliminary checklist 51, comp. by Garry D. Ryan. Wash., 1964. 4p.

1204. ———. Records of the United States Marine Corps, National Archives inventory record group 127, comp. by Maizie Johnson. Wash., 1970. 90p. (National Archives inventory series, no.2)

1205. ———. Supplement to Preliminary inventory No. 15, records of the War Production Board, comp. by Harry Schwartz. Wash., 1965. 9p.

1206. ———. Supplement to Preliminary inventory No. 33, records of the Bureau of Ordnance, comp. by Harry Schwartz. Wash., 1965. 5p.

1207. ———. Supplement to Preliminary inventory No. 142: records of the Office of the Chief of Finance (Army), comp. by Maizie H. Johnson. Wash., 1967. 4p.

Air Force

1208. Atkinson, Gloria L. "The archives of the USAF Historical Division." Special libraries, 59 (1968), 444-46.

Describes extensive historical archives of the U.S. Air Force at Air University, Maxwell AFB, Alabama.

1209. U.S. Air Force, Air University Library. Air University Library index to military periodicals. Maxwell AFB, Ala., 1961- . Quarterly, annual and triennial cumulations.

Subject index to 65-70 English-language military and aeronautical periodicals received by Air University Library.

1210. ——— ———. Guide to library services. Maxwell AFB, Ala., 1961- . Annual.

1211. U.S. Dept. of the Army Library. Missiles and ventures into space, 1960-1961 report. Wash., 1961. 81p.; Missiles and ventures into space, progress report, 1961-1962. 1962. 110p.; Missiles and ventures into space, progress report, 1962-1963. 1963. 123p.

1212. U.S. National Archives. Preliminary inventory of the records of Headquarters Army Air Forces, comp. by Kathleen E. Riley. Wash., 1962. 11p.

1213. ———. Preliminary inventory of the records of the Office of the Secretary of the Air Force, comp. by Jessie T. Midkiff and Olive K. Liebman. Wash., 1962. 8p.

1214. ———. Preliminary inventory of the textual records of the Army Air Forces, comp. by Maizie H. Johnson. Wash., 1965. 118p.

1215. ———. Supplement to Preliminary inventory No. NM 53: textual records of the Army Air Forces, comp. by Maizie H. Johnson and Sarah D. Powell. Wash., 1967. 11p.

Navy

1216. U.S. Naval Research Laboratory Library. Holdings of periodicals currently received in the Technical Library of the Naval Research Laboratory. Wash., 1961. 78p. Rev. ed., 1965. 135p.

1217. ———. Your library as a research tool: a guide to the resources and services of the Naval Research Laboratory Library. Wash.: U.S. Naval Research Laboratory, 1969. 54p.

Detailed descriptions of library's available resources and services.

1218. U.S. Dept. of the Navy, Naval Operations Office. United States naval history, a bibliography, 5th ed. Wash.: Govt. Print. Off., 1969. 34p.

Prepared by the Navy Department Library.

1219. ———, Office of the Chief of Naval Operations. U.S. naval history, naval biography, naval strategy and tactics, a selected and annotated bibliography, 3d ed. Wash.: Govt. Print. Off., 1963. 29p.

Prepared by the Navy Department Library.

1220. U.S. National Archives. Preliminary inventory of the records of the Office of the Chief of Naval Operations, comp. by Harry Schwartz and others. Wash., 1966. 111p.

1221. ———. Preliminary inventory of the records of the Office of the Chief Signal Officer, comp. by Mabel E. Deutrich. Wash., 1963. 26p. (Preliminary inventories, no.155)

1222. ———. Preliminary inventory of the textual records of Naval Districts and Shore Establishments, comp. by Harry Schwartz and Lee Saegesser. Wash., 1966. 81p.

1223. ———. Supplement to Preliminary checklist 32, records of the Office of the Judge Advocate General (Navy), comp. by Harry Schwartz. Wash., 1965. 6p.

1224. ———. Supplement to Preliminary checklist 41, records of the Bureau of Supplies and Accounts (Navy), comp. by Harry W. John. Wash., 1965. 4p.

1225. ———. Supplement to Preliminary inventory No. 105: records of the Office of the Chief Signal Officer, comp. by Mabel E. Deutrich. Wash., 1967. 10p.

1226. ———. Supplement to Preliminary inventory No. 123: records of the Bureau of Naval Personnel, comp. by Lee D. Saegesser and Harry Schwartz. Wash., 1967. 7p.

WELFARE AND SOCIAL ACTIVITIES

1227. Crabtree, Loren W. "The papers of the National Federation of Settlements and Neighborhood Centers." Social service review, 40 (1966), 317-18.

Describes collection in Social Welfare History Archives in University of Minnesota Libraries.

1228. Hinding, Andrea. "The papers of the Survey Associates." Social service review, 40 (June 1966), 213-15.

Description of collection in Social Welfare History Archives in University of Minnesota Libraries.

1229. Louisiana State Library. Break-through with books; a booklist for adult correctional institutional libraries. Baton Rouge, 1970. 67*l.*

1230. Michigan Historical Commission, Division of Archives. Finding aid for the records of the Michigan Social Welfare Department, 1881-1952, comp. by Geneva Kebler. Lansing, 1963. 12p. (Finding aid, no.11)

1231. ——— ———. Finding aid for the records of the Michigan State Prison, Jackson, Michigan, 1839-1906, comp. by Geneva Kebler. Lansing, 1962. 9p. (Finding aid, no.6)

1232. Minnesota, University, Social Welfare History Archives. Descriptive inventories of collections in the Social Welfare Library Archives. Westport, Conn.: Greenwood, 1970. 846p.

Composed primarily of historical records of social welfare organizations and papers of individuals prominent in social work.

1233. Washington State Library. Annotated bibliography; basic material in the field of public welfare. Olympia, 1968. 19p.

Secret Societies

1234. Cornell University Libraries. Bibliography of Cornell University's holdings of materials relative to the Anti-Masonic movement, by Jack Monroe Holl. Ithaca, N.Y., 1962. 20*l.*

Insurance

1235. Insurance Company of North America. The historical collection of Insurance Company of North America, 1792-1867, by M. J. McCosker. Philadelphia, 1967. 213p.

EDUCATION

General

1236. California State Library, Reference Section. Books, periodicals, and documents on education added to the State Library. Sacramento, Jan. 1958- . Monthly.

1237. Harvard University, Graduate School of Education, Library. Education Library guide. Cambridge, Mass., 1969. 16p.

1238. Harvard University Library. Education and education periodicals. Cambridge, Mass., 1968. 2v. (Widener Library shelflist, no. 16-17)

Lists more than 32,700 works in Widener Library by classification, author and title, and chronologically.

1239. Kentucky Dept. of Education Library. Archives report: a list of books in the Archives Room of the Kentucky State Department of Education. Frankfort, 1967. 14p.

1240. Michigan Historical Commission, Division of Archives. Finding aid for the records of the Boys' Vocational School, 1855-1954, comp. by Geneva Kebler. Lansing, 1963. 13p. (Finding aid, no.9)

1241. ——— ———. Finding aid for the records of the Girls' Training School, Adrian, Michigan, 1880-1941, comp. by Geneva Kebler. Lansing, 1962. 21p. (Finding aid, no.3)

1242. ——— ———. Finding aid for the records of the Michigan Department of Public Instruction, 1859-1957, comp. by Geneva Kebler. Lansing, 1963. 11p. (Finding aid, no.12)

1243. ——— ———. Records of the Michigan Children's Institute, 1871-1959. Lansing, 1966. 9p. (Finding aid, no.18)

1244. Michigan State Library. Bibliography for educators; bibliography on emotionally disturbed. Lansing, 1969? 54p.

1245. Michigan, University, William L. Clements Library. Education in early America; a guide to an exhibition in the Clements Library to commemorate the sesquicentennial of the University of Michigan, by Howard H. Peckham. Ann Arbor, 1967. 23p. (Bulletin, no.73)

1246. New York Division of Archives and History. Preliminary list of public education records in New York State. Albany, 1961. 31p.

1247. Rochester, University, Library. Selected list of education serials in the libraries of the University of Rochester as of October 15, 1968. Rochester, N.Y., 1969. 119p.

1248. Wisconsin State Historical Society. The history of education collections. Madison, 18p.

Textbooks

1249. Mattern, Margaret M. "Early Rochester textbooks, 1821-1850." University of Rochester Library bulletin, 22 (1966), 4-16.

Discussion and bibliography of school texts published and used in Rochester, New York, during first half of nineteenth century; copies now held by University of Rochester Library.

1250. Pittsburgh, University, Library. Old textbooks; spelling, grammar, reading, arithmetic, geography, penmanship, art, music—as taught in the common schools from colonial days to 1900, by John A. Nietz. Pittsburgh: Univ. Pr., 1961. 364p.

Most of textbooks listed are in University of Pittsburgh Library.

1251. Plimpton, Francis T. P. "The Plimpton library." Columbia Library columns, 10 (Feb. 1961), 25-36.

Library of historical textbooks and related works, containing 13,000 separate titles, 300 medieval and Renaissance manuscripts, 100 15th-century printed books, and later imprints; in Columbia University.

Colleges and Universities

1252. Harvard University Library. The Harvard University Archives. Cambridge, Mass., 1966. 11p. (Guides to the Harvard Libraries, no.4)

1253. Huber, George K. "Swarthmoreana; a collection of the serious and profound, the frivolous and lighthearted, and the how-to's from knot-tying to carving and cooking." Swarthmore College bulletin, Dec. 1969. p.29.

Description of Swarthmore College Library's Swarthmoreana collection.

1254. Kentucky, University, Libraries. University of Kentucky, the University Archives. Lexington, 1962. 6p. (Occasional contribution, no.131)

1255. Kuhn, Warren B. "The Earle D. Ross papers." Iowa State University Library, Notes for the faculty, 1 (Nov. 1968), 1.

Collection of manuscripts and papers on the history of Iowa State University and the land grant movement.

1256. Oregon State University. A guide to the archives of Oregon State University, by William F. Schmidt. Corvallis, 1966. 43*l.* (Archives bulletin, no.1)

1257. Shipton, Clifford K. "The Harvard University Archives in 1938 and in 1969." Harvard Library bulletin, 18 (1970), 205-11.

Traces development and use.

1258. Society of American Archivists, College and University Archives Committee. College and university archives in the United States and Canada. Ann Arbor, 1966. 108p.

Directory containing statistics and descriptions of collections, a total of about 375 institutions.

1259. Texas, University, Library. The University of

Texas Archives: a guide to the historical manuscripts collections in the University of Texas Library, comp. by Chester V. Kielman. Austin: Univ. of Tex. Pr., 1967. 594p.

1260. William and Mary College. Thomas Jefferson and the College of William and Mary; an exhibit of books, manuscripts, and artifacts prepared in observance of Charter Day. Williamsburg, Va., 1963. Unpaged.

CUSTOMS AND FOLKLORE

1261. Cleveland Public Library. The John G. White collection of folklore, Orientalia and chess. Cleveland, Ohio, 1970. 8p.

Description of collection containing 115,000 volumes and 1,500 manuscripts.

1262. ———, John G. White Dept. Catalog of folklore and folk songs. Boston: G. K. Hall, 1964. 2v.

Subject catalog of notable collection of 115,000 volumes relating to folklore, folktales, proverbs, superstitions, witchcraft, etc.

1263. Cleveland Public Library. Out-of-print books from the John G. White folklore collection at the Cleveland Public Library. Cleveland, Ohio: Micro Photo Division, Bell & Howell Co., 1966. 321p.

1264. Duke University Library. The Frank C. Brown collection of North Carolina folklore; the folklore of North Carolina, collected by Dr. Frank C. Brown during the years 1912 to 1943, in collaboration with the North Carolina Folklore Society. Durham, N.C: Duke Univ. Pr., 1952-64. 7v.

1265. [King's College Library, Wilkes-Barre, Pa. Korson collection] College & research libraries news, no.5 (May 1970), 146.

Collection of tapes, manuscripts, books, and letters of George Korson, American folklorist, acquired by King's College.

1266. Tennessee State Library and Archives, Manuscript Section. Highlander Folk School audio collection. Nashville, 1964. 41p. (Registers, no.9)

1267. ——— ———. Highlander Folk School manuscript records collection. Nashville, 1968. 21p. (Registers, no.9)

Covers period 1932-66.

Women

1268. James, Janet Wilson. "History and women at Harvard: the Schlesinger Library." Harvard Library bulletin, 16 (1968), 385-99.

1269. ———. "The Schlesinger Library at Radcliffe College." Bay State librarian, 56 (July 1966), 9-17.

On the history of women in America.

1270. Lord, Deane. "Remember the ladies: the Arthur and Elizabeth Schlesinger Library on the history of women in America." Harvard today (Autumn 1968), 18-22.

Account of Schlesinger Library at Radcliffe College.

1271. Solomon, Barbara M. "Women's archives, Radcliffe College." Social service review, 36 (1962), 325-27.

Material relating to role of women in the United States.

Science

GENERAL

1272. Academy of Natural Sciences of Philadelphia. Guide to the manuscript collections, comp. by Venia T. and Maurice T. Phillips. Philadelphia, 1963. 553p.

List of collections totaling about 185,000 items.

1273. ———. Guide to the microfilm publication of the minutes and correspondence of the Academy of Natural Sciences of Philadelphia, 1812-1924, comp. by Venia T. Phillips. Philadelphia, 1967. 92p.

1274. American Philosophical Society. Catalogue of instruments and models in the possession of the American Philosophical Society, by Robert P. Multhauf and David Davies. Philadelphia, 1961. 80p. (APS memoir 53)

1275. American Philosophical Society Library, Philadelphia. Catalog of books. Westport, Conn.: Greenwood, 1970. 23v.

Reproduced card catalog of printed books, outstanding for history of science and general American history.

1276. ———. Catalog of manuscripts in the American Philosophical Society Library, including the archival shelflist. Westport, Conn.: Greenwood, 1970. 10v.

Listing all collections and thousands of individual letters.

1277. ———. Guide to science and history of science resources in the Philadelphia area, by L. D. Gundry. Philadelphia, 1970. 63p. (Library publication, no.3)

1278. ———. Guide to the archives and manuscript collections of the American Philosophical Society, comp. by Whitfield J. Bell, Jr., and Murphy D. Smith. Philadelphia, 1966. 182p. (APS memoirs 66)

General description of 784 collections and manuscripts in the library.

1279. California State Library, Reference Section. Technical and scientific books received at the State Library. Sacramento, Jan. 1957- . Monthly.

1280. Columbia University Libraries, Science Division. The recorder. N.Y.: Semimonthly.

Listing of recent acquisitions of books and new serials received by Division.

1281. Georgia Institute of Technology Library. Literature of science and technology, by Edward Graham Roberts. Atlanta: Ga. Institute of Technology, 1966. 93p. 2d ed., 1969. 105p.

Textbook containing subject bibliographies in science, engineering, and management; based on Georgia Institute of Technology Library collection.

1282. Hawaii, Dept. of Planning & Economic Development. Directory of Hawaii's scientific resources. Honolulu, 1965. 56p.

Includes data on libraries.

1283. Hughes Aircraft Company, Technical Library Services Section. Bibliography of scientific and technical bibliographies, by M. Bloomfield and others. Culver City, Calif., 1968. 2v.

v.1, accession list; v.2, subject index.

1284. Idaho, University, Library. Evaluation of the holdings in science and technology in the University of Idaho Library, by Robert W. Burns, Jr. Moscow, 1968. 52p.

1285. International Science Foundation. Scientific resources of northern California. San Francisco, 1964. 1,136p.

Includes data on libraries.

1286. Jenkins, Frances Briggs. Science reference

sources, 5th ed. Cambridge, Mass.: M.I.T. Pr., 1969. 231p.

Comprehensive guide to scientific reference books and journals. University of Illinois Library call numbers added.

1287. Linda Hall Library. The book collection and services of the Linda Hall Library; an outline guide. Kansas City, Mo., 1967. 43p.

1288. National Academy of Sciences. Scientific and technical societies of the United States and Canada. Wash., 1961. 413p.

U.S. societies, p.1-413; limited data on libraries.

1289. National Science Foundation. Specialized science information services in the United States: a directory of selected specialized information services in the physical and biological sciences. Wash., 1961. 528p.

Includes data on libraries.

1290. North Carolina, University, Library. A survey of facilities for the sciences and social sciences in academic libraries of the United States. Chapel Hill, 1965. 16*l.*

1291. Northeastern University Library. A selective bibliography in science and engineering, Dodge Library, Northeastern University (Boston). Boston: G. K. Hall, 1964. 550p.

1292. Rochester, University, Library. Consolidated short-title catalog of books and journals of the science libraries: engineering, geology-geography, life sciences, physics-mathematics-astronomy. Rochester, N.Y., 1965. 394p.

1293. ———. Science libraries consolidated short-title catalog of books: engineering, geology-geography, life sciences, physics-mathematics-optics-astronomy, 3d ed. Rochester, N.Y., 1967. 406p.

1294. Shipman, Joseph C. "Linda Hall Library and its distinctive collections." MLA quarterly, 24 (March-June 1963), 23-32, 57-64.

1295. Tallman, Johanna E. "Physical sciences libraries at UCLA." Southern California Chapter, Special Libraries Association, bulletin, 29, no.1 (1967), 3-4.

1296. U.S. Federal Records Center. Preliminary inventory of the records of the U.S. Commission for the U.S. Science Exhibit at the Seattle World's Fair (1956-1963), comp. by Elmer W. Lingard. Seattle, 1966. 21p.

1297. U.S. Library of Congress, International Organizations Section. International scientific organizations; a guide to their library, documentation, and information services. Wash.: The Library, 1962. 794p.

1298. ———, National Referral Center for Science and Technology. A directory of information resources in the United States: Federal Government. With a supplement of government-sponsored information resources. Wash.: The Library, 1967. 411p.

1299. ——— ———. A directory of information resources in the United States: physical sciences, biological sciences, engineering. Wash.: Govt. Print. Off., 1965. 352p.

Describes collections and services of libraries, information centers, government agencies, professional societies, etc.

1300. ———, Science and Technology Division. Directories in science and technology: a provisional checklist. Wash.: Govt. Print. Off., 1963. 65p.

Lists 304 directories in Library of Congress and other locations.

1301. ——— ———. Mainland China organizations of higher learning in science and technology and their publications: a selected guide, comp. by Chi Wang. Wash.: Govt. Print. Off., 1961. 104p.

Publications available in Library of Congress are noted.

1302. ——— ———. Soviet science and technology, a bibliography on the state of the art, 1955-1961. Wash.: Govt. Print. Off., 1962. 209p.

Lists 2,000 annotated titles of periodicals and monographs.

1303. U.S. National Archives. Preliminary inventory of the records of the Office of Science and Technology, comp. by Norman D. Moore and John F. Simmons. Wash., 1964. 3p.

1304. ———. Preliminary inventory of the records of the Office of Scientific Research and Development, comp. by Forrest R. Holdcamper. Wash., 1965. 52p.

1305. ———. Preliminary inventory of the records of the President's Scientific Research Board, comp. by Marion M. Johnson. Wash., 1965. 3p.

1306. Walsh, John. "Linda Hall Library: Kansas City institution builds a reputation outside its own region." Science, 148 (1965), 1073-75.

General description of library outstanding for science and technology.

HISTORY

1307. American Philosophical Society Library. Science and medicine to 1870: pamphlets in the American Philosophical Society Library, comp. by Simeon J. Crowther and Marion Fawcett. Philadelphia, 1968. 164p. (Library publication, no.1)

1308. Bell, Whitfield J., Jr. "Rattlesnakes and hummingbirds: Philadelphia's resources for the history of science." Papers of the Bibliographical Society of America, 64 (1970), 13-27.

Descriptions of principal collections.

1309. Brasch, Frederick E. "The Isaac Newton collection." Publications of the Astronomical Society of the Pacific, 74 (1962), 366-91.

Describes Isaac Newton collection in Stanford University Library.

1310. Burndy Library. Heralds of science: as represented by two hundred epochal books and pamphlets selected from the Burndy Library, with notes by Bern Dibner. Cambridge, Mass.: M.I.T. Pr., 1969. 96p.

Detailed bibliographical descriptions of monuments in history of science.

1311. Cavanagh, G. S. T. "The Trent collection and the history of science." Gnomon (1970), 47-51. (Special number of Duke University Library's Library notes)

Describes collection in Duke Library.

1312. Grolier Club. One hundred books famous in science, based on an exhibition held at the Grolier Club. N.Y., 1964. 449p.

Notable exhibit drawn from 28 collections.

1313. Holland, Harold E. Academic libraries and the history of science. (Univ. of Ill., Graduate School of Library Science, Occasional papers, no.91, Jan. 1968)

p.14-18, "Academic library collections," describes history of science collections in U.S. university libraries.

1314. Indiana University, Lilly Library. Exhibition of original printings of some milestones of science from Pliny (1469) to Banting (1922); catalogue and notes by John Neu. Bloomington, 1963. 13p.

1315. Lehigh University Library. An exhibition of books and manuscripts by and relating to Galileo Galilei upon the quadricentennial of his birth, 1564-1964. Bethlehem, Pa., 1964. 32p.

Drawn mainly from private collection of Robert B. Honeyman.

1316. Linda Hall Library. Archimedes to Einstein; one hundred printed books and papers in the history of classical physics. Kansas City, Mo., 1965. 53p.

1317. Ohio State University Libraries. The Charles Henry Shaw memorial collection of the history of science: a centennial booklist, by Virginia E. Yagello. Columbus, 1970. 12p.

1318. Oklahoma, University, Library. Short-title catalog of the history of science collections, comp. by Duane H. D. Roller. Norman, 1969. 631p.

1319. Schullian, Dorothy May. "And the bones came together." Ithaca, N.Y., 1961-63. (Cornell University Library Associates, Occasional papers, 6-7)

Relates to Andreas Vesalius works in Cornell University Libraries' history of science collection.

1320. Southern Methodist University, DeGolyer Foundation Library. Subject guide and advice to users of the Library of the DeGolyer Foundation . . . Southern Methodist University. Dallas, Tex.: Southern Methodist Univ. Library, 1966. 7p.

Deals with history of science and technology.

1321. Stanford University Libraries. Sir Isaac Newton; an essay on Sir Isaac Newton and Newtonian thought as exemplified in the Stanford collection of books, manuscripts, and prints concerning celestial mechanics, optics, mathematics, and related disciplines as a history of natural philosophy, by Frederick E. Brasch. Stanford, Calif.: Stanford Univ. Pr., 1962. 28p.

1322. Syracuse University Library. Historical works in science and mathematics located in the Arents Rare Book Room, Syracuse University Library. Syracuse, 1964. 47*l.*

1323. Texas, University, History of Science Collection. John Herschel and Victorian science; exhibition of manuscripts, photographs, drawings and books, catalogue, comp. by James H. Leech. Austin: Univ. of Tex. Humanities Research Center, 1966. 36p.

1324. Union College Library. Early scientific books in Schaffer Library, Union College; a checklist by Wayne Somers. Schenectady, N.Y., 1971. 70p.

Annotated list of 307 works, arranged by broad fields.

1325. U.S. Military Academy Library. Landmarks in science; great rare books from the USMA collections, by

Edward P. Rich. West Point, N.Y., 1969. Unpaged. (USMA Library bulletin no.8)

Detailed descriptions of 18 rare works, 16th to 19th centuries.

PERIODICALS (GENERAL SCIENCE)

1326. Argonne National Laboratory, Library Services Dept. Argonne list of serials. Lemont, Ill., 1966. 233p.

1327. Bonn, George S. Japanese journals in science and technology, an annotated checklist. N.Y.: N.Y. Public Library, 1960. 119p.

Lists 660 titles; based on New York Public Library collections.

1328. California Institute of Technology. Serials and journals in the C.I.T. libraries. Pasadena, 1970. 156p.

1329. California, University, Visual Science Information Center, Berkeley. Vision union list of serials, 2d ed. Berkeley, 1970. 41p.

Locates holdings in 20 libraries in various parts of the United States.

1330. Center for Research Libraries. Rarely held scientific serials in the Midwest Inter-library Center. Chicago, 1963. 197p. Supplements 1-5. Chicago, 1964-68. 5v.

Titles included in Chemical abstracts and Biological abstracts not generally received; includes titles in chemistry, biology, agriculture, medicine, geology, and related fields.

1331. Franklin Institute Library. Serial titles in the Franklin Institute Library, 1969. Philadelphia, 1970. 377p.

Lists 8,000 titles. Collection dating from 1824, notable for science and technology. Updates 1963 and 1966 lists.

1332. Georgia Institute of Technology Library. Serials holdings list, April 1970. Atlanta, 1970. 317p.

Lists holdings for 11,000 serial publications; particular strength in science and technology.

1333. Harvard University Library. Current journals in the sciences, 4th ed. Cambridge, Mass., 1970. 108p.

List of 5,000 journals currently received in 15 science department libraries at Harvard.

1334. Houston list of scientific and technical serial publications. Houston, Tex.: P. Wilson, 1963. 304p.

Records holdings for about 8,000 titles in 50 Houston area libraries.

1335. John Crerar Library. List of current serials, 5th ed. Chicago, 1965. 286p. Supplement, 1967. 39p.

Lists about 7,500 titles.

1336. Johns Hopkins University, Applied Physics Laboratory, Silver Spring, Md. List of scientific-technical journal titles and holdings in the Washington-Baltimore area. Silver Spring? 1965. 119*l.*

Records holdings of 11 libraries.

1337. Joint University Libraries. Scientific serial publications in the Joint University Libraries, comp. by Eleanor F. Morrissey. Nashville, Tenn., 1968. 138p.

Lists about 6,000 titles.

1338. Linda Hall Library. A list of serial titles currently received. Kansas City, Mo., 1965. 85p. (Bulletin, no.11)

Revisions of lists issued in 1961 and 1963.

1339. ———. Serials holdings in the Linda Hall Library, February 1, 1967. Kansas City, Mo., 1967. 286p.

1340. Marine Biological Laboratory Library. Serial publications held by the Marine Biological Laboratory Library and the Woods Hole Oceanographic Institution. Woods Hole, Mass., 1965. 298p. Supplement 1, 1967. 24*l.*; supplement 2, 1968. 37*l.*

Alphabetical lists, with holdings.

1341. Massachusetts Institute of Technology Libraries. Current holdings of Communist Chinese journals in the M.I.T. Libraries, 2d ed. Cambridge, Mass., 1963. 44p.

Contains 138 entries, showing exact holdings; principally in natural and applied sciences.

1342. ———. International union list of Communist Chinese serials: scientific, technical and medical, with selected social science titles, comp. by Bernadette P. N. Shih and Richard L. Snyder. Cambridge, 1963. 148p.

Lists 874 titles; extent of holdings shown for 18 U.S. libraries.

1343. ———. Serials and journals in the M.I.T. Libraries, 12th ed. Cambridge, Mass.: M.I.T. Pr., 1970. 492p.

Lists detailed holdings.

1344. Michigan, University, Library. Union list of scientific and technical serials in the University of Michigan Library, 5th ed. Ann Arbor, 1970. 711p.

Contains 23,639 main entries.

1345. North Carolina union list of scientific serials, ed. by I. T. Littleton and Gloria W. Houser. Raleigh: N.C. State Univ. Library, 1967. 767p.

Includes holdings of libraries of Duke University, North Carolina State University, University of North Carolina, and Women's College of the University of North Carolina.

1346. Rochester, University, Library. Selected list of scientific periodicals in the libraries of the University of Rochester as of January 15, 1966. Rochester, N.Y., 1966. 130p.

1347. Slamecka, Vladimir. "Classified list of Czechoslovak scientific, technical, and trade serials, with indications of holdings in U.S. and Canadian libraries." In his: Science in Czechoslovakia. N.Y.: Columbia Univ. Pr., 1963, p.145-67.

Locates files of 279 titles in 214 libraries.

1348. Special Libraries Association, Boston Chapter, Science-Technology Group. Union list of serial holdings in sixty-eight libraries, ed. by Alice G. Anderson, 7th ed. Boston, 1967. 479p.

1349. ——— ——— ———. Union list of serial holdings, 8th ed. Boston, 1969. 273p.

Lists holdings of 68 libraries.

1350. ———. San Francisco Bay Region Chapter. Science-technology house journals. San Francisco, 1965. 31*l.*

Union list of 71 company-published serials held by 22 special libraries.

1351. Stanford University Libraries. The union list of serials currently received in the science libraries at Stanford University, 3d ed. Stanford, Calif., 1968. Unpaged.

1352. Technical serials in Kentucky. Lexington: Univ. of Kentucky Development Services Information Analysis Center, and Louisville: Univ. of Louisville Greater Louisville Technical Referral Center, 1970. 601p.

1353. Texas list of scientific and technical serial publications, ed. by Lois Bebout. Houston: Phil Wilson, 1965. 617p.

Lists over 12,000 titles with record of holdings in 96 libraries. Expansion and revision of Houston list, 1963. Quarterly with annual cumulations.

1354. U.S. Library of Congress, Science and Technology Division. Chinese scientific and technical serial publications in the collections of the Library of Congress, rev. ed., comp. by Joan Wu. Wash.: Govt. Print. Off., 1961. 107p.

Arranged by subject.

1355. ——— ———. Guide to the world's abstracting and indexing services in science and technology. Wash., 1963. 183p.

Lists 1,855 titles from 40 countries.

1356. ——— ———. Japanese scientific and technical serial publications in the collections of the Library of Congress. Wash., 1962. 247p.

Guide to the collections and holdings of the Library of Congress; contains about 1,700 entries.

1357. ——— ———. Journals in science and technology published in Japan and Mainland China: a selected list. Wash., 1961. 47p.

Lists 331 titles.

1358. ——— ———. List of Russian serials being translated into English and other Western languages, 4th ed. Wash., 1962. 53p.

Gives Library of Congress call numbers; records 189 entries.

1359. ——— ———. Scientific and technical serial publications of the Soviet Union, 1945-1960, prep. by Nikolay T. Zikeev. Wash.: Govt. Print. Off., 1963. 347p.

Library of Congress classification numbers given; includes 5,091 serials.

1360. U.S. Patent Office, Scientific Library. Periodicals in the Scientific Library, U.S. Patent Office. Wash.: U.S. Patent Office, 1962. 53p.

1361. Wagner, Frank S., and Moloney, Louis. Union list of scientific serials in the Corpus Christi area. Corpus Christi, Tex., 1961. 75p.

1362. Washington University Libraries. Scientific and technical periodicals currently received in the Washington University Library and the Missouri Botanical Garden Library as of December 1968, ed. by Elizabeth Hiza Roberts. St. Louis: Washington Univ., 1970. 123p. (Washington Univ. Library studies, no.6)

1363. West Virginia University Library. Union list of scientific, technical and social sciences serials in the West Virginia University Libraries, 3d ed., comp. by Michael

M. Reynolds, rev. by Lorise C. Boger. Morgantown, 1965. 188p.

ASTRONOMY

1364. San Diego State College Library. Astronomical literature in the Ernst Zinner collection, San Diego State College Library; a checklist, comp. by Gerald Johns. San Diego: Friends of the Library, 1969. 66p.

About 1,000 entries on the history of astronomy, 1485 to present.

1365. Carnegie Institution of Washington and the California Institute of Technology. Guide to the microfilm edition of the George Ellery Hale papers, 1882-1937, at the Mount Wilson and Palomar Observatories Library, Pasadena, California, ed. by Daniel J. Kevles. n.p., 1968. 47p.

1366. Linda Hall Library. Highlights of astronomy 1483-1850; an exhibit of printed books and papers. Kansas City, Mo., 1966. 24p.

1367. Reingold, Nathan. "A good place to study astronomy." Library of Congress quarterly journal of current acquisitions, 20 (1963), 211-17.

Cleveland Abbe papers acquired by Library of Congress.

1368. San Diego State College Library. Johann Kepler bibliography, holdings in the San Diego State College Library, comp. by Louis A. Kenney. San Diego, 1970. 14p.

In two sections: works by and works about Kepler.

1369. ———. Literature of time in the Ernst Zinner collection, San Diego State College Library; a checklist, comp. by Gerald Johns. San Diego, Calif.: Sciences and Engineering Library, San Diego State College, 1970. 25p.

Checklist on chronology and horology, dealing with sundials, clocks and watches, calendars, and other time devices.

1370. Taylor, Henry C. "Early books on navigation and piloting." Yale University Library gazette, 39 (1964), 57-66.

Describes collection of 16th- and 17th-century works in Yale University Library.

1371. U.S. National Archives. Supplement to Preliminary checklist 42, records of the Naval Observatory, comp. by Harry Schwartz. Wash., 1965. 3p.

METEOROLOGY

1372. U.S. Library of Congress, Science and Technology Division. United States IGY bibliography, 1953-1960, comp. by Frank M. Marson and Janet R. Terner. Wash.: National Academy of Sciences–National Research Council, 1963. 391p.

International Geophysical Year publications, based partly on Library of Congress holdings.

1373. ——— ———. Weather modification in the Soviet Union, 1946-1966; a selected annotated bibliography, by Nikolay T. Zikeev and George A. Doumani. Wash.: Govt. Print. Off., 1967. 78p.

List of 503 items received in the Library of Congress.

1374. U.S. National Archives. Preliminary inventory of operational and miscellaneous meteorological records of the Weather Bureau, comp. by Helen T. Finneran. Wash., 1962. 34p.

PHYSICS

1375. American Philosophical Society Library. Sources for the history of quantum physics: an inventory and report, by Thomas S. Kuhn and others. Philadelphia, 1967. 176p.

Index to large collection of manuscripts and printed materials, films, and taped recordings of interviews. Collection is duplicated at University of California, Berkeley.

1376. Hawaii, University, Library. Physics literature; a guide to sources available in University of Hawaii libraries, by Regina S. R. Liu. Honolulu, 1969. 75p.

1377. Massachusetts Institute of Technology, Lincoln Laboratory, Lexington, Library. Soviet books on radiotechnology and electronics in 1962. Lexington, Mass.? 1962. 44p. (Reference bibliography, no.13)

1378. U.S. Library of Congress. Nuclear science in mainland China: a selected bibliography, comp. by Chi Wang. Wash.: Govt. Print. Off., 1968. 70p.

Chinese and English references; 615 research reports, studies, articles, and related materials in Library of Congress collections.

1379. ———, Science and Technology Division. Selected foreign references on scatter propagation of ultrashort waves, 1956-1960. Wash.: The Library, 1961. 87p.

1380. Warnow, Joan Nelson. A selection of manuscript collections in American repositories. N.Y.: Niels Bohr Library, Center for History and Philosophy of Physics, American Institute of Physics, 1969. 73p. (National catalog of sources for history of physics, no.1)

CHEMISTRY

1381. Chemical Abstracts Service. Access; key to the source literature of the chemical sciences, 1969. Columbus, Ohio: American Chemical Society, 1969. 1,370p.

Supersedes Society's List of periodicals abstracted by chemical abstracts. Lists about 21,000 titles and shows holdings of 397 libraries in 28 countries.

1382. Cornell University Library. Antoine Laurent Lavoisier; an exhibition. Ithaca, N.Y., 1963. 31p.

Collection of books, manuscripts, and memorabilia relating to famous French chemist.

1383. [Delaware, University, Library. History of chemistry collection] College & research libraries news, no.4 (April 1969), 111.

Important collection of more than 2,000 volumes on history of chemistry, 1494-1960, acquired by University of Delaware.

1384. Linda Hall Library. Source materials in the history of chemistry, 1540-1900; an exhibit. Kansas City, Mo., 1968. 32p.

1385. MacPhail, Ian, and Witten, Laurence C., 2d. "The Mellon collection of alchemy and the occult." Yale University Library gazette, 41 (1966), 1-15.

Describes Yale Library's collection of early books and manuscripts relating to occult sciences.

1386. Newberry Library. An annotated reading list of the most important current material on the chemical deterioration and the chemical and physical preservation of paper, comp. by Paul N. Banks. Chicago, 1965. 15p.

1387. Ohio State University Libraries. Monographs written by the chemistry faculty 1870-1970: a centennial booklist, by Virginia E. Yagello. Columbus, 1970. 17p.

1388. Ohio University Libraries. The Morgan collection in the history of chemistry: a checklist, comp. by Roger W. Moss, Jr. Athens, 1965. 178p.

1389. Wisconsin, University, Library. Chemical, medical, and pharmaceutical books printed before 1800, in the collections of the University of Wisconsin Libraries, ed. by John Neu. Madison: Univ. of Wis. Pr., 1965. 280p.

Lists 4,442 items.

1390. Yale University Library. Alchemy and the occult; a catalogue of books and manuscripts from the collection of Paul and Mary Mellon given to Yale University Library, by Ian MacPhail. New Haven, Conn., 1968. 2v.

GEOLOGY

1391. California, University, Geology-Geophysics Library. Serials holding list. Los Angeles: Univ. of Calif. Library, 1970. Various paging.

1392. ———, Scripps Institution of Oceanography Library, La Jolla. Catalogs of the Scripps Institution of Oceanography Library: author-title catalog. Boston: G. K. Hall, 1970. 7v.

1393. ——— ———. Catalogs of the Scripps Institution of Oceanography Library; shelf list. Boston: G. K. Hall, 1970. 2v.

1394. ——— ———. Catalogs of the Scripps Institution of Oceanography Library: subject catalog. Boston: G. K. Hall, 1970. 2v.

1395. Geoscience Information Society. Guidebooks and Ephemeral Materials Committee. Geologic field trip guidebooks of North America: a union list incorporating monographic titles. Houston, Tex.: Phil Wilson, 1968. 97p.

1396. Illinois, University, Library. Early geology in the Mississippi Valley; an exhibition of selected works, by George W. White and Barbara O. Slanker. Urbana: 1962. 26p.

1397. Linda Hall Library. Historic books and papers in geology, 1546-1905. An exhibit. Kansas City, Mo., 1965. 24p.

1398. Maryland, University, Libraries. Fossil finds in Maryland; a retrospective bibliography, comp. by Mildred D. Donohue and Norma S. Gordon. College Park, 1967. 233p.

1399. Michigan Historical Commission, Division of Archives. List of cartographic records of the Michigan Department of Conservation, Geological Survey Division, comp. by Geneva Kebler and Elizabeth Rademacher. Lansing, 1962. 4p.

1400. [Oregon, University Library. Chaney papers] College & research libraries news, no.4 (April 1970), 105.

Collection of 12,000 letters and manuscripts of books and articles associated with Ralph W. Chaney, paleontologist and conservationist, received by University of Oregon Library.

1401. Rice University, Regional Information and Communication Exchange. Oceanography: a union catalog of selected Texas Gulf Coast library resources. Houston, 1970. 167p.

Lists monographs and serials with locations in 14 institutions.

1402. Syracuse University Libraries. Information sources in the earth sciences, comp. by Jessie B. Watkins. Syracuse, N.Y., 1967. 46p.

1403. ———. Reference sources in geology, comp. by Jessie B. Watkins. Syracuse, N.Y., 1964. 10p.

1404. U.S. Geological Survey Library. Catalog of the United States Geological Survey Library, Department of the Interior (Washington, D.C.). Boston: G. K. Hall, 1964. 25v.

Catalog of largest collection in its field.

1405. West Virginia University Library. The coal industry in America; a bibliography and guide to studies, by Robert F. Munn. Morgantown, 1965. 230p.

1406. ———. West Virginia geology, archeology, and pedology; a bibliography and index, by William H. Gillespie and John A. Clendening. Morgantown, 1964. 241p. (West Virginia Univ. bulletin, ser. 64, no. 124)

BIOLOGY AND ANTHROPOLOGY

1407. American Philosophical Society Library. Mendel newsletter. Philadelphia: American Philosophical Society, 1968- . Issued irregularly.

Cumulative record of archival material and information for the history of genetics and allied sciences, including embryology, cytology, evolution, and biochemistry.

1408. California, University, College Library. A guide to materials on ecology in UCLA's College Library. Los Angeles: Univ. of Calif. Library, 1970. 7p.

1409. ———, Library, Anthropology Library. Primate social behavior; a checklist. Berkeley, 1963. 9p. (Recent additions, v.6, no.2, Aug. 1963)

1410. Harvard University, Peabody Museum Library. Catalogue: subjects. Boston: G. K. Hall, 1963. 27v. First supplement. 1970. 12v.

1411. ——— ———. Catalogue: authors. Boston: G. K. Hall, 1963. 26v.

Relates to archeology and ethnology.

1412. [Hofstra University Library, Hempstead, N.Y. Paul Radin library] College & research libraries news, no.4 (April 1970), 101-2.

Collection of 5,500 items received by Hofstra from personal library of Paul Radin, American anthropologist.

1413. Kerker, Ann E., and Schlundt, Esther M. Literature sources in the biological sciences. Lafayette, Ind.: Purdue Univ. Libraries, 1961. 133p.

Based on Purdue Library collections.

1414. Oregon, University, Library. Biological serials, comp. by Alan W. Roecker. Eugene, 1966. 172p. (Univ. of Oregon Library occasional paper, no.4)

Records holdings of University of Oregon and Oregon State University Libraries, a total of 2,135 titles.

1415. Purdue University Libraries. Biological and biomedical resource literature, by Ann E. Kerker and Henry T. Murphy. Lafayette, Ind., 1968. 226p.

Bibliography based on Purdue Libraries' holdings.

1416. San Jose State College Library. The biology student's guide to the resources of San Jose State College Library, by John R. Douglas. San Jose, Calif., 1969. 44p.

1417. Shilling, Charles W., and Benton, Mildred C. Aquatic biology serials, their location and characteristics. Wash.: Biological Sciences Communication Project, George Washington Univ., 1964. 110p.

Lists 1,627 serials, with locations in 18 libraries.

1418. Syracuse University Libraries. Information

sources in the biological sciences; a guide to selected materials in the Natural Sciences Library, comp. by Jessie B. Watkins. Syracuse, N.Y., 1969. 35p.

1419. ———. Reference sources in the biological sciences; a guide to selected materials in the Natural Sciences Library, comp. by Jessie B. Watkins. Syracuse, N.Y., 1966. 18p.

1420. Williams College, Chapin Library. Landmarks of biology 1470-1859: four centuries of printed editions from Aristotle to Darwin in the Chapin Library. Williamstown, Mass.: Williams College, 1965. 24p.

BOTANY

1421. Carnegie Institute of Technology, Hunt Botanical Library. The Rachel McMasters Miller Hunt Botanical Library. Carnegie Institute of Technology; its collections, program, & staff. Pittsburgh, Pa., 1961. 35p.

Collection of incunabula, 16th- and 17th-century herbals, and 18th- and 19th-century color-plate books.

1422. Harvard University, Gray Herbarium. Gray Herbarium index. Boston: G. K. Hall, 1968. 10v.

Reproduction of 265,000 cards giving name and literature citations of plants of Western Hemisphere.

1423. Hunt, Rachel M. M. Catalogue of botanical books in the collection of Rachel McMasters Miller Hunt. Pittsburgh: Hunt Botanical Library, 1958-61. 2v. in 3.

Botanical works printed from 1477 to 1800.

1424. Kansas State University Library. Linneana, by G. A. Rudolph and Evan Williams. Manhattan, 1970. 225p. (Bibliography series, no.7)

Catalog of the MacKenzie Linneana collection in Kansas State University Library.

1425. [Kansas State University Library. Linneana collection] College & research libraries news, no.5 (July-Aug. 1966), 87.

Announcing acquisition of some 2,000 items by and about Carolus Linnaeus, 1707-78, Swedish botanist.

1426. Kansas, University, Libraries. A checklist of Linneana, 1735-1835, in the University of Kansas Libraries, comp. by Terrence Williams. Lawrence, 1964. 73p. (University of Kansas publications. Library series, no.20)

Works by and about Linnaeus.

1427. Linda Hall Library. One hundred herbals 1472-1671. A chapter in the history of botany; selections from printed works in the University of Kansas Libraries and the Linda Hall Library. Wichita, Kans.: Four Ducks, 1964. 6*l.*

1428. New York Botanical Garden Library. Biographical notes upon botanists, comp. by John H. Barnhart. Boston: G. K. Hall, 1965. 3v.

File maintained in New York Botanical Garden Library, on lives of botanists.

1429. New York Public Library. "Kelemen gift: early books in botany." Bulletin of the New York Public Library, 69 (1965), 73-76.

Description of 40 rare botanical works added to New York Public Library.

1430. New York State Library, Medical Library. Herbals in the New York State Medical Library. Albany, 1967. 17*l.*

1431. Pennsylvania State University Library. Report on the G. Weidman Groff collection: books, periodical publications and manuscript materials recording observations of the occurrence and use of plants in China and surrounding countries of Southeast Asia (1907-1947) in the University Library, by Henry S. Brunner and others. University Park: Pa. State Univ., 1961. 510p.

1432. Roylance, Dale R. "The art of botanical illustration; checklist of an exhibition." Yale University Library gazette, 43 (1968), 99-122.

Descriptions of 72 illustrated botanical works, 15th to 20th centuries.

1433. U.S. National Agricultural Library. Linneana in the collection of the National Agricultural Library. Wash., 1968. 43p. (Library list, no.89)

ZOOLOGY

1434. [Brown University Library. Audubon's Birds of America] College & research libraries news, no.9 (Sept. 1970), 242-43.

Announces Brown's acquisition of set of double elephant folio edition of Audubon's Birds of America.

1435. Creighton, Alice. "Creatures so very diminutive." Univ. of Rochester Library bulletin, 23 (Winter 1967-68), 25-33.

Description of rare books relating to microscopy in University of Rochester Medical Library.

1436. Cornell University Libraries. A survey of the John Henry Comstock Memorial Library of Entomology, Cornell University, Ithaca, New York, by James L. Craig. New Brunswick, N.J., 1964. 44*l.*

1437. Harvard University, Museum of Comparative Zoology Library. Catalogue. Boston: G. K. Hall, 1967. 8v.

Collection of 250,000 volumes.

1438. Louisiana State University Library. Seashells: conchology-malacology; a brief list of holdings in the LSU Library as of December 1968. Baton Rouge, 1968. 10*l.*

1439. Michigan, University, Library. Insecta; a synopsis of holdings as shown by the University Library shelf list. Ann Arbor, 1965. Unpaged.

1440. Reingold, Nathan. "Jacques Loeb, the scientist: his papers and his era." Library of Congress quarterly journal of current acquisitions, 19 (1962), 119-30.

Library of Congress acquisition. Loeb, 1859-1924, was a physiologist.

1441. Trinity College Library. "American ornithology before and after Audubon; a descriptive catalogue of an exhibition held in the Trumbull Rare Book Room of the Watkinson Library, Trinity College." Trinity College [Hartford, Connecticut] Library gazette, 3 (April 1966), 11-16.

Annotated list of works published from 1545 to 1962.

1442. U.S. National Agricultural Library. Oriental serial publications in the zoological sciences. Wash., 1963. 42p. (Library list, no.80)

1443. Yale University Library. Ornithological books in the Yale University Library, including the library of William Robertson Coe, comp. by S. Dillon Ripley and Lynette L. Scribner. New Haven, Conn.: Yale Univ. Pr., 1961. 338p.

Medicine

GENERAL

1444. Ash, Lee M. "The Michael M. Davis collection of social and economic aspects of medicine." Bulletin of the New York Academy of Medicine, 43 (1967), 598-608.

Describes collection in New York Academy of Medicine Library.

1445. California, University, Biomedical Library. Recent acquisitions in the Biomedical Library. Los Angeles, 1948- . Monthly.

1446. Crikelair, George F., and Gnudi, Martha T. "The Webster library of plastic surgery." Excerpta medica International Congress series, no.66 (1963), 756-66.

In Columbia University Medical Library.

1447. Darling, Louise. "Regional services for medical libraries." California librarian, 31 (Jan. 1970), 46-52.

Describes Pacific Southwest Regional Medical Library Service at the UCLA Biomedical Library.

1448. Dartmouth College Library. The health of the Eskimos, a bibliography, 1857-1967, by Robert Fortuine, M.D. Hanover, N.H., 1968. 86p.

1449. Graham, Ida Hervey. Medical collections in public libraries of the United States. University, Miss., 1968. 57p. (Thesis, M.L.S., Univ. of Miss.)

1450. John Crerar Library, Midwest Regional Medical Library. 1969 directory of health and allied sciences libraries and information sources, comp. by Sara L. Moreland. Chicago, 1969. 169p.

Describes resources and services; alphabetical list with subject index.

1451. Medical Library Association. Directory of health science libraries in the United States, 1969, ed. by Frank L. Schick and Susan Crawford. Chicago, 1970. 197p.

Lists 3,155 libraries.

1452. Oppenheimer, Gerald J. Regional medical library service in the Pacific Northwest. Seattle: Univ. of Wash. Library and School of Medicine, 1967. 167p.

1453. Purdue University Libraries. Bibliography of clinical medicine, surgery and animal management, comp. by Ann E. Kerker. Lafayette, Ind., 1965. 70*l.*

Selected materials available in the Purdue University Veterinary Science and Medicine Library.

1454. ———. Biomedical communication: a selected list of material available in the Veterinary Science and Medical Library, comp. by Ann E. Kerker. Lafayette, Ind., 1970. 2p.

1455. U.S. Library of Congress, National Referral Center for Science and Technology. A directory of information resources in the United States: general toxicology. Wash.: The Library, 1969. 293p.

1456. U.S. National Archives. Preliminary inventory of the records of the National Board of Health, comp. by Charles Zaid. Wash., 1962. 18p. (Preliminary inventories, no.141)

1457. ———. Supplement to Preliminary inventory No. 6, records of the Bureau of Medicine and Surgery, comp. by Harry Schwartz. Wash., 1965. 5p.

1458. U.S. National Library of Medicine. An annotated bibliography of biomedical computer applications, comp. by Ruth Allen. Bethesda, Md., 1969. 216p.

1459. ———. Film reference guide for medicine and allied sciences 1968. Wash.: Govt. Print. Off., 1968. Supplement, 1969. 2v. Annual.

1460. ———. Guide to MEDLARS services; a brief description of the system with emphasis on the automated bibliographic search service. Bethesda, Md., 1970. 21p.

1461. ———. Prints relating to dentistry. Bethesda, Md., 1967. 36p.

Illustrates 67 prints from library's collection; includes bibliography on dentistry in art.

1462. ———. Soviet medical research related to human stress, review of literature, ed. by William H. Fitzpatrick and Chester W. DeLong. Wash.: Public Health Service, 1961. 121p.

Contains lists of references to literature cited.

1463. ———. Toxicity bibliography. Wash.: Govt. Print. Off., 1968- . Quarterly.

1464. U.S. Public Health Service. Bibliography on smoking and health with English language abstracts of foreign terms, 1969 cumulation. Wash.: Govt. Print. Off., 1969. 321p.

Catalog of items added to Library of the National Clearinghouse for Smoking and Health.

1465. U.S. Social Security Administration. Medicare, a bibliography of selected references 1966-1967. Wash.: Govt. Print. Off., 1968. 88p.

Prepared by and based on collections of Social Security Administration Library.

1466. U.S. Veterans Administration, Medical and General Reference Library. Medical care of the veteran in the United States, 1870-1960; a bibliography. Wash.: Govt. Print. Off., 1963. 106p.

Lists 1,872 references.

1467. ——— ———. Selected readings in techniques of stereotaxic brain surgery, a bibliography through 1967, comp. by John L. Fox. Wash.: Govt. Print. Off., 1968. 35p.

Lists 578 titles. Supplement through 1968: Wash.: Govt. Print. Off., 1969. 37p.

1468. Wannarka, Marjorie Bernice. "Medical collections in public libraries of the United States: a brief historical study." Medical Library Association bulletin, 56 (Jan. 1968), 1-14.

1469. ———. Medical collections in public libraries of the United States: a historical study. Minneapolis, 1967. 107p. (Master's thesis, Univ. of Minn.)

1470. Wayne State University Libraries. The Florence Nightingale collection at Wayne State University; an annotated bibliography, comp. by Howard A. Sullivan. Detroit, 1963. 20p.

1471. Yale University Medical Library. Users' guide; services and resources. New Haven, Conn., 1970. 19p.

Brief description of holdings.

HISTORY

1472. Alabama, University, Medical Center Library. Reynolds Historical Library; rare books and collections of the Reynolds Historical Library; a bibliography, comp. by Martha Lou Thomas. University: Univ. of Ala. Pr., 1968. 495p.

Collection dealing with history of medicine and science, in Birmingham, Alabama.

1473. Austin, Robert B. Early American medical imprints: a guide to works printed in the United States, 1668-1820. Wash.: U.S. Govt. Print. Off., 1961. 240p.

Locates copies in large number of U.S. academic and research libraries.

1474. Boston University, Mugar Memorial Library. Nursing archive exhibit on history of nursing. Boston, 1968. 6p.

Descriptive catalog.

1475. ——— ———. Nursing archive exhibit on history of public health nursing. Boston, 1969. 6p.

Descriptive catalog.

1476. California, University, Library. Catalogue of the medical history collection presented to the Biomedical Library UCLA. Los Angeles, 1964. 56p. Supplements 1-2. 1966, 1968.

Includes manuscripts and books dealing with history of urology and with landmarks in general history of medicine and science.

1477. ———. The John A. Benjamin collection of medical history presented to UCLA, 2d supplement, comp. by Martha Teach Gnudi. Los Angeles, 1968. 8p.

1478. Cantu, Jane Q. "American medical literary firsts, 1700-1820, in the Countway Library." Medical Library Association bulletin, 54 (1966), 48-61.

In Harvard University's medical library.

1479. ———, and Esterquest, Ralph T. "Treasures in the Countway." Harvard Library bulletin, 15 (1967), 301-7.

Discussion of rare books in Harvard Medical Library.

1480. Cavanagh, G. S. T. "The Osler, Clendening and Trent collections." North Carolina libraries, 23 (Fall 1964), 21-26.

Medical history collections in Duke University Library.

1481. Duke University Library. Early American medical imprints at Duke University. Durham, N.C.: Duke Univ. Medical Center Library, 1970. 46p.

Includes 500 entries.

1482. Duke University, Medical Center Library. From Hammurabi to Gesell, an exhibition of books on the history of pediatrics, from the Trent collection, by Henry Schuman. Wash.: 2d International Congress on Medical Librarianship, 1963. 64p.

1483. Gordan, John D. "Doctors as men of letters: English and American writers of medical background: an exhibition in the Berg collection." Bulletin of the New York Public Library, 68 (1964), 574-601. Reprinted. 32p.

In New York Public Library.

1484. Guerra, Francisco. American medical bibliography, 1639-1783. N.Y.: Lathrop C. Harper, 1962. 885p.

Chronological catalog of books, pamphlets, broadsides, and periodical articles relating to medical sciences; locates copies in various U.S. libraries.

1485. Hawes, Lloyd E. "Harvard's new collection in the history of radiology." Harvard Library bulletin, 18 (1970), 254-66.

1486. Indiana University, Lilly Library. Medicine; an exhibition of books relating to medicine and surgery. Bloomington: 1966? 100p. (Lilly Library publications, no.2)

1487. Michigan Historical Commission. Records of the Board of Registration in Medicine, 1899-1958. Lansing, 1966. 16p. (Finding aid, no.16)

1488. Michigan Historical Commission Archives. Finding aid for the records of the Department of Mental Health, 1922-1961, comp. by Geneva Kebler. Lansing, 1963. 19p. (Finding aid, no.10)

1489. Midwest Regional Medical Library. A guide to the location of titles listed in Garrison and Morton's "Medical bibliography," [2d ed., 1965] in twenty Midwest libraries, ed. by Sara L. Moreland and Ella Donaldson. Chicago, 1970. 184p.

Locates titles regarded as landmarks in medical history.

1490. Stanton, Madeline E. "Medical Historical Library on the hundredth birthday of Harvey Cushing." Yale University Library gazette, 44 (July 1969), 30-37.

1491. U.S. National Library of Medicine. Bibliography of the history of medicine, no.1, 1965. Wash.: Govt. Print. Off., 1966. 290p.

First in a planned series of annual bibliographies.

1492. ———. Bibliography of the history of medicine, no.2, 1966. Wash.: Govt. Print. Off., 1967. 218p.

1493. ———. Bibliography of the history of medicine, no.3, 1967. Wash.: Govt. Print. Off., 1969. 316p.

1494. ———. Bibliography of the history of medicine, no.4, 1968. Wash.: Public Health Service, 1970. 299p.

1495. ———. A catalogue of sixteenth century printed books in the National Library of Medicine, comp. by Richard J. Durling. Wash., 1967. 698p.

Lists more than 4,800 imprints.

1496. ———. Early American medical imprints; a guide to works printed in the United States, 1668-1820, comp. by Robert B. Austin. Wash.: U.S. Dept. of Health, Education, and Welfare, 1961. 240p.

Lists more than 2,100 works, indicating library holdings.

1497. ———. Medical symbolism in books of renaissance and baroque, exhibit in National Library of Medicine. Wash., 1966. 22p.

1498. ———. Pre-Columbian medicine; an exhibit of selected figures from the Weisman collection, November 14-December 31, 1966. Bethesda, Md.: U.S. Public Health Service, 1966. 15p.

1499. ———. A summary checklist of medical manuscripts on microfilm held by the National Library of Medicine. Bethesda, Md., 1968. 14p.

Microfilms of medieval manuscripts in European libraries.

1500. Washington University, School of Medicine Library. Index to the William Beaumont, M.D. (1785-1853) manuscript collection, by Phoebe A. Cassidy and Roberta A. Sokol. St. Louis, 1968. 165p.

1501. Wayne State University, Medical Library. Short title listing of the historical collection, Wayne State University, Medical Library, comp. by Fanny Anderson and Vern M. Pings. Detroit, 1966. 43*l.*

1502. Yale University. Exhibitions in Yale University on the occasion of the sesquicentennial celebration of the School of Medicine. New Haven, Conn., 1960. 60p.

Describes manuscripts and books from the Yale Medical Library, 1100-1700, and other collections relating to history of medicine.

1503. Yale University Medical Library. The Library of the Medical Institution of Yale College and its catalogue of 1865. New Haven, Conn., 1960. 74p.

Includes catalog of library as of 1865, arranged by subjects.

1504. ———. Mental illness illustrated from the Clements C. Fry collection of medical prints and drawings. New Haven, Conn., 1962. 12p.

Exhibition of 76 items, 17th to 20th centuries, relating to mental illness, as depicted by artists.

1505. ———. Users' guide; historical collections. New Haven, Conn., 1970. 20p.

Describes holdings under manuscripts, authors, subjects, theses, chronological periods, etc.

1506. ———. Yale Medical Library; the formation and growth of its historical library, by John F. Fulton, Frederick G. Kilgour, and Madeline E. Stanton. New Haven, Conn., 1962. 29p.

CATALOGS AND SURVEYS OF COLLECTIONS

1507. California, University, Biomedical Library. A brief guide to the Biomedical Library. Los Angeles: Univ. of Calif. Library. 1970. 21p. Annual.

1508. Harvard University Library. The Francis A. Countway Library of Medicine, rev. ed. Cambridge, Mass., 1969. 33p. (Guides to the Harvard Libraries, no.9)

1509. New Mexico, University, School of Medicine, Library. Book catalog, 1963-1964. Albuquerque, 1965. 2v.

Includes Bernalillo County Medical Society Library.

1510. New York Academy of Medicine Library. Author catalog of the Library of the New York Academy of Medicine. Boston: G. K. Hall, 1969. 43v.

1511. ———. Illustration catalog, 2d ed. Boston: G. K. Hall, 1965. 238p.

Index to illustrative material in medical works, early and recent.

1512. ———. Portrait catalog. Boston: G. K. Hall, 1960. 5v. (4,564p.). Supplement. 1965. 842p.

Lists 10,784 separate portraits in Academy Library and 151,792 portraits in books and periodicals.

1513. Titley, Joan. "Printed catalogue of American medical libraries before 1850: a check list." Journal of the history of medicine, 19 (Jan. 1964), 61-65.

Locations in National Library of Medicine and elsewhere.

1514. U.S. Dept. of Agriculture. Index-catalogue of medical and veterinary zoology, 1932 to date. Wash.: Govt. Print. Off., 1931- . v.1- .

Basic catalog issued 1932-52 in 18 volumes, kept up to date by supplements. Gives locations.

1515. U.S. National Library of Medicine. Current catalog, annual cumulation, 1966 to date. Wash.: Dept. of HEW Public Health Service, 1967- . Monthly and quarterly issues.

Includes all publications printed after 1800 cataloged during year by National Library of Medicine, Harvard Medical Library, and Upstate Medical Center Library of State University of New York at Syracuse.

1516. ———. Current catalog proof sheets. Chicago: Medical Library Association, 1970- .

Semiweekly author list of recent English-language publications cataloged at National Library of Medicine, Harvard Medical Library, and Upstate Medical Center Library of State University of New York.

1517. ———. Index-catalogue of the Library of the Surgeon General's Office, National Library of Medicine, 5th series. Wash.: Govt. Print. Off., 1959-61. 3v.

Conclusion of monumental bibliography which began publication in 1880.

1518. ———. Index medicus. Wash., 1960- . n.s. v.1- . Monthly. Cumulates annually into Cumulated index medicus.

Comprehensive index to world's medical literature.

1519. ———. National Library of Medicine catalog; a list of works represented by the National Library of Medicine cards 1960-1965. N.Y.: Rowman and Littlefield, 1966. 6v.

Authors v.1-3; subjects, v.4-6.

1520. Washington University, School of Medicine Library. Catalog of books plus a complete catalog of reserve books. St. Louis, 1965. 275p.

1521. ——— ———. Catalog of books, 1965-1967. St. Louis: Washington Univ. 1967. 336p.

1522. ——— ———. Catalog of books, 1967. St. Louis, 1968. 239p.

1523. ——— ———. Catalog of books, 1968. St. Louis, 1969. 299p.

1524. ——— ———. Quinquennial catalog of books, 1965-1969. St. Louis, 1970. 2v.

1525. Wayne State University Medical Library. Union catalog of monographs of Metropolitan Detroit medical libraries, 1965-1966 imprints. Detroit, Mich., 1966. 53*l*.

PERIODICALS

1526. Anderl, Robert G. Bio-medical serials held in Nevada libraries. Las Vegas: Univ. of Nevada, 1970. 74*l*.

1527. Auburn University Library. Periodicals of medicine and allied sciences received on Auburn University campus, comp. by Allen W. Hahn. Auburn, Ala., 1961. 25p. (Occasional bibliographies, no.7)

1528. California, University, Biomedical Library. Serials holdings list, UCLA Biomedical Library. Los Angeles: Pacific Southwest Regional Medical Library Service, 1969. 265p.

1529. ——— ———. Serials holdings list, UCLA Biomedical Library. Los Angeles: Pacific Southwest Regional Medical Library Service, Biomedical Library, Univ. of Calif., 1970. 275p.

1530. Cleveland Health Sciences Library. Biomedical serials in 44 metropolitan libraries, 2d ed. Cleveland, Ohio: Medical Library Asso. of Northern Ohio, 1970. 868p.

Union list of holdings.

1531. Cleveland Medical Library Association. Biomedical serials in twenty-four metropolitan Cleveland libraries, prepared under the auspices of the Cleveland Medical Library. Cleveland, Ohio, 1963. 267p.

1532. Columbia University Libraries. Union list of serials currently received in the Medical and Science Divisions, 2d ed. N.Y., 1970. 187p.

No holdings reported.

1533. Frost, Anaclare. An evaluation of the biomedical serial resources in southeastern Michigan. Detroit: Wayne State Univ. School of Medicine, 1965. 13*l*.

1534. Harvard University, Francis A. Countway Library of Medicine. Periodicals in the Countway Library, a list of the serial publications to be found in the Francis A. Countway Library of Medicine. Boston, 1967. 2v.

1535. Indiana University, School of Medicine Library. InU-M serial holdings, 2d ed. Indianapolis, 1968. 74p.

1536. Jones, Claud Lee. Evaluation of the serial holdings of 24 biomedical libraries in Texas. Galveston: Univ. of Texas Medical Branch Library, 1968. 120*l*.

1537. Kentucky, University, Medical Center Library. Union list of periodicals currently received in medical libraries in the Lexington area, comp. by Omer Hamlin, Jr. Lexington, 1965. 93*l*.

1538. Lovelace Foundation for Medical Education and Research, Lassetter-Foster Memorial Library. Serials holdings list, 1969-1970. Albuquerque, New Mexico, 1960. 114, 82p.

List of medical serial holdings, with KWIC index.

1539. Medical Library Association. Vital notes on medical periodicals. Chicago, 1952- . v.1- . (3 nos. per year)

Lists new journals, changes of title, mergers, cessations, and other bibliographic data in biomedicine; includes locations with holdings for many entries.

1540. ———, Southern Regional Group. Checklist of periodical titles currently received by the medical libraries in the Southern region, 3d ed., ed. by Mayo Drake. Gainesville, Fla., 1967. 180*l*.

Locates files in 134 libraries in 13 Southern states; 2d ed., comp. by John P. Ische, New Orleans, La., 1964. 178*l*., locates files in 150 libraries.

1541. Medical Library Center of New York. Union catalog of medical periodicals, 4th ed. N.Y., 1970. 1,173p.

Lists selected periodicals and serials; records holdings of libraries in New York metropolitan area.

1542. Minnesota, University, Libraries. Bio-Medical Library catalog of serial holdings. Minneapolis, 1968. 225p.

1543. Northwestern University Dental School Library. Foreign serial holdings. Chicago, 1965. 63*l.*

1544. Pizer, Irwin H., and Steuernagel, Harriet. "Medical journals in St. Louis before 1900." Missouri Historical Society bulletin, 20 (1964), 221-56.

Records 140 titles with holdings in 17 U.S. libraries.

1545. Steuernagel, Harriet, and O'Leary, Francis B. "Medical journals in St. Louis before 1900: union list of medical journals. Supplement." Medical Library Association bulletin, 55 (Jan. 1967), 85-89.

Entries for 22 titles with holdings located in 5 St. Louis libraries.

1546. UCMP-II. N.Y.: Medical Library Center of New York, 1969. 515p.

Union list of selected medical periodicals and serials published prior to 1950; holdings of 83 libraries in New York metropolitan area.

1547. U.S. National Agricultural Library. Veterinary medical periodicals currently received in National Agricultural Library, comp. by Ruth M. Salmons. Wash., 1963. 10p. (Library list, no.76)

1548. U.S. National Library of Medicine. Biomedical serials, 1950-1960; a selective list of serials in the National Library of Medicine, comp. by Lela M. Spanier. Wash., 1962. 503p. (Public Health Service publ. no.910)

Lists 8,939 titles.

1549. ———. Chinese mainland journals; current NLM holdings, January 1961. Wash., 1961. 15*l.*

Entries for 69 journals; files also located in Library of Congress, National Agricultural Library, and Massachusetts Institute of Technology.

1550. ———. Current holdings of mainland Chinese journals, comp. by Stephen Kim. Bethesda, Md., 1966. 26p.

Lists 92 Communist Chinese journals relating to biomedical sciences.

1551. ———. International bibliography of medicolegal serials, 1736-1967, comp. by Jaroslav Nemec. Wash.: Govt. Print. Off., 1969. 110p.

Based on National Library of Medicine collection.

1552. U.S. Public Health Service. Bibliography of medical reviews. Wash.: Govt. Print. Off., 1955- . Annual.

Prepared by National Medical Library.

1553. ———. Periodicals currently received in the NIH Library, 1966. Wash.: Govt. Print. Off., 1966. 134p.

1554. U.S. Veterans Administration Libraries. Union list of periodicals in the medical libraries of the Veterans Administration, 3d ed. Wash., 1965. 138p.

Records holdings of 179 libraries.

1555. Virginia union list of biomedical serials. Charlottesville: Univ. of Va. Medical School Library, 1969. 229p.

Contains serial holdings of 16 medical and biomedical libraries in Virginia.

1556. Virginia, University, Medical Center. Serial holdings, School of Medicine, School of Nursing. Charlottesville, 1968. 105p.

1557. Walter Reed Army Medical Center. Union list of biomedical periodicals. Cooperating libraries: Walter Reed Army Institute of Research, Walter Reed General Hospital, Armed Forces Institute of Pathology. Wash., 1963. 28p.

1558. Washington University, School of Medicine Library. Philsoms: periodical holdings in the Library of the School of Medicine by subject. St. Louis, 1963-1970. 8v.

1559. Wayne State University, Medical Library. Availability of biomedical serials titles in four resource libraries in Michigan, spring 1966, by Anaclare Frost. Detroit, 1966. 23*l.*

1560. ——— ———. A list of medical serials and annual reports of medical institutions and agencies published in Michigan before 1900, by Fanny J. Anderson. Detroit, 1965. 12*l.*

1561. ——— ———. Selected list of biomedical serials in

twelve metropolitan Detroit libraries. Detroit, 1963. 105p.; 2d ed., Detroit, 1964. 135p.

Second edition shows holdings for 23 libraries.

1562. Wisconsin, University, Power Pharmaceutical Library. Periodicals and annual publications currently received at the F. B. Power Pharmaceutical Library, rev. by Dolores Nemec. Madison: School of Pharmacy, Univ. of Wis. 1964. 119*l.*

Holdings shown for University of Wisconsin libraries and Center for Research Libraries in Chicago.

Technology

GENERAL

1563. New York Public Library. New technical books; a selected list of books on industrial arts and engineering, recently added to the Library. N.Y., 1915- . Bimonthly.

1564. Special Libraries Association. Technical book review index. Pittsburgh, Pa., 1935- . Monthly.

Periodicals indexed are in Carnegie Library of Pittsburgh, Technology Dept.

ENGINEERING

1565. Auburn University. A study of the holdings and services of the Auburn University Library, including comparisons with other libraries having curricula approved by the Engineering Council for Professional Development. Auburn, Ala., 1965. 82p.

1566. California, University, Engineering and Mathematical Sciences Library. Guide to the Engineering and Mathematical Sciences Library, 1970-71. Los Angeles: Univ. of Calif. 1970. 12p.

1567. ——— ———. Periodical and serial holdings, 2d ed. Los Angeles: Univ. of Calif. Library, 1969. 295p.

Lists about 6,000 titles in engineering, mathematics, meteorology, and astronomy.

1568. ———, Water Resources Center. Dictionary catalog of the Water Resources Center archives, University of California, Berkeley. Boston: G. K. Hall, 1970. 5v.

1569. Detroit Public Library. The automotive history collection of the Detroit Public Library; a simplified guide to its holdings. Boston: G. K. Hall, 1966. 2v.

1570. Engineering Societies Library, New York. Bibliography on filing, classification and indexing systems, and thesauri, for engineering offices and libraries. N.Y., 1966. 37p. (ESL bibliography, no.15)

Lists 176 annotated references.

1571. ———. Bibliography on flow of granular materials from bins, bunkers and silos. N.Y., 1967. 34p.

Bibliography of 187 selected references to books, theses, and articles.

1572. ———. Classed subject catalog. Boston: G. K. Hall, 1963. 14v. Supplements 1-6. 1964-70. 6v.

A collection of 180,000 volumes covering all branches of engineering.

1573. ———. Periodicals currently received as of Dec. 31, 1968. N.Y., 1969. 166p.

1574. ———. The reference collection of the Engineering Societies Library. N.Y., 1970. 74p.

Lists over 600 titles found most valuable in engineering library reference work.

1575. Harvard University, Division of Engineering and Applied Physics Library. A guide to the Gordon McKay Library, Division of Engineering and Applied Physics, Harvard University, rev. ed. Cambridge, Mass., 1967. 5p. (Guides to the Harvard Libraries, no.8)

1576. ——— ———. Journals and serials currently received in the Gordon McKay Library and in the Blue Hill Observatory collection. Boston, 1962. 26p.

1577. Hawaii, University, Library. Electrical engineering literature; a reference guide, by Paula Szilard. Honolulu, 1969. 69*l.*

1578. Rochester, University, Library. Short-title catalog of books in the Engineering Library, University of

Rochester, as of January 1962. Rochester, N.Y., 1962. 75p.

1579. U.S. Federal Records Center. Preliminary inventory of the records of the North Pacific Division, Corps of Engineers, Portland, Oregon, comp. by Elmer W. Lingard. Seattle, Wash., 1968. 2p.

1580. ———. Preliminary inventory of the records of the Portland District, Corps of Engineers, comp. by Elmer W. Lingard. Seattle, Wash., 1968. 8p.

1581. ———. Preliminary inventory of the records of the Seattle District, Corps of Engineers, comp. by Elmer W. Lingard. Seattle, Wash., 1968. 4p.

1582. U.S. Library of Congress, National Referral Center for Science and Technology. A directory of information resources in the United States: water. Wash.: Govt. Print. Off., 1966. 248p.

1583. U.S. National Archives. Preliminary inventory of the textual records of the Office of the Chief of Engineers. Part II, Records of engineer divisions and districts, comp. by Maizie H. Johnson. Wash., 1965. 160p.

1584. ———. Supplement to Preliminary inventory No. NM-19: textual records of the Office of the Chief of Engineers, Part I, comp. by Maizie H. Johnson. Wash., 1967. 7p.

1585. ———. Supplement to Preliminary inventory No. MN-45: textual records of the Office of the Chief of Engineers, Part II, comp. by Maizie H. Johnson. Wash., 1967. 4p.

1586. Wisconsin, University, Engineering Library. Union list of serials and periodicals held at the Physical Sciences [and] Engineering Libraries, University of Wisconsin–Madison. Madison, 1966. 173*l.* First supplement, 1966.

AERONAUTICS

1587. Aerospace Corporation Aerospace Library. Serials and journals currently received by the Aerospace Corporation libraries. El Segundo, Calif., 1963. 92p.

Union list of 834 titles, relating primarily to aerospace sciences.

1588. [Alabama, University, Library, Huntsville. Rockets and space travel collection] College & research libraries news, no.8 (Sept. 1970), 241.

Describes collection of 4,500 volumes on rockets and space travel, assembled by Willy Ley, acquired by Alabama.

1589. Chase, Lawrence B. "Space travel since 1640." Princeton University Library chronicle, 30 (1968), 1-24.

Surveys Pendray collection in Princeton University Library.

1590. Michigan Historical Commission, Division of Archives. Finding aid for the records of the Michigan Department of Aeronautics, 1946-1952, comp. by Geneva Kebler. Lansing, 1962. 11p. (Finding aid, no.7)

1591. Purdue University Libraries. Guide to research reports in the fields of aeronautics, astronautics, and the engineering sciences, with a list of current serial publications in the same subject areas, comp. by Ivan Kvakovsky. Lafayette, Ind., 1965. Unpaged.

1592. Smith, Maurice H. "Travel by air before 1900, the Harold Fowler McCormick collection of aeronautica." Princeton University Library chronicle, 27 (1966), 143-55.

1593. U.S. Dept. of the Air Force. Judge Advocate General activities, space law bibliography: 20 July 1961. Wash.: Govt. Print. Off., 1961. 79p.

Lists books, periodicals, etc., available in the Library of Congress, Army Library, and other governmental depository libraries in Washington area.

1594. U.S. Library of Congress, Aerospace Technology Division. Chinese-English technical dictionaries. v.1, Aviation and space. Wash., 1969. 694p.

1595. ———, Science and Technology Division. Aeronautical and space serial publications; a world list. Wash., 1962. 255p.

Lists 4,551 titles, based in part on Library of Congress holdings.

1596. ——— ———. Air Force scientific research bibliography. Wash.: Govt. Print. Off., 1961-67. 5v.

1597. ——— ———. Space science and technology books, 1957-1961; a bibliography with contents noted. Wash.: Govt. Print. Off., 1962. 133p.

1598. ——— ———. UFOs and related subjects: an annotated bibliography, comp. by Lynn E. Catoe. Wash.: Govt. Print. Off., 1969. 401p.

Lists more than 2,400 items; based principally on Library of Congress' extensive holdings.

1599. ——— ———. Wilbur and Orville Wright, a bibliography commemorating the hundredth anniversary of the birth of Wilbur Wright—April 16, 1867, comp. by Arthur G. Renstrom. Wash.: Govt. Print. Off., 1968. 187p.

Contains 2,055 references to books, pamphlets, periodical articles, etc.

1600. U.S. National Archives. Preliminary inventory of the records of the Civil Aeronautics Administration, comp. by Forrest R. Holdcamper. Wash., 1962. 5p.

1601. ———. Preliminary inventory of the textual records of the National Advisory Committee for Aeronautics, comp. by Sarah D. Powell. Wash., 1967. 8p.

1602. ———. Supplement to Preliminary inventory no. 26, records of the Bureau of Aeronautics, comp. by Harry Schwartz. Wash., 1965. 6p.

HOME ECONOMICS

1603. Kansas State University Library. The Kansas State University receipt book and household manual, by G. A. Rudolph. Manhattan, 1968. 230p. (Bibliography series, no.4)

Cookery books and manuals covering the years 1541-1898, in Kansas State University Library; 803 titles.

1604. Lackschewitz, Gertrud. Interior design and decoration: a bibliography. N.Y.: New York Public Library, 1961. 86p.

Based, with rare exceptions, on New York Public Library collection; includes classification numbers.

1605. U.S. Library of Congress, Science and Technology Division. Fish protein concentrate: a comprehensive bibliography. Springfield, Va.: Clearinghouse for Federal Scientific and Technical Information, 1970. 77p.

1606. U.S. National Agricultural Library. Freeze-drying of foods, a list of selected references. Wash.: Govt. Print. Off., 1963. 79p.

Lists 638 entries, with National Agricultural Library call numbers.

1607. ———. School lunches, 1952-61; list of selected references, comp. by Ruth M. Salmons. Wash., 1963. 43p. (Library list, no.74)

1608. ———. School lunches and other school feeding programs, 1962-July 1967, list of selected references, comp. by Betty B. Baxtresser. Wash., 1968. 28p.

AGRICULTURE

General

1609. Finneran, Helen T. "Records of the National Grange in its Washington office." American archivist, 27 (1964), 103-11.

Records of the National Grange of the Patrons of Husbandry, 1867- , in Washington, D.C.

1610. Jennings, Pauline W. "U.S. National Agricultural Library: outstanding special collections." IAALD quarterly bulletin, 7 (April 1962), 103-15.

1611. Oregon State Library, Division of State Archives. Records of agricultural agencies in the Oregon State Archives. Salem, 1968. 9*l.*

1612. Petersen, Peter L. "Some research opportunities in the papers of Edwin T. Meredith, 1876-1928." Books at Iowa, 7 (Nov. 1967), 32-40.

Papers of founder of Successful farming and Better homes and gardens, a land developer and U.S. Secretary of Agriculture.

1613. Reeves, Dorothea D. "Resources on agricultural history in the Kress Library." Agricultural history, 36 (1962), 171-73.

In Harvard University Graduate School of Business Administration.

1614. U.S. Dept. of Agriculture, Economic Research Service. Parity prices, a list of selected references, comp. by Ruth M. Salmons. Wash., 1962. 6p.

Contains 48 references with National Agricultural Library classification numbers.

1615. U.S. Library of Congress, African Section. Agricultural development schemes in Sub-Saharan Africa, a bibliography, comp. by Ruth S. Freitag. Wash.: Govt. Print. Off., 1963. 189p.

Copies located in Library of Congress and elsewhere.

1616. U.S. National Agricultural Library. Aircraft in agriculture; supplement for 1958-1963. Wash., 1965. 93p. (Library list, no.65)

1617. ———. Beauty for America, January 1966-May 1968. Wash., 1968. 32p. (Library list, no.94)

1618. ———. Bibliography of agriculture. Wash.: Govt. Print. Off., 1942-69. N.Y.: CCM Information Corp., 1970- . Monthly.

Lists current literature, domestic and foreign, received by National Agricultural Library.

1619. ———. Biological effects of barometric and/or atmospheric pressure. Wash., 1970. 17p.

1620. ———. Books on cooperatives: a general reading list, comp. by Nellie G. Larson. Wash., 1965. 2p.

1621. ———. Business side of cooperatives. Wash., 1964. 5p.

1622. ———. Chinese agricultural publications from the Republic of China since 1947. Wash., 1964. 55p. (Library list, no.82)

1623. ———. Closing the gap in cooperative communications. Wash., 1965. 3p.

1624. ———. Communist Chinese monographs in the USDA Library, comp. by Leslie Tse-Chiukuo and Peter B. Schroeder. Wash., 1961. 87p. (Library list, no.71)

1625. ———. Communist Chinese periodicals in the agricultural sciences. Wash., 1963. 33p. (Library list, no.70)

Gives holdings for 115 titles.

1626. ———. Contract farming and vertical integration, 1953-1962, a list of selected references. Wash.: Govt. Print. Off., 1963. 77p. (Library list, no.64)

Includes class numbers for publications in National Agricultural Library.

1627. ———. Cooperation in agriculture, 1954-1964, a list of selected references, supplement 2, comp. by G. J. Kubal. Wash., 1966. 115p. (Library list, no.41)

1628. ———. DDT (1, 1-Dichloro-2, 2-Bis (P-Chlorophenyl) Ethylene). A list of references selected and compiled from the files of the Pesticides Information Center National Agricultural Library 1960-1969. Wash., 1970. 143p. (Library list, no.97)

1629. ———. Developments in financing cooperatives. Wash., 1965. 3p.

1630. ———. Dictionary catalog of the National Agricultural Library, 1862-1965. N.Y.: Rowman & Littlefield, 1968-70. 73v.

More than 1,500,000 entries. Supplemented by monthly, annual, and quinquennial cumulations.

1631. ———. Drainage of agricultural land, 1956-1964. Wash., 1968. 524p. (Library list, no.91)

1632. ———. Historic books and manuscripts concerning general agriculture in the collection of the National Agricultural Library, comp. by Mortimer L. Naftalin. Wash., 1967. 94p. (U.S. National Agricultural Library, Library list, no.86)

Lists 586 items with NAL call numbers and LC printed card numbers.

1633. ———. Historic books and manuscripts concerning horticulture and forestry in the collection of the National Agricultural Library, by Mortimer L. Naftalin. Wash., 1968. 106p. (U.S. National Agricultural Library list, no.90)

1634. ———. How cooperatives help develop stronger rural communities. Wash., 1964. 5p.

1635. ———. Japanese serial publications in the National Agricultural Library, comp. by Peter B. Schroeder, Wash., 1963. 172p. (Library list, no.72)

Titles listed in agricultural and biological sciences and related fields.

1636. ———. Korean publications in the National Agricultural Library, comp. by Peter B. Schroeder. Wash., 1963. 25p. (Library list, no.79)

1637. ———. Non-urban patterns of land utilization, 1963-1968. Wash., 1968. 39p. (Library list, no.93)

1638. ———. Pesticides documentation bulletin. Wash., 1965-69. 5v.

Compilation of current literature on pests in all aspects.

1639. ———. Publications on Chinese agriculture prior to 1949, comp. by W. J. C. Logan and P. B. Schroeder. Wash., 1966. 142p.

Based on National Agricultural Library's collection; lists 186 serials and 888 monographs in Chinese and Western languages.

1640. ———. Role of cooperatives in new economic opportunity program. Wash., 1964. 3p.

1641. ———. Rural electrification in the United States 1954-1964. Wash., 1966. 74p. (Library list, no.84)

1642. ———. Selected list of American agricultural books in print and current agricultural periodicals. Wash., 1967. 66p. (Library list, no.1)

1643. ———. Serial publications indexed in Bibliography of agriculture, rev. ed. Wash., 1965. 79p.

1644. ———. Significant books about U.S. agriculture, 1860-1960, comp. by Elizabeth Gould Davis. Wash., 1962. 10p. (Reprinted from Department of Agriculture yearbook, 1962, p.646-51)

1645. ———. Toxicity of herbicides to mammals, aquatic life, soil micro-organisms, beneficial insects and cultivated plants, 1950-65, comp. by Patricia A. Condon. Wash., 1968. 161p. (Library list, no.87)

Based on National Agricultural Library holdings.

1646. ———. What cooperatives contribute to the consumer. Wash., 1964. 3p.

1647. U.S. National Archives. Preliminary inventory of the records of the Agricultural Marketing Service, comp. by Virgil E. Baugh. Wash., 1965. 37p.

1648. ———. Preliminary inventory of the records of the Agricultural Research Service, comp. by William F. Sherman. Wash., 1965. 3p.

1649. ———. Preliminary inventory of the records of the Agricultural Stabilization and Conservation Service, comp. by William F. Sherman and others. Wash., 1966. 7p.

1650. ———. Preliminary inventory of the records of the Bureau of Agricultural and Industrial Chemistry, comp. by Helen T. Finneran. Wash., 1962. 35p. (Preliminary inventories, no.149)

1651. ———. Preliminary inventory of the records of the Bureau of Entomology and Plant Quarantine. Wash., 1965. 20p. (Supplementary to Preliminary inventory, no.94)

1652. ———. Preliminary inventory of the records of the Consumers' Counsel Division of the Agricultural Adjustment Administration, comp. by Truman R. Strobridge. Wash., 1963. 12p.

1653. ———. Preliminary inventory of the records of the Farm Credit Administration, comp. by Daniel T. Goggin. Wash., 1963. 53p.

1654. ———. Preliminary inventory of the records of the Foreign Agricultural Service, comp. by James E. Primas. Wash., 1965. 6p.

1655. ———. Preliminary inventory of the records of the Office of Experiment Stations, comp. by Edward E. Hill. Wash., 1965. 18p.

1656. ———. Writings relevant to farm management in the records of the Bureau of Agricultural Economics, comp. by Vivian Wiser. Wash., 1963. 80p. (Special list, no.17)

Animal Culture

1657. Cornell University, James E. Rice Memorial Poultry Library. Books on poultry husbandry, comp. by Lucille N. Wright. Ithaca, N.Y.: Cornell Univ. Pr., 1961. 79p. (Cornell University, James E. Rice Memorial Poultry Library, Publication, no.2)

1658. Dyce, E. J. "Cornell receives Armbruster library." Gleanings in bee culture, 91 (Feb. 1963), 107-8.

1659. Marston, Thomas E. "Books on horses." Yale University Library gazette, 39 (1965), 105-34.

Describes Yale Library's collection of early and rare books, American and foreign, relating to horses.

1660. [Texas A&M University Library. Livestock collection] College & research libraries news, no.4 (April 1970), 105, 107.

Describes collection of 4,182 items relating to various aspects of range livestock industry, acquired by Texas A&M Library.

1661. U.S. National Agricultural Library. Marketing of livestock, meat, and meat products, 1962-June 1967, comp. by Minnie N. Fuller and Betty B. Baxtresser. Wash., 1968. 73p. (Library list, no.92)

1662. U.S. National Archives. Preliminary inventory of the records of the Bureau of Dairy Industry. Wash.: 1965. 8p. (Revision of Preliminary checklist, no.56)

1663. ———. Preliminary inventory of the records of the Fish and Wildlife Service, comp. by Edward E. Hill. Wash., 1965. 28p.

Plant Culture

1664. Boston Public Library. Waiting for spring: a catalog of an exhibition of books and manuscripts for the gardener, in the Boston Public Library. Boston, 1966. 28p.

Selection of 99 rare items, with brief annotations.

1665. Kansas, University, Libraries. International bibliography of vegetation maps, ed. by A. W. Küchler. Lawrence, 1965-68. 3v.

1666. ---. Vegetation maps of North America, comp. by A. W. Küchler and Jack McCormick. Lawrence, 1965. 453p.

1667. Marin, Carmen M. Tobacco literature; a bibliography of publications in the United States Library of Congress. Raleigh: N.C. Agricultural Experiment Station, Tobacco Literature Service, 1970. 303p. (Station's bulletin, no.439)

1668. Massachusetts Horticultural Society Library. Dictionary catalog of the Library of the Massachusetts Horticultural Society (Boston). Boston: G. K. Hall, 1963. 3v.

Catalog of 31,000-volume library established in 1829.

1669. Michigan State Library. Roots and references; a selected bibliography for the retail florists and growers of Michigan. Lansing, n.d. 36p.

1670. New York Public Library. "The Arents tobacco collection." Bulletin of the New York Public Library, 65 (1961), 661-70.

Descriptive catalog of exhibition illustrating scope and variety of collection.

1671. ---. Tobacco; a catalogue of the books, manuscripts and engravings acquired since 1942 in the Arents tobacco collection . . . from 1507 to the present, comp. by Sarah A. Dickson. N.Y.: 1958- , pts. 1- . (In progress)

1672. Southwestern Louisiana, University, Libraries. Guide to Southwestern archives and manuscripts collection. Lafayette, La., 1968. 23*l.*

Includes collection of material relating to rice industry.

1673. U.S. Dept. of Agriculture, Economic Research Service. Bibliography of tree nut production and marketing research, 1960-65, comp. by M. Lundquist and J. V. Powell. Wash.: Govt. Print. Off., 1967. 39p.

Lists 587 items; call numbers given for titles in National Agricultural Library.

1674. U.S. National Agricultural Library. Safflower, 1900-60; list of selected references, comp. by Nellie G. Larson. Wash., 1962. 31p. (Library list, no.73)

1675. ---. Soybean processing and utilization, a selected list of references, 1955-1965. Wash.: Govt. Print. Off., 1966. 183p.

Contains 2,218 entries, foreign and domestic.

1676. ---. Sunflower: a literature survey, January 1960-June 1967, comp. by Merne H. Posey. Wash., 1969. 133p. (Library list, no.95)

1677. U.S. National Archives. Preliminary inventory of the records of the United States Grain Corporation, comp. by Philip R. Ward and Carolyn K. Fagan. Wash., 1966. 32p.

1678. ---. Records of the Bureau of Plant Industry, Soils, and Agricultural Engineering, comp. by Herbert J. Horwitz. Wash., 1965. 22p. (Supplement to Preliminary inventory, no.66)

Forestry

1679. Berner, Richard C. "Sources for research in forest history; the University of Washington manuscripts collection." Business history review, 35 (1961), 420-25.

1680. Idaho, University, Library. Serial holdings in forestry in the University of Idaho Library, comp. by Robert W. Burns, Jr. Moscow, 1966. 19p.

1681. Oregon State College Library. "Forestry theses accepted by colleges and universities in the United States, 1960-1969." Forest science, 7- . 1961- .

Annual listing.

1682. Oregon, University, Library. Supplementary bibliography of books and reports of the forest products industries. Eugene, 1965? 5*l.*

1683. Society of American Foresters. Checklist for a basic forestry library, comp. by Lora I. Kelts and Bernice F. Smith. Wash., 1969. 39p.

Based on Forest Resources Library, University of Washington.

1684. Syracuse University, State University College of Forestry Library. List of serials in the Library. Syracuse, N.Y., 1964. 55p.

1685. U.S. National Archives. A preliminary inventory of cartographic records of the Forest Service (Record group 95), comp. by Charlotte M. Ashby. Wash., 1967. 71p. (Preliminary inventories, no.167)

1686. ---. Preliminary inventory of the records of

the Forest Service (Record group 95), comp. by Harold T. Pinkett, rev. by Terry W. Good. Wash., 1969. 23p. (Preliminary inventories, no.18 rev.)

1687. Washington, University, College of Forest Resources Library. Forestry economics: selected sources for business and statistics material in periodical literature in the Forest Resources Library, University of Washington, comp. by Bernice F. Smith. Seattle, 1970. 8p.

1688. ——— ———. A selected list of reference tools in forestry. Seattle, n.d. 6p.

1689. ——— ———. The tropics and tropical forestry: selected references in the Forest Resources Library, University of Washington, comp. by Bernice F. Smith. Seattle, 1969. 4p.

1690. ——— ———. Woodworking machinery: selected references in the Forest Resources Library, University of Washington, comp. by Bernice F. Smith. Seattle: 1970. 2p.

1691. Washington, University, Libraries. Theses in forestry, comp. by Bernice Ferrier Smith. Seattle: Institute of Forest Products, College of Forest Resources, Univ. of Wash., 1967. 36p. Supplement, 1967-69. Seattle, 1970. 7p.

Listing of master's theses and doctoral dissertations.

1692. West Virginia University Library. Forests and forestry in West Virginia—a bibliography, by Michael M. Reynolds. Morgantown, 1962. 78p.

1693. Yale University, School of Forestry Library. Dictionary catalogue of the Yale Forestry Library. Boston: G. K. Hall, 1962. 12v.

1694. ——— ———. Handbook Yale University Forestry Library. New Haven, Conn.: 1965. 32p.

CHEMICAL TECHNOLOGY

1695. Carnegie Library of Pittsburgh. Review of iron and steel literature; a classified list of the more important books, serials and trade publications during the year. Pittsburgh, 1919- . Annual.

Compiled in and based upon collections of Carnegie Library of Pittsburgh.

1696. Hicks, Carroll Ann. "Ceramics library begun in Charlotte." North Carolina libraries, 26 (Summer 1968), 111-12.

Description of library and gallery of the Mint Museum of Art, Charlotte, N.C.

1697. Illinois, University, Library. Racheff metallurgical studies; index to collections in the University of Illinois Library. Urbana, 1968. 238p.

1698. John Crerar Library. Crerar metal abstracts. Chicago, Aug. 1952- . Monthly.

Prepared by John Crerar Library's Research Information Service from library's current acquisitions.

1699. U.S. National Agricultural Library. Activated charcoal, 1953-64; list of selected references, comp. by Patricia A. Condon. Wash., 1966. 51p. (Library list, no.82)

POLLUTION AND ENVIRONMENTAL CONTROL

1700. Cleveland Public Library. Environmental crisis. Cleveland, Ohio, 1970. 17p.

Resources on air, water, and noise pollution available in Cleveland Public Library.

1701. Northwestern University Library. A selected list of U.S. government publications on environmental pollution. Evanston, Ill., 1970. 34p.

1702. Oregon State University Library. Environmental pollution and related topics; a partial list of bibliographies and indexes in the OSU Library as of July 1, 1969, prep. by Rita McDonald and Rod Waldron. Corvallis: OSU Environmental Sciences Center, 1969. 29p.

1703. Pennsylvania State Library. Water pollution; a selected bibliography of recent material in the Pennsylvania State Library, comp. by Marjory H. Hetrick. Harrisburg, 1969. 7*l.*

1704. U.S. Library of Congress, Science and Technology Division. Air pollution publications: a selected bibliography with abstracts, 1966-1968. Wash.: Govt. Print. Off., 1969. 522p.

Contains over 1,000 entries on all major aspects of subject.

1705. Yale University Library. Bibliography: air pollution and water pollution, comp. by Solomon C. Smith. New Haven, Conn.: Yale Law Library, 1969. 34*l.* (Yale Law Library, Selected new acquisitions, v.12, no.16, pt.2, March 1969)

Fine Arts

GENERAL

1706. American Philosophical Society. Catalogue of portraits and other works of art in the possession of the American Philosophical Society. Philadelphia, 1961. 173p. (APS memoirs 54)

1707. Archives of American Art. "A preliminary guide to the collections of the Archives of American Art." Archives of American art, 5, no.1 (1965), 20p.

Located in, but not a part of, Detroit Institute of Arts. Consists of personal papers and institutional and business records relating to history of visual arts in U.S.

1708. Art Institute of Chicago, Ryerson Library. Index to art periodicals. Boston: G. K. Hall, 1962. 11v.

Based on Ryerson Library's holdings.

1709. California, University. Library. The decorative designers, 1895-1932: an essay, for an exhibition of the work of Lee Thayer, Henry Thayer, and Jay Chambers, by Charles B. Gullans and John J. Espey. Los Angeles, 1970. 9p.

Based partly on UCLA Library's collections.

1710. Crask, Catherine. "An art reference library for children." Top of the news, 22 (Nov. 1965), 93-95.

Describes Junior Museum Library in Metropolitan Museum of Art, New York, a collection of several thousand volumes emphasizing art and book illustration.

1711. Faigel, Martin. "Berenson Library (Biblioteca Berenson)." Encyclopedia of library and information science, 2 (1969), 335-43.

Fine arts library near Florence, Italy, now branch of Harvard University Library.

1712. Fehl, Philipp. A bibliographical guide to the study of the history of art, 2d ed. Chapel Hill, N.C.: Ackland Art Center, 1969. 48*l.*

Based on University of North Carolina Library collection.

1713. Fisher, Oneita. "The journals of George Henry Yewell." Books at Iowa, 5 (Nov. 1966), 3-10.

Record of life in Iowa and abroad by Iowa City artist, 1847-75; in University of Iowa Library.

1714. Freer Gallery of Art, Washington, D.C. Dictionary catalog of the library. Boston: G. K. Hall, 1967. 6v.

Records collection of 40,000 books, pamphlets, and periodicals.

1715. Harvard University, Fine Arts Library. Fine arts: a selected list of reference materials prepared by the librarians of the Fine Arts Library, 2d ed. Cambridge, Mass., 1968. 32*l.*

1716. Jenkins, Marianna D. "Resources for the study of art history." Gnomon (1970), 43-46. (Special number of Duke University Library's Library notes)

Describes Duke Library's holdings.

1717. McCoy, Garnett. "The Archives of American Art." American archivist, 30 (1967), 443-51.

Description of collection centered on history of visual arts in U.S., housed in Detroit Institute of Arts.

1718. McDarrah, Fred W. Museums in New York. N.Y.: Dutton, 1967. 319p.

Includes descriptions of libraries.

1719. Metropolitan Museum of Art Library, New York. Library catalog. Boston: G. K. Hall, 1960. 25v. Supplements 1-4, 1962-70. 4v.

v.1-23, books and periodicals; v.24-25, sales catalogs. First supplement, 1962, reproduces 21,000 cards for additions since 1900; 2d supplement, 1966, adds 21,000 cards for 7,000 titles.

1720. Pennsylvania State University Library. Checklist of holdings in art and architectural history. University Park, 1968. 7p.

1721. Princeton University Library. Baroque art: illustrated books of the 17th century; checklist of books in the exhibition. Princeton, N.J., 1964. 33*l.*

1722. Quenzel, Carrol H., and Carder, Marguerite L. Principal holdings on art and architecture in the Library of Mary Washington College of the University of Virginia. Fredericksburg, Va., 1967. 249p.

1723. Rochester, University, Library. Selected list of fine arts serials in the libraries of the University of Rochester as of August 15, 1970. Rochester, N.Y., 1970. 51p.

1724. Schnorrenberg, John M. "Holdings of art books in Southeastern libraries: a survey." Southeastern librarian, 15 (1965), 186-97.

A statistical study.

1725. Special Libraries Association, Picture Division. Picture sources, 2d ed., ed. by Celestine G. Frankenberg. N.Y., 1963. 224p.

Descriptions of about 700 collections of pictures in libraries, museums, etc., arranged by subject.

1726. Washington, University, Libraries. A list of serials in the fields of art, archaeology and decorative arts—the University of Washington Libraries and Seattle Public Library, comp. by Marietta Ward and Karen Wise. Seattle, 1968. 77p.

LANDSCAPE ARCHITECTURE AND URBAN PLANNING

1727. Eastern Michigan University Library. City and regional planning. Pt.1. An annotated bibliography of books and U.S. documents available in the University Library, comp. by Hannelore B. Rader. Ypsilanti, 1970. 39*l.*

1728. [Emory University Library. Charles Forrest Palmer collection] College & research libraries news, no.1 (Jan. 1970), 5.

Letters and other documents, numbering about 15,000, relating to slum clearance, low-cost housing, town planning, and related topics.

1729. Harvard University, Graduate School of Design Library. Catalogue of the Library of the Graduate School of Design. Boston: G. K. Hall, 1968. 44v. First supplement. 1970. 2v.

Reproduction of 611,000 cards on architecture, landscape architecture, and urban planning.

1730. Shillaber, Caroline. "The Charles Mulford Robinson collection." Harvard Library bulletin, 15 (1967), 281-86.

Describes collection in Harvard Library on city planning and related subjects.

1731. U.S. Dept. of Housing and Urban Development Library. Bibliography on housing, building and planning for use of overseas missions of the U.S. Agency for International Development. Wash.: Govt. Print. Off., 1969. 43p.

Prepared by HUD Library; lists about 400 items.

1732. ———. Books about cities. Wash.: Govt. Print. Off., 1969. 24p.

Selected bibliography on urban problems, planning, and housing.

1733. ———. 60 books on housing and urban planning. Wash.: Govt. Print. Off., 1966. 19p.

Includes HUD Library call numbers.

1734. U.S. Dept. of Housing and Urban Development, Office of the Secretary, Library. Housing and planning references. Wash.: Govt. Print. Off., 1966. 89p.

Publications acquired in the HUD libraries.

1735. U.S. Housing and Home Finance Agency Library. Periodicals currently received in the Housing and Home Finance Library. Wash., 1965. 33p.

Covers variety of subjects relating to housing and urban development.

1736. U.S. Library of Congress. The grand design; an exhibition tracing the evolution of the L'Enfant plan and subsequent plans for the development of Pennsyivania Avenue and the Mall area, organized jointly by the Library of Congress and the President's Temporary Commission on Pennsylvania Avenue. Wash.,1967. 25p.

Catalog of the exhibition.

1737. U.S. National Archives. List of records relating to the White House in the records of the Office of Public Buildings and Grounds, comp. by Kenneth W. Munden. Wash.: 1963. 11p.

ARCHITECTURE

1738. Boston University, Mugar Memorial Library. Holdings in American architectural history. Boston, 1968. 18p.

List of books and periodicals in collection.

1739. Cogswell, George Ralston. Library collections of accredited schools of architecture in Texas: a comparison based on a sample of entries from the catalog of the Avery Memorial Architectural Library of Columbia University. Austin, 1965. 76p. (Master's thesis, Graduate School of Library Science, Univ. of Tex.)

1740. Columbia University, Avery Architectural Library. Avery index to architectural periodicals. Boston: G. K. Hall, 1963. 12v.

Reproduction of library's card file. Supplements 1-5. Boston: G. K. Hall, 1965-70. 5v.

1741. ——— ———. Avery obituary index of architects and artists. Boston: G. K. Hall, 1963. 338p.

File maintained since 1943 by Avery Architectural Library, Columbia University.

1742. ——— ———. Catalog of the Avery Memorial Architectural Library of Columbia University, 2d ed. Boston: G. K. Hall, 1968. 19v.

1743. Gilchrist, Agnes Addison. "Notes for a catalogue of the John McComb (1763-1853) collection of architectural drawings in the New-York Historical Society." Journal of the Society of Architectural Historians, 28 (Oct. 1969), 201-10.

1744. Hitchcock, Henry R. American architectural books; a list of books, portfolios, and pamphlets on architecture and related subjects published in America before 1895. Minneapolis: Univ. of Minn. Pr., 1962. 130p.

Lists 1,461 items with locations in about 130 public and private libraries.

1745. Johns Hopkins University Library. The Fowler architectural collection of the Johns Hopkins University; catalogue, comp. by Lawrence Hall Fowler and Elizabeth Baer. Baltimore: Evergreen House Foundation, 1961. 388p.

1746. New York Public Library. Contemporary theatre architecture; an illustrated survey, by Maxwell Silverman, and a checklist of publications 1946-1964, by Ned A. Bowman. N.Y., 1965. 100p.

1747. Placzek, Adolf K. "The Frank Lloyd Wright collection of Sullivan drawings." Columbia Library columns, 14 (May 1965), 43-45.

Collection of drawings by Louis Henry Sullivan (1856-1924), famous American architect, acquired by Avery Library, Columbia University.

1748. Robison, Andrew. "Giovanni Battista Piranesi: prolegomena to the Princeton collections." Princeton University Library chronicle, 31 (1970), 165-206.

Extended discussion of Princeton's holdings on Piranesi, with detailed bibliographic descriptions of rare editions.

1749. U.S. National Archives. Preliminary inventory of the general records of the Housing and Home Finance Agency, comp. by Katherine H. Davidson. Wash., 1965. 28p. (Preliminary inventories, no. 164)

1750. ———. Preliminary inventory of the records of the Federal Housing Administration, comp. by Kathleen E. Riley and Charlotte M. Ashby. Wash., 1965. 8p.

1751. ———. Preliminary inventory of the records of the United States Housing Corporation, comp. by Katherine H. Davidson. Wash., 1962. 98p. (Preliminary inventories, no.140)

1752. Western Reserve University Library. Library resources in architecture and art at University Circle. Cleveland, Ohio, 1964. 1v. Unpaged.

DRAWING

1753. Boston Public Library. David Claypool Johnston, American graphic humorist, 1798-1865, by Malcolm Johnson; an exhibition jointly held by the American Antiquarian Society, Boston College, the Boston Public Library, and the Worcester Art Museum. Boston, 1970. 48p.

1754. Paluka, Frank, and Bush, Cynthia B. G. "The SUI Ding Darling cartoon collection." Iowa alumni review, 17 (Dec. 1963), 7-9.

Collection of 6,000 original cartoons, indexed by subject, caption, and date, in University of Iowa Libraries.

1755. Syracuse University Libraries. American political cartoons, 1865-1965, by Martin H. Bush. Syracuse, N.Y., 1966. 55p.

Exhibition catalog.

PAINTING AND SCULPTURE

1756. Bond, John W. "The Augustus Saint-Gaudens collection." Dartmouth College Library bulletin, n.s. 8 (1967), 2-9.

Collection in Dartmouth Library relating to famous American sculptor.

1757. Columbia University Libraries. The centenary of Arthur Rackham's birth, September 19, 1867: an appreciation of his genius and a catalogue of his original sketches, drawings, and paintings in the Berol collection, by Roland Baughman. N.Y., 1967. 48p.

Collection owned by Columbia Libraries.

1758. Massachusetts Institute of Technology, Charles Hayden Memorial Library. Jack Butler Yeats, 1871-1957. Boston, 1965. 32p.

Collection relating to Irish painter, in MIT Library.

1759. New York Public Library. Pen and brush: the author as artist, by Lola L. Szladits and Harney Simmonds. N.Y., 1969. 59p.

Catalog of exhibition from Berg collection, New York Public Library.

1760. Pennsylvania State University Library. George Grey Barnard, centenary exhibition, 1863-1963. University Park, 1964. 39p.

Relates to Barnard, 1863-1938, American sculptor.

1761. Pierpont Morgan Library. Audubon watercolors and drawings, by Edward H. Dwight. N.Y., 1965. 57p.

Illustrated exhibition catalog of 95 original watercolors and drawings of portraits, birds, and mammals by Audubon.

1762. Shaw, Renata V. "Japanese picture scrolls of the first Americans in Japan." Quarterly journal of the Library of Congress, 25 (1968), 134-53.

Report on Library of Congress acquisitions.

ENGRAVING

1763. Bentley, G. E., Jr. "Notes on the early editions of Flaxman's classical designs." Bulletin of the New York Public Library, 68 (1964), 277-307; 361-380. Reprinted. 1965. 60p.

Copies located. John Flaxman, 1755-1826, English sculptor, did series of engravings for editions of classical authors.

1764. Florida, University, Libraries. An abbreviated list: John Buckland Wright's engravings, books, etc., including a group of the artist's unpublished letters. Gainesville, 1964. 8p.

1765. [Illinois, University, Library. The Bishop collection] College & research libraries news, no.1 (Jan. 1970), 6.

Describes following work added to library: The Bishop collection—investigations and studies in jade. N.Y., 1906. 2v., from edition of 100 copies.

1766. Museum of Graphic Art. American printmaking, the first 150 years. N.Y., 1969. 180p. Issued also by Smithsonian Institution Press.

Exhibition sponsored in part by John Carter Brown Library, Brown University.

1767. Princeton University Library. William Blake, engraver; a descriptive catalogue of an exhibition, by Charles Ryskamp. Princeton, N.J., 1969. 61p.

Exhibition in Princeton Library.

1768. Rothrock, O. J. "The Janet Munday Gordon collection of French portrait engraving." Princeton University Library chronicle, 28 (1967), 178-84.

Collection received by Princeton Library.

1769. Scott-Elliot, A. H. "The etchings by Queen Victoria and Prince Albert." Bulletin of the New York Public Library, 65 (1961), 139-53.

Examples in Prints Division of New York Public Library are indicated.

1770. Syracuse University Libraries. The fine line of Rembrandt, 13 original etchings. Syracuse, N.Y., 1966. 3p.

An exhibition catalog.

1771. U.S. Library of Congress, Prints and Photographs Division. American prints in the Library of Congress; a catalog of the collection. Baltimore: Johns Hopkins Pr., 1970. 568p.

Contains entries for about 12,000 prints by 1,250 artists.

1772. ——— ———. Catalog of the 20th national exhibition, held at the Library of Congress. Wash.: The Library, 1966. 15p.

1773. ——— ———. Catalog of the 21st national exhibition of prints, held at the Library of Congress. Wash.: The Library. 1969. 16p.

1774. --- ---. "Prints and photographs." Library of Congress quarterly journal of current acquisitions, 19 (1961), 48-62; 20 (1962), 68-79; 21 (1964), 49-62; 22 (1965), 65-76; 23 (1966), 51-74.

Annual reports on Library's current acquisitions.

NUMISMATICS

1775. American Numismatic Society Library. Dictionary and auction catalogues of the Library of the American Numismatic Society. Boston: G. K. Hall, 1962. 7v. Supplement. 1967. 819p.

1776. "UCLA gains Gans." Numismatist, 81 (1968), 330-31.

Edward Gans numismatic collection of 10,000 titles acquired by University of California at Los Angeles Library.

CALLIGRAPHY

1777. Brown University Library. The working calligrapher and lettering artist; an international exhibition of contemporary design, prep. by Alexander Nesbitt. Providence, R.I.: Annmary Brown Memorial, 1961. 23p.

1778. Peabody Institute Library, Baltimore. Calligraphy and handwriting in America, 1710-1962, comp. by P. W. Filby. Caledonia, N.Y.: Italimuse, 1963. 83p.

Catalog of exhibition drawn from various U.S. collections.

1779. Pierpont Morgan Library. Chinese calligraphy and painting in the collection of John M. Crawford, Jr., ed. by Lawrence Sickman. N.Y., 1962. 306p.

1780. Walters Art Gallery. 2,000 years of calligraphy; a three-part exhibition organized by the Baltimore Museum of Art, the Peabody Institute Library and the Walters Art Gallery. Baltimore: Walters Art Gallery, 1965. 201p.

Detailed descriptions of 218 items drawn from various libraries.

PHOTOGRAPHY

1781. Boston Public Library. Photographs from the Boston Public Library, by Rachel Johnston Homer. Boston, 1970. 32p.

A survey of the library's photograph collections.

1782. Kuiper, John P. "Opportunities for film study at the Library of Congress." Film library quarterly, 1 (Winter 1967-68), 30-32.

1783. Syracuse University Libraries. Margaret Bourke-White's people. Syracuse, N.Y.: Syracuse Univ. School of Journalism, n.d. 8p.

Exhibition catalog of Margaret Bourke-White photographs.

1784. Texas, University, Humanities Research Center, Gernsheim Collection of Photography. The Gernsheim collection, the University of Texas. Austin, 1965. 24p.

Educational Film Catalogs (the following are examples of numerous catalogs of educational films issued by libraries, universities, etc.)

1785. Arizona, University, Bureau of Audiovisual Services. 16mm educational motion pictures, 1968. Tucson: Univ. of Ariz. Pr., 1968. 172p.

1786. Boston Public Library. Film catalog, 4th ed. Boston, 1970. 106p.

Catalog describing more than 2,800 films in Library.

1787. Boston University School of Education. Boston University instructional films available from Krasker Memorial Film Library. Boston, 1969. 292p.

1788. Cleveland Public Library. Film catalog. Cleveland, Ohio, 1968. 174p.

List of 2,600 16mm films available.

1789. California, University, Extension Media Center (Berkeley). 16mm films. Berkeley, 1969. 362p.

1790. Illinois, University, Visual Aids Service, Division of University Extension. Education films. 1969-72. Urbana, n.d. 599p.

1791. Indiana University, Audio-visual Center. 1970 catalog, educational motion pictures, 1970. 1,120p.

1792. Minnesota, University, Dept. of Audio-visual Extension. Educational resources bulletin; descriptive catalog of 16mm films with subject index. Minneapolis, 1969. 314p.

1793. Mountain Plains Educational Media Council. Joint film catalog 1971-1973. n.p. 492p.

Collections held by Universities of Colorado, Nevada, Utah, and Wyoming.

1794. New York University Film Library. The film library, 1969-70; general catalogue. N.Y., 1969. 84p. Triennial with annual supplements.

MUSIC

General

1795. Arizona State University, International Percussion Reference Library. Catalogue No. III. Tempe, 1968. 26p.

1796. Beck, Sydney, and Roth, Elizabeth. Music in prints; fifty-two prints illustrating musical instruments from the 15th century to the present. N.Y.: New York Public Library, 1965. 15p. and 52 plates.

Prints from the New York Public Library's collections.

1797. Benton, Rita. "The Music Library of the University of Iowa." Fontes artis musicae, 16 (1969), 124-29.

Description, history, and holdings.

1798. Boston Public Library, Gorokhoff Collection. Collection of Russian music; 450 pieces of liturgical music, 40 pieces of secular music. Liturgical music based on Slavic sources, rather than Italian. Boston, 1965. 12*l.*

1799. Bowen, Jean. "Buried in the stacks." Opera news, 26 (Dec. 30, 1961), 8-13.

Describes opera libretti and scores in New York Public Library collections.

1800. Bowles, Edmund A. "Musical instruments in illuminated manuscripts at the New York Public Library." Bulletin of the New York Public Library, 70 (1966), 86-92.

Discussion with illustrations.

1801. Brown, Howard M. Instrumental music printed before 1600; a bibliography. Cambridge, Mass.: Harvard Univ. Pr., 1965. 559p.

Chronological list; locates copies.

1802. Bryan, Mina R., and Morgan, Paula. "Music exhibition." Princeton University Library chronicle, 28 (1967), 106-24.

Annotated catalog of 120 musical works from ancient to modern times in Princeton Library.

1803. California, University, Library. The George Pullen Jackson collection of Southern hymnody; a bibliography, comp. by Paul J. Revitt. Los Angeles, 1964. 26p. (UCLA Library, occasional papers, no.13)

1804. ———, Music Library, Berkeley. A collection of Italian libretti, comp. by Dennis J. Dufalla. Berkeley, 1967. 5v.

Serial, title, poet, composer, and set designer indexes.

1805. ——— ———. G. H. Hooper libretto collection. Berkeley, 1965. 7*l.*

1806. ——— ———. Thematic catalog of a manuscript collection of eighteenth-century Italian instrumental music in the University of California, Berkeley, Music Library, by Vincent Duckles and Minnie Elmer. Berkeley: Univ. of Calif. Pr., 1963. 403p.

1807. Cohen, Selma Jeanne. "Freme di gelosia! Italian ballet librettos, 1766-1865." Bulletin of the New York Public Library, 67 (1963), 555-64.

In New York Public Library's Music Division.

1808. Fontes artis musicae, 16 (July-December, 1969), 107-50.

Essays describing resources of American music libraries.

1809. Harvard University Library. The romantic ballet; catalogue of an exhibition, Harvard theatre collection, 1966, comp. by P. D. Hull. Cambridge, Mass., 1966. 28p.

1810. Indiana University Library. The Apel collection of early keyboard sources in photographic reproduction in the Indiana University Music Library. Bloomington, 1961. 22*l.*

1811. International Association of Music Libraries, Commission of Research Libraries. Directory of music research libraries. Part 1: Canada and the United States, comp. by Rita Benton. Iowa City: Univ. of Iowa, 1967. 70p.

Brief descriptions of resources of 295 U.S. libraries.

1812. Krummel, Donald W. "The Newberry Library, Chicago." Fontes artis musicae, 16 (1969), 119-24.

Emphasis on music holdings.

1813. ———. "Observations on library acquisitions of

music." Music Library Association notes, n.s. 23 (1966), 5-16.

Concerning the Newberry Library.

1814. Marco, Guy A. "Beginnings of the Newberry Library music collection: background and personal influences." In: Approaches to library history. Tallahassee, Fla.: Journal of library history, 1966, p.197-208.

1815. Minniear, John Mohr. An annotated catalogue of the rare music collection in the Baylor University Library. Waco, Tex. 1963. 241p. (Master's thesis, Baylor Univ.) First supplement, by George G. Townsend. Waco, 1966. 162p. (Master's thesis) Second supplement, by Alberteen Ratliff. Waco, 1969. 200p. (Master's thesis)

1816. Nece, Bernice M. "The Kirsten Flagstad memorial collection." American archivist, 30 (1967), 477-82.

Describes collection of varied types of materials in California Historical Society.

1817. New York Public Library. Dictionary catalog of the music collection. Boston: G. K. Hall, 1964. 33v. Supplement 1. Boston: G. K. Hall, 1966. 811p.

1818. ———. "Musical treasures in American libraries; an exhibition in the Vincent Astor Gallery." Bulletin of the New York Public Library, 72 (1968), 428-41.

Detailed descriptions of 33 items, dated from 11th to 20th centuries, with locations.

1819. Oberlin College, Conservatory of Music Library. Mr. and Mrs. C. W. Best collection of autographs in the Mary M. Vial music library. Oberlin, Ohio, 1967. 55p.

Catalog of 110 autographs and holographs relating to music.

1820. O'Meara, Eva J. "Lowell Mason library of music." Yale University Library gazette, 40 (1965), 57-74.

Describes collection received by Yale in 1873, principally church music, assembled by leading figure in musical life of America in 19th century.

1821. Pierpont Morgan Library. Liturgical manuscripts for the mass and the divine office, by John Plummer. N.Y., 1964. 80p.

Illustrated catalog of principal types of liturgical manuscripts in Morgan Library.

1822. ———. The Mary Flagler Cary music collection; printed books and music, manuscripts, autograph letters, documents, portraits. N.Y.: Spiral, 1970. 105p.

Illustrated catalog of collection now in Morgan Library.

1823. [Princeton University Library. Music collection] College & research libraries news, no.5 (May 1969), 165.

Orchestral parts and conductor's scores for several thousand popular songs used in vaudeville and movie houses from about 1900 to 1930, received by Princeton.

1824. Reti-Forbes, Jean. "The Olin Downes papers." Georgia review, 21 (Summer 1967), 165-71.

Papers of music critic of the New York times; collection held by University of Georgia Library.

1825. [Rogers and Hammerstein Archives of Recorded Sound. Recordings collection] College & research libraries news, no.2 (Feb. 1970), 29.

Collection of 9,000 operatic and concert recordings, 1900- , received in Research Library of the Performing Arts, Lincoln Center, New York.

1826. Seidler, Richard D. A descriptive catalog of the Harold Bauer collection of the Library of Congress Music Division. Wash., 1964. 319p. (Master's thesis, Dept. of Library Science, Catholic Univ. of America)

Collection of correspondence, programs, music, articles, pamphlets, etc., in Library of Congress Music Division.

1827. Speer, Klaus. "Notes on liturgical books in the Sibley Music Library." University of Rochester Library bulletin, 23 (1967-68), 35-42.

Description of early liturgical works in University of Rochester's Music Library.

1828. Syracuse University Libraries. The "A to Z" of musical history, comp. by Walter L. Welch. Syracuse, N.Y., 1965. 110p.

Partial catalog of Bell collection in Syracuse University Audio Archives; recordings of popular music and folk song; political and theatrical celebrities.

1829. U.S. Library of Congress. Library of Congress catalog: music and phonorecords; a cumulative list of works represented by Library of Congress printed cards. Wash., 1953- . Semiannual and annual cumulations.

1830. ———. The national union catalog; a cumulative author list representing Library of Congress printed cards and titles reported by other American libraries, 1958-1962, v.51-52: music and phonorecords. N.Y.: Rowman and Littlefield, 1963. 2v.

Part 1, author list, part 2, subject index.

1831. ———. The national union catalog; a cumulative author list representing Library of Congress printed cards and titles reported by other American libraries,

1963-1967: music and phonorecords. Ann Arbor, Mich.: J.W. Edwards, 1969. 3v.
v.1-2, author catalog; v.3, subject index.

1832. ---, African Section. African music: a briefly annotated bibliography, comp. by Darius L. Thieme. Wash.: Govt. Print. Off., 1964. 55p.
Bibliography of 597 items.

1833. ---, Music Division. A guide to the music of Latin America, by Gilbert Chase, 2d ed. Wash.: The Library, 1962. 411p.
Lists 3,784 items.

1834. --- ---. "Music." Library of Congress quarterly journal of current acquisitions, 19 (1961), 17-47; 20 (1962), 30-67; 21 (1964), 15-48; 22 (1965), 29-64; 23 (1966), 11-50; 24 (1967), 47-82; 25 (1968), 50-91; 26 (1969), 21-47; 27 (1970), 51-83.
Annual reports on acquisitions.

1835. --- ---. The Sousa Band: a discography, comp. by James R. Smart. Wash.: Govt. Print. Off., 1970. 123p.
Sousa Band recordings in Music Division.

1836. Watanabe, Ruth. "The Danish historical series." University of Rochester Library bulletin, 18 (Winter, 1963), 30-35.
Describes series of music compositions, published by Society for Publishing Danish Music, acquired by University of Rochester's Music Library.

1837. ---. "The Sibley Music Library of the Eastman School of Music" (University of Rochester). Fontes artis musicae, 16 (July-Dec. 1969), 143-44.

1838. Winfrey, Dorman H. "The Toscanini archives." American archivist, 30 (1967), 465-70.
Describes two archival depositories in New York City of Arturo Toscanini materials: Toscanini Memorial Archives (New York Public Library) and the Toscanini Archives of Riverdale.

1839. Wofford College Library. Hymns and hymnody, comp. by Frank J. Anderson. Spartanburg, S.C.: Wofford Library Pr., 1970. 26p. (Special collections checklists, no.1)
List of 168 titles in Wofford Library's special collection.

Folk Music

1840. Indiana University Folklore Institute. Archives of traditional music; catalog of Afroamerican music and oral data holdings, comp. by Philip M. Peek. Bloomington, 1970. 28p.

1841. Jabbour, Alan A., and Hickerson, Joseph C. "African recordings in the Archive of Folk Song." Quarterly journal of the Library of Congress, 27 (1970), 283-88.

1842. Oster, Harry. "The Edwin Ford Piper collection of folksongs." Books at Iowa, 1 (Oct. 1964), 28-33.
In University of Iowa Libraries.

1843. U.S. Library of Congress, Music Division. Folk music, a catalog of folk songs, ballads, dances, instrumental pieces, and folk tales of the United States and Latin America on phonograph records. Wash.: The Library, 1964. 107p.
Lists 166 discs, with a total of 1,240 titles, from Archive of American Folk Song in Library of Congress.

Periodicals

1844. Coover, James B. "A bibliography of East European music periodicals." Fontes artis musicae, 3 (1956), 219-26; 4 (1957), 97-102; 5 (1958), 44-55, 93-99; 6 (1959), 27-28; 7 (1960), 16-21, 69-70; 8 (1961), 75-90; 9 (1962), 78-80; 10 (1963), 60-71.
Lists 653 titles, locating holdings in U.S. libraries wherever possible.

1845. McClellan, William M. A checklist of music serials in nine libraries of the Rocky Mountain region. Boulder: Univ. of Colo. Libraries, 1963. 21p.
Extent of holdings shown.

1846. Music Library Association, Northern California Chapter. Union list of music periodicals in the libraries of Northern California, ed. by C. R. Nicewonger. Berkeley, 1965. 141*l.*
Records holdings of 24 libraries.

1847. Weichlein, William J. A checklist of American music periodicals, 1850-1900. Detroit, Information Coordinators, 1970. 103p. (Detroit studies in music bibliography, no.16)
Bibliographical details on 309 titles, with locations.

1848. Wunderlich, Charles E. A history and bibliography of early American musical periodicals, 1782-1852. Ann Arbor, Mich., 1962. 2v. (Ph.D. thesis, Univ. of Mich.)
Entries for 66 periodicals with holdings for 73 U.S. libraries.

Music–American

1849. Brown University Library. A study and catalogue of Presidential campaign songsters in the Harris collection of American poetry and plays and the McClellan Lincoln collection at Brown University. Providence, R.I., 1964. 354*l.* (Master's thesis, Brown University)

1850. Edmunds, John. A general report on the New York Public Library's Americana music collection and its proposed development in Lincoln Center for the Performing Arts. N.Y., 1961. 28p.

Examination of various facets of New York Public Library's extensive and important holdings of musical Americana.

1851. Heintze, James R. "Music of the Washington family: a little known collection." Musical quarterly, 56 (April 1970), 283-93.

Description of collection in George Washington Masonic Museum, Alexandria, Virginia.

1852. Indiana University, Lilly Library. American patriotic songs: Yankee Doodle to the Conquered Banner with emphasis on the Star-Spangled Banner; an exhibition held at the Lilly Library. Bloomington, 1968. Unpaged. (Lilly Library publication, no.6)

1853. Library Company of Philadelphia. American song sheets, ship ballads, and poetical broadsides, 1850-1870: a catalogue of the collection of the Library Company of Philadelphia, by Edwin Wolf, 2nd. Philadelphia, 1963. 205p.

1854. Schroeder, Rebecca. Manuscript collections of Ohio folk song. Kent, Ohio, 1964. 152p. (Master's thesis, School of Library Science, Kent State Univ.)

Describes in detail collections of Ohio folksong material, mainly in Ohio institutions, but including Library of Congress.

1855. Sherr, Paul C. "Bibliography: libretti of American musical productions of the 1930s." Bulletin of the New York Public Library, 70 (1966), 318-24.

Copies located in several libraries and private collections.

1856. Sonneck, Oscar G. A bibliography of early secular American music, 18th century, rev. and enlarged. N.Y.: Da Capo Press, 1964. 616p.

Locates copies.

1857. Soule, Edmund P. "Tutta la forza imaginevole." The call number, published by the University of Oregon Library, 28 (Spring 1967), 5-20.

Essay descriptive of University of Oregon Library's extensive holdings of American sheet music produced during past 150 years.

1858. Spottswood, Richard K. A catalog of American folk music on commercial recordings at the Library of Congress, 1923-40. Wash., 1962. 440p. (Master's thesis, Dept. of Library Science, Catholic Univ. of America)

1859. Virginia, University, Library. The folksongs of Virginia: a checklist of the WPA holdings, Alderman Library, University of Virginia, comp. by Bruce A. Rosenberg. Charlottesville: Univ. Pr. of Va., 1969. 145p.

Checklist of folksong and other folklore material on deposit in University of Virginia Library; records 1,604 items.

1860. Wolfe, Richard J. Secular music in America, 1801-1825; a bibliography. N.Y.: New York Public Library, 1964. 3v.

Lists about 10,000 titles and editions with locations of copies in 44 American collections.

Individual Composers

1861. Bator, Victor. The Béla Bartók Archives; history and catalogue. N.Y.: Bartók Archives, 1963. 39p.

Includes checklist of contents.

1862. California, University, Library. Autograph manuscripts of Ernest Bloch at the University of California. Berkeley, 1962. 20p.

Collection relating to U.S. composer, 1880-1959.

1863. ———, Music Library. Materials for Mozart research; an inventory of the Mozart Nachlass of Alfred Einstein, comp. by John Emerson. Berkeley, 1963. 28*l.*

1864. DeLerma, Dominique-René. Charles Edward Ives, 1874-1954: a bibliography of his music. Kent, Ohio: Kent State Univ. Pr., 1970. 212p.

Based primarily on Ives collection in Yale School of Music.

1865. Epstein, Dena J. "Lucy McKim Garrison, American musician." Bulletin of the New York Public Library, 67 (1963), 529-46.

Description of McKim papers in New York Public Library's Music Division.

1866. Kimball, Robert E. "The Cole Porter collection

at Yale." Yale University Library gazette, 44 (1969), 8-15.

Music, manuscripts, scrapbooks, photographs, recordings, librettos, and other material associated with Porter, now in Yale Library.

1867. Lowens, Irving. "New Beethoveniana." Library of Congress quarterly journal of current acquisitions, 20 (1962), 1-11.

Description of Library of Congress acquisitions.

1868. Picker, Martin. "Handeliana in the Rutgers University Library." Journal of the Rutgers University Library, 29 (1965), 1-12.

Listing of large collection of 18th-century editions and original manuscripts of George Frederick Handel in Rutgers Library.

1869. Watanabe, Ruth. "Music manuscripts of Weldon Hart." University of Rochester Library bulletin, 19 (1964), 27-30.

Annotated list of 35 manuscripts of the works of Hart (1911-1957) in University of Rochester's Sibley Music Library.

1870. ———. "The Percy Grainger manuscripts." University of Rochester Library bulletin, 19 (1964), 21-26.

Description of group of Grainger manuscripts received by University of Rochester's Sibley Music Library.

1871. Williams, Philip L. Music by John Powell in the John Powell music collection at the University of Virginia: a descriptive bibliography. Charlottesville, Va., 1968. 99p. (Master's thesis, Dept. of Music, Univ. of Va.)

1872. Yale University School of Music Library. A temporary mimeographed catalogue of the music manuscripts and related materials of Charles Edward Ives, 1874-1954, given by Mrs. Ives to the Library of the Yale School of Music, Sept. 1955, comp. by John Kirkpatrick. New Haven, Conn., 1960. 279*l*.

AMUSEMENTS

Theater, Moving Pictures, etc.

1873. Anderson, Jack. "Towards a dance film library." Dance magazine, 39 (Sept. 1965), 40-42.

Describes New York Public Library's holdings of dance film material.

1874. Black, Matthew W., and Miller, William E. "Some letters from actors and actresses to Dr. Horace Howard Furness." University of Pennsylvania Library chronicle, 29 (1963), 105-15; 30 (1964), 10-22.

In University of Pennsylvania Library; Furness was an eminent Shakespearean scholar.

1875. California, University, Library. Jack Benny checklist: radio, television, motion pictures, books and articles, by David R. Smith. Los Angeles, 1970. 33p.

Based in part on extensive collection of scripts, films, phonograph records, tape recordings, and other archival materials in UCLA Library.

1876. Cleveland Public Library. The library sets the stage. Cleveland, Ohio, 1969. 8p.

Describes theatre collection of 50,000 volumes in Cleveland Public Library.

1877. Crawford, Dorothy. "Crawford theatre collection at Yale." Yale University Library gazette, 41 (1967), 131-35.

1878. Dallas Public Library, Fine Arts Dept. An exhibit of selected material from the W. E. Hill theatre collection. Dallas, Tex., 1966. 40p.

Collection contains letters, programs, photographs, clippings, autographs, broadsides, etc., from the 18th century to date.

1879. Finley, Katherine P., and Nolan, Paul T. "Mississippi drama between wars, 1870-1916; a checklist and an argument." Journal of Mississippi history, 26 (Aug.-Nov. 1964), 219-28, 299-306.

Locates copies in Library of Congress.

1880. Freedley, George. "The New York Public Library's theatre collection." Wilson Library bulletin, 38 (1964), 637-39.

General description.

1881. Harvard University Library, Theatre Collection. An exhibition to honor William Van Lennep, curator of the Harvard theatre collection from 1940 to 1960. Cambridge, Mass.: Houghton Library, 1963. 30p.

1882. Hunter, Frederick J. "Drama and theatre arts resources at TxU." Library chronicle of the University of Texas, 7, no.4 (1964), 55-59.

Survey of University of Texas Library's research materials in drama and theatre history.

1883. Kaiser, Barbara J. "Resources in the Wisconsin

Center for Theatre Research." American archivist, 30 (1967), 483-92.

Primarily concerned with American theatre since 1900.

1884. Moore, Lillian. "Buried treasure." Dance magazine, 38 (April 1964), 42-47.

Description of New York Public Library's dance collection.

1885. New York Public Library. Catalog of the theatre and drama collections, the New York Public Library, Reference Department. Boston: G. K. Hall, 1967. 21v.

Part I: drama, listed by cultural origin; part II: drama, listed by authors; part III: theatre collection.

1886. ———. Dancing in prints 1634-1870; a portfolio of twelve fine etchings, engravings, and color lithographs assembled from the archives of the dance collection, with commentary by Marian Eames. N.Y., 1964. 20p. and 12 plates.

From New York Public Library's dance collection.

1887. ———. Images of the dance: historical treasures of the dance collection 1581-1861, by Lillian Moore. N.Y., 1965. 86p.

Material in New York Public Library's dance collection.

1888. ———. The Library and Museum of the Performing Arts [Lincoln Center] N.Y., 1965. 52p.

1889. ———. Stravinsky and the theatre: a catalogue of decor and costume designs for stage productions of his works, 1910-1962. N.Y., 1964. 60p.

1890. Rood, Arnold. "Edward Gordon Craig, artist of the theatre 1872-1966; a memorial exhibition in the Amsterdam Gallery: the catalogue." Bulletin of the New York Public Library, 71 (1967), 445-67, 524-41.

Copies located in public and private collections.

1891. "Scholar and screen." Quarterly journal of the Library of Congress, 21 (1964), 265-69.

Notes on Library of Congress' motion picture collection.

1892. Southern California, University. Radio and television: holdings of the University Library. n.p., 1961. 1v. Unpaged.

1893. Stratman, Carl J. American theatrical periodicals, 1789-1967; a bibliographical guide. Durham, N.C.: Duke Univ. Pr., 1970. 133p.

Entries for 685 titles with holdings shown for 138 U.S. and 2 Canadian libraries and British Museum.

1894. ———. A bibliography of British dramatic periodicals, 1720-1960. N.Y.: New York Public Library, 1962. 58p.

Entries for 674 periodicals chronologically arranged; files located in 53 U.S. libraries and in British and Canadian libraries.

1895. ———. Bibliography of the American theatre, excluding New York City. Chicago: Loyola Univ. Pr., 1965. 397p.

Includes all types of publications and all aspects of theatre. Arranged by states and cities, with author-subject index; one or more locations for each title listed.

1896. ———. "Dramatic play lists, 1591-1963." Bulletin of the New York Public Library, 70 (1966), 71-85, 169-88.

Lists 99 titles, with detailed annotations and some locations.

1897. Texas, University, Hoblitzelle Theatre Arts Collection. A guide to the theatre and drama collections at the University of Texas, comp. by Frederick J. Hunter. Austin: Univ. of Tex. Humanities Research Center, 1967. 84p.

1898. ———, Humanities Research Center. Theatre and drama during the Restoration and eighteenth century; an exhibit of early prints and early editions. Austin, 1964. 16p.

1899. ——— ———. Twentieth century drama in manuscript: an exhibit of plays and libretti, comp. by Kim Taylor. Austin, 1962. Unpaged.

1900. U.S. Library of Congress. The national union catalog; a cumulative author list representing Library of Congress printed cards and titles reported by other American libraries, 1958-1962, v.53-54: motion pictures and filmstrips. N.Y.: Rowman and Littlefield, 1963. 2v.

Part 1, title list; part 2, subject index.

1901. ———. The national union catalog; a cumulative author list representing Library of Congress printed cards and titles reported by other American libraries, 1963-1967: motion pictures and filmstrips. Ann Arbor, Mich.: J. W. Edwards, 1967. 2v.

v.1, titles; v.2, subject index.

1902. Whitmore, Eugene. "Hertzberg collection in the

San Antonio Public Library offers a ticket to the circus." Texas libraries, 30 (Spring 1968), 37-39.

Collection relating to circuses.

1903. Willard, Helen D. "The Harvard theatre collection." Restoration and 18th century theatre research, 3 (May 1964), 14-22.

Sports and Games

1904. Brown University Library. Fly fishing; an exhibit for those who love fly fishing and for those who would be fly fishermen. Providence, R.I.: Foremost Lithograph Co., 1968. 14p.

1905. Cleveland Public Library, John G. White Department. Catalog of the chess collection (including checkers). Boston: G. K. Hall, 1964. 2v.

"The largest body of chess literature in the world"; about 26,000 entries.

1906. Di Cesare, Mario A. "Vida's game of chess: a bibliography." Bulletin of the New York Public Library, 68 (1964), 493-516.

Lists 135 editions, 1525-1933, with locations.

1907. Goff, Frederick R. "TR's big-game library." Library of Congress quarterly journal of current acquisitions, 21 (1964), 167-71.

Theodore Roosevelt's collection of hunting literature received by Library of Congress.

1908. U.S. National Archives. Preliminary inventory of the records of the National Conference on Outdoor Recreation, 1924-29, comp. by Kenneth W. Munden and Richard Bartlett. Wash., 1962. 23p.

Linguistics

GENERAL

1909. Alston, R. C. A bibliography of the English language from the invention of printing to the year 1800; a systematic record of writings on English, and other languages in English, based on the collections of the principal libraries of the world. Leeds, England: Printed for the author by E. J. Arnold, 1965-69- . (In progress)

Locations shown.

1910. Bako, Elemer. "The minor Finno-Ugrian languages." Library of Congress quarterly journal of current acquisitions, 23 (1966), 117-37.

Survey of Finno-Ugrian holdings in Library of Congress, emphasizing minor languages.

1911. California, University, Library. The English dictionary before Webster: fifty landmarks in the history of the English language, by Robert L. Collison. Los Angeles, 1969. 9p.

Describes exhibit drawn from the UCLA Library's collections.

1912. Howren, Robert. "Iowa materials for the Linguistic atlas of the Upper Midwest." Books at Iowa, 6 (April 1967), 29-35.

In University of Iowa Library.

1913. Lewanski, Richard C. A bibliography of Slavic dictionaries. N.Y.: New York Public Library, 1959-63. 3v.

Based on New York Public Library's collections.

1914. Nadela, Ernestina C. An annotated bibliography on Philippine linguistics in the Library of Congress. Wash., 1967. 55*l.* (Master's thesis, Dept. of Library Science, Catholic Univ. of America)

1915. Ohio State University Libraries. French language dictionaries in the Ohio State University Libraries: a bibliographic guide, by Ana R. Llorens and Rosemary L. Walker. Columbus, 1970. 56p.

1916. Peck, Charles R. A subject and descriptive catalog of the holdings of the Clementine collection of the Catholic University of America Library in the field of language and languages. 1968. 88p. (Master's thesis, Dept. of Library Science, Catholic Univ. of America)

1917. Swanson, Donald C. E. Modern Greek studies in the West; a critical bibliography of studies on modern Greek linguistics, philology, and folklore, in languages other than Greek. N.Y.: N.Y. Public Library, 1960. 93p.

Includes holdings of New York Public Library and University of Minnesota Library.

Literature

GENERAL

1918. Boston University, Mugar Memorial Library, Division of Special Collections. Twentieth century archives. Boston, 1968. 11p.

List of writers and public figures whose literary and personal papers are in Library's archives.

1919. Chicago, University, Library. Scholars and scholarship of the Renaissance; an exhibition from the collections of the University of Chicago Library. Chicago, 1964. 22p.

1920. Harvard University, Houghton Library. Bibliotheca chimaerica; a catalogue of an exhibition of catalogues of imaginary books. Cambridge, Mass., 1962. 12p.

1921. ——— ———. An exhibition of books published when they were 21 or younger by one hundred authors who later became famous. Cambridge, Mass., 1961. 28p.

1922. Harvard University Library. Literature: general and comparative; classification schedule, classified listing by author or title, chronological listing. Cambridge, Mass.: 1968. 189p. (Widener Library shelflist, no.18)

Lists about 5,100 titles.

1923. Huntington Library. The Huntington Library as a literary research center, by James Thorpe. San Marino, Calif., 1968. 8p.

1924. Idaho, University, Library. Humanities literature; a selected bibliography of sources by George Kellogg. Moscow, 1965. 42p. (Supplement to the Bookmark, v.18, no.1)

1925. Indiana University, Lilly Library. Five centuries of familiar quotations in their earliest appearances in print. Exhibition. Bloomington, 1968. 6p.

1926. Morrison, Julia M. "A checklist of literary journals in Minnesota, November 1850-April 1961." Minnesota libraries, 20 (Sept. 1961), 83-87.

Files located in 2 Minnesota libraries and 1 Wisconsin library.

1927. New York Public Library. The Arents collection of books in parts and associated literature; a supplement to the checklist, 1957-1963, comp. by Perry O'Neil. N.Y., 1964. 38p. (Reprinted from Bulletin of the New York Public Library, 68 (1964), 141-52, 259-69)

Original checklist issued in 1957.

1928. Ohio State University Libraries. Periodicals in the Romance languages and literatures at the Ohio State University Libraries, comp. by Ana R. Llorens. Columbus, 1969. 43p.

Selective list of 1,000 journals of research importance.

1929. Oregon State Library. Master book catalog of adult non-fiction and adult fiction in foreign languages in the Oregon State Library as of November 1965. Salem, 1967. 25v.

Author-title-subject catalog of 190,000 titles.

1930. Peabody Institute Library. Crime and the literati: fraud and forgery in literature, by P. W. Filby. Baltimore, 1962. 35*l.*

Catalog of an exhibition.

1931. Pennsylvania State University Library. Checklist of holdings in emblem books. University Park, 1965. 7p.

1932. Pennsylvania, University, Library. Catalog of the programmschriften collection. Boston: G. K. Hall, 1961. 377p.

Lists 16,555 pamphlets from Graz, Austria, of scholarly papers by gymnasium faculty members, 1850-1918, in humanities, history of science, etc.

1933. Rice, Howard C., Jr. "Sylvia Beach collection."

Princeton University Library chronicle, 26 (1964), 7-13.
In Princeton University Library; extensive collection of books and manuscripts relating to 20th-century literature.

Fiction

1934. California, University, Library. The boys in the black mask: an exhibit in the UCLA Library. Los Angeles, 1961. 13p.
Collection of detective novels and magazines in UCLA Library.

1935. Gribbin, Lenore S. Who's whodunit; a list of 3,218 detective story writers and their 1,100 pseudonyms. Chapel Hill: Univ. of N.C. Library, 1968. 174p.
Based on University of North Carolina Library collection.

1936. Indiana University, Lilly Library. Eighty-nine good novels of the sea, the ship, and the sailor; a list compiled by J. K. Lilly. An account of its formation by David A. Randall. Bloomington, 1966. 29p. (Lilly Library Publication, no.4)

1937. Minnesota, University, Libraries. Nick Carter, master detective; an exhibition from the George H. Hess collection. Minneapolis, 1968. 9p.
Leaflet descriptive of extensive collection of dime novels and similar works in University of Minnesota Libraries.

1938. [New York University Libraries. Dime novel collection] College & research libraries news, no.4 (April 1970), 102, 105.
Describes collection of 8,000 19th-century dime novels, story papers, and fiction magazines acquired by N.Y.U. Libraries.

1939. North Carolina, University, Library. "UNC detective collection," by Mary S. Cameron. The bookmark, Friends of the University of North Carolina Library, 38 (Sept. 1968), 1-6.
Description of 4,000-volume collection of detective, mystery, spy, and crime novels in University of North Carolina Library.

1940. Syracuse University Library. Fictional accounts of trips to the moon, by Lester G. Wells, 2d ed. Syracuse, N.Y., 1962. 30p.

1941. Syracuse University Libraries. Science fiction collections in the George Arents Research Library at Syracuse University, comp. by Philip F. Mooney. Syracuse, N.Y., 1970. 14p.

Poetry

1942. U.S. Library of Congress, General Reference and Bibliography Division. Archive of recorded poetry and literature; a checklist. Wash., 1961. 132p.
List of recordings in the Library's archive, arranged by recording artist.

1943. ——— ———. Literary recordings; a checklist of the Archive of Recorded Poetry and Literature in the Library of Congress. Wash., 1966. 190p.
Updates 1961 checklist; contains 853 entries.

AMERICAN

General

1944. American Antiquarian Society. American penmanship, 1800-1850, a history and bibliography of writing masters and copy books, by Ray Nash. Worcester, Mass., 1969. 304p.
Locates copies in 38 libraries.

1945. Blanck, Jacob N. Bibliography of American literature. New Haven, Conn.: Yale Univ. Pr., 1955-69. v.1-5, Adams-Longfellow. (In progress)
To include comprehensive bibliographics for 300 selected authors from beginning of federal period to 1930. Locates copies of works examined.

1946. Bush, Alfred L. "Literary landmarks of Princeton." Princeton University Library chronicle, 29 (1967), 1-90. Reprinted. 88p.
Exhibition catalog of works of 132 authors associated with Princeton University, 18th to 20th centuries.

1947. Byrns, Lois. Recusant books in America, 1700-1829. New York: Peter Kavanagh Hand-Press, 1964. 71p.
Books by authors who refused to comply with or conform to some regulation or practice. A union list.

1948. Clark, Charles E. "The literature of the New England earthquake of 1755." Papers of the Bibliographical Society of America, 59 (1965), 295-305.
Detailed bibliographical descriptions of 27 contemporary publications, with locations.

1949. DeWaal, Ronald B. "Colorado State University: Western American literature collection." Mountain-Plains library quarterly, 12 (Summer 1967), 29.

1950. Gallup, Donald. "The Yale collection of American literature." Yale University Library gazette, 38 (1964), 151-59.

General description, followed by summaries of holdings for individual authors.

1951. Gohdes, Clarence. "The American literature collection." Gnomon, (1970), 11-16. (Special number of Duke University Library's Library notes)

Describes Duke Library's holdings.

1952. Grolier Club. Italian influence on American literature . . . a catalogue of an exhibition of books, manuscripts and art showing this influence on American literature and art. N.Y., 1962. 131p.

1953. Harvard University Library. American literature. Cambridge, Mass., 1970. 2v. (Widener Library shelflist, no.26-27)

Lists 61,000 titles.

1954. Kansas State College of Pittsburg Library. Kansas authors of best sellers: a bibliography, comp. by Gene DeGruson. Pittsburg, 1970. 30p.

Includes works of Martin and Osa Johnson, Margaret Hill McCarter, Charles M. Sheldon, and Harold Bell Wright.

1955. New York Public Library. First fruits; an exhibition of first editions of first books by American authors, by John D. Gordan. N.Y., 1968. 25p.

1956. Paluka, Frank. Iowa authors: a bio-bibliography of sixty native writers. Iowa City: Friends of the Univ. of Iowa Libraries, 1967. 243p.

Describes manuscript holdings of University of Iowa Libraries.

1957. Pennsylvania State University Library. Arthur S. Hoffman; calendar of papers for editor of Adventure, Romance, and the Delineator. University Park, 1968. 27p.

1958. Rusk, Ralph L. The literature of the middle western frontier. N.Y.: Columbia Univ. Pr., 1925. 2v. Reprinted. N.Y., Ungar, 1963.

Locates copies.

1959. Szladits, Lola L. "New in the Berg collection: 1962-1964." Bulletin of the New York Public Library, 73 (1969), 227-52.

Manuscripts and early editions of works of American and British authors acquired by New York Public Library.

1960. Virginia, University, Library. The American writer in England: an exhibition arranged in honor of the sesquicentennial of the University of Virginia; with a foreword by Gordon N. Ray. Charlottesville: Univ. Pr. of Va., 1969. 137p.

Drawn from the University of Virginia's rare book collections.

1961. ———. "Manuscripts in the Clifton Waller Barrett Library of American literature in the University of Virginia Library." Thoreau Society bulletin, no.90 (Winter 1965), 1-2.

Listing of letters, manuscripts, and other material relating to Thoreau.

1962. ———. The Virginia author, 1819-1969; an exhibition in commemoration of the sesquicentennial of the University of Virginia. Charlottesville, 1969. 26p.

1963. West Virginia University Library. The Southern mountaineer in literature; an annotated bibliography, by Lorise C. Boger. Morgantown, 1964. 105p.

Poetry

1964. Brown University Library. "The Harris collection of American poetry and plays; report of acquisitions." Books at Brown, 19 (1963), 161-75; 20 (1965), 111-30; 21 (1966), 157-96.

1965. Indiana University, Lilly Library. Three centuries of American poetry; an exhibition of original printings, at the Lilly Library. Bloomington, 1965. 30, 6p.

All except about "two dozen volumes" drawn from Lilly Library.

1966. Northwestern State College of Louisiana Library. The poets of Louisiana; a handlist. Natchitoches, 1966. 22*l*.

1967. Rosenfeld, Alvin H. "Yiddish poets and playwrights of America: a preliminary report on a recent addition to the Harris collection." Books at Brown, 22 (1968), 161-81.

Collection of 635 volumes of Yiddish poetry and 293 volumes of and about Yiddish drama acquired by Brown University Library.

1968. Stoddard, Roger E. "A catalogue of books and pamphlets unrecorded in Oscar Wegelin's Early American poetry, 1650-1820." Books at Brown, 23 (1969), 1-84.

Annotated list of 262 titles with locations in numerous libraries.

1969. ———. "The Harris collection of American poetry and plays." Books at Brown, 19 (May 1963), 161-75.
Brown University Library collection.

1970. Virginia, University, Library, The Barrett Library. The Wegelin collection of later nineteenth-century minor American poetry, 1821-1899, comp. by Lucy T. Clark, Charlottesville: Univ. of Va. Pr., 1962. 107p.

Drama

1971. Brown University Library. Two hundred years of American plays, 1765-1964; catalogue of an exhibition. Providence, R.I., 1965. 51p.

Fiction

1972. Coad, Oral S. New Jersey in the Revolution: a bibliography of historical fiction, 1784-1963. New Brunswick, N.J.: New Brunswick Historical Club, 1964. 39p.
Based primarily on Rutgers University Library holdings.

1973. Ohio State University Libraries. The William Charvat American fiction collection, I; an exhibition of selected works, 1787-1850, comp. by Richard A. Ploch. Columbus, 1967. 37p.
Detailed bibliographical descriptions of 75 rare works selected from the Ohio State University Library collection.

1974. ———. The William Charvat American fiction collection, II; an exhibition of selected works, 1851-1875, comp. by Richard A. Ploch. Columbus, 1967. 37p.
Detailed bibliographical descriptions of 75 rare works selected from the Ohio State University Library collection.

1975. ———. The William Charvat American fiction collection, III; an exhibition of selected works, 1876-1900, comp. by Richard A. Ploch. Columbus, 1968. 43p.
Detailed bibliographical description of 75 rare works selected from the Ohio State University Library collection.

1976. Thorp, Willard. "Whit Burnett and Story magazine." Princeton University Library chronicle, 27 (1966), 107-12.
Summarizes contents of Burnett papers in Princeton Library.

1977. Wright, Lyle H. American fiction, 1774-1850: a contribution toward a bibliography. San Marino, Calif.: Huntington Library, 1969. 411p.

1978. ———. American fiction, 1851-1875; a contribution toward a bibliography. Additions and corrections appended. San Marino, Calif.: Huntington Library, 1968. 438p.
Reprint of 1957 edition with additions and corrections; locates copies.

1979. ———. American fiction, 1876-1900. San Marino, Calif.: Huntington Library, 1966. 638p.
Companion to earlier volumes covering 1774-1875. Reports locations in 15 American libraries of 6,175 items.

Individual Authors

Agee, James

1980. Kramer, Victor A. "James Agee papers at the University of Texas." Library chronicle of the University of Texas, 8, no.2 (1966), 33-36.
Description of manuscripts, mostly written after 1946, in University of Texas Library.

Alcott, Louisa May

1981. U.S. Library of Congress, Children's Book Section. Louisa May Alcott: a centennial for Little women; an annotated, selected bibliography, comp. by Judith C. Ullom. Wash.: Govt. Print. Off., 1969. 91p.
Includes Library of Congress call numbers for 171 items by and about author; catalog of an exhibition.

Algren, Nelson

1982. Ohio State University Libraries. Nelson Algren—Samuel Beckett; an exhibition of books and manuscripts selected from the Ohio State University Libraries collections. Columbus, 1966. 13p.
Contemporary novelists, American and Irish.

Anderson, Maxwell

1983. Avery, Laurence G. "The Maxwell Anderson papers." Library chronicle of the University of Texas, 8, no.1 (1965), 21-33.
Description of manuscripts, letters, and diaries in University of Texas Library.

1984. Texas, University, Humanities Research Center.

A catalogue of the Maxwell Anderson collection at the University of Texas, comp. by Laurence G. Avery. Austin, Univ. of Tex. Pr., 1968. 175p. (Tower bibliographical series, no.6)

Bonner, Amy

1985. Pennsylvania State University Library. Amy Bonner, calendar of papers of poet, reviewer, and Eastern representative for Poetry magazine. University Park, 1969. 27p.

Brooks, Van Wyck

1986. Westlake, Neda M. "The Van Wyck Brooks collection." University of Pennsylvania Library chronicle, 31 (1965), 25.

Van Wyck Brooks correspondence and manuscript material in the University of Pennsylvania Library.

Brown, Charles Brockden

1987. Krause, Sydney J. "A census of the works of Charles Brockden Brown." The Serif, Kent State University Library quarterly, 3 (Dec. 1966), 27-55.

Locates 93 books, pamphlets, and works in periodicals by Brown, 1771-1810, first prominent American novelist, in 30 libraries.

Bryant, William Cullen

1988. Catholic University of America. William Cullen Bryant, an annotated checklist of the exhibit held in the Mullen Library of the Catholic University of America, by Thomas H. Voss. Wash., 1967. 18p.

Bynner, Edwin Lassetter

1989. Virginia, University, Library, The Barrett Library. Edwin Lassetter Bynner; a checklist of printed and manuscript works of Edwin Lassetter Bynner in the Library of the University of Virginia, comp. by Lucy T. Clark. Charlottesville: Univ. of Va. Pr., 1961. 9p.

Works by American novelist, printed 1877-93, in University of Virginia Library.

Cabell, James Branch

1990. Dorbin, Sanford. "Collecting James Branch Cabell." California librarian, 31 (1970), 77-80.

Description of special collection in University of California Library, Santa Barbara.

Cather, Willa

1991. Cary, Richard. "A Willa Cather collection." Colby Library quarterly, 8, no.2 (1968), 82-95.

Books, periodicals, letters, and manuscripts by and about Willa Cather in Colby College Library.

Cooper, James Fenimore

1992. Barnes, Warner. "American first editions at T x U. XIII. James Fenimore Cooper (1789-1851)." Library chronicle of the University of Texas, 7, no.2 (1962), 15-18.

Crane, Hart

1993. Katz, Joseph, and others, eds. Twenty-one letters from Hart Crane to George Bryan. Columbus: Ohio State Univ. Libraries, 1968. 22p. (Ohio State University Libraries publications, no.4)

Collections owned by Ohio State University Libraries.

1994. Lohf, Kenneth A. The literary manuscripts of Hart Crane. Columbus: Ohio State Univ. Pr., 1967. 152p. (Calendars of American literary manuscripts)

Records holdings of Hart Crane manuscripts and correspondence in the Ohio State University and several other libraries.

Crapsey, Adelaide

1995. Smith, Susan Sutton. "Adelaide Crapsey: materials for a biographical and textual study." University of Rochester Library bulletin, 25 (Autumn-Winter, 1969-70), 3-32.

Description of collection of papers relating to poetess.

Davenport, Marcia

1996. [U.S. Library of Congress, Manuscript Division. Marcia Davenport papers] College & research libraries news, no.5 (May 1969), 165.

Description of important group of literary manuscripts and correspondence presented to Library of Congress by Marcia Davenport, novelist and biographer.

Davis, Richard Harding

1997. Virginia, University, Library. The Barrett Library: Richard Harding Davis; a checklist of printed and manuscript works of Richard Harding Davis in the Library of the University of Virginia, comp. by Fannie Mae Elliott and Lucy Clark, manuscripts by Marjorie D. Carver. Charlottesville: Univ. of Va. Pr., 1963. 31p.

American novelist, 1864-1916.

Dickinson, Emily

1998. [Princeton University Library. Emily Dickinson collection] College & research libraries news, no.8 (Sept. 1969), 272-74.

Describes outstanding collection of works by and about New England poet Emily Dickinson, presented to Princeton.

1999. Princeton University Library. The Margaret Jane Pershing collection of Emily Dickinson, presented to the Princeton University Library. Catalogue comp. by Robert S. Fraser. Princeton, N.J., 1969. 23p.

Downing, J. Hyatt

2000. Wadden, Anthony T. "J. Hyatt Downing: the chronicle of an era." Books at Iowa, 8 (April 1968), 11-18, 23.

Manuscripts of a novelist and short-story writer in University of Iowa Libraries.

Eliot, T. S.

2001. Gallup, Donald. "The 'lost' manuscripts of T. S. Eliot." Bulletin of the New York Public Library, 72 (1968), 641-52.

Description and collection of "The Waste Land" manuscripts in New York Public Library's Berg collection.

2002. Northwestern University Library. A list of books by and about T. S. Eliot, James Joyce, D. H. Lawrence, Dylan Thomas, and W. B. Yeats in Deering Library. Evanston, Ill., 1961. 73*l.*

2003. Sackton, Alexander. "T. S. Eliot at Texas." Library chronicle of the University of Texas, 8, no.3 (1967), 22-26.

Description of special collection of Eliot books and manuscripts in University of Texas Library.

2004. Texas, University, Humanities Research Center. An exhibition of manuscripts and first editions of T. S. Eliot. Austin, 1961. 48p.

Emerson, Ralph Waldo

2005. Harding, Walter. Emerson's library. Charlottesville: Univ. Pr. of Va., 1967. 338p.

Catalog of Emerson's books; almost all are in Concord (Mass.) Antiquarian Society Library.

Faulkner, William

2006. Princeton University Library. The literary career of William Faulkner: a bibliographical study, by James B. Meriwether. Princeton, N.J., 1961. 192p.

Catalog of an exhibition in the Princeton Library.

2007. [Virginia, University, Library. Faulkner collection] College & research libraries, no.6 (June 1970), 184-85.

Brief description of William Faulkner manuscripts, typescripts, books, and other materials, presented to University of Virginia Library.

2008. Virginia, University, Library. William Faulkner: "Man working," 1919-1962; a catalogue of the William Faulkner collections at the University of Virginia, comp. by Linton R. Massey. Charlottesville: Univ. Pr. of Va., 1968. 2v.

Frost, Robert

2009. New York University Libraries, Division of Special Collections. Checklist of Robert Frost library. N.Y., 1970. 99p.

2010. U.S. Library of Congress, Reference Dept. Robert Frost: a backward look by Louis Untermeyer, with selective bibliography of Frost manuscripts, separately published works, recordings, and motion pictures in the collections of the Library of Congress. Wash.: The Library, 1964. 40p.

2011. Virginia, University, Library. Clifton Waller Barrett Library: Robert Frost, 1874-1963; an exhibition of books, manuscripts and memorabilia. Charlottesville, 1966. 18p.

Gardner, Isabella

2012. [Washington University Libraries, St. Louis. Isabella Gardner papers] College & research libraries news, no.4 (April 1970), 101.

About 1,000 letters from prominent writers received by Isabella Gardner, American poetess, in Washington University Libraries.

Garland, Hamlin

2013. Huntington Library. Hamlin Garland's diaries, ed. by Donald Pizer. San Marino, Calif., 1968. 281p.

Selections from 43 manuscript volumes in Huntington Library.

2014. Southern California, University, Library. Hamlin Garland: centennial tributes and a checklist of the Hamlin Garland papers in the University of Southern California Library, ed. by Lloyd A. Arvidson. Los Angeles, 1962. 159p. (Library bulletin, no.9)

Glasgow, Ellen

2015. Kelly, William W. Ellen Glasgow: a bibliography, ed. by Oliver L. Steele. Charlottesville: Univ. Pr. of Va., 1964. 330p.

Catalog of collection of Glasgow correspondence and manuscripts in University of Virginia Library.

Hawthorne, Julian

2016. Bassan, Maurice. "Papers of Julian Hawthorne at Yale." Yale University Library gazette, 39 (1964), 85-89.

Describes collection, now in Yale Library, of notebooks, letters, and diary of Nathaniel Hawthorne's son.

Hawthorne, Nathaniel

2017. Bowdoin College Library. Hawthorne and Longfellow, a guide to an exhibit, by Richard B. Harwell. Brunswick, Maine, 1966. 65p.

Based primarily on Bowdoin's holdings, but supplemented by other collections.

2018. [Bowdoin College Library, Brunswick, Maine. Hawthorne collection] College & research libraries news, no.4 (April 1970), 97.

Extensive collection of books from Nathaniel Hawthorne's library, acquired by Bowdoin.

2019. Ohio State University Libraries. An exhibition of books, manuscripts, and letters of Nathaniel Hawthorne. Columbus, 1964. 8p.

Hellman, Lillian

2020. Texas, University, Humanities Research Center. The Lillian Hellman collection at the University of Texas, comp. by Manfred Triesch. Austin: Univ. of Tex. Pr., 1968. 167p.

2021. Triesch, Manfred. "The Lillian Hellman collection." Library chronicle of the University of Texas, 8, no.1 (1965), 17-20.

Description of collection of manuscripts, containing drafts of all dramas thus far released, in University of Texas Library.

Hemingway, Ernest

2022. Baker, Carlos. "Letters from Hemingway." Princeton University Library chronicle, 24 (1963), 101-7.

Summarizes contents of Princeton's collection of Hemingway letters.

2023. Davies, John D. "New Hemingway letters." Princeton alumni weekly, 63 (16 Nov. 1962), 11.

Describes collection of 150 letters written by Hemingway, 1945-61, to Major General Charles T. Lanham, in Princeton Library.

2024. Westbrook, Max. "Necessary performance: The Hemingway collection at Texas." Library chronicle of the University of Texas, 7, no.4 (1964), 26-31.

Description of books, manuscripts, and inscriptions to Lee Samuels in University of Texas Library.

Hergesheimer, Joseph

2025. Slate, Joseph E. "The Joseph Hergesheimer collection." Library chronicle of the University of Texas, 7, no.1 (1961), 24-31.

Description of special collection of books and manuscripts in University of Texas Library.

2026. Texas University, Humanities Research Center. Joseph Hergesheimer, American man of letters, 1880-1954; an exhibition. Austin, 1961. 34p.

Higginson, Thomas Wentworth

2027. Cary, Richard. "More Higginson letters." Colby Library quarterly, 7, no.1 (1965), 33-48.

Letters of Thomas Wentworth Higginson, 1823-1911, American author, reformer, and soldier, in Colby College Library.

Hillyer, Robert Silliman

2028. Syracuse University Library. Robert Silliman

Hillyer, comp. by John S. Patterson. Syracuse, N.Y., 1964. 117p. (Manuscript register series, no.5)

Poet and English professor, Pulitzer prize winner, and president of Poetry Society of America.

Holmes, John

2029. Erdelyi, Gabor, and Glavin, Mary A. "John Holmes: a bibliography of published and unpublished writings in the special collections of the Tufts University Library." Bulletin of the New York Public Library, 73 (1969), 375-97.

New England poet (1904-62).

Howells, William Dean

2030. Cary, Richard. "William Dean Howells to Thomas Sergeant Perry." Colby Library quarterly, 8, no.4 (1968), 157-215.

Howells letters to Perry in Colby College Library.

2031. Kirk, Rudolf, and Kirk, Clara M. "Kirk-Howells collection." University of Pennsylvania Library chronicle, 35 (1969), 67-74.

Description of a collection of books and manuscripts by and about William Dean Howells in University of Pennsylvania Library.

2032. Reeves, John K. "The literary manuscripts of W. D. Howells, a supplement to the descriptive finding list." Bulletin of the New York Public Library, 65 (1961), 465-76.

Copies located; supplements list published in 1958.

James, Henry

2033. Bixler, J. Seelye. "James family letters in Colby College Library." Colby Library quarterly, 9, no.1 (1970), 35-47.

Family of Henry and William James.

2034. Donovan, Alan B. "My dear Pinker: the correspondence of Henry James with his literary agent." Yale University Library gazette, 36 (1961), 78-88.

Describes collection of 480 letters in Yale Library.

2035. Virginia, University, Library. Clifton Waller Barrett Library: Henry James, 1843-1916; an exhibition of books, manuscripts and portraits arranged on the fiftieth year of his death. Charlottesville, 1966. 31p.

Jarrell, Randall

2036. U.S. Library of Congress. Randall Jarrell, lecture by Karl J. Shapiro, with a bibliography of Jarrell materials in the collections of the Library of Congress. Wash., 1967. 47p.

Jeffers, Robinson

2037. Alabama, University, Library. The Robinson Jeffers collection in the rare book room, University of Alabama Library, comp. by Sarah A. Verner and Catherine T. Jones. University, 1961. Unpaged.

Jewett, Sarah Orne

2038. Colby College Library. Sarah Orne Jewett letters, enlarged and revised edition, ed. by Richard Cary. Waterville, Maine: Colby College Pr., 1967. 186p.

Collection in Colby College Library.

Johnson, Josephine

2039. [Washington University Libraries, St. Louis. Josephine Johnson papers] College & research libraries news, no.6 (June 1970), 182.

Brief description of correspondence and literary manuscripts of Pulitzer-prize-winning novelist, presented to Washington University.

Lewis, Wyndham

2040. Cornell University Libraries. Wyndham Lewis at Cornell; a review of the Lewis papers presented to the University by William G. Mennen, by William K. Rose. Ithaca, N.Y., 1961. 18p.

Papers of American-British literary critic and author, 1886-1957.

Longfellow, Henry Wadsworth

2041. Bush, Sargent, Jr. "Longfellow's letters to Cornelia Fitch." Books at Iowa, 6 (April 1967), 13-18, 23.

Concerns 8 unpublished letters owned by University of Iowa Library.

Masters, Edgar Lee

2042. Robinson, Kee. "The Edgar Lee Masters collection: sixty years of literary history." Library chronicle of the University of Texas, 8, no.4 (1968), 42-49.

Description of manuscripts, notebooks, and some 12,000 items of correspondence in University of Texas Library.

Melville, Herman

2043. Star, Morris. "A checklist of portraits of Herman

Melville." Bulletin of the New York Public Library, 71 (1967), 468-73.

Copies located.

Mencken, Henry Louis

2044. Adler, Betty. "Mencken room." Maryland libraries, 32 (Spring 1966), 11-13.

Describes H. L. Mencken collection in Enoch Pratt Free Library, Baltimore.

2045. ———, and Wilhelm, Jane. HLM: The Mencken bibliography. Baltimore: Johns Hopkins Univ. Pr., 1961. 367p.

Based in part on Enoch Pratt Free Library collection, Baltimore.

Miller, Arthur

2046. Wilkinson, Richard T. Arthur Miller manuscripts at the University of Texas. 1964. 78p. (Master's thesis, Graduate School of Library Science, Univ. of Tex.)

More, Paul Elmer

2047. Hanford, James H. "The Paul Elmer More papers." Princeton University Library chronicle, 22 (1961), 163-68.

Describes More manuscripts and correspondence in Princeton collection; More was an American literary critic and philosopher, 1864-1937.

Morley, Christopher

2048. Bracker, Jon. "The Christopher Morley collection." Library chronicle of the University of Texas, 7, no.2 (1962), 19-35.

Description of University of Texas' extensive holdings of books, manuscripts, letters, and Morley's personal library of some 10,000 volumes.

2049. Kuehl, John. "The Armstrong Morley collection." Princeton University Library chronicle, 23 (1961), 130-32.

Describes Christopher Morley collection in Princeton Library.

2050. Texas, University, Humanities Research Center. An exhibition of C. D. M. manuscripts & first editions, comp. by Jon Bracker. Austin, 1961. 48p.

Catalog of Christopher D. Morley exhibition drawn from Texas collection.

O'Hara, John

2051. Mann, Charles. "The John O'Hara manuscripts at Penn State." Manuscripts, 20, no.4 (1968), 47-49.

O'Neill, Eugene

2052. [New York Public Library. Eugene O'Neill collection] College & research libraries news, no.1 (Jan. 1970), 8.

Collection of unpublished letters and poems presented to New York Public Library.

Pattee, Fred Lewis

2053. Pennsylvania State University Library. Fred Lewis Pattee; calendar of papers for pioneer critic and historian of American literature. University Park, 1969. 89p.

Poe, Edgar Allan

2054. Indiana University, Lilly Library. The J. K. Lilly collection of Edgar Allan Poe; an account of its formation, by David A. Randall. Bloomington, 1964. 62p.

2055. Todd, William B. "The early . . . issues of Poe's Tales (1845)." Library chronicle of the University of Texas, 7 (Fall 1961), 13-18.

Critical analysis of variant editions in University of Texas Library.

2056. Virginia, University, Library. Guide to the microfilm edition of John Henry Ingraham's Poe collection, ed. by Paul P. Hoffman. Charlottesville, 1967. 31p. (Microfilm publication, no.4)

Pound, Ezra

2057. Texas, University, Humanities Research Center. Ezra Pound, an exhibition, comp. by David Farmer. Austin, 1967. 62p.

Rexroth, Kenneth

2058. California, University, Library. Kenneth Rexroth: a checklist of his published writings, by James Hartzell and Richard Zumwinkle. Los Angeles: Friends of the UCLA Library, 1967. 67p.

Largely represents materials in UCLA Library relating to contemporary American author, critic, and painter.

Richards, Laura E.

2059. Cary, Richard. "Some Richards manuscripts and correspondence." Colby Library quarterly, 5, no.12 (1961), 344-56.

Autograph materials by and to Laura E. Richards in Colby College Library.

Robinson, Edwin Arlington

2060. Cary, Richard, ed. Edwin Arlington Robinson letters to Edith Brower. Cambridge, Mass.: The Belknap Pr. of the Harvard Univ. Pr., 1968. 226p.

Collection in Colby College Library.

2061. Cary, Richard. "The library of Edwin Arlington Robinson: addenda." Colby Library quarterly, 7, no.9 (1967), 398-415.

Recent additions to special collection in Colby College Library.

2062. ———. "Robinson books and periodicals." Colby Library quarterly, 8, no.5 (1969), 266-77; 8, no.6 (1969), 334-43; 8, no.7 (1969), 399-413; 8, no.8 (1969), 479-87.

Edwin Arlington Robinson collection in Colby College Library.

2063. U.S. Library of Congress. Edwin Arlington Robinson: a reappraisal by Louis Untermeyer; with a bibliography by William J. Studer, and a list of materials in the Edwin Arlington Robinson exhibit on display at the Library of Congress. Wash.: Govt. Print. Off., 1963. 39p.

Sandburg, Carl

2064. [Dickinson College Library, Carlisle, Pa. Sandburg collection] College & research libraries news, no.11 (Dec. 1969), 387-88.

Description of collection of Carl Sandburg manuscripts, letters, books, photographs, and other memorabilia, acquired by Dickinson Library.

2065. Flanagan, John T. "Presentation copies in the Sandburg library." College & research libraries, 24 (1963), 47-52.

Based on Carl Sandburg collection, University of Illinois Library.

2066. U.S. Library of Congress. Carl Sandburg: with a bibliography of Sandburg materials in the collections of the Library of Congress, by Mark Van Doren. Wash., 1969. 83p.

2067. [Virginia, University, Library. Carl Sandburg collection] College & research libraries news, no.10 (Nov. 1970), 297.

Brief description of collection of early Sandburg letters acquired by Virginia.

Simms, William Gilmore

2068. Welsh, John R. "The Charles Carroll Simms collection." South Atlantic bulletin, 31 (Nov. 1966), 1-3.

Collection of personal notebooks, scrapbooks, manuscripts, and printed editions of writings of William Gilmore Simms, in University of South Carolina Library.

Sinclair, Upton

2069. Indiana University, Lilly Library. A catalogue of books, manuscripts, and other materials from the Upton Sinclair archives. Bloomington, 1963. 56p.

The extensive Upton Sinclair archives were acquired by Indiana University in 1957.

Smith, Logan Pearsall

2070. Heaney, Howell J. "A Logan Pearsall Smith collection." Princeton University Library chronicle, 23 (1961), 181-83.

Describes material in Princeton Library relating to American author and critic, 1865-1946.

Steinbeck, John

2071. Texas, University, Humanities Research Center. John Steinbeck; an exhibition of American and foreign editions. Austin, 1963. 31p.

Stevens, Wallace

2072. Dartmouth College Library. "A supplementing list of items in the Wallace Stevens collection at Dartmouth College." Dartmouth College Library bulletin, n.s. 4 (1961), 67-71.

Collection relating to Stevens, 1879-1955, American poet.

Stockton, Frank Richard

2073. Virginia, University, Library. The Barrett Library: Frank Richard Stockton; a checklist of printed and manuscript works of Frank Richard Stockton in the Library of the University of Virginia, comp. by Lucy Trimble Clark, manuscripts by Marjorie D. Carver. Charlottesville: Univ. of Va. Pr., 1963. 24p.

Stockton was an American novelist, 1834-1902.

Street, Julian

2074. Clark, Alexander P. "The papers of Julian Street." Princeton University Library chronicle, 23 (1961), 28-32.

Examines contents of Princeton Library collection relating to American writer, 1879-1947.

Suckow, Ruth

2075. Paluka, Frank. "Ruth Suckow: a calendar of letters." Books at Iowa, 1 (Oct. 1964), 34-40; 2 (April 1965), 31-40.

Letters, 1918-60, in University of Iowa Libraries.

Thoreau, Henry David

2076. St. Armand, Barton L. "Thoreau comes to Brown." Books at Brown, 22 (1968), 121-41.

Description of Lownes collection of Thoreauviana, including original autographed letters and manuscripts, in Brown University Library.

2077. Wayne State University Libraries. Henry David Thoreau, 1817-1862; books, manuscripts, and association items in Detroit and Ann Arbor; catalogue of a centennial exhibition, by Leo Stoller. Detroit, 1962. 13p.

Thurber, James

2078. Bowden, Edwin T. James Thurber: a bibliography. Columbus: Ohio State Univ. Pr., 1968. 353p.

Records holdings of Ohio State University Libraries on Thurber, though without specific locations.

2079. Ohio State University Libraries. James Thurber; an exhibition of books, manuscripts and drawings selected from the Thurber collection of the Ohio State University Libraries. Columbus, 1966. 12p.

2080. [Ohio State University Libraries. Thurber collection] College & research libraries news, no.6 (June 1969), 195.

Extensive collection of letters, drafts of manuscripts, typescripts, etc., relating to James Thurber, received by O.S.U. Libraries.

Ticknor, George

2081. Dartmouth College Library. The George Ticknor Room in Baker Memorial Library at Dartmouth College. Hanover, N.H., 1964. 4p.

Brief description of collection in Dartmouth Library, relating to George Ticknor, 1791-1871, American literary historian and educator.

Twain, Mark

2082. [Illinois, University, Library. Mark Twain collection] College & research libraries news, no.9 (Oct. 1969), 335.

Describes extensive collection of Mark Twain's published writings and many Twain memorabilia acquired by Illinois, the Franklin J. Meine collection.

2083. Northeast Missouri State College Library. Mark Twain holdings in the Missouriana Library, comp. by David S. Webb and Paul O. Selby. Kirksville, 1968. 62, 31p.

2084. ———, Missouriana Library. Theses on Mark Twain, 1910-1967, comp. by P. O. Selby. Kirksville, 1969. Unpaged.

2085. [Wake Forest University Library. Mark Twain collection] College & research libraries news, no.9 (Oct. 1970), 275.

Describes collection of first editions, letters, and other materials relating to Twain, acquired by Wake Forest University Library, Winston-Salem, North Carolina.

2086. Welland, Dennis. "Mark Twain's last travel book." Bulletin of the New York Public Library, 69 (1965), 31-48.

Manuscript, typescript, and related correspondence in Berg collection, New York Public Library.

Viereck, George Sylvester

2087. Johnson, Neil M. "George Sylvester Viereck: poet and propagandist." Books at Iowa, 9 (Nov. 1968), 22-24, 29-36.

Papers of controversial early 20th-century journalist and poet, in University of Iowa Library.

Wharton, Edith

2088. West Virginia University Library. Edith Wharton: a bibliography, by Vito J. Brenni. Morgantown, 1966. 99p.

Includes about 700 titles by and about Edith Wharton; locates rare items.

White, William Allen

2089. Kansas State Teachers College Library. A bibliography of William Allen White, prep. . . .from the William Allen White collection, William Allen White Library, Kansas State Teachers College. Emporia: Teachers College Pr., 1969. 2v.

Whitman, Walt

2090. [Boston University Library. Whitman collection] College & research libraries news, no.6 (June 1970), 182.

Describes "one of the largest Walt Whitman collections in the country" given to Boston University.

2091. Broderick, John C. "The greatest Whitman collector and the greatest Whitman collection." U.S. Library of Congress quarterly journal, 27 (April 1970), 109-28.

Charles E. Feinberg collection in Library of Congress.

2092. Duke University Library. A bibliography of Walt Whitman: being the catalog of the Trent collection of Duke University, comp. by Ellen F. Frey, and a concise bibliography of the works of Walt Whitman by Carolyn Wells and Alfred F. Goldsmith. Port Washington, N.Y.: Kennikat, 1965. 2v. in 1.

2093. Golden, Arthur. "New light on Leaves of grass: Whitman's annotated copy of the 1860 (third) edition." Bulletin of the New York Public Library, 69 (1965), 283-306.

Study of the "Blue Book" in New York Public Library's Lion-Whitman collection.

2094. [U.S. Library of Congress. Whitman collection] College & research libraries news, no.9 (Oct. 1969), 337.

Major assemblage of Walt Whitman manuscripts, books, and memorabilia, Charles E. Feinberg collection, "probably the largest and most important collection of Whitman material ever assembled."

2095. Virginia, University, Library. The Barrett Library: Walt Whitman; a checklist of printed and manuscript works of Walt Whitman in the Library of the University of Virginia, comp. by Fannie Mae Elliott and Lucy T. Clark. Manuscripts section by Marjorie D. Carver. Charlottesville: Univ. of Va. Pr., 1961. 97p.

2096. "Walt Whitman: the man and the poet: catalog of the sesquicentennial exhibit held in the Library of Congress." Quarterly journal of the Library of Congress, 27 (1970), 171-76.

2097. Whitman, Walt. Walt Whitman's Blue book; the 1860-61 Leaves of grass containing his manuscript additions and revisions. Vol. I Facsimile of the unique copy in the Oscar Lion collection [New York Public Library]; Vol. II Textual analysis by Arthur Golden. N.Y.: New York Public Library, 1968. 2v.

Williams, William Carlos

2098. Westlake, Neda M. "William Carlos Williams; an exhibition of a collection." University of Pennsylvania Library chronicle, 32 (1966), 74-78.

Collection of inscribed first editions in University of Pennsylvania Library.

Winslow, Anne Goodwin

2099. Memphis State University Library. Anne Goodwin Winslow; an annotated checklist of her published works and of her papers, ed. by Helen White. Memphis, Tenn., 1969. 57p.

Collection in Mississippi Valley Collection, Memphis State University Library, of American poetess' works.

Wister, Owen

2100. Mason, Julian D. "Owen Wister, boy librarian." Quarterly journal of the Library of Congress, 26 (1969), 200-12.

The Owen Wister papers are in Library of Congress.

Wright, Richard

2101. Kent State University Libraries. Richard Wright: letters to Joe C. Brown, ed. by Thomas Knipp. Kent, Ohio, 1968. 16p.

Based upon collection of Wright's letters in Kent State Library.

CANADIAN

2102. Pennsylvania State University Library. An exhibit of selected papers of Dorothy Roberts, March 20-June 1, 1967. University Park, 1967. 8p.

Papers of Canadian poetess.

ENGLISH

General

2103. Auburn University Library. A partial checklist of bibliographical sources in the Auburn University Library for students of English and American literature, prep. by John E. Warner and others. Auburn, Ala., 1961. 46p. (Occasional bibliographies, no.6)

2104. Boston Public Library. English literary manuscripts in the Boston Public Library: a checklist. Boston, 1966. 25p.

2105. Boyce, Benjamin. "English literature, 1600-1900." Gnomon (1970), 17-23. (Special number of Duke University Library's Library notes)

Describes Duke Library's holdings.

2106. Brigham Young University Library. The Roy E. Christensen collection of Victorian literature. Provo, Utah, 1970. 7p.

Description of collection of 2,000 books, letters, manuscripts, and drawings.

2107. California, University, Library, San Diego. A selected catalog of books from the library of Don Cameron Allen, Mandeville Department of Special Collections, University of California, San Diego, comp. by J. M. Edelstein. San Diego, 1968. 41p.

Sampling of 5,000 volumes of 16th- and 17th-century books relating to English and Italian literature and Renaissance.

2108. Columbia University Libraries. The Engel collection, presented by Solton and Julia Engel. N.Y.: 1967. 42p.

About 500 books, manuscripts, and original drawings; contains first and early editions of English and American authors.

2109. Harvard University Library. Catalogue of English and American chapbooks and broadside ballads in Harvard College Library, comp. by Charles Welsh and William H. Tillinghast. Detroit: Singing Tree, 1968. 171p. (Harvard University Library bibliographical contributions, no.56)

2110. ———. Celtic literatures. Cambridge, Mass., 1970. 192p. (Widener Library shelflist series, no.25)

Lists about 8,000 titles for Irish, Gaelic, Welsh, Cornish, Manx, and Breton.

2111. Indiana University. Lilly Library. Grolier; or, 'Tis sixty years since; a reconstruction of the exhibit of 100 books famous in English literature. Bloomington, 1963. 48p.

Based on Lilly Library collection.

2112. [Kansas, University, Library. Eighteenth-century English literature collection] College & research libraries news, no.7 (July-Aug. 1970), 212.

Description of collection of English literature acquired by Kansas, composed primarily of 17th- and 18th-century periodicals.

2113. New York Public Library. An anniversary exhibition: the Henry W. and Albert A. Berg collection 1940-1965, by John D. Gordan. N.Y., 1965. 48p. (Reprinted from Bulletin of the New York Public Library, 69 [1965], 537-54, 597-608, 665-77)

Rare editions and manuscripts of English and American authors in New York Public Library.

2114. ———. Dictionary catalog of the Albert A. and Henry W. Berg collection of English and American literature. Boston: G. K. Hall, 1969. 5v.

2115. ———. New in the Berg collection, 1959-61; an exhibition, by John D. Gordan. N.Y., 1964. 36p. (Reprinted from Bulletin of the New York Public Library, 67 [1963], 625-38; 68 [1964], 6-12, 73-82)

Rare editions and manuscripts of English and American authors acquired by New York Public Library.

2116. Pennsylvania State University Library. Checklist of holdings in English literature before 1641. University Park, 1964. 6p.

2117. Pondrom, Cyrena N. English literary periodicals: 1885-1918. Ann Arbor, Mich.: University Microfilms, 1966. 370*l.* (Ph.D. thesis, Columbia Univ.)

Chronological listing; locates files in 6 U.S. and 3 English collections.

2118. Princeton University Library. Landmarks of English literature; an exhibition. Princeton, N.J., 1964? 7p.

2119. Schulz, Herbert C. "English literary manuscripts in the Huntington Library." Huntington Library quarterly, 31 (1968), 251-302.

2120. Southern Illinois University Library. The Irish collection. Carbondale, 1970. 10p.

Description of manuscript and book holdings in modern Irish literature: Joyce, O'Casey, O'Nolan, Yeats, etc.

2121. Taylor, Charles E. A bibliographical study of the University of Iowa Special Collections Department holdings of English books within the period 1475-1700, with analyses of selected editions of literary interest. Iowa City, 1967. 196*l.* (M.A. thesis, Dept of English, Univ. of Iowa).

Poetry

2122. Brown, Carleton F., and Robbins, Rossell H. The index of Middle English verse. Supplement. Lexington: Univ. of Ky. Pr., 1965. 551p.

Supplement to work published in 1943; expands 2,300 entries and adds 1,500 new entries; locates manuscripts.

Drama

2123. Bush, Alfred L. "The Jacobean and Caroline stage; quartos from Princeton collections." Princeton University Library chronicle, 30 (1969), 77-89.

Notes on exhibit at Princeton.

2124. Omans, Stuart. "Newberry Library: English Renaissance drama from the Silver collection." In: Research opportunities in Renaissance drama, 11 (1968), 59-63.

2125. Stratman, Carl J. Bibliography of English printed tragedy, 1565-1900. Carbondale: Southern Ill. Univ. Pr., 1966. 843p.

Includes locations for collections, anthologies, and extant manuscripts; 6,852 entries for 1,483 titles.

2126. ———. "Survey of the Huntington Library's holdings in the field of English printed drama." Huntington Library quarterly, 24 (1961), 171-74.

Fiction

2127. Booth, Bradford A. "An analytical subject-index to the Sadleir collection." Nineteenth-century fiction, 23 (1968), 217-20.

Discussion of subject index proposed for the Sadleir collection of 19th-century fiction in University of California Library at Los Angeles Library.

2128. Gordan, John D. "Novels in manuscript; an exhibition from the Berg collection." Bulletin of the New York Public Library, 69 (1965), 317-29, 396-413. Reprinted. 40p.

Manuscripts of works by well-known English and American authors in New York Public Library.

2129. Illinois, University Library. English prose fiction, 1700-1800, in the University of Illinois Library, comp. by William H. McBurney and Charles M. Taylor. Urbana: Univ. of Ill. Pr., 1965. 162p.

Records 966 titles or variants.

2130. Kelly, Doris B. "A checklist of nineteenth-century English fiction about the decline of Rome." Bulletin of the New York Public Library, 72 (1968), 400-13.

Copies located in a half dozen U.S. libraries.

2131. New York University Libraries. Checklist of the Fales collection of the English and American novel, ed. by Joel W. Egerer. N.Y., 1963. 2v.

2132. ———. The Fales collection, a record of growth, by John T. Winterich. N.Y., 1963. 31p.

Collection of American and English fiction in New York University Libraries.

2133. Princeton University Library. "Manuscripts additions to the Parrish collection." Princeton University Library chronicle, 23 (1961), 32-33.

Collection of Victorian novels in Princeton Library.

2134. Ray, Gordon N. Bibliographical resources for the study of nineteenth century English fiction. Los Angeles: School of Library Service, Univ. of Calif., 1964. 31p.

Details of holdings of 130 selected books in U.S. and British libraries, according to total titles held and titles held in original condition.

2135. Sadleir, Michael. Passages from the autobiography of a bibliomaniac. Los Angeles: Univ. of Calif. Library, 1962. 38p.

Marking exhibit of books from Sadleir collection of 19th-century fiction, in UCLA Library.

Individual Authors

Barrie, J. M.

2136. Mott, Howard S. "The Walter Beinecke Jr. J. M. Barrie collection." Yale University Library gazette, 39 (1965), 163-67.

Collection acquired by Yale Library.

Bennett, Arnold

2137. Gordan, John D. "Arnold Bennett, the centenary of his death." Bulletin of the New York Public Library, 72 (1968), 72-112. Reprinted. 60p.

Catalog of exhibition of manuscripts and first editions drawn from the New York Public Library's Berg collection.

Blake, William

2138. Huntington Library. Catalogue of William Blake's drawings and paintings in the Huntington Library, by C. H. C. Baker, rev. by R. R. Wark. San Marino, Calif., 1969. 55p.

Blunden, Edmund

2139. Lacey, Henry C. The Iowa Blunden collection: a catalogue. Iowa City, 1967. 278*l.* (Master's thesis, Dept. of English, Univ. of Iowa)

Description of literary manuscripts and letters of Edmund Blunden, English poet, in University of Iowa Libraries.

Bridges, Robert

2140. South Carolina, University, Library. The Ewelme collection of Robert Bridges, a catalogue, by William S. Kable. Columbia: Dept. of English, Univ. of S.C., 1967. 35p.

Exhibit catalog based on collection acquired by University of South Carolina Library.

Browning, Robert and Elizabeth

2141. Barnes, Warner. A bibliography of Elizabeth Barrett Browning. Austin: Univ. of Tex. Humanities Research Center and Baylor Univ. Armstrong Browning Library, 1967. 179p.

Based on holdings of Baylor and University of Texas Libraries.

2142. ———. "The Browning collection." Library chronicle of the University of Texas, 7, no.3 (1963), 12-13.

Description of University of Texas' comprehensive Robert and Elizabeth Barrett Browning collection.

2143. Baylor University Library. The Pied Piper of Hamelin in the Armstrong Browning Library, Baylor University; a catalogue of materials relating to Browning's poem. Waco, Tex., 1968? 27p.

2144. Texas, University, Humanities Research Center. Catalogue of the Browning collection, comp. by Warner Barnes. Austin, 1966. 120p. (Bibliographical series, no.3)

Includes Robert and Elizabeth Barrett Browning books, manuscripts, and letters.

Buchan, John

2145. Hanna, Archibald, Jr. "A John Buchan collection." Yale University Library gazette, 37 (1962), 25-29.

Describes collection of 400 volumes relating to Buchan, 1875-1940, acquired by Yale Library; relates to English author and governor general of Canada.

Bunyan, John

2146. Smith, David E. "Publication of John Bunyan's works in America." Bulletin of the New York Public Library, 66 (1962), 630-52.

Checklist of American editions, p.644-52, locates copies in New York Public Library and American Antiquarian Society Library.

Burns, Robert

2147. Nevada, University, Library. Robert Burns; an exhibition in the Noble H. Getchell Library of the University of Nevada, catalog by G. Ross Roy. Reno: Univ. of Nev. Pr., 1962. 27p.

Byron, George Gordon

2148. Marshall, William H. "The Byron collection in memory of Meyer Davis, Jr." University of Pennsylvania Library chronicle, 33 (1967), 8-29.

Chaucer, Geoffrey

2149. Huntington Library. The Ellesmere manuscript of Chaucer's Canterbury tales, by Herbert C. Schulz. San Marino, Calif., 1966. 26p.

Clough, Arthur Hugh

2150. New York Public Library: Arthur Hugh Clough; a descriptive catalogue: poetry, prose, biography, and criticism, by Richard M. Gollin, Walter E. Houghton, and Michael Timko. N.Y., 1968. 117p.

Works of British writer, 1819-61, in New York Public Library.

Cobbett, William

2151. Osborne, John W. "Recent acquisitions of the William Cobbett collection in the Rutgers University Library." Journal of the Rutgers University Library, 26 (1963), 60-64.

Additions to outstanding collection of Cobbettiana in Rutgers University Library.

Coleridge, Samuel Taylor

2152. Stephens, Fran. "The Coleridge collection: a sample." Library chronicle of the University of Texas at Austin, n.s. no.1 (1970), 33-38.

Description of Coleridge family papers, particularly those of Hartley Coleridge, in University of Texas Library.

Congreve, William

2153. [Tennessee, University, Library. Congreve collection] College & research libraries news, no.10 (Nov. 1968), 345.

Important collection of works by and about William Congreve, 1670-1729, English dramatist, and concerning English drama and theatre of 16th and 17th centuries, acquired by Tennessee.

2154. Tennessee, University, Library. The John C. Hodges collection of William Congreve in the University of Tennessee Library: a bibliographical catalog, by Albert M. Lyles and John Dobson, Knoxville, 1970. 135p.

Cowper, William

2155. Ryskamp, Charles. "William Cowper and his circle; a study of the Hannay collection." Princeton University Library chronicle, 24 (1962), 3-26.

Describes books and manuscripts by and about Cowper in Princeton Library.

De la Mare, Walter

2156. Temple University Libraries. Walter De la Mare, an exhibition of books, letters, manuscripts. Philadelphia, 1969. 11p.

Defoe, Daniel

2157. Boston Public Library. A catalog of the Defoe collection in the Boston Public Library. Boston: G. K. Hall, 1966. 200p.

Represents 360 Defoe titles in about 900 editions or variants.

Dickens, Charles

2158. California, University, Library. An Oliver Twist exhibition, by Richard A. Vogler. Los Angeles, 1970. 16p.

2159. Collins, Philip. "The texts of Dickens' readings." Bulletin of the New York Public Library, 74 (1970), 360-80.

Descriptions of Dickens' personal copies of texts from which he gave public readings; now in Berg collection, New York Public Library.

2160. Gimbel, Richard. "An exhibition of 150 manuscripts, illustrations, and first editions of Charles Dickens to commemorate the 150th anniversary of his birth." Yale University Library gazette, 37 (1962), 45-93.

Catalog of 150 items with detailed descriptions, shown in Yale Library.

2161. Huntington Library. Charles Dickens 1812-1870: an anniversary exhibition. San Marino, Calif., 1962. 8p.

2162. New York Public Library. Charles Dickens, 1812-1870: an anthology. N.Y.: New York Public Library and Arno Press, 1970. 165p.

Based on exhibition of material from Berg collection, New York Public Library.

2163. New York University Libraries. Charles Dickens in the Fales library, by Joel W. Egerer. N.Y.: 1965. 44p. (NYU Libraries bibliographical series, no.3)

2164. Szladits, Lola L. "Dickens and his illustrators." Bulletin of the New York Public Library, 74 (1970), 350-80.

Describes material in Berg collection, New York Public Library.

2165. Texas, University, Humanities Research Center. Catalogue of the Dickens collection, comp. by Mary Callista Carr. Austin, 1961. 195p. (Bibliographical series, no.1)

Lists first editions, manuscripts, and Dickensiana in University of Texas Library.

2166. ——— ———. A catalogue of the Vander Poel Dickens collection, 2d ed., comp. by Lucile Carr, Austin: Univ. of Tex. Pr., 1968. 274p. (Tower bibliographical series, no.1)

Dunsany, Lord

2167. Stoddard, F. G. "The Lord Dunsany collection." Library chronicle of the University of Texas, 8, no.3 (1967), 27-32.

Description of University of Texas Library's collection of some 870 items, including 13 manuscripts and 43 manuscript notebooks.

Durrell, Lawrence

2168. California, University Library. Lawrence Durrell: a checklist, comp. by Robert A. Potter and Brooke Whiting. Los Angeles, 1961. 50p.

UCLA holdings indicated by asterisks; relates to contemporary British author.

Fielding, Henry

2169. Pennsylvania State University Library. Checklist of holdings for Henry Fielding. University Park, 1966. 1p.

Ford, Ford Madox

2170. Ludwig, Richard M. "Ford Madox Ford letters." Princeton University Library chronicle, 24 (1963), 148.
Describes letters by and to English novelist in Princeton collection.

Hardy, Thomas

2171. Bowden, Ann. "The Thomas Hardy collection." Library chronicle of the University of Texas, 7, no.2 (1962), 7-14.
Description of University of Texas' collection of books, manuscripts, and architectural drawings relating to Thomas Hardy.

Hopkins, Gerard Manley

2172. Gonzaga University Library. Hopkins collected at Gonzaga, by Ruth Seelhammer. Chicago: Loyola Univ. Pr., 1970. 272p.
Lists 3,301 items in Gerard Manley Hopkins collection in Gonzaga University Library; relate to English poet and critic, 1844-89.

Hopkins, Kenneth

2173. Texas, University, Library. A checklist of Kenneth Hopkins, by Anthony Newnham. Austin: Univ. of Tex. Humanities Research Center, 1961. 12p.
Lists University of Texas Library's holdings of works of contemporary British writer.

Housman, A. E.

2174. Indiana University, Lilly Library. A. E. Housman; a collection of manuscripts, letters, proofs, first editions, etc., prep. by David A. Randall. Bloomington, 1961. 37p.

2175. ———. The John Carter collection of A. E. Housman. Bloomington, 1965? 6p.

Hudson, William Henry

2176. Hill, James J., Jr. and Brack, O. M., Jr. "First editions of William Henry Hudson." Library chronicle of the University of Texas, 8, no.1 (1965), 45-46.
Description of special collection of books in University of Texas Library, by Hudson, 1841-1922, English author and naturalist.

Hunt, Leigh

2177. Brewer, Luther. "Leigh Hunt association books." Books at Iowa, 1 (Oct. 1964), 4-10.
In University of Iowa Library.

2178. Colburn, Gail C. A bibliographical description of the Leigh Hunt collection at the University of Iowa. Iowa City, 1965. 157*l.* (Master's thesis, Univ. of Iowa)

Huxley, Aldous

2179. California, University, Library. Aldous Huxley at UCLA; a catalogue of the manuscripts in the Aldous Huxley collection, ed. by George Wickes. Los Angeles, 1964. 36p.

2180. [New York State University, College of Arts and Sciences Library, Geneseo. Aldous Huxley collection] College & research libraries news, no.4 (April 1970), 102.
Comprehensive collection of Huxley's published works, first editions, etc., received at Geneseo.

2181. Woodman, Edwin R., Jr. "The University of Houston Aldous Huxley collection." Aldus, 5 (Aug. 1966), 4-12.

Johnson, Samuel

2182. Harvard University, Houghton Library. An exhibit of books and manuscripts from the Johnsonian collection. Cambridge, Mass., 1966. 39p.

2183. Pennsylvania State University Library. Checklist of Samuel Johnson literature. University Park, 1964. 5p.

Joyce, James

2184. Appel, Alfred. James Joyce, an appreciation. Stanford, Calif.: Stanford Univ. Pr., 1964. 5p.
Essay based upon Joyce exhibition in Stanford University Libraries.

2185. Buffalo, University, Library. James Joyce's manuscripts and letters at the University of Buffalo: a catalogue. Buffalo, N.Y., 1962. 241p.
Describes about 450 items held by library.

2186. Cornell University Library. The Cornell Joyce

collection, a catalogue, by Robert E. Scholes. Ithaca, N.Y.: Cornell Univ. Pr., 1961. 225p.

Manuscripts, letters, and papers dealing primarily with James Joyce's life to 1920.

2187. Kansas, University, Libraries. A bibliography of James Joyce studies, by Robert H. Deming. Lawrence, 1964. 180p.

Largely contained in the University of Kansas Libraries.

2188. Thornton, Weldon. "Books and manuscripts by James Joyce." Library chronicle of the University of Texas, 7, no.1 (1961), 19-23.

Description of about 290 Joyce items, mainly books and pamphlets, in University of Texas Library.

Kingsley, Charles

2189. Martin, Robert B. "Manuscript sermons of Charles Kingsley." Princeton University Library chronicle, 23 (1961), 181.

Items from Princeton Library collection.

Kipling, Rudyard

2190. Princeton University Library. Something of Kipling, 1865-1965; an exhibition in the Princeton University Library. Princeton, N.J., 1965. 8p.

2191. Rice, Howard C., Jr. "Into the hold of remembrance." Princeton University Library chronicle, 22 (1961), 105-17.

Describes Rudyard Kipling material in special collection at Princeton.

2192. Syracuse University Libraries. The search for Rudyard Kipling, by Morton N. Cohen. Syracuse, N.Y., 1966. 6p.

Lawrence, D. H.

2193. Stanford University Libraries. Lawrence in the war years, by Mark Schorer. Stanford, Calif.: Stanford Univ. Pr., 1968. 15p.

Essay, with checklist of D. H. Lawrence correspondence in Stanford University Libraries.

Lawrence, T. E.

2194. Texas, University, Humanities Research Center. T. E. Lawrence: fifty letters, 1920-35; an exhibition. Austin, 1962. 42p.

Machen, Arthur

2195. Texas, University, Library. A bibliography of Arthur Machen. Austin: Univ. of Tex. Pr., 1965. 180p. (University of Texas Humanities Research Center bibliographical series, no.2)

A record of University of Texas Library's holdings.

2196. Thom, Ian W. "The Arthur Machen collection." Princeton University Library chronicle, 26 (1965), 113-14.

Describes collection received by Princeton Library.

MacNeice, Louis

2197. Stoddard, F. G. "The Louis MacNeice collection." Library chronicle of the University of Texas, 8, no.4 (1968), 50-54.

Description of books and manuscripts in University of Texas Library. Collection of material by and about MacNeice, 1907-63, British poet and dramatist.

Milton, John

2198. Indiana University, Lilly Library. An exhibit of seventeenth-century editions of writings, by John Milton. Bloomington, 1969. 24p. (Lilly Library publication, no.7)

Annotated list of 92 items drawn from Lilly Library. Includes table of American and English libraries holding more than 30 copies of separate 17th-century editions of Milton's works.

2199. Kelley, Maurice. "Milton's Dante-Della Casa-Varchi volume." Bulletin of the New York Public Library, 66 (1962), 499-504.

Work from Milton's private library now in New York Public Library.

More, Sir Thomas

2200. Gibson, Reginald W., and Patrick, J. Max. St. Thomas More, a preliminary bibliography of his works and of Moreana to the year 1750; with a bibliography of utopiana. New Haven, Conn.: Yale Univ. Pr., 1961. 499p.

Locations in American and foreign libraries.

O'Casey, Sean

2201. [New York Public Library. Sean O'Casey collection] College & research libraries news, no.8 (Sept. 1969), 274; no.9 (Oct. 1969), 335-36.

Describes "largest known assemblage of Sean O'Casey literary papers," now held by New York Public Library.

Priestley, J. B.

2202. Teagarden, Lucetta J. "The J. B. Priestley collection." Library chronicle of the University of Texas, 7, no.3 (1963), 27-32.

Description of manuscripts and letters in University of Texas Library.

2203. Texas, University, Humanities Research Center. J. B. Priestley, an exhibition of manuscripts and books. Austin, 1963. 32p.

Roberts, Morley

2204. Boll, T. E. M. "A note on Storm Jameson's presentation of the papers of Morley Roberts." University of Pennsylvania Library chronicle, 27 (1961), 125-27.

List of printed and manuscript material by and about English author in the University of Pennsylvania Library.

Sassoon, Siegfried

2205. Texas, University, Humanities Research Center. Siegfried Sassoon, a memorial exhibition, by David Farmer. Austin: Academic Center Library, Univ. of Tex., 1969. 68p.

Sassoon, 1886-1967, was English poet and novelist.

Scott, Walter

2206. Idaho, University, Library. The Earl Larrison collection of Sir Walter Scott. Moscow, 1967. Unpaged.

2207. Larrison, Earl J. "Larrison collection of Sir Walter Scott." Bookmark, 15 (1962), 5-9.

In University of Idaho Library.

2208. New York University Libraries. Sir Walter Scott in the Fales library. N.Y., 1969. 44p. (NYU Libraries bibliographical series, no.4)

2209. Peterson, Walter F. "Sir Walter Scott—a unique collection." Wisconsin Library bulletin, 65 (1969), 99-100.

Describes special collection relating to Scott in Lawrence University Library.

Shakespeare, William

2210. Alden, John. "America's first Shakespeare collection." Papers of the Bibliographical Society of America, 58 (1964), 169-73.

Description of Thomas Pennant Barton collection in Boston Public Library.

2211. Bentley, Gerald E. "Eleven Shakespeare quartos." Princeton University Library chronicle, 30 (1969), 69-76.

Bibliographical descriptions of collection received by Princeton.

2212. Gordan, John D. "The bard and the book, editions of Shakespeare in the seventeenth century, an exhibition." Bulletin of the New York Public Library, 68 (1964), 462-76. Reprinted. 23p.

Based on New York Public Library's holdings.

2213. Hastings, William T. "The richest Shakespeare collection." Books at Brown, 19 (1963), 113-42.

Description and listing of collection by and about Shakespeare acquired in 1845 in London by Brown University Library. Copies located also in Harvard, Yale, and Library Company of Philadelphia.

2214. Huntington Library. William Shakespeare 1564-1616: an exhibition. San Marino, Calif., 1964. 26p.

2215. Illinois, University, Library. An exhibition of books presented to the University of Illinois Library by Ernest Ingold—Class of 1909. Urbana, 1969. 11p.

Primarily Shakespeareana.

2216. [Princeton University Library. Shakespeare collection] College & research libraries news, no.7 (July-Aug. 1969), 236.

Describes collection of 11 first editions and other 17th-century quartos of Shakespeare plays, received by Princeton.

2217. Shattuck, Charles H. The Shakespeare promptbooks; a descriptive catalogue. Urbana: Univ. of Ill. Pr., 1965. 553p.

Locates copies; includes register of libraries with promptbook holdings.

2218. Willard, Helen D. "Shakespeare in the Harvard theatre collection." Wilson library bulletin, 38 (1963-64), 640-44.

Shaw, George Bernard

2219. Cornell University Libraries. Bernard Shaw; an

exhibition of books and manuscripts from the collection presented by Mr. Bernard Bergunder, prep. by Alison (Kyle) Kerr. Ithaca, N.Y., 1963. 19p.

2220. Masterton, Isabel Van Rensselaer. The Archibald Henderson collection of books and other materials relating to George Bernard Shaw. 1964. 211p. (Master's thesis, Univ. of N.C.)

Collection in University of North Carolina Library.

Sinclair, May

2221. Boll, T. E. M. "On the May Sinclair collection." University of Pennsylvania Library chronicle, 27 (1961), 1-15.

Collection of letters, manuscripts, and miscellanea relating to English novelist, in University of Pennsylvania Library.

Stephens, James

2222. Cary, Richard. "James Stephens at Colby College." Colby Library quarterly, 5, no.9 (1961), 224-52.

Books, periodicals, letters, and manuscripts by and about Stephens, Irish poet and novelist, 1882-1950, in Colby College Library.

Sterne, Laurence

2223. Indiana University, Lilly Library. Laurence Sterne (1713-1768); an exhibition of his writings from the collection formed by H. Bacon Collamore. Bloomington, 1962. 4p.

2224. Rousseau, G. S. "Harvard's holdings on Laurence Sterne." Harvard Library bulletin, 16 (1968), 400-1.

Brief summary of collection of manuscripts, early editions, and supporting materials.

Stevenson, Robert Louis

2225. Yale University Library. Stevenson and Kino; manuscripts from the Edwin J. Beinecke collection of Robert Louis Stevenson and the Frederick W. and Carrie S. Beinecke collection of Western Americana. New Haven, Conn., 1963? 16p.

2226. ———. Stevenson library; catalogue of a collection of writings by and about Robert Louis Stevenson, formed by Edwin J. Beinecke, comp. by George L. McKay. New Haven, Conn., 1956-61. 5v.

Swift, Jonathan

2227. Halsband, Robert. "Jonathan Swift and Swiftiana at Columbia." Columbia Library columns, 16 (May 1967), 19-23.

Description of manuscript poem and letters received by Columbia University.

2228. Huntington Library. Rage or raillery: the Swift manuscripts at the Huntington Library, by George P. Mayhew. San Marino, Calif., 1967. 190p.

An examination of more than 70 pieces of Swiftiana held by the Huntington Library.

Tennyson, Alfred, Lord

2229. Virginia, University, Library. The Tennyson collection presented to the University of Virginia in honor of Edgar Finley Shannon, Jr. Charlottesville: Univ. of Va. Pr., 1961. 52p.

Primarily a bibliography.

Tennyson, Frederick

2230. Collins, Rowland L. "The Frederick Tennyson collection." Tennyson Society publications, no.1 (1963), 57-76.

Manuscripts and memorabilia, poetry, prose works, letters, photographs, business papers, etc., of Alfred, Lord Tennyson's brother, acquired in 1961 by Lilly Library, Indiana University.

Wilde, Oscar

2231. Princeton University Library. Wilde and the nineties; an essay and an exhibition, by Richard Ellmann and others. Princeton, N.J., 1966. 64p.

Exhibition of items from Princeton Library's collection.

Wilson, Angus

2232. Iowa, University, Libraries. The Angus Wilson manuscripts in the University of Iowa Libraries, by Frederick P. W. McDowell and E. Sharon Graves. Iowa City: Friends of the University of Iowa Libraries, 1969. 16p.

Papers of contemporary British novelist and critic; description and exhibition catalog.

Wordsworth, William

2233. Cornell University Library. Wordsworth and his circle; books and manuscripts from the Cornell Wordsworth collection exhibited at the Pierpont Morgan Library. N.Y.: Spiral, 1965. 57p.

Annotated list of 58 first editions, manuscripts, etc.

2234. Indiana University, Lilly Library. The Indiana Wordsworth collection; a brief account of the collection together with a catalogue of the exhibit held in the Lilly Library on the occasion of the bicentenary of Wordsworth's birth. Bloomington, 1970. Unpaged. (Lilly Library publication, no.9)

GERMAN

2235. Faber du Faur, Curt von. "German literature collection." Yale University Library gazette, 38 (1964), 138-44.
In Yale University Library.

2236. Pennsylvania State University Library. Checklist of German literature. University Park, 1965. 19p.

2237. Yale University Library. German baroque literature: a catalogue of the collection in the Yale University Library, by Curt von Faber du Faur. New Haven, Conn.: Yale Univ. Pr., 1958-1969. 2v.

Individual Authors

Mann, Thomas

2238. Cary, Richard. "A Thomas Mann collection." Colby Library quarterly, 7, no.7 (1966), 313-33.
Books, periodicals, letters, and manuscripts by and about Mann in Colby College Library.

2239. Princeton University Library. The Thomas Mann commemoration at Princeton University October 24, 1964. Princeton, N.J., 1965. 36p.

Rilke, Rainer Maria

2240. Harvard University, Houghton Library. Katalog der Rilke-Sammlung Richard von Mises, hearb. und hrsg. von Paul Obermüller and Herbert Steiner unter Mitarbeit von Ernst Zinn. Frankfurt am Main: Insel-Verlag, 1966. 431p.
Rilke collection in Harvard Library.

2241. Kansas, University Libraries. Rilke's last year, by George C. Schoolfield. Lawrence, 1969. 73p.
"The Henry Sagan Rilke collection," p.55-73, University of Kansas Libraries.

Traven, B.

2242. Texas, University, Humanities Research Center. Catalogue of B. Traven's "Treasure of Sierra Madre," comp. by David Farmer. Austin, 1968. 22p.

SCANDINAVIAN

2243. Fancher, Pauline M. "Svenska collection at James Prendergast Free Library." The Bookmark (New York State Library), 22 (1963), 288-89.
Describes special collection of Swedish literature in Jamestown, N.Y., Public Library.

FRENCH

2244. Baldner, Ralph W. Bibliography of seventeenth-century French prose fiction. N.Y.: Columbia Univ. Pr., 1967. 197p.
Locates copies.

2245. Kentucky, University, Libraries. French plays in the University of Kentucky Library. Lexington, 1964. 26p. (Occasional contribution, no.145)

2246. Sutherland, D. M. Modern language libraries, a rapid survey of their resources in French. Oxford: Blackwell, 1963. 54p.
International list describing holdings of libraries in French studies.

Individual Authors

Balzac, Honoré de

2247. George, Albert J. Books by Balzac; a checklist of books by Honoré de Balzac, comp. from the papers of William Hobart Royce, presently in the Syracuse University collection. Syracuse, N.Y.: Syracuse Univ. Pr., 1960. 90p.
Royce collection acquired by Syracuse University Library.

Camus, Jean Pierre

2248. Syracuse University Library. The Syracuse University Library's holdings of books by Jean Pierre Camus; a description by Robert S. Fraser. 1967. 50*l.*

Maupassant, Guy de

2249. Heiman, Monica. "Maupassant and others: the Artinian collection." Library chronicle of the University of Texas, 8, no.4 (1968), 56-57.
Description of collection of books, manuscripts,

and letters of Maupassant and other 19th- and 20th-century French literary authors acquired by University of Texas Library.

Proust, Marcel

2250. Illinois, University, Library, Rare Book Room. Marcel Proust: a centennial exhibit. Urbana, 1971. 15p.

Manuscripts, letters, photographs, and other documents drawn from extensive Proust collection held by University of Illinois Library.

Rimbaud, Arthur

2251. Southwest Missouri State College Library. The William J. Jones Rimbaud collection, comp. by F. C. St. Aubyn. Springfield, 1965. 63p.

Collection relating to Jean Nicolas Arthur Rimbaud, French poet, 1854-91, in Southwest Missouri State College Library.

ITALIAN

2252. Cerreta, Florindo. "Italian plays of the Renaissance." Books at Iowa, 2 (April 1965), 26-30.

Record of University of Iowa Library's holdings.

2253. Duke University Library. An index to the pamphlets in the Guido Mazzoni collection. Durham, N.C., 1970. 24v. in 25.

Contents: Italian classics, 19th-century verse and prose, critical and biographical studies, opera librettos.

2254. Folger Shakespeare Library. Italian plays (1500-1700) in the Folger Library: a bibliography, comp. by Louise George Clubb. Florence, Italy: Leo S. Olschki, 1968. 267p.

Describes 890 titles in full bibliographical detail.

2255. Illinois, University, Library. Italian plays, 1500-1700, in the University of Illinois Library, comp. by Marvin T. Herrick. Urbana: Univ. of Ill. Pr., 1966. 92p.

Checklist of collection.

2256. Pennsylvania State University Library. Checklist of holdings in Italian books before 1600. University Park, 1967. 9p.

SPANISH, PORTUGUESE, AND LATIN AMERICAN

2257. Aguilera, Francisco. "An archive–20 years later." Library of Congress quarterly journal of current acquisitions, 20 (1963), 218-22.

The Archive of Hispanic Literature on Tape, Library of Congress.

2258. Ashcom, Benjamin B. A descriptive catalogue of the Spanish comedias sueltas in the Wayne State University Library and the private library of Professor B. B. Ashcom. Detroit: Wayne State University Libraries, 1965. 103p.

Lists 566 titles.

2259. Beardsley, Theodore S., Jr. "Hispano-classical translations (1491-1693) at the Library of the University of Pennsylvania." University of Pennsylvania Library chronicle, 29 (1963), 16-29.

Accompanied by an annotated catalog of 42 individual works and 5 collections.

2260. Boston Public Library. Catalogue of the Spanish Library and of the Portuguese books bequeathed by George Tichnor together with the collection of Spanish and Portuguese literature in the General Library, by James L. Whitney. Boston: G. K. Hall, 1970. 550p.

Reprint of 1879 edition with an appendix of "short-title listing of materials acquired since the original publication."

2261. California, University, Library. The Portuguese collection at UCLA, by Frances Zeitlin. Los Angeles, 1966. 3p.

2262. Dartmouth College Library. The Bryant Spanish collection in the Dartmouth College Library. Hanover, N.H., Undated. 4p.

Collection of about 3,000 volumes, comprehensive of history, literature, language, archeology, regional printing, etc., of Spain.

2263. Fernández, Oscar. A preliminary listing of foreign periodical holdings in the United States and Canada which give coverage to Portuguese and Brazilian language and literature. Iowa City: Univ. of Iowa, 1968. 28*l.*

Lists holdings of 106 U.S. and Canadian libraries for some 200 titles.

2264. Kentucky, University, Libraries. Spanish plays in the University of Kentucky Library. Lexington, 1964. 25p. (Occasional contribution, no.152)

2265. North Carolina, University, Library. A catalogue of "comedias sueltas" in the Library of the University of North Carolina, by William A. McKnight and Mabel B. Jones. Chapel Hill, 1965. 240p. (Library studies, no.4)

Golden Age and 18th century, representing 400 playwrights and 300 anonymous works.

2266. [Southern Methodist University Library. Spanish collection] College & research libraries news, no.1 (Jan. 1970), 10.

Collection of Spanish books, 1499-1966, relating to history of printing and bookmaking in Spain and other subjects received by Southern Methodist University Library.

2267. Texas, University, Library. A tentative list of Mexican journals in the field of humanities in the Latin American collection of the University of Texas Library. Austin, 1968. 136p.

2268. Thompson, Lawrence S. A bibliography of Spanish plays on microcards. Hamden, Conn.: Shoestring, 1968. 490p.

Lists about 6,000 plays from 16th century to present. Originals in University of Kentucky Library.

2269. U.S. Library of Congress, Hispanic Foundation. Spanish and Portuguese translations of United States books 1955-1962, a bibliography. Wash., 1963. 506p.

Individual Authors

Cervantes, Miguel de

2270. Dartmouth College Library. "The Don Quixote collection." Dartmouth College Library bulletin, n.s. 6 (1966), 85-88.

2271. Ohio State University Libraries. A catalogue of the Talfourd P. Linn collection of Cervantes materials on deposit in the Ohio State University Libraries, comp. by Dorothy Petersen Ackerman, ed. by Paul J. Kann and Rolland E. Stevens. Columbus: Ohio State Univ. Pr., 1963. 90p. (Ohio State University Libraries publication, no.1)

Gómez de la Serna, Ramón

2272. [Pittsburgh, University, Libraries. Gómez de la Serna collection] College & research libraries news, no.3 (March 1970), 76-77.

Manuscripts of books, published works, and papers of Ramón Gómez de la Serna, 1888-1963, Spanish writer, received by Pittsburgh.

Hernandez, José

2273. Benson, Nettie Lee. "Martín Fierro at the University of Texas." Library chronicle of the University of Texas, 8, no.4 (1968), 13-27.

Description of most complete collection of José Hernandez's "Martín Fierro" and related materials in University of Texas Library.

GREEK AND LATIN

2274. Alevizos, Theodore. "The modern Greek collection at Harvard University." C.N.H.S. bulletin [Center for Neo-Hellenic Studies, Austin, Texas], 3 (Winter 1969-70), 12-14.

2275. [California, University, Library. San Diego. Romero collection] College & research libraries news, no.1 (Jan. 1970), 5.

Description of 4,100-volume collection strong in Latin works of classical authors printed in 16th and 17th centuries and in Spanish history.

2276. Jackson, Donald F. "Sixteenth-century Greek editions at Iowa." Books at Iowa, 12 (April 1970), 3-12.

In University of Iowa Library.

2277. Kristeller, Paul O. Latin manuscript books before 1600; a list of the printed catalogues and unpublished inventories of extant collections, 3d ed. N.Y.: Fordham Univ. Pr., 1965. 284p.

Guide to public collections, U.S. and European.

2278. O'Donnell, Hugh F. Subject and descriptive catalog of the classical holdings of the Clementine collection of the Catholic University of America Library. 1964. 144p. (Master's thesis, Catholic Univ. of America, Dept. of Library Science)

2279. Pack, Roger A. The Greek and Latin literary texts from Greco-Roman Egypt, 2d ed. Ann Arbor: Univ. of Mich. Pr., 1965. 165p.

Locates items in libraries and museums throughout the world.

2280. Pennsylvania, University, Library. Aristotle texts and commentaries to 1700 in the University of Pennsylvania Library: a catalogue, by Lyman W. Riley. Philadelphia: Univ. of Pa. Pr., 1961. 109p.

Includes printed books and manuscripts.

2281. Stanley, D. Keith, Jr. "The Duke collections and the program in classical studies." Library notes, a bulletin issued for the Friends of Duke University Library, 39 (April 1965), 10-14.

Lists early and rare editions of classical works in Duke University Library.

2282. Willis, William H. "The Duke manuscripts in Latin." Library notes, a bulletin issued for the Friends of Duke University Library, 39 (April 1965), 15-25.

Illustrated article describing Duke University Library's collection of medieval Latin manuscripts; includes list of 40 examples, 13th to 15th centuries.

2283. ———. "Primary sources for classical, mediaeval, and Renaissance studies." Gnomon (1970), 71-81. (Special number of Duke University Library's Library notes)

Describes Duke Library's holdings.

2284. Yale University Library. Plato manuscripts: a catalogue of microfilms in the Plato microfilm project, Yale University Library, ed. by Robert S. Brumbaugh and Rulon Wells. New Haven, Conn.: 1962. 2v.

2285. ———. The Plato manuscripts; a new index. New Haven: Yale Univ. Pr., 1968. 163p.

Records extant pre-1500 Plato manuscripts, listed by library and by dialogue.

FINNO-UGRIAN

2286. Bako, Elemer. "Finno-Ugrian materials." Quarterly journal of the Library of Congress, 21 (1964), 113-23.

Report on acquisitions, Library of Congress.

JUVENILE

2287. Barnes, Bonnie J. Dorothy Cross collection of early children's books: a partial listing with annotations. Kent, Ohio, 1967. 71p. (Master's research paper, School of Library Science, Kent State Univ.)

2288. Beck, Lucy. A bibliography of juvenile holdings in the Library of Congress in classification BT10-315 (Doctrinal Theology). 1963. 100p. (Master's thesis, Dept. of Library Science, Catholic Univ. of America)

2289. Blankinship, Anne G. A bibliography of juvenile holdings in the Library of Congress in classification, DS: (History of Asia) DS5-DS902. Wash., 1961. 96p. (Master's thesis, Dept. of Library Science, Catholic Univ. of America)

2290. California Library Association, Children's and Young People's Section. Illustrations for children: the Gladys English collection. Los Angeles: Ward Ritchie Pr., 1967. 45p.

Collection of original illustrations for children's books, held at California Library Association headquarters in Berkeley.

2291. California, University, Library. The child, the artist & the book, by Donnarae MacCann. Los Angeles, 1962. 18p.

Exhibit of contemporary art in children's books, based on UCLA's collections.

2292. Canada, Mary W. "Some notes on Confederate children's books in Duke University Library." North Carolina libraries, 21 (Summer 1963), 104-6.

2293. Cao, Myra. "Some children's books by Iowa writers." Books at Iowa, 9 (Nov. 1968), 3-21.

Checklist of books by 16 authors in University of Iowa collection.

2294. Chicago, University, Library. Science in nineteenth-century children's books; an exhibition based on the Encyclopaedia Britannica historical collection of books for children. Chicago, 1966. 18p.

2295. Cole, Joan E. Bibliography of juvenile holdings in the Library of Congress in classifications E11-99 (America–General, North America, Aboriginal America, Indians of North America); F2251-2659 (Colombia, Venezuela, the Guianas, Brazil). Wash., 1963. 193*l.* (Master's thesis, School of Library Science, Catholic Univ. of America)

2296. Danes, Doris L. A bibliography of juvenile holdings in the Library of Congress in the classification CT–biography. Wash., 1961. 105p. (Master's thesis, Dept. of Library Science, Catholic Univ. of America)

2297. Danforth, Margaret V. A bibliography of juvenile holdings in the Library of Congress in classifications: BT317-1490 (Doctrinal Theology), BV1-110 (Practical Theology), F1201-1392 (Mexico), and DS903-935 (Korea). Wash., 1963. 123p. (Master's thesis, Dept. of Library Science, Catholic Univ. of America)

2298. Feldman, Mary Helen. A bibliography of juvenile holdings in the Library of Congress in classifications, BV3591 through BV4571. Wash., 1965. 91p. (Master's thesis, Dept. of Library Science, Catholic Univ. of America)

2299. Field, Carolyn W. Subject collections in children's literature. N.Y.: Bowker, 1969. 142p.

Collections listed and described alphabetically by subject, p.1-91; "Directory of collections," p.93-130, in U.S. and Canadian libraries; "Bibliography of books and articles relating to the special collections listed," p.117-30.

2300. Florida State University Library. Childhood in poetry; a catalogue, with biographical and critical annotations, of the books of English and American poets comprising the Shaw Childhood in Poetry collection in the Library of Florida State University. Detroit: Gale, 1967-68. 5v.

2301. ———. The Lois Lenski collection in the Florida State University Library, comp. by Nancy Bird, with foreword and other material by Lois Lenski. Tallahassee: Friends of the Fla. State Univ. Library, 1966. 42p.

2302. ———. What the poets have to say about childhood; an exhibition of one hundred books, opened to passages written for or about children, ed. by John Mackay Shaw. Tallahassee, 1966. 18*l.*

Collection in Florida State University Library.

2303. Gardner, Ralph D. "Alger heroes, the Merriwells, et al!" Princeton University Library chronicle, 30 (1969), 103-9.

Describes collection of juvenile hero fiction in Princeton University Library.

2304. Girsch, Mary Louise. A selected annotated bibliography of books from the Dorothy Cross collection of early children's books. Kent, Ohio, 1966. 20p. (Master's research paper, School of Library Science, Kent State Univ.)

In Kent State University Library.

2305. Gyulahazi, Maria. A bibliography of juvenile holdings in the Library of Congress in classification DC54-801. Wash., 1962. 83p. (Master's thesis, Dept. of Library Science, Catholic Univ. of America)

2306. Haviland, Virginia. "Serving those who serve children; a national reference library of children's books." Quarterly journal of the Library of Congress, 22 (1965), 301-16. Reprinted. 16p.

Analysis of Library of Congress' extensive holdings of children's books.

2307. Huckabee, Gloria Comstock. A bibliography of juvenile holdings in the Library of Congress in classification HF1-HQ100 (Economics and Sociology). Wash., 1963. 60p. (Master's thesis, Dept. of Library Science, Catholic Univ. of America)

2308. Ikena, Richard J. A bibliography of juvenile holdings in the Library of Congress in classification P-PH (except PG2000-2850): Philology–Modern European Languages. 1962. Wash., 78p. (Master's thesis, Dept. of Library Science, Catholic Univ. of America)

2309. Jenkins, Gwendolyn. A bibliography of juvenile holdings in the Library of Congress in the classification Q-QD (Science). Wash., 1963. 115p. (Master's thesis, Dept. of Library Science, Catholic Univ. of America)

2310. King, Dorothy. A bibliography of juvenile holdings in the Library of Congress in classification F, British North America–Canada–F1001-1199. Wash., 1962. 92p. (Master's thesis, Dept. of Library Science, Catholic Univ. of America)

2311. King, Frances. A bibliography of juvenile holdings in the Library of Congress in the classification GR-GT: Folklore, Manners and Customs. Wash., 1961. 91p. (Master's thesis, Dept. of Library Science, Catholic Univ. of America)

2312. Krug, Adele Jensen. A bibliography of juvenile holdings in the Library of Congress in classification G (Geography) 150-190. Wash., 1961. 104p. (Master's thesis, Dept. of Library Science, Catholic Univ. of America)

2313. Leary, Bernice M. "Milestones in children's books." Books at Iowa, 12 (April 1970), 18-22, 27-39.

In University of Iowa Libraries.

2314. Levy, Sharon. A description of non-circulating special collections of children's literature in the public libraries of the Washington Metropolitan Area. Wash., 1966. 41p. (Master's thesis, Dept. of Library Science, Catholic Univ. of America)

2315. McDonald, Murry Frank. Analysis of the American Sunday School Union publications in the old juvenile collection in the Brooklyn Public Library. 1963. 50p. (Master's thesis in Library Science, Univ. of N.C.)

2316. McLay, Hannah H. A bibliography of juvenile holdings in the Library of Congress in the classification E101-170. Wash., 1962. 94p. (Master's thesis, Dept. of Library Science, Catholic Univ. of America)

2317. Marcoux, Clara W. A bibliography of juvenile holdings in the Library of Congress classifications BS552-BS2970.S3 (the Bible and Exegesis) and H-HD (Social Sciences and Economics). Wash., 1963. 114*l.*

(Master's thesis, Dept. of Library Science, Catholic Univ. of America)

2318. Meier, Kathleen. A bibliography of juvenile holdings in the Library of Congress in classifications F2661-3799 (History of Paraguay, Uruguay, the Argentine Republic, Chile, Bolivia, Peru and Ecuador), and HE (Transportation and Communication). Wash., 1962. 75p. (Master's thesis, Dept. of Library Science, Catholic Univ. of America)

2319. Michigan, University, Library. Children's books around the world; an exhibit arranged . . . by Doreen Graham and Sarita Davis. Ann Arbor, 1966. 14*l.*

2320. Minnesota, University, Libraries. Roger Duvoisin, children's book illustrator, an exhibition from the Kerlan collection. Minneapolis, 1967. 8p.

2321. Morales, Phylliss. "Milner Library, Illinois State University Library." Illinois libraries, 47 (1965), 834-41.

Includes descriptions of several special collections of children's books, current and historical.

2322. Moses, Richard G. A bibliography of juvenile holdings in the Library of Congress in the classification ML, Literature of Music. Wash., 1961. 98p. (Master's thesis, Dept. of Library Science, Catholic Univ. of America)

2323. Nelson, Karen. "The Kerlan collection." Top of the news, 24 (1968), 181-86.

Describes major collection of children's books in University of Minnesota Library.

2324. New York Public Library. Books for the teenage, 1970. N.Y., 1970. 45p.

2325. Odland, Norine. "The Kerlan collection of children's literature in the University of Minnesota Library." Elementary English, 44 (Nov. 1967), 749-52.

2326. O'Hanlon, Mary Catherine. Bibliography of American Catholic juvenile literature, 1850-1890. Wash., 1960. 186p. (Unpublished master's thesis, Dept. of Library Science, Catholic Univ. of America)

Locates copies.

2327. Oklahoma, University, Library. The Lois Lenski collection in the University of Oklahoma Library, with a complete bibliography of her works, comp. by Esther G. Witcher. Norman: The Library and School of Library Science, 1963. 33p.

Includes books, manuscripts, and original works of art.

2328. Owen, Doris H. A bibliography of juvenile holdings in the Library of Congress in classifications CB-CS (History—Auxiliary Sciences) and QK (Botany). Wash., 1963. 96*l.* (Master's thesis, Dept. of Library Science, Catholic Univ. of America)

2329. Paine, Barbara A. A bibliography of juvenile holdings in the Library of Congress in the classification BV110-BV3540: Practical Theology. Wash., 1963. 94*l.* (Master's thesis, Dept. of Library Science, Catholic Univ. of America)

2330. Philadelphia Free Library. Children's books; reference and research collections of the Free Library of Philadelphia. Philadelphia, 1962. 16p.

Brochure defining scope of library's important special collections of children's literature.

2331. Presson, Mary Louise. A bibliography of juvenile holdings in the Library of Congress in classification F1401-2239 (Latin America). Wash., 1962. 128p. (Master's thesis, Dept. of Library Science, Catholic Univ. of America)

2332. Quinnam, Barbara. The Rachel Field collection of old children's books in the District of Columbia Public Library: a catalogue. Wash., 1962. 100p. (Master's thesis, Dept. of Library Science, Catholic Univ. of America)

2333. Seawell, Mary Robert. Children's book collections in North Carolina college and university libraries. North Carolina libraries, 21 (1963), 98-103.

2334. Shaffer, Ellen. "Children's books in the Free Library of Philadelphia." Top of the news, 25 (1969), 176-83.

2335. Shaw, John MacKay. "The Shaw collection—childhood in poetry." Top of the news, 24 (1967), 19-27.

Description of major collection of poetry for or about children, now in Florida State University Library.

2336. Shih, Maria Huang. A bibliography of juvenile holdings in the Library of Congress in classification QL605-739 (Zoology). Wash., 1965. 119p. (Master's thesis, Dept. of Library Science, Catholic Univ. of America)

2337. Southern Connecticut State College Library. The Carolyn Sherwin Bailey historical collection of children's books: a catalogue, ed. by Dorothy R. Davis. New Haven: Southern Conn. State College, 1966. 232p.

Describes 1,880 items, published from 1657 to 1930, in library's collection.

2338. Stiles, Jeanne N. A bibliography of juvenile holdings in the Library of Congress in section QE (Geology) and QH (Natural History). Wash., 1963. 132p. (Master's thesis, Dept. of Library Science, Catholic Univ. of America)

2339. Strohecker, Edwin C. American juvenile literary periodicals, 1789-1826. 1969. 321*l.* (Thesis, Univ. of Mich. School of Library Science)

2340. Tanzy, C. E. "The John MacKay Shaw collection of 'childhood in poetry.' " Journal of library history, 1 (1966), 220-23. Reprinted. 15p.

Descriptive article on 10,000-volume collection in Florida State University Library.

2341. U.S. Library of Congress, Children's Book Section. Children and poetry, a selective, annotated bibliography, comp. by Virginia Haviland and William Jay Smith. Wash.: Govt. Print. Off., 1969. 67p.

Includes Library of Congress class numbers.

2342. ——— ———. Children's books 1964, a list of 200 books for preschool through junior high school age, comp. by V. Haviland and Lois B. Watt. Wash.: Govt. Print. Off. 1964–. (Annual)

2343. ——— ———. Children's literature, a guide to reference sources, comp. by Virginia Haviland. Wash.: Govt. Print. Off., 1966. 341p.

Contains 1,073 entries with location of copies.

2344. ——— ———. Fables from incunabula to modern picture books, a selective bibliography, comp. by Barbara Quinnam. Wash.: Govt. Print. Off., 1966. 85p.

Based on Library of Congress holdings.

2345. ——— ———. Folklore of the North American Indians; an annotated bibliography, comp. by Judith C. Ullom. Wash., 1969. 126p.

2346. Uzdrowski, Rev. Mel R. A bibliography of juvenile holdings in the Library of Congress in classification U (Military Science) and V (Naval Science). Wash., 1965. 109p. (Master's thesis, Dept. of Library Science, Catholic Univ. of America)

2347. Wayne State University Libraries. The Eloise Ramsey collection of literature for young people: a catalogue, comp. by Joan Cusenza. Detroit: Wayne State Univ. Pr., 1967. 389p.

2348. Welch, d'Alte A. "A bibliography of American children's books printed prior to 1821." Proceedings of the American Antiquarian Society, 73 (1963), 121-324, 465-596; 74 (1964), 260-382; 75 (1965), 273-476; 77 (1967), 44-190, 281-535.

Locations in numerous American and foreign libraries.

2349. Wofford College Library. Children's literature, comp. by Elizabeth Sabin. Spartanburg, S.C.: Wofford Library Pr., 1970. Unpaged. (Special collections checklist, no.3)

List of 200 titles, principally 19th century.

2350. Zens, Mildred L. A bibliography of juvenile holdings in the Library of Congress in classifications Q and Z (Zoology, Anatomy, Physiology, Bacteriology; Library Science): QL801-991, QM, QP, QR, Z. Wash., 1963. 96p. (Master's thesis, Dept. of Library Science, Catholic Univ. of America)

2351. Zugby, Lillian C. A bibliography of juvenile holdings in the Library of Congress in classifications B (Philosophy-Religion) BR-BS551.2, (America) E11-E45 and N (Fine Arts) NE-NK. Wash., 1964. 165*l.* (Master's thesis, Dept. of Library Science, Catholic Univ. of America)

Geography and Maps

GENERAL

2352. American Geographical Society, New York. Current geographical publications; additions to the Research catalogue of the American Geographical Society, 1938- . v.1- .

Classified index to current books, pamphlets, government publications, and periodical articles relating to geography.

2353. American Geographical Society of New York, Map Dept. Index to maps in books and periodicals. Boston: G. K. Hall, 1968. 10v.

Records about 160,000 cards from society's catalog.

2354. American Geographical Society Library of New York. Research catalogue. Boston: G. K. Hall, 1962. 15v.

Photographic reproduction of cards listing books, pamphlets, government publications, and periodical articles.

2355. Armstrong, Charles E. "Copies of Ptolemy's Geography in American libraries." Bulletin of the New York Public Library, 66 (1962), 105-14.

Editions from 1475 to 1730 located.

2356. Brown University, John Carter Brown Library. Early maps and their uses; an exhibition illustrating some of the practical uses found for maps in daily life. Providence, R.I., 1963. 15*l.*

2357. ——— ———. Maps of the Renaissance and the discovery of America; an exhibition held in the John Carter Brown Library. Providence, R.I., 1961. 10*l.*

2358. California, University, Bancroft Library, Berkeley. Index to printed maps. Boston: G. K. Hall, 1964. 521p.

Catalog of Bancroft Library's map collection.

2359. Cline, Howard F. "The Oztoticpac lands map of Texcoco, 1540." Quarterly journal of the Library of Congress, 23 (1966), 77-115.

Library of Congress acquisition.

2360. Hafstad, Margaret R. "The Society's map collection." Wisconsin magazine of history, 52 (Spring 1969), 223-38.

Describes State Historical Society of Wisconsin's holdings.

2361. Huntington Library. Early maps 1482-1690: an exhibition. San Marino, Calif., 1963. 6p.

2362. Indiana University, Lilly Library. The Bernardo Mendel collection; an exhibit. Bloomington, 1964. 83p.

Relates to geography and Latin America.

2363. ——— ———. Discovery; an exhibition of books relating to the age of geographical discovery and exploration. Bloomington, 1965. 40p. (Publication, no.1)

2364. Kansas, University, Libraries. Maps of Costa Rica: an annotated cartobibliography, by Albert E. Palmerlee. Lawrence, 1965. 358p. (Univ. of Kans. publications, Library series, no.19)

Also includes locations in some other U.S. and Latin American libraries.

2365. ———. Maps of the 16th to 19th centuries in the University of Kansas Libraries, by Thomas R. Smith and Bradford L. Thomas. Lawrence, 1963. 137p. (Univ. of Kans. publications, Library series, no.16)

Describes 254 maps.

2366. Koeman, Cornelis. Atlantes Neerlandici; bibliography of terrestrial, maritime and celestial atlases and pilot books, published in the Netherlands up to 1880. Amsterdam: Theatrum Terrarum, 1967- , v.1- . (In progress, to be completed in 5 volumes)

Locates copies in a half dozen U.S. libraries.

2367. North Carolina, University, Institute of Government. North Carolina's map resources; problems and needs; special study, by Robert E. Stipe. Chapel Hill, 1962. 77*l.*

2368. Ristow, Walter W. "Recent facsimile maps and atlases." Quarterly journal of the Library of Congress, 24 (1967), 213-29.

Report on Library of Congress acquisitions.

2369. ———. "Theatrum Orbis Terrarum, 1570-1970." Quarterly journal of the Library of Congress, 27 (1970), 316-31.

In Map Division, Library of Congress.

2370. Southern Illinois University Library. American travelers abroad; a bibliography of accounts published before 1900, comp. by Harold F. Smith. Carbondale, 1969. 166p.

2371. Special Libraries Association, Geography and Map Division. Map collections in the United States and Canada: a directory, 2d ed. N.Y., 1970. 159p.

Lists 605 collections, describing area and subject specializations, special collections, etc.

2372. Syracuse University Libraries. Selected bibliography of maps in libraries, comp. by Jessie B. Watkins. Syracuse, N.Y., 1967. 18p.

2373. U.S. Library of Congress, Map Division. A descriptive list of treasure maps and charts, comp. by Richard S. Ladd. Wash.: Govt. Print. Off., 1964. 29p.

Maps and charts in Library of Congress collection.

2374. ———, Geography and Map Division. Facsimiles of rare historical maps; a list of reproductions for sale by various publishers and distributors, 3d ed., comp. by Walter W. Ristow. Wash., 1968. 20p.

2375. ———, Map Division. A guide to historical cartography; a selected, annotated list of references on the history of maps and map making, 2d ed., comp. by Walter W. Ristow and Clara E. LeGear. Wash., 1961. 22p.

Lists 67 items, with Library of Congress call numbers.

2376. ——— ———. A list of geographical atlases in the Library of Congress, with bibliographical notes, comp. by Clara Egli LeGear. Wash.: Govt. Print. Off., 1963. v.6 (681p.)

2377. ——— ———. "Maps." Library of Congress quarterly journal of current acquisitions, 18 (1961), 207-17; 19 (1962), 181-91; 20 (1963), 225-34; 21 (1964), 273-84; 22 (1965), 216-25; 23 (1966), 231-42.

Annual reports on Library's current acquisitions.

2378. ——— ———. Three-dimensional maps; an annotated list of references relating to the construction and use of terrain models, 2d ed., comp. by Walter W. Ristow. Wash.: Govt. Print. Off., 1964. 38p.

Works in Library of Congress are identified by classification numbers.

2379. U.S. National Archives. Preliminary inventory of the records of the Office of Geography, comp. by Laura E. Kelsey. Wash., 1965. 8p.

2380. Wofford College Library. Geography and travels, ed. by Frank J. Anderson. Spartanburg, S.C.: Wofford Library Pr., 1970. 55p. (Special collections checklist, no.1)

Checklist of books dealing with geography and travel in special collection in Wofford Library.

2381. Yonge, Ena L. A catalogue of early globes made prior to 1850 and conserved in the United States; a preliminary listing. N.Y.: American Geographical Soc., 1968. 118p. (American Geographical Soc. Library series, no.6)

Locates early globes.

AMERICAN

2382. Bernson, Alexander. "Panama: a bibliography of 20th century general maps and atlases of the Republic of Panama in the Library of Congress." Special Libraries Association, Geography and Map Division bulletin, 75 (March 1969), 21-25.

2383. Brown University, John Carter Brown Library. A map of 1782 showing Friends meetings in New England; a list of eighteenth-century manuscript maps of New England yearly meetings, by Thomas R. Adams. Providence, R.I., 1963. 8p. (Reprinted from Quaker history, v.3, Spring 1963)

2384. Burton, Arthur G., and Stephenson, Richard W. "John Ballendine's eighteenth-century map of Virginia." Quarterly journal of the Library of Congress, 21 (1964), 174-78.

Acquisition by Library of Congress.

2385. Cumming, William P. The Southeast in early maps, with an annotated checklist of printed and manuscript regional and local maps of Southeastern North America during the colonial period. Chapel Hill: Univ. of N.C. Pr., 1962. 284p.

Locates copies.

2386. Day, James M., and Dunlap, Ann B. "The map collection of the Texas State Archives." Southwestern historical quarterly, 65 (1962), 399-439, 539-74; 66 (1962), 103-32, 271-303. Reprinted. 1962. 156p.

Covers period 1527-1900.

2387. Guthorn, Peter J. American maps and map makers of the Revolution. Monmouth Beach, N.J.: Philip Freneau Press, 1966. 48p.

Lists over 500 maps with descriptions and locations.

2388. ———. "Some notable New Jersey maps of the Dutch colonial period." Proceedings of New Jersey Historical Society, 80 (April 1962), 102-10.

Mainly in New York Public Library and Library of Congress; locations cited in notes.

2389. Lind, Genevieve R. "Nineteenth-century cadastral maps of New Hampshire and Vermont." Dartmouth College Library bulletin, n.s. 9 (1968), 20-28.

Lists and describes Dartmouth Library holdings of 19th-century county, township, and city ownership maps and county atlases.

2390. Lunny, Robert M. Early maps of North America. Newark: New Jersey Historical Society, 1961. 48p.

Checklist of exhibition; items loaned from institutions and private collections.

2391. Michigan Historical Commission, Division of Archives. List of cartographic records of the Michigan Department of Conservation, Lands Division, comp. by Geneva Kebler and Elizabeth Rademacher. Lansing, 1962. 17p.

2392. New York State Library. A checklist of New York State county maps published 1779-1945, by Albert Hazen Wright. Albany, 1965. 87p.

2393. Pennsylvania State University Library. Checklist of Pennsylvania maps. University Park, 1970. 9p.

2394. Princeton University Library. New Jersey road maps of the 18th century. Princeton, N.J., 1964. 48p.

Based in part on original manuscripts in Princeton Library.

2395. Ristow, Walter W. "John Melish and his Map of the United States." Library of Congress quarterly journal of current acquisitions, 19 (1962), 159-78.

Library of Congress acquisition.

2396. ———. "Seventeenth century wall maps of America and Africa." Library of Congress quarterly journal of current acquisitions, 24 (1967), 3-17.

General discussion with specific descriptions of examples in Library of Congress.

2397. ———. "United States fire insurance and underwriters maps, 1852-1968." Library of Congress quarterly journal of current acquisitions, 25 (1968), 194-218.

Survey of Library of Congress holdings.

2398. Scheffler, Emma M. "Maps in the Illinois State Archives." Illinois libraries, 44 (1962), 418-26.

2399. Sifton, Paul G. "The Walker-Washington map." Quarterly journal of the Library of Congress, 24 (1967), 90-96.

Copied by George Washington from Dr. Thomas Walker's map; in Library of Congress.

2400. Texas State Library, Archives Division. Maps of Texas, 1527-1900; the map collection of the Texas State Archives, comp. by James M. Day and others. Austin: Pemberton, 1964. 178p.

Catalog of maps of, or including, Texas.

2401. U.S. Library of Congress, Geography and Map Division. Detroit and vicinity before 1900: an annotated list of maps, comp. by Alberta G. Auringer Koerner. Wash.: Govt. Print. Off., 1968. 84p.

Describes 239 maps and atlases, most of which are in Library of Congress Map Division; others located in libraries.

2402. ——— ———. Land ownership maps: a checklist of nineteenth century United States county maps in the Library of Congress, comp. by Richard W. Stephenson. Wash., 1967. 86p.

Records 1,449 maps in the Geography and Map Division.

2403. ——— ———. Panoramic maps of American cities, prep. by John R. Hébert. Wash., 1970. 7pts.

Describes nearly 1,000 maps, 1865 to end of World War I, in Library of Congress collection; each part is devoted to separate region.

2404. ——— ———. Maps showing explorers' routes, trails and early roads in the United States; an annotated list, comp. by Richard S. Ladd. Wash.: Govt. Print. Off., 1962. 137p.

Selective bibliography of 300 entries; includes Library of Congress call numbers.

2405. Washington, University, Library, Seattle. Reference guide to early maps in the Pacific Northwest collection, the Suzzallo library, University of Washington, 1966. 69p.

2406. Wheat, James Clements, and Brun, Christian F. Maps and charts published in America before 1800: a bibliography. New Haven, Conn.: Yale Univ. Pr., 1969. 215p.

Lists 915 maps with locations in the United States and Britain.

Biography and Genealogy

GENERAL

2407. Allen, Edison B. "The hands of history." The Tulanian, 40 (Oct. 1966), 1-7.
Description of Davis collection of letters, documents, pictures, and books of famous Americans, in Tulane University Library.

2408. California, University, Library. Letters & documents of American statesmen: an exhibit, by James V. Mink. Los Angeles, 1965. 12p.
Materials from UCLA Library collections.

2409. Cary, Richard. "Rounding the presidential cycle." Colby Library quarterly, 6, no.2 (1962), 74-80.
Letters of U.S. presidents in Colby College Library.

2410. Davies, John D. "A center for 20th century studies." Princeton alumni weekly, 64 (June 2, 1964), 8-9, 13.
Describes collections of papers of Bernard Baruch, James Forrestal, John Foster Dulles, Adlai Stevenson, and others in Princeton University Library.

2411. Kaplan, Louis. A bibliography of American autobiographies. Madison: Univ. of Wis. Pr., 1961. 372p.
Contains 6,377 titles, published before 1945, arranged alphabetically by authors, with library locations.

2412. Lancour, Harold. A bibliography of ship passenger lists, 1538-1825; being a guide to published lists of early immigrants to North America, 3d ed. rev. and enlarged by Richard J. Wolfe, with a list of passenger arrival records in the National Archives by Frank E. Bridgers. N.Y.: New York Public Library, 1963. 137p.

2413. Newman, John. "The presidential letters collection of the University of Iowa Libraries." Manuscripts, 22 (Fall 1970), 273-76.
Description of collection.

2414. Pennsylvania Historical and Museum Commission, Division of Public Records. Military service records in the State Archives. Harrisburg, 1962. 4p.

2415. Pennsylvania State Library. Pennsylvania in autobiography. Harrisburg, 1967. 19p.
Locates copies in libraries.

2416. Syracuse University Library. The Lorenzo collection, comp. by Howard L. Applegate and Paul H. McCarthy. Syracuse, N.Y., 1964. 13p. (Manuscript register series, no.3)
Papers of the Ledyard, Lincklaen, Fairchild, Fitzhugh, Forman, Krumbhaar, Remington, Seymour, Stebbins, and Strawbridge families.

2417. Tennessee State Library and Archives, Manuscript Section. Registers, No. 1-9. Nashville, 1959-64. 9v.
Contents: 1, Jacob McGavock Dickinson papers; 2, Joseph Buckner Killebrew papers; 3, Walter Wagner Faw papers; 4, McIver collection; 5, J. Emerick Nagy collection; 6, Zilphia Horton folk music collection; 7, Buell-Brien papers; 8, John Trotwood Moore papers; 9, Highlander Folk School audio collection.

2418. U.S. Library of Congress, General Reference and Bibliography Division. Biographical sources for the United States, comp. by Jane Kline. Wash.: The Library, 1961. 58p.
Library of Congress call numbers included.

2419. ——— ———. The Presidents of the United States, 1789-1962; a selected list of references, comp. by Donald H. Mugridge. Wash.: U.S. Govt. Print. Office, 1963. 159p.
Contains 1,453 references with locations.

2420. U.S. National Archives. Age and citizenship records in the National Archives. Wash., 1967. 7p.

2421. ———. Preliminary inventory of pension case files of the Bureau of Pensions and the Veterans Administration, 1861-1942, comp. by Frank E. Bridgers and others. Wash., 1963. 11p.

2422. ———. Preliminary inventory of the records of the Immigration and Naturalization Service, comp. by Marion M. Johnson. Wash., 1965. 11p.

2423. Vecoli, Rudolph J. "The immigration studies collection of the University of Minnesota." American archivist, 32 (April 1969), 139-45.

Describes immigration archives in University of Minnesota Libraries relating to immigrants from Southern and Eastern Europe.

2424. Wofford College Library. Biography, comp. by Elizabeth Sabin, ed. by Frank J. Anderson. Spartanburg, S.C.: Wofford Library Pr., 1970. Unpaged.

List of about 200 biographies of 19th-century figures in Wofford Library.

2425. Wolfe, Richard J. "Early New York naturalization records in the Emmet collection, with a list of aliens naturalized in New York 1802-1814." Bulletin of the New York Public Library, 67 (1963), 211-17.

Collection in New York Public Library.

INDIVIDUAL BIOGRAPHY

Adams, Randolph G.

2426. Michigan, University, William L. Clements Library. A bibliography of Randolph G. Adams. Ann Arbor, 1962. 35p.

American historian, 1892-1951, director of Clements Library.

Adams, Sherman

2427. Shewmaker, Kenneth E. "The Sherman Adams papers." Dartmouth College Library bulletin, n.s. 9 (1969), 88-92.

Governor of New Hampshire, U.S. congressman, and assistant to President Dwight Eisenhower.

Aitchison, Clyde Bruce

2428. Oregon, University, Library. Inventory of the Clyde Bruce Aitchison papers, comp. by Martin Schmitt. Eugene, 1962. 8p. (University of Oregon Library occasional paper, no.1)

Papers held by University of Oregon Library, of Aitchison, 1875-1962, Oregon lawyer.

Allen, James E., Jr.

2429. New York State Library. A guide to the papers of James E. Allen, Jr., president of the University of the state of New York and commissioner of education, 1955-1969. Albany, 1970. 68p.

Anderson Family

2430. Kansas State Historical Society. Guide to the microfilm edition of the Anderson family papers 1802-1905 in the Kansas State Historical Society, ed. by Joseph W. Snell. Topeka, 1967. 8p.

Correspondence and papers of John Anderson, 1768-1835, two sons and a grandson, clergyman, educators, and businessmen associated with Kansas history in 19th century.

Andrews, T. Coleman

2431. Oregon, University, Library. Inventory of the papers of T. Coleman Andrews, comp. by Martin Schmitt. Eugene, 1967. 28p. (University of Oregon Library occasional paper, no.5)

Papers held by University of Oregon Library of public accountant for federal government.

Arthur, Chester A.

2432. U.S. Library of Congress, Manuscript Division. Index to the Chester A. Arthur papers. Wash., 1961. 13p.

Lists 1,413 items, with index to 1,900 names.

Bagley Family

2433. Washington, University, Libraries. The Bagley family papers 1859-1932, comp. by Judith Johnson. Seattle, 1966. 33p. (Univ. of Wash. Libraries, manuscript series, no.4)

In University of Washington Libraries.

Ballinger, Richard A.

2434. Washington, University, Libraries. Richard A. Ballinger papers, 1907-1920. Seattle, 1965. 26p.

In University of Washington Libraries. Ballinger, 1853-1922, was a lawyer and jurist, mayor of Seattle, and U.S. Secretary of the Interior in Taft administration.

Barlow, Samuel Latham Mitchill

2435. House, Albert V. "The Samuel Latham Mitchill Barlow papers in the Huntington Library." Huntington Library quarterly, 28 (Aug. 1965), 341-52.

Barlow, 1826-1889, was New York lawyer.

Barnum, P. T.

2436. Neafie, Nellie. P. T. Barnum bibliography. Bridgeport, Conn.: Bridgeport Public Library, 1968. 55p.

Primarily listing of works found in Bridgeport Public Library and Barnum Museum, also in Bridgeport.

Berrien, John MacPherson

2437. North Carolina, University, Library. The John MacPherson Berrien papers in the Southern Historical Collection of the University of North Carolina Library, ed. by Margaret Lee Neustadt. Chapel Hill, 1967. 14p.

Papers of Berrien, 1781-1856, U.S. Senator from Georgia and Southern political leader in pre-Civil War era.

Booth, John Wilkes

2438. Fingerson, Ronald L. "John Wilkes Booth in the Bollinger Lincoln collection." Books at Iowa, 2 (April 1965), 9-16.

Bragg, Thomas

2439. North Carolina, University, Library. Thomas Bragg diary, 1861-1862, in the Southern Historical Collection of the University of North Carolina Library, ed. by Clyde E. Pitts. Chapel Hill, 1966. 10p.

Papers of Bragg, 1810-72, lawyer and Confederate statesman from North Carolina.

Braithwaite, William Stanley

2440. Syracuse University Library. William Stanley Braithwaite, comp. by John S. Patterson. Syracuse, N.Y.: 1964. 18p. (Manuscript register series, no.7)

Braithwaite, 1878-1962, literary critic and anthologist.

Brien, John Smith

2441. Tennessee State Library and Archives. Buell-Brien papers. Nashville, 1964. 21p. (Registers, no.7)

Papers of John Smith Brien, 1807-67, and George Pearson Buell, 1833-83, Tennesseeans; about 10,000 items for 19th century, relating to military and nonmilitary affairs.

Bristow, Joseph Little

2442. Kansas State Historical Society. Guide to the microfilm edition of the Joseph Little Bristow papers 1894-1925 in the Kansas State Historical Society, ed. by Joseph W. Snell. Topeka, 1967. 16p.

Bristow, 1861-1944, was U.S. Senator from Kansas.

Brown, John, Jr.

2443. Ohio Historical Society. Inventory and calendar of the John Brown, Jr., papers, 1830-1932. Columbus, 1962. 32p.

Collection includes many papers of John Brown, of Civil War fame.

Brown, John Stillman

2444. Kansas State Historical Society. Guide to the microfilm edition of the John Stillman Brown family papers, 1818-1907 in the Kansas State Historical Society, ed. by Joseph W. Snell. Topeka, 1967. 8p.

Brown, 1806-1902, was a native of New Hampshire, who migrated to Kansas in 1857, where he was a Unitarian minister and secretary of the Kansas State Agricultural Society.

Brown, Walter F.

2445. Ohio Historical Society. Inventory and calendar of the Walter F. Brown papers, 1907-1950. Columbus, 1962. 52*l.* (Inventory and calendar series, no.2)

Brown, 1869-1961, was an Ohio political leader, lawyer, and railroad executive.

Brown, William Compton

2446. Washington State University Library. William Compton Brown: a calendar of his papers in the Washington State University Library. Pullman, 1966. 25p.

Attorney, historian, and superior court judge, state of Washington.

Brownson, Orestes Augustus

2447. Notre Dame, University, Archives. Guide to the

microfilm edition of the Orestes Augustus Brownson papers. Notre Dame, Ind., 1966. 47p.

Papers of Brownson, 1803-76, author, magazine editor, and Catholic convert, in Notre Dame Archives.

Burke, Thomas

2448. North Carolina, University, Library. The Thomas Burke papers in the Southern Historical Collection of the University of North Carolina Library, ed. by Clyde E. Pitts. Chapel Hill, 1967. 11p.

Papers of Burke, c. 1747-83, governor of North Carolina in Revolutionary period and member of Continental Congress.

Butler, Benjamin F.

2449. Cary, Richard. "A dozen Ben Butler letters." Colby Library quarterly, 6, no.11 (1964), 486-96.

Letters of General Benjamin F. Butler of Civil War fame.

Butler, Smedley Darlington

2450. Lyon, Eunice M. The unpublished papers of Major General Smedley Darlington Butler, United States Marine Corps; a calendar. Wash., 1962. 602p. (Master's thesis, Dept. of Library Science, Catholic Univ. of America)

Located in Marine Corps Historical Library, Arlington, Virginia.

Callan, John Lansing

2451. U.S. Library of Congress, Manuscripts Division. John Lansing Callan [and] John Crittenden Watson, a register of their papers in the Library of Congress. Wash., 1968. 6, 8*l.*

Callan (1886-1958), early aviator, pioneer in aeronautics industry, and naval officer; Watson (1842-1923), naval officer.

Carnegie, Andrew

2452. U.S. Library of Congress, Manuscript Division. Andrew Carnegie: a register of his papers in the Library of Congress. Wash., 1964. 21p.

Carter, Landon

2453. Virginia, University, Library. The Landon Carter papers in the University of Virginia Library, a calendar and biographical sketch, by Walter Ray Wineman. Charlottesville: Univ. of Va. Pr., 1962. 99p.

Carter, 1710-78, colonial and Revolutionary leader from Virginia.

Carter Family

2454. Virginia, University, Library. Guide to the microfilm edition of the Carter family papers, 1659-1797, in the Sabine Hall collection, ed. by Paul P. Hoffman. Charlottesville, 1967. 26p. (Microfilm publications, no.3)

Carty, William Edward

2455. Washington State University Library. William Edward Carty: an indexed register of his papers, 1898-1963, in the Washington State University Library, comp. by Elaine G. White. Pullman, 1967. 42p.

Dairy farmer and legislator, state of Washington.

Casey, Silas

2456. U.S. Library of Congress, Manuscript Division. Silas Casey [and] Stanford Caldwell Hooper; a register of their papers in the Library of Congress. Wash.: The Library, 1968. 5, 9*l.*

Silas Casey (1841-1913), naval officer, and Stanford Caldwell Hooper (1884-1955), naval officer and "father of naval radio."

Cattell, James McKeen

2457. U.S. Library of Congress, Manuscript Division. James McKeen Cattell; a register of his papers in the Library of Congress. Wash., 1962. 24p.

American psychologist and editor, 1860-1944.

Chaffee, Edmund B.

2458. Syracuse University Library. Edmund B. Chaffee, comp. by Walter Timms. Syracuse, N.Y., 1968. 185p. (Manuscript register series, no.11)

Chaffee, 1887-1936, was a Presbyterian clergyman, editor of the Presbyterian Tribune, social reformer and director of the Labor Temple, New York City, 1921-36.

Chambers, Washington Irving

2459. U.S. Library of Congress, Manuscript Division. Washington Irving Chambers; a register of his papers in the Library of Congress. Wash., 1967. 15p.

Papers of Chambers (1856-1934), naval officer and pioneer in development of naval aviation.

Chapman, Samuel M.

2460. Nebraska State Historical Society. Samuel M. Chapman papers, 1866-1906, ed. by Douglas A. Bakken. Lincoln, 1966. 6p.

Guide to the microfilm edition of papers of Chapman, 1839-1907, Nebraska lawyer, jurist, and state senator.

Church, George Earl

2461. Hauke, Lewis. "A note on the life and publications of Colonel George Earl Church." Books at Brown, 20 (1965), 131-63.

Contains bibliographies of Church materials in U.S. State Department and several foreign depositories; relates to American civil engineer, explorer, and writer, 1835-1910.

Churchill, Winston

2462. Mortlake, Harold, & Co. Sir Winston Leonard Spencer Churchill. Catalogue no.132. London, 1969. 144p.

Lists 1,580 items by or about Winston Churchill; collection acquired by University of Illinois Library.

Clark, Grenville

2463. Wight, Ruth N. "Papers of Grenville Clark." Dartmouth College Library bulletin, n.s. 9 (1968), 57-61.

Clark, 1882-1967, was a New York lawyer and promoter of world peace.

Cleveland, Grover

2464. U.S. Library of Congress, Manuscript Division. Index to the Grover Cleveland papers. Wash., 1965. 345p.

Index to 87,027 letters and other manuscripts, 1828-1908, in Library of Congress collection.

Cochrane, Henry Clay

2465. U.S. Marine Corps Museum. Register of the Henry Clay Cochrane papers 1809-1957 and undated, in the United States Marine Corps Museum, Quantico, Virginia, by C. F. W. Coker. Quantico, Va.: 1968. 86p. (Manuscript register series, no.1)

Brigadier general in Marine Corps after Civil War.

Cloutier Family

2466. Northwestern State College of Louisiana Library. The Cloutier collection, Louisiana Room, Russell Library; a calendar, by Katherine F. Bridges. Natchitoches, 1966. 35*l.*

Manuscripts relating to Cloutier family of Louisiana.

Colhoun, Edmund Ross

2467. U.S. Library of Congress, Manuscript Division. Edmund Ross Colhoun [and] Charles O'Neil: a register of their papers in the Library of Congress. Wash., 1967. 8, 9*l.*

Colhoun (1821-97), naval officer, and O'Neil (1842-1927), naval officer and pioneer in naval ordnance and armor.

Colmer, William M.

2468. Southern Mississippi, University, Library. The William M. Colmer papers, 1933-62, comp. by Walter Batson. Hattiesburg: Univ. of Southern Miss. Pr., 1970. 220p.

Papers of long-time member of U.S. House of Representatives.

Cook, Captain James

2469. California, University, Library. Captain James Cook & his voyages of discovery in the Pacific, by Norman J. W. Thrower. Los Angeles, 1970. 12p.

Describes Sir Maurice G. Holmes collection of Cook materials in UCLA Library.

Cook, Roy Bird

2470. West Virginia University Library. Catalogue of the Roy Bird Cook collection. Morgantown, 1964. 36p.

Collection of writings of West Virginia historian, 1886-1961, in West Virginia University Library; concerns West Virginia history, Confederacy, and Stonewall Jackson.

Coolidge, Calvin

2471. U.S. Library of Congress, Manuscript Division. Index to the Calvin Coolidge papers. Wash., 1965. 34p.

Index to about 175,000 manuscripts in Library of Congress' Coolidge collection, 1921-29.

Corsi, Edward

2472. Syracuse University Library. Edward Corsi, comp. by Roberta Thibault. Syracuse, N.Y., 1969. 32p. (Manuscript register series, no.13)

Corsi, 1896-1965, was a writer and speaker, Commissioner of Immigration and Naturalization, and Industrial Commissioner of New York State Labor Department.

Culbertson, William S.

2473. U.S. Library of Congress, Manuscript Division. William S. Culbertson; a register of his papers in the Library of Congress. Wash., 1963. 12*l.*

Culbertson, 1884-1966, was a lawyer, diplomat, army officer, and university professor.

David, Charles Wendell

2474. Riggs, John B. Charles Wendell David: scholar, teacher, librarian. Philadelphia: Union Library Catalogue of the Philadelphia Metropolitan Area, 1965. 68p.

Davis, David

2475. Illinois State Historical Library. The David Davis family papers, 1816-1943; a descriptive inventory, by Robert L. Brubaker. Springfield, 1965. 60p. (Manuscripts in the Illinois State Historical Library, no.3)

Davis, Jefferson

2476. Joyner, Fred B. "A brief calendar of the Jefferson Davis papers in the Samuel Richey Confederate collection of Miami University Library, Oxford, Ohio." Journal of Mississippi history, 25 (Jan. 1963), 15-32.

Day, Jerome J.

2477. Idaho, University, Library. Jerome J. Day collection, a bibliography, comp. by Charles A. Webbert. Moscow: 1963. 66p. (Bookmark, v.15, no.3, supplement)

Collection relating to Day, 1876-1941, Idaho industrialist and state senator.

Dibdin, Thomas Frognall

2478. Harvard University Library. An annotated list of the publications of the Reverend Thomas Frognall Dibdin, D.D., based mainly on those in the Harvard College Library, with notes of others. Cambridge, Mass.: Houghton Library, 1965. 63p.

Dickinson, Jacob McGavock

2479. Tennessee State Library and Archives, Manuscript Section. The Jacob McGavock Dickinson papers. Nashville, 1964. 35p. (Registers, no.1)

Papers of Dickinson, 1851-1928, Tennessee lawyer and Secretary of War in Taft cabinet.

Donnelly, Ignatius

2480. Minnesota Historical Society. Guide to a microfilm edition of the Ignatius Donnelly papers, ed. by Helen McCann White. St. Paul, 1968. 34p.

Papers of Donnelly, 1831-1901, Minnesota congressman and political leader, in Minnesota Historical Society.

Douglas, Stephen A.

2481. Felt, Thomas E. "The Stephen A. Douglas letters in the [Illinois State] Historical Library." Journal of the Illinois State Historical Society, 56 (1963), 677-91.

Dromgoole, Edward

2482. North Carolina, University, Library. The Edward Dromgoole papers in the Southern Historical collection of the University of North Carolina Library, ed. by Clyde E. Pitts. Chapel Hill, 1966. 13p.

Papers of Dromgoole, 1751-1815, merchant, planter, and preacher of Virginia, and of his family.

Dulany, Bladen

2483. U.S. Library of Congress, Manuscript Division. Bladen Dulany, Gustavus R. B. Horner, Daniel Todd Patterson: a register of their papers in the Library of Congress. Wash., 1970. 4, 8, 4*l.*

U.S. naval officers.

Erasmus, Desiderius

2484. Harvard University, Houghton Library. Erasmus on the 500th anniversary of his birth, prep. by James E. Walsh. Cambridge, Mass., 1969. 38p.

Exhibition catalog.

Ewing, Thomas, Sr. and Jr.

2485. Notre Dame, University, Archives. Guide to the microfilm edition of the Thomas Ewing, Sr., papers, ed. by Lawrence J. Bradley. Notre Dame, Ind., 1967. 25p.

Ewing, 1789-1871, was U.S. senator from Ohio, Secretary of Treasury and Secretary of Interior.

2486. Kansas State Historical Society. Guide to the microfilm edition of the Thomas Ewing, Jr., papers, 1856-1908, in the Kansas State Historical Society, ed. by Joseph W. Snell. Topeka, 1967. 6p.

Chief justice of Kansas supreme court and brigadier general.

Fairchild, Herman LeRoy

2487. Rochester, University, Library. Register of the Herman LeRoy Fairchild papers, 1869-1943, comp. by Joan C. Tinkler. Rochester, N.Y., 1962. 125*l.*

Fairchild, 1850-1943, was an educator and geologist.

Falk, Sawyer

2488. Syracuse University Library. Sawyer Falk, comp. by David C. Maslyn and Judy Woolcock. Syracuse, N.Y., 1965. 55p. (Manuscript register series, no.8)

Falk, 1898-1961, was director of drama, Syracuse University, 1927-61; nationally prominent in theater organizations.

Farragut, David G.

2489. [U.S. Library of Congress, Manuscript Division. Farragut papers] College & research libraries news, no.3 (March 1970), 75.

Collection of papers of Admiral David G. Farragut, 1801-70, of Civil War fame, received by Library of Congress.

Faw, Walter Wagner

2490. Tennessee State Library and Archives. Walter Wagner Faw papers. Nashville, 1961. 34p. (Registers, no.3)

Papers of Faw (1867-1956), Tennessee jurist.

Fiske, Minnie Maddern

2491. U.S. Library of Congress, Manuscript Division. Minnie Maddern Fiske; a register of her papers in the Library of Congress. Wash., 1962. 16p.

American actress, 1865-1932.

Flanders, Ralph E.

2492. Schmavonian, Arsiné. "The Ralph E. Flanders papers at Syracuse University," Vermont history, 37 (Spring 1969), 128-31.

U.S. Senator from Vermont, 1946-58, engineer and business leader.

2493. Syracuse University Library. Ralph E. Flanders; a register of his papers in the Syracuse University Library, comp. by Howard L. Applegate and others. Syracuse, N.Y., 1964. 56p. (Manuscript register series, no.4)

Papers of U.S. Senator from Vermont, 1946-58.

Flick, Alexander C.

2494. Syracuse University Library. Alexander C. Flick; a calendar of his papers in the Syracuse University Library. Syracuse, N.Y., 1963. 11p. (Manuscript register series, no.1)

Flick papers, consisting of 2,552 items, relate to Pennsylvania state historian, 1895-1942.

Flynn, John T.

2495. Oregon, University, Library. Inventory of the papers of John T. Flynn, comp. by Martin Schmitt. Eugene, 1966. 32p. (University of Oregon Library occasional paper, no.3)

Papers held by University of Oregon Library of Flynn, 1882-1964, author and journalist.

Forbes, Robert Bennett

2496. Massachusetts Historical Society. Guide to the microfilm edition of the Forbes papers, ed. by Frederick S. Allis, Jr. Boston, 1969. 68p.

Papers of Robert Bennett Forbes, Francis Blackwell Forbes, and other members of family prominent in Massachusetts commerce and business, 1825-1930.

Force, Manning Ferguson

2497. Washington, University, Libraries. Manning Ferguson Force papers, 1835-1885. Seattle, 1965. 4p.

In University of Washington Libraries. Force, 1824-99, was Civil War general, lawyer, and Ohio political leader.

Foster, O. D.

2498. Starkes, M. Thomas. "The O. D. Foster collection." Books at Iowa, 6 (April 1967), 24-28.

Personal diaries, notebooks, and correspondence concerning religious education, interfaith cooperation, and religious life in Mexico, Latin America, and Spain.

Frankfurter, Felix

2499. [U.S. Library of Congress, Manuscript Division. Frankfurter papers] College & research libraries news, no.3 (March 1970), 76.

Papers of Justice Felix Frankfurter, numbering about 70,000, received by Library of Congress.

Fulton, William Savin

2500. Arkansas History Commission. Catalogue of the Fulton-Wright papers, 1825-1891, by John L. Ferguson. Little Rock, 1963. 5*l.*

Papers of William Savin Fulton, 1795-1844, 4th territorial governor of Arkansas.

Furnas, Robert W.

2501. Nebraska State Historical Society. Robert W. Furnas papers, 1844-1905, ed. by Douglas A. Bakken. Lincoln, 1966. 9p.

Papers of Furnas, 1824-1905, soldier, governor of Nebraska, and agriculturist, in Nebraska State Historical Society.

Gallatin, Albert

2502. New York University Libraries. Guide to the microfilm edition of the papers of Albert Gallatin, ed. by Carl E. Prince. N.Y.: N.Y. Univ., Rhistoric Pubs., 1970. 29p.

Papers of Gallatin, 1761-1849, U.S. Secretary of the Treasury, 1801-14, and diplomat.

Garford, Arthur Lovett

2503. Ohio Historical Society. Inventory of the Arthur Lovett Garford papers, 1877-1933. Columbus, 1962. 20*l.*

Papers of Ohio manufacturer and Progressive Party candidate for governor of Ohio in 1912.

Gaston, William

2504. North Carolina, University, Library. The William Gaston papers in the Southern Historical collection of the University of North Carolina Library, ed. by Clyde E. Pitts. Chapel Hill, 1966. 13p.

Papers of Gaston, 1778-1844, North Carolina congressman and jurist.

Gesner, Conrad

2505. U.S. National Library of Medicine. Conrad Gesner, physician, scholar, scientist, 1516-1565; a quarter centenary exhibit held November-December 1965 in the National Library of Medicine, catalog by Richard J. Durling. Bethesda, Md., 1965. 20p.

Gest, Erasmus

2506. Ohio Historical Society. Inventory of the Erasmus Gest papers, 1834-1885. Columbus, 1962. 21*l.* (Inventory and calendar series, no.4)

Gest, 1820-1908, was an Ohio surveyor, engineer, railroad magnate, and street railway entrepreneur.

Gleaves, Albert

2507. U.S. Library of Congress, Manuscript Division. Albert Gleaves; a register of his papers in the Library of Congress. Wash.: 1968. 12p.

Albert Gleaves (1858-1937) was a naval officer, author, and historian.

Goethals, George Washington

2508. U.S. National Archives. Preliminary inventory of the records of the Goethals Memorial Commission, comp. by Kathryn M. Murphy. Wash., 1966. 3p.

George Washington Goethals, 1858-1928, directed building of Panama Canal.

Grant, Ulysses

2509. U.S. Library of Congress, Manuscript Division. Index to the Ulysses S. Grant papers. Wash.: Govt. Print. Off., 1965. 83p.

Index to 20,108 letters, orders, and other manuscripts in Library of Congress' Grant collection.

Green, Duff

2510. North Carolina, University, Library. The Duff Green papers in the Southern Historical collection of the University of North Carolina Library, ed. by Ritchio O. Watson. Chapel Hill, 1967. 26p.

Papers of Green, 1791-1875, Southern journalist, politician, and industrial promoter.

Griffin, Ray B.

2511. Fingerson, Ronald L. "Letters to an Iowa lawyer, 1855-1870." Books at Iowa, 5 (Nov. 1966), 38-46.

Correspondence in Ray B. Griffin papers concerning Civil War, westward expansion, Indian conflicts, etc.

Hale, John P.

2512. Sewell, Richard H. "The John P. Hale papers." Dartmouth College Library bulletin, n.s. 10 (1970), 70-80.

Hale, 1806-73, was lawyer, politician, diplomat, and U.S. Senator from New Hampshire.

Hamond, Sir Andrew Snape

2513. Virginia, University, Library. Guide to the Naval papers of Sir Andrew Snape Hamond, Bart., 1766-1783 and Sir Graham Eden Hamond, Bart., 1799-1825, ed. by Paul P. Hoffman and others. Charlottesville, 1966. 41p. (Microfilm publication, no.2)

Hamond, 1738-1828, was British naval captain and governor of Nova Scotia.

Harding, Warren G.

2514. Ohio Historical Society, Archives and Manuscripts Division. The Warren G. Harding papers; an inventory to the microfilm edition, ed. by Andrea D. Lentz. Columbus, 1970. 283p.

Harriman, Averell

2515. Syracuse University Library. Averell Harriman, an inventory of his gubernatorial papers in the papers in the Syracuse University Library, comp. by James K. Owens. Syracuse, N.Y.: 1967. 77p. (Manuscript register series, no.10)

Harrison, Benjamin

2516. U.S. Library of Congress, Manuscript Division. Index to the Benjamin Harrison papers. Wash.: Govt. Print. Off., 1964. 333p.

Records 69,612 items of correspondence and other materials with 76,985 entries in name index.

2517. Wright, Marcia. "The Benjamin Harrison papers." Library of Congress, Quarterly journal of current acquisitions, 18 (1961), 121-25.

Hay, John

2518. Brown University Library. The life and works of John Hay, 1838-1905; a commemorative catalogue of an exhibition shown at the John Hay Library of Brown University in honor of the centennial of his graduation at the commencement of 1858. Providence, R.I., 1961. 51p.

Hayes, Rutherford B.

2519. Marchman, Walt P., and Rodabaugh, James H. "Collections of the Rutherford B. Hayes State Memorial." Ohio history, 71 (1962), 151-57.

Herbert, Hilary Abner

2520. North Carolina, University, Library. The Hilary Abner Herbert papers in the Southern Historical Collection of the University of North Carolina Library, ed. by Margaret Lee Neustadt. Chapel Hill, 1966. 13p.

Papers of Herbert, 1834-1919, Confederate soldier, congressman, and Secretary of the Navy.

Hill, Knute

2521. Washington State University Library. Knute Hill: a register of his papers in the Washington State University Library. Pullman, 1966. 6p.

U.S. congressman, state of Washington.

Hoover, Herbert

2522. Stanford University, Hoover Institution. Genealogy of the Herbert Hoover family, by Hulda Hoover McLean. Stanford, Calif., 1967. 486p. (Bibliographical series, no.30)

Horan, Walt

2523. Washington State University Library. Walt Horan: a register of his papers, 1943-1965, in the Washington State University Library. Pullman, 1965. 20p.

U.S. congressman, state of Washington.

Horton, S. Wentworth

2524. Syracuse University Library. S. Wentworth Horton; a register of his papers in the Syracuse University Library, comp. by Jill Kopp and others. Syracuse, N.Y., 1963. 45p. (Manuscript register series, no.2)

Collection of 35,000 items, 1933-56, from New York state senator, 1885-1960.

Houston, William Churchill

2525. Nash, Gary B. "William Churchill Houston papers." Princeton University Library chronicle, 24 (1965), 119-22.

Material relating to Receiver of Taxes in New Jersey, 1782-85, in Princeton Library.

Hunter, R. M. T.

2526. Virginia, University, Library. Guide to the microfilm edition of the papers of R. M. T. Hunter, 1817-1887, ed. by James Anderson and Mary F. Crouch. Charlottesville, 1967. 44p. (Microfilm publications, no.6)

Virginia lawyer, speaker of U.S. House of Representatives, and political leader, 1809-87.

Hyatt, Thaddeus

2527. Kansas State Historical Society. Guide to the microfilm edition of the Thaddeus Hyatt papers 1843-1898 in the Kansas State Historical Society, ed. by Joseph W. Snell. Topeka, 1967. 11p.

Hyatt, 1816-1901, was a New York manufacturer, an active Free-State Party supporter, and chairman of the National Kansas Committee, 1856-57.

Ingersoll, Robert G.

2528. Stein, Gordon. Robert G. Ingersoll: a checklist. Kent, Ohio: Kent State Univ. Pr., 1969. 128p.

Union list of works by and about Ingersoll to be found in about 90 institutions.

Jackson, Andrew

2529. Owsley, Harriet C. "Jackson manuscripts in the Tennessee Historical Society and the Manuscript Division of the Tennessee State Library and Archives: a bibliographical note." Tennessee historical quarterly, 26 (1967), 97-100.

2530. U.S. Library of Congress, Manuscript Division. Index to the Andrew Jackson papers. Wash.: Govt. Print. Off., 1967. 111p.

Guide to 22,449 letters and other manuscripts in Library of Congress' Jackson collection, 1775-1885.

Jewett, George Frederick

2531. Idaho, University, Library. Descriptive inventory of the papers of George Frederick Jewett, Sr. Moscow, 1969. 45p.

Jewett, 1896-1956, was lumberman and business man in Idaho, Minnesota, and Washington.

Johnson, Andrew

2532. U.S. Library of Congress, Manuscript Division. Index to the Andrew Johnson papers. Wash.: Govt. Print. Off., 1963. 154p.

Record of 23,477 papers, with 33,850 entries in name index.

Johnson, George F.

2533. Syracuse University Library. George F. Johnson, comp. by Mona F. Atlas and John Janitz. Syracuse, N.Y., 1969. 23p. (Manuscript register series, no.12)

Johnson, 1857-1948, was a philanthropist and industrialist, developer of idea of "industrial democracy" in labor-management relations.

Johnson, Lon

2534. Washington State University Library. Lon Johnson: a register of his papers in the Washington State University Library. Pullman, 1966. 12p.

Attorney, judge, and lieutenant governor, state of Washington.

Jones Family

2535. Tennessee State Library and Archives, Manuscript Division. Jones family papers. Nashville, 1967. 37p. (Registers, no.12)

Jordan, David Starr

2536. Stanford University Libraries. Guide to the microfilm edition of the David Starr Jordan papers, 1861-1964. Stanford, Calif.: Stanford Univ. Pr., 1964. 31p.

Kaltenborn, H. V.

2537. Wisconsin Mass Communications History Center. The H. V. Kaltenborn collection. Madison, 1961. 32p.

Papers of Kaltenborn, 1878-1965, U.S. radio commentator and journalist.

Kennedy, John Fitzgerald

2538. U.S. Library of Congress, General Reference and Bibliography Division. John Fitzgerald Kennedy, 1917-1963; a chronological list of references. Wash.: U.S. Govt. Print. Office, 1964. 68p. Supplement. 1964. 25p.

Locates copies in Library of Congress and elsewhere of writings by and about Kennedy.

Killebrew, Joseph Buckner

2539. Tennessee State Library and Archives. Joseph Buckner Killebrew papers. Nashville, 1961. 6, 5p. (Registers, no.2)

Papers of Killebrew (1831-1906), Tennessee agriculturist, editor, and author.

King Family

2540. Illinois State Historical Library. The King family

papers, 1798-1927, comp. by Robert L. Brubaker. Springfield, 1963. 24p.
Papers in Illinois State Historical Library.

Kitchin, Claude

2541. North Carolina, University, Library. The Claude Kitchin papers in the Southern Historical Collection of the University of North Carolina Library, ed. by Margaret Lee Neustadt. Chapel Hill, 1966. 29p.
Papers of Kitchin, 1869-1923, North Carolina congressman.

Kurtz, Charles L.

2542. Ohio Historical Society. Inventory and calendar of the Charles L. Kurtz papers, 1873-1899. Columbus, 1963. 31*l.* (Inventory and calendar series, no.5)
Kurtz, 1854-1929, was an Ohio political leader and manufacturer.

Lafayette, Marquis de

2543. Cornell University Libraries. Lafayette, an exhibition, comp. by Edward W. Fox. Ithaca, N.Y., 1964. 26p.

Langmuir, Irving

2544. U.S. Library of Congress, Manuscript Division. Irving Langmuir; a register of his papers in the Library of Congress. Wash., 1962. 9p.
U.S. chemist and physicist, 1881-1957.

Larkin, Thomas Oliver

2545. California, University, Bancroft Library. The Larkin papers: personal, business, and official correspondence of Thomas Oliver Larkin, merchant and United States Consul in California, index, ed. by George P. Hammond. Berkeley: Univ. of Calif. Pr., 1968. 80p.
Describes collection of 4,000 letters and other documents, obtained by library in 1905.

Lee, Samuel P.

2546. U.S. Library of Congress. Manuscript Division. Samuel P. Lee, a register of his papers in the Library of Congress. Wash., 1967. 15p.
Papers of Samuel Phillips Lee (1812-97), naval officer.

Lee Family

2547. Virginia, University, Library. Guide to the microfilm edition of the Lee family papers, 1742-1795, ed. by Paul P. Hoffman and John L. Molyneaux. Charlottesville, 1966. 51p. (Microfilm publications, no.1)

Lehman, Herbert

2548. Columbia University, School of International Affairs. The Herbert H. Lehman papers; an introduction, checklist and guide, by William B. Liebmann. N.Y., 1968. 30p.
Papers of New York governor and U.S. senator.

Lincoln, Abraham

2549. California, University, Library, Santa Barbara. William Wyles collection. Westport, Conn.: Greenwood, 1970. 5v.
Collection devoted to Abraham Lincoln, Civil War, and Western expansion in America.

2550. Hrdlicka, Adolph E. "St. Procopius College Library." Illinois Libraries, 47 (1965), 586-93.
Describes Library's Lincoln collection.

2551. Edelstein, J. M. "Lincoln papers in the Stern bequest." Library of Congress quarterly journal of current acquisitions, 19 (1961), 7-14.
Description of Library of Congress acquisition.

2552. Illinois State Historical Library. "Library adds five Lincoln manuscripts to collection." Journal of the Illinois State Historical Society, 59 (1966), 172-74.

2553. Walton, Clyde C. "Illinois' Lincoln letters." Illinois blue book, 1961-62, p.49-71.

Lincoln, Benjamin

2554. Massachusetts Historical Society. Guide to the microfilm edition of the Benjamin Lincoln papers, ed. by Frederick S. Allis, Jr., and Wayne A. Frederick. Boston, 1967. 10p.
Papers of Lincoln, 1733-1810, Revolutionary soldier, in Massachusetts Historical Society.

Long, Chester I.

2555. Kansas State Historical Society. Guide to the microfilm edition of the Chester I. Long papers 1890-1928 in the Kansas State Historical Society, ed. by Joseph W. Snell. Topeka, 1967. 10p.
Long, 1860-1934, was U.S. senator from Kansas.

Long, Huey P.

2556. Williams, T. Harry, and Price, John M. "The

Huey P. Long papers at Louisiana State University." Journal of Southern history, 36 (May 1970), 256-61.

Lowndes, William

2557. North Carolina, University, Library. The William Lowndes papers in the Southern Historical Collection of the University of North Carolina Library, ed. by Clyde E. Pitts. Chapel Hill, 1967. 13p.

Papers of Lowndes, 1782-1822, congressman from South Carolina.

Lynd, Robert S.

2558. U.S. Library of Congress, Manuscript Division. [Lynd papers] College & research libraries news, no.4 (April 1969), 112.

Papers of Robert S. and Helen M. Lynd, authors of Middletown, presented to Library of Congress.

McCoy, Isaac

2559. Kansas State Historical Society. Guide to the microfilm edition of the Isaac McCoy papers 1808-1874 in the Kansas State Historical Society, ed. by Joseph W. Snell. Topeka, 1967. 9p.

McCoy, Indian agent and missionary, 1784-1846.

McGilvra, John J.

2560. Washington, University, Libraries. John J. McGilvra papers, 1861-1903. Seattle: 1965. 7p.

In University of Washington Libraries. McGilvra, 1827-1903, was U.S. attorney for Washington Territory. 1861-66, legislator, business leader, and civic reformer in Seattle.

McIntosh, Lacklan

2561. Georgia, University, Libraries. Lacklan McIntosh papers in the University of Georgia Libraries, ed. by Lilla Mills Hawes. Athens: Univ. of Ga. Pr., 1968. 141p. (Miscellanea publications, no.7)

Papers of McIntosh, 1725-1806, Revolutionary War soldier.

McIver, John

2562. Tennessee State Library and Archives, Manuscript Section. McIver collection. Nashville, 1962. 9p. (Registers, no.4)

John McIver, 1764-1828, was Tennessee Secretary of State and Register of the U.S. Treasury.

McKinley, William

2563. U.S. Library of Congress, Manuscript Division. Index to the William McKinley papers. Wash.: Govt. Print. Off., 1963. 482p.

Record of 105,832 items; name index contains 108,636 entries.

Madison, James

2564. U.S. Library of Congress, Manuscript Division. Index to the James Madison papers. Wash.: Govt. Print. Off., 1965. 61p.

Index to 12,320 letters and other manuscripts in Library of Congress collection.

Marshall, George C.

2565. Pogue, Forrest C. "General Marshall and the Pershing papers." Quarterly journal of the Library of Congress, 21 (1964), 1-11.

Materials on General George C. Marshall, 1919-30, in John J. Pershing papers, Library of Congress.

Martin, Joseph W., Jr.

2566. [Stonehill College Library, North Easton, Mass. Joseph W. Martin, Jr. papers] College & research libraries news, no.1 (Jan. 1970), 6.

Letters, speeches, photographs, and scrapbooks associated with Martin, 1884-1968, speaker of U.S. House of Representatives and Republican minority leader, received by Stonehill College.

Maxey, Samuel Bell

2567. Texas State Library and Archives. Samuel Bell Maxey papers; an inventory, prep. by Louise Horton. Austin, 1969. 17*l.*

Papers of Maxey (1825-95), Confederate general and U.S. senator.

Maxwell, Samuel

2568. Nebraska State Historical Society. Samuel Maxwell papers, 1853-1901, ed. by Douglas A. Bakken. Lincoln, 1966. 6p.

Papers of Maxwell, 1825-1901, Nebraska jurist, congressman, and author of legal treatises, in Nebraska State Historical Society.

Meeker, Jotham

2569. Kansas State Historical Society. Guide to the

microfilm edition of the Jotham Meeker papers 1825-1864, in the Kansas State Historical Society, ed. by Joseph W. Snell. Topeka, 1967. 5p.

Jotham Meeker, 1804-55, Baptist missionary to Indians and printer.

Memminger, Christopher Gustavus

2570. North Carolina, University, Library. The Christopher Gustavus Memminger papers in the Southern Historical Collection of the University of North Carolina Library, ed. by Clyde E. Pitts. Chapel Hill, 1966. 9p.

Papers of Memminger, 1803-88, South Carolina legislator and Secretary of the Treasury of the Confederacy.

Miller, Samuel

2571. U.S. Marine Corps Museum. Register of the Samuel Miller papers 1814-1856 in the United States Marine Corps Museum, Quantico, Virginia, comp. by Doris S. Davis and Jack B. Hilliard. Quantico, Va., n.d. 50p. (Manuscript register series, no.3)

Officer in Marine Corps who saw action in War of 1812 and in Indian Wars in 1836-37.

Mires, Austin

2572. Washington State University Library. Austin Mires: an indexed register of his papers, 1872-1936, in the Washington State University Library, comp. by Terry P. Abraham. Pullman, 1968. 110p.

Attorney, mayor, legislator, and judge, state of Washington.

Monroe, James

2573. U.S. Library of Congress, Manuscript Division. Index to the James Monroe papers. Wash.: Govt. Print. Off., 1963. 25p.

Lists 3,821 items, with index of 4,642 names.

2574. Virginia, University, Library. Guide to the microfilm edition of James Monroe papers in Virginia repositories, ed. by Curtis W. Garrison and David L. Thomas. Charlottesville, 1969. 86p. (Microfilm publications, no.7)

Moore, John Trotwood

2575. Tennessee State Library and Archives. John Trotwood Moore papers. Nashville, 1964. 33p. (Registers, no.8)

Papers of Moore (1858-1929), Tennessee author and journalist.

Morton, J. Sterling

2576. Nebraska State Historical Society. J. Sterling Morton papers 1849-1902, ed. by Douglas A. Bakken. Lincoln, 1968. 16p.

Guide to microfilm edition of papers of Nebraska agriculturist, political leader, and journalist.

Muir, John

2577. [University of the Pacific, Pacific Center for Western Historical Studies, Stuart Library. John Muir papers] College & research libraries news, no.6 (June 1970), 178.

Describes "the world's largest collection of John Muir papers," placed on permanent loan in library; relates to "the father of the national park movement."

Murphy, Edgar Gardner

2578. North Carolina, University, Library. The Edgar Gardner Murphy papers in the Southern Historical Collection of the University of North Carolina Library, ed. by Margaret Lee Neustadt. Chapel Hill, 1966. 10p.

Papers of Murphy, 1869-1913, Southern Episcopal clergyman and publicist.

Napoleon Bonaparte

2579. Perdue, Albert. "Hertzberg's Napoleonana." Books at Iowa, 10 (April 1969), 3-18.

Set of Sloane's Life of Napoleon Bonaparte, with 1,250 extra illustrations and 45 manuscript letters, in University of Iowa Libraries.

Nicholson, John

2580. Pennsylvania Historical and Museum Commission. Guide to the microfilm of the John Nicholson papers in the Pennsylvania State Archives, ed. by Donald Kent. Harrisburg, 1967. 52p.

Nicholson (died 1800) papers; comptroller general of Pennsylvania and land-company promoter.

O'Connor, William Van

2581. Syracuse University Library. The achievement of William Van O'Connor; a checklist of publications and an appreciation, by Robert S. Phillips, with an inventory of his manuscripts in the George Arents Research

Library at Syracuse University, comp. by Glenn B. Skillin. Syracuse, N.Y., 1969. 48*l.*

Guide to printed works and manuscripts of O'Connor (1915-66), author and educator.

Olmsted, Frederick Law

2582. U.S. Library of Congress, Manuscript Division. Frederick Law Olmsted: a register of his papers in the Library of Congress. Wash.: 1963. 13*l.*

U.S. landscape architect, 1822-1903.

Outlaw, David

2583. North Carolina, University, Library. The David Outlaw papers in the Southern Historical Collection of the University of North Carolina Library, ed. by Margaret Lee Neustadt. Chapel Hill, 1966. 10p.

Outlaw, 1806-68, was a Whig congressman, lawyer, and political leader from North Carolina.

Parker, Theodore

2584. Broderick, John C. "Problems of the literary executor: the case of Theodore Parker." Quarterly journal of the Library of Congress, 23 (1966), 261-73.

Papers of Theodore Parker in Library of Congress.

Penn, Thomas

2585. Pennsylvania Historical Society. Guide to the microfilm edition of the Thomas Penn papers, ed. by John D. Kilbourne. Philadelphia, 1968. 16p.

Papers of Penn, 1702-75, Pennsylvania proprietor and son of William Penn.

Penn, William

2586. Robbins, Caroline. "The papers of William Penn." Pennsylvania magazine of history and biography, 93 (Jan. 1969), 3-12.

References to major repositories.

2587. Wainwright, Nicholas B. "The Penn collection." Pennsylvania magazine of history and biography, 87 (Oct. 1963), 393-419.

In Historical Society of Pennsylvania.

Perry, Benjamin Franklin

2588. North Carolina, University, Library. The Benjamin Franklin Perry papers in the Southern Historical Collection of the University of North Carolina Library, ed. by Clyde E. Pitts. Chapel Hill, 1967. 8*l.*

Papers of Perry, 1805-86, Governor of South Carolina after Civil War.

Pickering, Timothy

2589. Massachusetts Historical Commission. Guide to the microfilm edition of the Timothy Pickering papers, ed. by Frederick S. Allis, Jr., and Roy Bartolomei. Boston, 1966. 46p.

Papers of Pickering, 1745-1829. American soldier, administrator, and politician.

Pierce, Franklin

2590. U.S. Library of Congress, Manuscript Division. Index to the Franklin Pierce papers. Wash.: Govt. Print. Off., 1962. 16p.

Lists 2,340 items, with index to 3,200 names.

Polk, James K.

2591. U.S. Library of Congress, Manuscript Division. Index to the James K. Polk papers. Wash.: Govt. Print. Off., 1969. 91p.

Guide to collection of 20,435 manuscripts in Library of Congress, dated 1775-1891.

Porter, Peter B.

2592. Buffalo and Erie County Historical Society. Guide to the microfilm edition of the Peter B. Porter papers in the Buffalo and Erie County Historical Society, ed. by Arthur C. Detmers, Jr. Buffalo, N.Y., 1968. 22p.

Porter, 1773-1844, was a congressman, major general, and Secretary of War under John Quincy Adams.

Pratt, John G.

2593. Kansas State Historical Society. Guide to the microfilm edition of the John G. Pratt papers 1834-1899, in the Kansas State Historical Society, ed. by Joseph W. Snell. Topeka, 1967. 10p.

John Gill Pratt, 1814-1900, was a Kansas missionary to Indians, teacher and printer.

Pyper, George Dollinger

2594. Utah, University, Libraries, Western Americana Dept. Register of the papers of George Dollinger Pyper (1860-1943). Salt Lake City, 1970. 24p.

Pyper, 1860-1943, Mormon leader, general superintendent of L.D.S. Deseret Sunday School Union, in charge of Salt Lake Theater, and Utah judge.

Reid, George C.

2595. U.S. Marine Corps Museum. Register of the George C. Reid papers 1898-1960 in the United States Marine Corps Museum, comp. by Doris S. Davis and others. Quantico, Va., undated. 37p. (Manuscript register series, no.4)

Marine general, 1876-1961; papers at Quantico, Virginia.

Ridgely, Charles Goodwin

2596. U.S. Library of Congress, Manuscript Division. Charles Goodwin Ridgely, Francis Asbury Roe, John Grimes Walker: a register of their papers in the Library of Congress. Wash., 1970. 4, 5, 5*l.*

U.S. naval officers.

Ridgely Family

2597. Delaware State Archives. A calendar of Ridgely family letters, 1742-1899, in the Delaware State Archives, comp. by Leon de Valinger, Jr., and Virginia E. Shaw. Dover, 1961. 362p. (v.3)

Riis, Jacob A.

2598. [New York Public Library. Jacob A. Riis collection] College & research libraries news, no.4 (April 1970), 102.

Manuscripts of books, diaries, correspondence, and other materials associated with Riis, 1849-1914, acquired by New York Public Library.

Robinson, Charles

2599. Kansas State Historical Society. Guide to the microfilm edition of the private papers of Charles and Sara T. D. Robinson 1834-1911 in the Kansas State Historical Society, ed. by Joseph W. Snell. Topeka: 1967. 14p.

Papers of first governor of Kansas, 1818-94, and wife.

Roosevelt, Franklin D.

2600. U.S. National Archives. Franklin D. Roosevelt Library, era of Franklin D. Roosevelt, selected bibliography of periodical and dissertation literature, 1945-66, comp. by William J. Stewart. Hyde Park, N.Y.: Franklin D. Roosevelt Library, 1967. 175p.

Roosevelt, Theodore

2601. Harvard University Library. Theodore Roosevelt collection; dictionary catalogue and shelflist. Cambridge, Mass., 1970. 5v.

Reproduces 65,000 cards; a comprehensive bibliography of writings by and about Roosevelt.

2602. U.S. Library of Congress, Manuscript Division. Index to the Theodore Roosevelt papers. Wash.: Govt. Print. Off., 1970. 3v.

2603. Virginia, University, Library. The Barrett Library: Theodore Roosevelt; a checklist of printed and manuscript works of Theodore Roosevelt in the Library of the University of Virginia, comp. by Anita Rutman and Lucy T. Clark. Manuscripts section by Marjorie D. Carver. Charlottesville: Univ. of Va. Pr., 1961. 44p.

Rosecrans, William Starke

2604. California, University, Library. The papers of General William Starke Rosecrans and the Rosecrans family: a guide to collection 663, by James V. Mink. Los Angeles, 1961. 39p. (UCLA Library occasional paper, no.12)

Relates to U.S. army officer and Civil War general, 1819-98.

Russell, Carl Porcher

2605. Washington State University Library. Carl Porcher Russell: an indexed register of his scholarly and professional papers, 1920-1967, in the Washington State University Library. Pullman, 1970. 149p.

National Park officer, historian, and author of Western books.

Rutledge, John

2606. North Carolina, University, Library. The John Rutledge papers in the Southern Historical Collection of the University of North Carolina Library, ed. by Clyde E. Pitts. Chapel Hill, 1967. 12p.

Papers of Rutledge, 1739-1800, Revolutionary War Governor of South Carolina and Supreme Court justice.

Sargent, Winthrop

2607. Massachusetts Historical Society. Guide to the microfilm edition of the Winthrop Sargent papers, ed. by Frederick S. Allis, Jr., and Roy Bartolomei. Boston, 1965. 55p.

Papers of Sargent, 1753-1820, first governor of Mississippi Territory, in Massachusetts Historical Society.

Sayre, Francis Bowes

2608. U.S. Library of Congress, Manuscript Division. Francis Bowes Sayre: a register of his papers in the Library of Congress. Wash., 1965. 11*l.*

American public official and diplomat, 1885- ; son-in-law of Woodrow Wilson.

Schurz, Carl

2609. U.S. Library of Congress, Manuscript Division. Carl Schurz: a register of his papers in the Library of Congress. Wash., 1966. 17p.

Papers of Carl Schurz (1829-1906), soldier, senator, Secretary of the Interior, editor, and reformer.

Schweitzer, Albert

2610. Bixler, J. Seelye. "Letters from Dr. Albert Schweitzer in the Colby Library." Colby Library quarterly, 6, no.9 (1964), 373-82.

Selfridge, Thomas Oliver

2611. U.S. Library of Congress, Manuscript Division. Thomas Oliver Selfridge, Sr. [and] Thomas Oliver Selfridge, Jr.: a register of their papers in the Library of Congress. Wash., 1969. 8, 7*l.*

T. O. Selfridge, Sr. (b. 1804) and T. O. Selfridge, Jr. (b. 1837), U.S. naval officers.

Sellers, David Foote

2612. U.S. Library of Congress, Manuscript Division. David Foote Sellers [and] Stephen B. Luce: a register of their papers in the Library of Congress. Wash., 1969. 7, 8*l.*

Sellers, 1874-1949, and Luce, 1827-1917, U.S. naval officers.

Semple, Eugene

2613. Washington, University, Libraries. The Eugene Semple papers 1865-1907, ed. by Richard C. Berner and Alan A. Hynding. Seattle: 1967. 18p. (Manuscript series, no.5)

In University of Washington Libraries.

Seward, William Henry

2614. Rochester, University, Library. Register of the William Henry Seward papers, comp. by Catherine D. Hayes. Rochester, N.Y.: 1963. 67*l.*

Papers of Seward, 1801-72, Secretary of State in Lincoln's cabinet.

Sheridan, Philip H.

2615. U.S. Library of Congress, Manuscript Division. Philip H. Sheridan; a register of his papers in the Library of Congress. Wash., 1962. 18p.

Union general, 1831-88.

Sherman, William T.

2616. Notre Dame, University, Archives. Guide to the microfilm edition of the William Tecumseh Sherman family papers (1808-91), ed. by Lawrence J. Bradley. Notre Dame, Ind., 1967. 24p.

Papers of Civil War general and family.

2617. U.S. Library of Congress, Manuscript Division. William T. Sherman, a register of his papers in the Library of Congress. Wash., 1965. 12p.

Union general, 1820-91.

Shufeldt, Robert Wilson

2618. U.S. Library of Congress, Manuscript Division. Robert Wilson Shufeldt, a register of his papers in the Library of Congress. Wash., 1969. 12p.

Naval officer, shipmaster, explorer, and diplomat, 1822-95.

Snow, Elliot

2619. U.S. Library of Congress, Manuscript Division. Elliot Snow, Leonard F. Cushing: a register of their papers in the Library of Congress. Wash., 1969. 5, 8*l.*

Snow, 1866-1939, was naval officer and author; Cushing, 1901-62, was naval architect.

Southcott, Joanna

2620. Texas, University, Humanities Research Center. A catalogue of the Joanna Southcott collection at the University of Texas, comp. by Eugene P. Wright. Austin: Univ. of Tex. Pr., 1968. 138p. (Tower bibliographical series, no.7)

Relates to English prophetess, 1750-1814.

Sterling, George

2621. Virginia, University, Library. The Barrett Library: George Sterling; a checklist of printed and manuscript works of George Sterling in the Library of the University of Virginia, comp. by Lucy T. Clark. Manuscripts section by Marjorie D. Carver. Charlottesville: Univ. of Va. Pr., 1961. 28p.

American poet, 1869-1926.

Stevens, Isaac Ingalls

2622. Washington, University, Library. Isaac Ingalls Stevens papers, 1831-1862, at the University of Washington Libraries. Seattle, 1965. 7p. (Guides to the microfilmed papers in the University of Washington Libraries, no.5)

Stevens, 1818-62, was territorial governor of Washington (1853-57), and a Union general in the Civil War.

Stevens Family

2623. New Jersey Historical Society. Guide to the microfilm edition of the Stevens family papers, ed. by Miriam V. Studley and others. Newark, 1968. 32p.

Stewart, Ethelbert

2624. North Carolina, University, Library. The Ethelbert Stewart papers in the Southern Historical Collection of the University of North Carolina Library, ed. by Margaret Lee Neustadt. Chapel Hill, 1966. 10p.

Stewart, 1857-1936, was a pioneer in field of labor statistics.

Taft, William Howard

2625. [Syracuse University Library. William Howard Taft collection] College & research libraries news, no.9 (Oct. 1970), 275.

Describes collection of 28,000 letters and other papers relating to political contest between William Howard Taft and Theodore Roosevelt for Republican presidential nomination in 1912.

Talbot, Silas

2626. Marine Historical Association Library. Inventory of the Silas Talbot papers 1767-1867. Mystic, Conn.: The Association for the G. W. Blunt White Library, Mystic Seaport, 1965. 43p.

Talbot, 1751-1813, was Revolutionary War soldier and naval officer.

Taliaferro, Lawrence

2627. Minnesota Historical Society. Guide to a microfilm edition of the Lawrence Taliaferro papers, ed. by Helen McCann White. St. Paul, 1966. 12p.

Papers of Taliaferro, 1794-1871, Indian agent, in Minnesota Historical Society.

Taylor, James Wickes

2628. Minnesota Historical Society. Guide to a microfilm edition of the James Wickes Taylor papers, ed. by Constance J. Kadrmas. St. Paul, 1968. 16p.

Papers of Taylor, 1819-93, Minnesota consular officer, author, and journalist, in Minnesota Historical Society.

Thompson, Dorothy

2629. Syracuse University Libraries. Dorothy Thompson; an inventory of American journalist's papers in Syracuse University Library, comp. by Stephanie Leon and Susan D'Angelo. Syracuse, N.Y., 1966. 144p. (Manuscript register series, no.9)

Tilton, McLane

2630. U.S. Marine Corps Museum. Register of the McLane Tilton papers 1861-1914 in the United States Marine Corps Museum, comp. by Charles A. Wood and Jack B. Hilliard. Quantico, Va., n.d. 45p. (Manuscript register series, no.2)

Captain Tilton, Asiatic Fleet Marine officer, took prominent part in 1871 Korean engagement.

Tourgée, Albion W.

2631. Chautauqua County Historical Society. An index to the Albion W. Tourgée papers in the Chautauqua County Historical Society, Westfield, New York, by Dean H. Keller. Kent, Ohio: Kent State Univ. bulletin, 1964. 59p. (Research series, no.7)

Tourgée, 1838-1905, was Union soldier, lawyer, jurist, and politician.

Twiggs, Levi

2632. U.S. Marine Corps Museum. Register of the Levi Twiggs papers 1834-1850 in the United States Marine Corps Museum, comp. by Doris S. Davis. Quantico, Va., n.d. 28p. (Manuscript register series, no.5)

Major Twiggs, veteran of the War of 1812, was killed in war with Mexico, 1847.

Tyler, John

2633. U.S. Library of Congress, Manuscript Division. Index to the John Tyler papers. Wash., 1961. 10p.

Lists 1,410 items with about 1,500 name entries.

van Gulik, R. H.

2634. Boston University, Mugar Memorial Library. Bibliography of Dr. R. H. van Gulik. Boston, 1967. 82p.
Relates to Robert Hans van Gulik, diplomat, sinologue, author.

Vinci, Leonardo da

2635. Merritt, Howard S. "The Anthony J. and Frances A. Guzzetta collection of Vinciana." University of Rochester Library bulletin, 18 (1963), 35-40.
Extensive collection of works by and about Leonardo da Vinci acquired by University of Rochester Library.

2636. Rochester University. Library. Leonardo da Vinci: list of books given to the University of Rochester Library, by Anthony J. Guzzetta. Rochester, N.Y., 1966. 33*l.*

Wallace, William H.

2637. Washington, University, Libraries. William H. Wallace papers, 1851-1878, at the University of Washington Libraries. n.p., n.d. 6p.
Whig congressman from Washington Territory, Wallace, 1811-79, was prominent in Territory of Washington affairs from 1853 until his death.

Ward, Artemas

2638. Massachusetts Historical Society. Guide to the microfilm edition of the Artemas Ward papers, 1721-1953. Boston, 1967. 30p.
Ward, 1727-1800, colonial American and U.S. military and political figure from Massachusetts.

Ward, Elizabeth Stuart Phelps

2639. Virginia, University, Library. The Barrett Library: Elizabeth Stuart Phelps Ward; a checklist of printed and manuscript works of Elizabeth Stuart Ward in the Library of the University of Virginia, comp. by Fannie Mae Elliott and Lucy T. Clark. Manuscripts section by Marjorie D. Carver. Charlottesville: Univ. of Va. Pr., 1961. 24p.
New England novelist, 1844-1911.

Warmoth, Henry Clay

2640. North Carolina, University, Library. The Henry Clay Warmoth papers in the Southern Historical Collection of the University of North Carolina Library, ed. by Margaret Lee Neustadt. Chapel Hill, 1967. 21p.
Papers of Warmoth, 1842-1931, Union soldier, lawyer, and Governor of Louisiana.

Washington, George

2641. Eaton, Dorothy S. "George Washington Papers." Library of Congress quarterly journal of current acquisitions, 22 (1965), 3-26.
Description of Washington papers in Library of Congress.

2642. Jackson, Donald. "The Papers of George Washington." Manuscripts, 22 (Winter 1970), 3-12.
Discussion of several private collections.

2643. U.S. Library of Congress, Manuscript Division. Index to the George Washington papers. Wash.: Govt. Print. Off., 1964. 294p.
Records 64,786 items of correspondence and other materials, with 67,107 entries in name index.

Weeks, Stephen Beauregard

2644. Powell, William S. Stephen Beauregard Weeks, 1865-1918: a preliminary bibliography. Chapel Hill: North Carolina collection, Univ. of N.C., 1965. 19p.
Relates to Weeks, 1865-1918, North Carolina historian and bibliographer; based on University of North Carolina Library collection.

Weeks Family

2645. Dartmouth College Library. A guide to the papers of the Weeks family of Lancaster, New Hampshire. Hanover, N.H.: 1969. 170p.
Papers cover 6 generations and over 2 centuries, 1660-1890, of prominent New Hampshire family.

Werfel, Alma Mahler

2646. Klarman, Adolf, and Hirsch, Rudolf. "Notes on the Alma Mahler Werfel collection." University of Pennsylvania Library chronicle, 35 (1969), 33-35.
Account of Alma Mahler Werfel correspondence and papers, University of Pennsylvania Library; wife, first, of Gustav Mahler and later of Franz Werfel.

Whitaker, John Mills

2647. Utah, University, Libraries, Western Americana Dept. Register of the papers of John Mills Whitaker (1863-1960). Salt Lake City, 1969. 31p.

Whitaker was prominent Mormon missionary, bishop, patriarch, teacher, and speaker.

Wilson, Woodrow

2648. Davies, John D. "New Wilson letters." Princeton alumni weekly, 63 (Feb. 8, 1963), 9, 15.

Describes collection of 1,460 letters from Woodrow Wilson to his wife, received by Princeton Library.

Yancey, Benjamin Cudworth

2649. North Carolina, University, Library. The Benjamin Cudworth Yancey papers in the Southern Historical Collection of the University of North Carolina Library, ed. by Clyde E. Pitts. Chapel Hill, 1967. 13p.

Papers of Yancey, 1817-91, South Carolina lawyer and diplomat, in University of North Carolina Library.

GENEALOGY

2650. American Society of Genealogists. Genealogical research; methods and sources, ed. by Milton Rubincam. Wash., 1960. 456p.

Discusses regional, state, and local records.

2651. California Secretary of State. Genealogical research in the California State Archives. Sacramento, 1969. 7p.

2652. Cappon, Lester J. American genealogical periodicals; a bibliography with a chronological finding list. N.Y.: New York Public Library, 1964. 32p.

Includes a "geographical finding-list by states."

2653. Chow, Dorothy Wei. A selective bibliography of books on American genealogy in the Enoch Pratt Free Library, the Maryland Historical Society Library, and the Peabody Institute Library in Baltimore, Maryland. Wash., 1965. 208p. (Master's thesis, Dept. of Library Science, Catholic Univ. of America)

2654. Church of Jesus Christ of Latter-Day Saints Genealogical Society. Major genealogical record sources in the United States. Salt Lake City, 1967. 10p.

2655. Gleason, Margaret. Printed resources for genealogical searching in Wisconsin: a selective bibliography. Detroit: Detroit Society for Genealogical Research, 1964. 96p.

Based on State Historical Society of Wisconsin holdings.

2656. National Genealogical Society. Long Island genealogical source material, comp. by Herbert F. Seversmith and Kenn Stryker-Roda. Wash., 1962. 121p. (Special publications, no.24)

Author list of 845 printed and manuscript works, with locations.

2657. New Jersey State Library. Genealogical research, a guide to source materials in the Archives and History Bureau of the New Jersey State Library and other state agencies. Trenton, 1966. 33*l.*

2658. North Carolina State Dept. of Archives and History. Genealogical research in the North Carolina Department of Archives and History. Raleigh, 1962. 8p.

2659. Pennsylvania State Library. Heraldry; a bibliography of books in the Pennsylvania State Library with a subject-place index, comp. by Carol Carolson. Harrisburg, 1970. 18p.

2660. St. Louis Public Library. Genealogical material and local histories in the St. Louis Public Library, rev. ed. by Georgia Gambrill. St. Louis, 1965. 356p.

2661. Tennessee State Library and Archives. Genealogical source materials in the Tennessee State Library and Archives. Nashville, n.d. 7p.

2662. ———. Guide to the use of genealogical material in the Tennessee State Library and Archives. Nashville, 1964. 24p.

2663. Texas State Library and Historical Commission. Catalog of genealogical materials in Texas libraries, comp. by John B. Corbin. Austin: Tex. State Library, 1965-66. 2v.

Part I, Virginia; part II, Kentucky. Locates copies in 20 libraries.

2664. U.S. National Archives. Genealogical records in National Archives. Wash., 1967. 12p.

2665. ———. Genealogical sources outside National Archives. Wash., 1970. 12p. (General information leaflet, no.6)

2666. ———. Guide to genealogical records in the National Archives, by Meredith B. Colket and Frank E. Bridgers. Wash.: Govt. Print. Off., 1964. 145p. (National Archives pub. no. 64-8)

2667. Utah, University, Libraries. A representative list

of genealogical materials held in the University of Utah Libraries, Western Americana collection, by Elva Dean. Salt Lake City, 1969. 9p. (Univ. of Utah Libraries news letter, v.1, no.10, Aug. 5, 1969)

2668. Wright, Norman E. North American genealogical sources; Southern states. Provo, Utah: Brigham Young Univ. Pr., 1968. 158p.

DIRECTORIES

2669. American Antiquarian Society. Bibliography of American directories through 1860, by Dorothea N. Spear. Worcester, Mass., 1961. 389p.

About 70 percent of 1,647 entries in American Antiquarian Society; locations in other libraries also shown.

History

GENERAL

2670. Colorado, University, Libraries, Social Sciences Library. Social sciences general references: History; a selective and annotated bibliographical guide, by Lubomyr R. Wynar. Boulder, 1963. 348p.
Limited to University of Colorado Library holdings.

2671. Hale, Richard W. Guide to photocopied historical materials in the United States and Canada. Ithaca, N.Y.: Cornell Univ. Pr., 1961. 241p.
Lists government records, personal papers, church records, educational records, ships' logs, etc., with locations; union list of 11,000 entries.

2672. Princeton University Library. Princeton University Library microform holdings of historical interest, comp. by Earle E. Coleman. Princeton, N.J., 1968. 51p. Supplement, Aug. 1968-Aug. 1970. 5p.

2673. Southern Methodist University, Bridwell Library. The modern spirit: an exhibit of printed materials charting the intellectual adventure of the last fifty years (1915-1965). Dallas, Tex., 1966. 52p. (Bridwell broadside, no.4)

ORAL HISTORY

2674. Association for Recorded Sound Collections. Preliminary directory of sound recordings collections in the United States and Canada. N.Y.: New York Public Library, 1967. 157p.

2675. California, University, Library. The oral history program at UCLA: a bibliography, by Elizabeth I. Dixon. Los Angeles, 1966. 30p.
Collection of tape recordings and typescripts of oral history interviews, 1959-66, including subject index.

2676. Columbia University. The oral history collection, recent acquisitions and a report for 1966. N.Y., 1966. 30p.

2677. Columbia University, Oral History Research Office. The oral history collection of Columbia University. N.Y., 1964. 181p.
Transcripts of interviews with persons prominent in U.S. political, cultural, social, and economic life.

2678. North Carolina, University, Library. Catalog of the collection of spoken-word recordings in the Undergraduate Library of the University of North Carolina at Chapel Hill. Chapel Hill, 1968. 93*l*.

2679. Princeton University Library. A descriptive catalogue of the Dulles oral history collection. Princeton, N.J., 1967. 82p.
A catalog of taped memoirs of individuals who knew John Foster Dulles and events in which he participated. Includes brief descriptions of the extensive collection of Dulles papers in Princeton Library.

2680. Stanford University Libraries, Archive of Recorded Sound. Sounds of the past. Stanford, Calif.: Stanford Univ. Pr., 1970. Unpaged.
Descriptive brochure.

2681. Tracy, Lorna. "Echoes in a bottle." Books at Iowa, 8 (April 1968), 24-29.
Collection of oral recordings in University of Iowa Libraries.

EUROPEAN

General

2682. California State College Library, San Diego. Bibliography on European integration; list of the books, documents, and periodicals on European integration in San Diego State College Library, comp. by Andrew Szabo and Walter H. Posner. San Diego, 1967. 62p.

2683. Harvard University Library. General European and world history. Cambridge, Mass., 1970. 959p. (Widener Library shelflist, no.32)

Lists about 37,000 titles.

2684. Stanford University, Hoover Institution. Western Europe: a survey of holdings at the Hoover Institution on War, Revolution and Peace, by Agnes F. Peterson. Stanford, Calif., 1970. 60p.

Medieval and Renaissance

2685. California, University, Library. Medieval and Renaissance studies; a selected list of recent additions to the collections, by J. M. Edelstein. Los Angeles, Sept. 1962-May 1964. 14 issues.

2686. Harvard University Library. Crusades. Cambridge, Mass., 1965. 23, 19, 19p. (Widener Library shelflist, v.1)

Listing by call number, author or title, and chronologically.

2687. North Carolina, University, Library. Medieval and Renaissance studies; a location guide to selected reference works and source collections in the libraries of the University of North Carolina at Chapel Hill and Duke University, prep. by Louise McG. Hall. Chapel Hill, 1965. 226p.

2688. ---, Humanities Division. Medieval and Renaissance studies; a location guide to selected reference works and source materials in the libraries of the University of North Carolina at Chapel Hill and Duke University, comp. by Louise McG. Hall. Chapel Hill: Univ. of N.C., 1967. 322p.

Bibliographical guide to entire field.

2689. Ohio State University Libraries. Arabic culture in the medieval West: a reading list based on a selection from the holdings of the OSU Libraries, by Margaret Anderson. Columbus, 1969. 33p.

2690. Syracuse University Libraries. Medieval and Renaissance history serials in Syracuse University Libraries, comp. by Margery Ganz. Syracuse, N.Y., 1970. 15p.

Great Britain

2691. [Brigham Young University Library. "Brigham Young University has purchased a unique collection"] College and research libraries news, no.8 (Sept. 1969), 276-77.

Announces the acquisition of a major collection relating to Queen Victoria and her times.

2692. Chicago, University, Library. Handlist of Bacon manuscripts in the University of Chicago Library. Chicago, 1965? 434p.

Concerns Sir Nicholas Bacon collection of court and manorial records in Department of Special Collections.

2693. Hamilton, William B. "British historical materials." Gnomon (1970), 24-30. (Special number of Duke University Library's Library notes)

Describes Duke Library's holdings.

2694. Huntington Library. The Huntington Library as a research center for the study of British history, by James Thorpe. San Marino, Calif., 1968. 8p.

2695. Magee, David B. Victoria R.I.; a collection of books, manuscripts, autograph letters, original drawings, etc., by the lady herself and her loyal subjects, produced during her long and illustrious reign. San Francisco: David Magee, 1969-70. 3v.

Catalog of collection relating to Queen Victoria, acquired by Brigham Young University Library.

2696. New York State, Secretary of State. Calendar of British historical manuscripts in the Office of the Secretary of State, Albany, New York, 1664-1776. Ridgewood, N.J.: Gregg, 1968. 893p.

2697. Pennsylvania State University Libraries. Checklist of English Civil War pamphlets. University Park, 1963. 4p.

2698. Preston, Jean. "Collections of English historical manuscripts in the Huntington Library." Archives, the journal of the British Records Association, 6 (1963), 95-107.

2699. Texas, University, Library. British heritage; an exhibition of books, manuscripts and iconography from the collections at the University of Texas at Austin. Austin, 1967. 59p.

2700. Weller, Sam and Lila. "Magee's Victoria R.I. collection." AB bookman's weekly, 45 (1970), 1775-81.

Describes collection relating to Queen Victoria, acquired by Brigham Young University Library.

Germany

2701. Price, Arnold H. "German history: a review of

some recent publications." Quarterly journal of the Library of Congress, 23 (1966), 139-46.

Report on acquisitions, Library of Congress.

2702. U.S. Library of Congress, Slavic and Central European Division. East Germany; a selected bibliography, comp. by Arnold H. Price. Wash., 1967. 133p.

Principally works published since 1958; cites 833 monographs, articles, dissertations, atlases, etc.

Austria and Austria-Hungary

2703. Harvard University, Houghton Library. Vienna, 1888-1938. Cambridge, Mass., 1967. 30p.

Catalog of an exhibition.

2704. Peterson, Agnes F. "Austro-Hungarian materials 1867-1918 in the Hoover Institution." Austrian history news letter, no.2 (1961), 25-32. (Univ. of Tex., Dept. of History)

2705. Price, Arnold H. "Austria: a survey." Quarterly journal of the Library of Congress, 21 (1964), 105-12.

Report on acquisitions, Library of Congress.

2706. [Rice University Library. Austro-Hungarian collection] College & research libraries news, no.10 (Nov. 1968), 345.

Collection of 3,600 items on Austro-Hungarian history, acquired by Rice Library.

2707. Stanford University Libraries. A list of materials for the study of the history of Austria; with a note of holdings in the libraries of Stanford University, comp. by Kenneth W. Rock. Stanford, Calif., 1963. 50*l.*

2708. U.S. National Archives. Records of Department of State relating to internal affairs of Austria-Hungary and Austria, 1910-1929, prep. by James E. Primas. Wash., 1968. 12p.

2709. ———. Records of Department of State relating to political relations between United States and Austria-Hungary and Austria, 1910-29 and between Austria-Hungary and Austria and other states, 1910-29, prep. by James E. Primas. Wash., 1969. 11p.

France

2710. Hardy, James D., Jr., and Jensen, John H. "Maclure collection serials: a descriptive catalogue." University of Pennsylvania Library chronicle, 29 (1963), 30-42.

Essay describing 39 serial publications (677 volumes) in French Revolutionary collection at University of Pennsylvania.

2711. Haubold, Marcia Ann. "The French Revolution collection." Books at Iowa, 3 (Nov. 1965), 5-9.

Description of pamphlet collection of over 8,000 pieces in University of Iowa Library.

2712. Lindsay, Robert O., and Neu, John. French political pamphlets, 1547-1648: a catalog of major collections in American libraries. Madison: Univ. of Wis. Pr., 1969. 510p.

Describes 6,800 pamphlets in 15 U.S. research libraries.

2713. McDonough, John, and O'Neill, James E. "France in the Manuscript Division of the Library of Congress." French historical studies, 4 (Spring 1965), 95-102.

2714. Ohio State University Libraries. France—(1870-1945)—the Third Republic and Vichy governments; a bibliography of works at Ohio State University Library. Columbus, 1964. 2pts. in 1.

2715. Oregon, University, Library. A selective bibliography of materials on the French seventeenth century in the University of Oregon Library, based on the Cabeen-Brody-Edelman bibliography. Eugene, 1963. 33, 5*l.*

2716. Pennsylvania, University, Library. The Maclure collection of French Revolutionary materials, ed. by James D. Hardy, Jr., and others. Philadelphia: Univ. of Pa. Pr., 1966. 456p.

Lists 25,000 items of serials, pamphlets, etc., with indexes of authors, committees, and commissions.

2717. Roylance, Dale R. "Royal association books in the Bliss collection." Yale University Library gazette, 39 (1965), 174-83; 40 (1966), 160-67.

Collection relating to French history in Yale Library.

2718. Stanford University, Hoover Institution. The French Fifth Republic; establishment and consolidation, 1958-1965; an annotated bibliography of the holdings at the Hoover Institution, by Grete Heinz and Agnes F. Peterson. Stanford, Calif., 1970. 170p. (Bibliographical series, no.44)

Lists 2,134 books and serial publications.

Belgium

2719. U.S. National Archives. Records of Department

of State relating to internal affairs of Belgium, 1910-29, prep. by Ralph E. Huss. Wash., 1967. 16p.

Netherlands

2720. New York State, Secretary of State. Calendar of Dutch historical manuscripts in the Office of the Secretary of State, Albany, New York, 1630-1664, ed. by Edmund B. O'Callaghan. Ridgewood, N.J.: Gregg, 1968. 423p.

2721. U.S. National Archives. Records of Department of State relating to political relations between United States and Netherlands and between Netherlands and other states, 1910-29, prep. by Frank S. Soriano. Wash., 1970. 11p.

Switzerland

2722. Price, Arnold H. "German-language Helvetica." Library of Congress quarterly journal of current acquisitions, 19 (1961), 1-6.

Report on acquisitions, Library of Congress.

Scandinavia

2723. Klesment, Johannes. "Scandinavia—a 10-year survey." Library of Congress quarterly journal of current acquisitions, 21 (1964), 63-80.

Review of acquisitions by Library of Congress from Scandinavian countries.

Italy

2724. Baron, Hans. "A forgotten chronicle of early fifteenth-century Venice: the copy in Newberry Library F. 87." In Essays in history and literature presented . . . to Stanley Pargellis, Chicago: Newberry Library, 1965, p.19-36.

2725. Dennis, George T. "An inventory of Italian notarial documents in the Sutro Library, San Francisco." Manuscripta, 9 (July 1965), 89-103.

2726. Lansing, Elizabeth. "Opuscoli; the pamphlets in the Guido Mazzoni collection." Library notes, a bulletin issued for the Friends of Duke University Library, no.38 (April 1964), 1-6.

Extensive collection of Italian pamphlets in Duke Library.

2727. Syracuse University Libraries. A selection from the library of Leopold von Ranke, an exhibition of manuscripts. Syracuse, N.Y., 1970. 10p.

Exhibition catalog of 16th-18th-century manuscripts dealing with history of Venice and its relationships with European powers and Ottoman Empire; collection acquired by Syracuse in 1887.

2728. ———. A short description of Leopold von Ranke's manuscripts, nos. 101-209, by Joseph Della Grotte. Syracuse, N.Y., 1966. 48p.

Collection dealing with Republic of Venice, 16th-18th centuries, its colonial possessions and relations with other powers.

2729. U.S. National Archives. Record of Department of State relating to political relations between United States and Italy, 1910-29, and between Italy and other states, 1910-29, prep. by Ernestine S. Cognasso. Wash., 1969. 11p.

Portugal and Spain

2730. California, University, Library. Spain and Spanish America in the libraries of the University of California; a catalogue of books. N.Y.: B. Franklin, 1969. 2v.

Reprint of 1928-30 edition.

2731. Catholic University of America Library. Catalog of the Oliveira Lima Library. Boston: G. K. Hall, 1970. 2v.

Major collection on Portuguese and Brazilian history and literature, acquired by Catholic University in 1916.

2732. Lanning, John T. "The Hispanic collection." Gnomon, (1970), 82-94. (Special number of Duke University Library's Library notes)

Describes Duke Library's holdings.

2733. Ramalho, Américo da Costa. "The Portuguese pamphlets." Library of Congress quarterly journal of current acquisitions, 20 (1963), 157-62.

Description of collection of 28,500 books, pamphlets, reprints, and manuscripts relating to Portugal, acquired by Library of Congress.

Slavic and East European

2734. Brooklyn College Library. A cumulative catalog of titles in the Slavic languages in the Brooklyn College Library as of April 30, 1966. Brooklyn, N.Y., 1966. 180, 64*l.*

2735. Carlton, Robert G. "Recent sources of information on Eastern Europe." Quarterly journal of the Library of Congress, 21 (1964), 207-11.

Report on acquisitions, Library of Congress.

2736. Gredler, Charles R. "The Slavic collection at Harvard." Harvard Library bulletin, 17 (1969), 425-33.

General description.

2737. Harvard University Library. Slavic history and literatures. Cambridge, Mass., 1971. 4v. (Widener Library shelflist, no. 28-31)

Lists 95,000 titles.

2738. Horecky, Paul L. "Slavic and East European resources and facilities of the Library of Congress." Slavic review, 23 (1964), 309-27.

2739. Indiana University Library. Slavic and East European materials in the Indiana University Libraries. Bloomington: Russian and East European Institute, 1963. 5*l.*

2740. Pidhainy, Oleh Semenovych. "East-European and Russian studies in the South: Auburn University." New review, 10 (Sept. 1970), 69-102.

Includes checklists of major collections and current serials in Auburn Library.

2741. Readex Microprint Corporation. Cyrillic union catalog of the Library of Congress: description and guide to the microprint edition. N.Y., 1964. 12p.

2742. U.S. Dept. of the Army Library. Communist Eastern Europe; analytical survey of literature. Wash.: Govt. Print. Off., 1971. 367p. (DA pamphlet 550-8)

2743. U.S. House of Representatives. Hungarians in Rumania and Transylvania, a bibliographical list of publications in Hungarian and West European languages compiled from the holdings of the Library of Congress, by Elemer Bako and William Solyom-Fekete. Wash.: Govt. Print. Off., 1969. 192p.

2744. U.S. Library of Congress. Cyrillic union catalog. N.Y.: Readex Microprint Corp., 1963. 1,244 microprint cards.

Includes authors, titles, and subjects for more than 700,000 cards, representing 178,226 titles for works in Russian and other Cyrillic-alphabet languages; locations in 186 American libraries.

2745. ———. "Slavica." Library of Congress quarterly journal of current acquisitions, 18 (1961), 99-116, 153-65; 19 (1962), 223-47; 20 (1963), 200-9; 21 (1964), 203-31; 22 (1965), 226-73.

Annual reports on Library's current acquisitions; covers subject fields (e.g., technology and social sciences), and areas (Czechoslovakia, Poland, Baltic states, etc.), and forms of material.

2746. ———. "Southeast Europe." Library of Congress quarterly journal of current acquisitions, 18 (1961), 166-85.

Report on Library's current acquisitions for Yugoslavia, Bulgaria, Rumania, and Albania.

2747. ———, Processing Dept. East European accessions list. Wash.: Govt. Print. Off., 1951- . Monthly.

Monographs published since 1944 and periodicals since 1950 currently received by Library of Congress and numerous other U.S. libraries.

Soviet Union

2748. Chicago, University, Library. Ucrainiana; an exhibition of Ukrainian books and books about Ukraine. Chicago, Ill., 1971. Unpaged.

Lists 142 items.

2749. City College Library, City University of New York. Russian area studies at the City College Library, by Peter A. Goy. N.Y., 1964. 25*l.*

2750. Foster, Ludmila A. Bibliography of Russian emigré literature, 1918-1968. Boston: G. K. Hall, 1970. 2v.

Based on Harvard University Library collection; contains about 17,000 entries, primarily for belles lettres—poetry, prose, drama—memoirs, and literary criticism.

2751. Granovsky, A. A. "Immigrant gift to America: Ukrainian library given to Immigrant Archives, University of Minnesota." Minnesota libraries, 21 (1966), 299-302.

2752. Harvard University Library. Russian history since 1917. Cambridge, Mass., 1966. 698p. (Widener Library shelflist, no.4)

Lists 13,772 titles, arranged by classification schedule, author or title, and chronologically.

2753. ———. Twentieth century Russian literature. Cambridge, Mass., 1965. 142p., 139p., 140p. (Widener Library shelflist, no.3)

Lists 9,430 titles, mainly after 1917, in classified, author-title, and chronological arrangements.

2754. Kasinec, Edward. "Eighteenth-century Russian publications in the New York Public Library: a preliminary catalogue." Bulletin of the New York Public Library, 73 (1969), 599-614.

Lists 166 titles.

2755. Neiswender, Rosemary. Guide to Russian reference and language aids. N.Y.: Special Libraries Association, 1962. 92p.

Based on University of California Library, Los Angeles, collections.

2756. Newberry Library. Check list of the Russian collections of the Newberry Library, comp. by Judd Gershenson. Chicago, 1965. 231*l*.

2757. Princeton University Library. Russian bibliographic aids (selected bibliography), Princeton University Library, Slavic collections. Princeton, N.J., 196–. 20*l*.

2758. Stanford University, Hoover Institution. Menshevik collection of newspapers, periodicals, pamphlets, and books relating to the Menshevik Movement. Stanford, Calif., 1967. 29p.

Detailed listing.

2759. ——— ———. Nikolai I. Bukharin; a bibliography, with annotations, including the locations of his works in major American and European libraries, comp. by Sidney Heitman. Stanford, Calif., 1969. 181p. (Bibliographical series, no.37)

Lists 937 items.

2760. ——— ———. "The Okhrana": the Russian Department of Police, a bibliography, by Edward E. Smith. Stanford, Calif., 1967. 280p. (Bibliographical series, no.33)

Guide to books, pamphlets, articles, and manuscripts on Imperial Russian secret police, based on Hoover Institution holdings.

2761. ——— ———. Russian language journals and books on microfilm (including some other East European publications). Stanford, Calif., 1965. 35p.

2762. ——— ———. Russian social democracy: the Menshevik Movement, comp. by Anna Bourguina. Stanford, Calif., 1968. 391p. (Bibliographical series, no.36)

2763. ——— ———. Stalin's works: an annotated bibliography, comp. by Robert H. McNeal. Stanford, Calif., 1967. 197p. (Bibliographical series, no.26)

Lists 1,018 titles.

2764. U.S. Dept. of the Army Library. Soviet Russia: strategic survey. Wash., 1963. 223p. (DA pamphlet 20-64)

2765. ———. USSR: strategic survey; a bibliography. Wash., 1968. 238p. (DA pamphlet 550-6)

2766. U.S. Library of Congress. Monthly index of Russian accessions, 1948- . v.1- . Wash.: Govt. Print. Off., 1948- .

Records of publications in Russian language currently received by Library of Congress and a group of cooperating libraries.

2767. ———, Slavic and Central European Division. Eighteenth century Russian publications in the Library of Congress, a catalog, prep. by Tatiana Fessenko. Wash., 1961. 157p.

Baltic States

2768. Balys, John P. "The Baltic states: a 10-year survey." Library of Congress quarterly journal of current acquisitions, 20 (1962), 80-92.

Description of Library of Congress acquisitions from Baltic states.

2769. ———. "The Baltic states." Quarterly journal of the Library of Congress, 21 (1964), 212-16.

Report on acquisitions, Library of Congress.

2770. ———. Lithuania and Lithuanians; a selected bibliography. N.Y.: Praeger, 1961. 190p.

Cites 1,182 items with locations, usually in Library of Congress.

Bulgaria

2771. Pundeff, Marin V. "Sources for Bulgarian biography." Quarterly journal of the Library of Congress, 24 (1967), 97-102.

Report on acquisitions, Library of Congress.

2772. Stanford University Libraries. A list of materials for the study of the history of Bulgaria, with a note of holdings in the Libraries of Stanford University, by Roger V. Paxton. Stanford, Calif., 1963. 14*l*.

2773. U.S. Library of Congress, Slavic and Central European Division. Bulgaria; a bibliographic guide, by

Marin V. Pundeff. Wash.: Govt. Print. Off., 1965. 98p.
Locations in Library of Congress and other American libraries.

Czechoslovakia

2774. Stanford University Library. A list of materials for the study of the history of Czechoslovakia, with a note of holdings in the Libraries of Stanford University, comp. by Sybil Halpern. Stanford, Calif., 1964. 33*l.*

2775. U.S. Library of Congress, Slavic and Central European Division. Czechoslovakia; a bibliographic guide, by Rudolf Sturm. Wash., 1967. 157p.
Lists and discusses 1,500 items in Library of Congress and other locations.

Hungary

2776. Maryland, University, Library. An annotated bibliography of Stephen I, King of Hungary; his reign and his era, by Michael J. Horvath. College Park, 1969. 28p.
Prepared for exhibit in University of Maryland Library.

2777. Solyom-Fekete, William. "The Hungarian constitutional compact of 1867." Quarterly journal of the Library of Congress, 24 (1967), 287-308.
Collection of Hungarian parliamentary records and documents in Library of Congress.

2778. Stanford University, Hoover Institution. The Hungarian Soviet Republic: 1919; an evaluation and a bibliography, by Ivan Völgyes. Stanford, Calif., 1970. 90p. (Bibliographical series, no.43)

2779. Stanford University Libraries. A list of materials for the study of the history of Hungary, with a note of holdings in the Libraries of Stanford University, comp. by Roger V. Paxton. Stanford, Calif., 1962. 18*l.*

2780. Tezla, Albert. Hungarian authors; a bibliographical handbook. Cambridge, Mass.: Harvard Univ. Pr., 1970. 792p.
Lists 84 "scholarly and literary periodicals" with locations in 81 U.S. libraries.

2781. ———. An introductory bibliography to the study of Hungarian literature. Cambridge, Mass.: Harvard Univ. Pr., 1964. 290p.
Appendix, "Scholarly and literary periodicals," p.237-60, lists 72 titles, with holdings in 112 U.S. and 18 foreign libraries.

2782. U.S. Library of Congress. "Hungarica." Library of Congress quarterly journal of current acquisitions, 18 (1961), 186-91; 19 (1962), 152-57; 20 (1963), 101-10; 21 (1964), 119-23; 22 (1965), 108-10.
Annual reports on Library's current acquisitions.

2783. U.S. National Archives. Preliminary inventory of the President's Committee for Hungarian Refugee Relief, comp. by Kathryn M. Murphy. Wash., 1965. 16p.

Poland

2784. Nitecki, André. "Polish books in America and the Farmington Plan." College and research libraries, 27 (1966), 439-49.
Quantitative study of holdings of Polish titles issued in 1957 in 33 U.S. libraries.

2785. Stanford University Libraries. A list of materials for the study of the history of Poland, with a note of holdings in the Libraries of Stanford University, by Roman Szporluk. Stanford, Calif., 1962. 32*l.*

2786. U.S. Library of Congress. Poland in the collections of the Library of Congress; an overview, by Kazimierz Grzybowski. Wash.: Govt. Print. Off., 1968. 26p.

Rumania

2787. Carlton, Robert G. "Published research on Rumania." Quarterly journal of the Library of Congress, 21 (1964), 228-31.
Annual report on acquisitions, Library of Congress.

2788. [Pittsburgh, University, Libraries. Rumanian collection] College and research libraries news, no.6 (June 1969), 195-96.
Describes 500-volume collection relating to various aspects of Rumanian culture and history, received by Pittsburgh.

2789. Stanford University Libraries. A list of materials for the study of the history of Romania, showing holdings in the Libraries of Stanford University, comp. by Kenneth W. Rock. Stanford, Calif., 1962. 45*l.*

2790. U.S. Library of Congress, Slavic and Central European Division. Rumania, a bibliographic guide, by Stephen A. Fischer-Galati. Wash.: Govt. Print. Off., 1963. 75p.
Lists 748 titles, locating copies.

2791. U.S. National Archives. Materials in National

Archives relating to Rumania, comp. by James F. Vivian. Wash., 1970. 18p. (Reference information paper, no.46)

Yugoslavia

2792. Price, Robert F. "The Matica Srpska and Serbian cultural development." Quarterly journal of the Library of Congress, 22 (1965), 259-64.

Report on acquisitions, Library of Congress.

ASIAN

General

2793. Asia Society. Libraries in New York City with collections of materials on Asia, and notes on other sources of information, including bibliographies. N.Y., 1962. 23p.

2794. International Colloquium on Luso-Brazilian Studies. Europe informed; an exhibition of early books which acquainted Europe with the East. Cambridge, Mass.: Harvard College Library, New York Public Library, Columbia University Library, Library of the Hispanic Society of America, 1966. 192p.

2795. Mary Washington College Library. A bibliography of books, periodicals and recordings pertaining to Asia in the Library of Mary Washington College, comp. by Carrol H. Quenzel. Fredericksburg, Va., 1966. 160*l.*

2796. Michigan State University Library, International Library. Asia: select recent acquisitions. East Lansing, 1965- . No.1- .

Works in all languages relating to Asia acquired by Michigan State University Library.

2797. Michigan, University, Asia Library. List of new acquisitions. Ann Arbor, 1961- . No. 1- .

2798. Nunn, G. Raymond. Resources for research on Asia at the University of Hawaii and in Honolulu. Honolulu: East-West Center Library, 1965. 16*l.* (East-West Center Library, Occasional papers, no.1)

2799. Pearson, James D. Oriental and Asian bibliography; an introduction with some references to Africa. Hamden, Conn.: Archon Books, 1966. 261p.

One of three sections deals with libraries holding outstanding collections in these areas.

2800. Princeton University Library. Public affairs in Asia; serials (periodicals, monographs in series, documents) in the Princeton University Library in Western languages. Princeton, N.J.: Woodrow Wilson School of Public and International Affairs, 1964. 24*l.*

2801. Syracuse University Library. A survey of Asian materials in the Syracuse University Library with some recommendations. Syracuse, 1961. 33*l.*

2802. ———. Theses and dissertations on Asia, comp. by Donn V. Hart. Syracuse, N.Y., 46p.

2803. U.S. Library of Congress, Orientalia Division. "Orientalia." Library of Congress quarterly journal of current acquisitions, 18 (1961), 61-98; 19 (1962), 79-118; 20 (1963), 111-55; 21 (1964), 105-66; 22 (1965), 119-47, 274-86; 23 (1966), 147-83; 24 (1967), 103-37; 25 (1968), 155-75; 26 (1969), 91-123.

Annual reports on Library's current acquisitions. Covers China, Korea, Japan, South and Southeast Asia, Near and Middle East, Hebraica, etc.

2804. U.S. National Archives. Records of Department of State relating to internal affairs of Asia, 1910-29, prep. by Frank S. Soriano. Wash., 1969. 13p.

2805. ———. Records of Department of State relating to internal affairs of British Asia, 1910-29, prep. by Frank S. Soriano. Wash., 1969. 15p.

2806. ———. Records of Department of State relating to political relations between United States and Asia, 1920-29, and between Asia and other states, 1914-29, prep. by Frank S. Soriano. Wash., 1969. 11p.

2807. Washington, University, Libraries. Shu Hu: news letter from the University of Washington Libraries, Asiatic collections, Seattle, Washington, Oct. 15, 1970- . No. 1- .

Each issue contains annotated bibliography of selected new acquisitions.

2808. Yang, Winston and Teresa. Asian resources in American libraries; essays and bibliographies. N.Y.: Foreign Area Materials Center, Univ. of the State of N.Y., 1968. 122p.

Bibliographical guide to published information on library resources and a directory of Asian library resources in U.S.

Near and Middle East

2809. Buchanan, Briggs. "The Newell collection of Oriental seals: an important addition to the Yale Babylonian collection." Yale University Library gazette, 43 (1968), 91-97.

Description of Yale Library's collection of 1,400 cylinder seals from ancient Babylonia.

2810. Harvard University Library. Catalogue of Arabic, Persian, and Ottoman Turkish books. Cambridge, Mass., 1968. 5v.

Collection of more than 40,000 volumes: 31,000 in Arabic, 6,000 in Persian, and 4,000 in Ottoman Turkish, with author, title, and subject entries.

2811. ———. Catalogue of Persian books, prelim. ed., ed. by Labib Zuwiyya Yamak. Cambridge, Mass., 1964. 218p.

2812. Krek, Miroslav. A catalogue of Arabic manuscripts in the Oriental Institute of Chicago. New Haven, Conn.: American Oriental Society, 1961. 46p.

2813. Matta, Seoud. "Arabic resources in American research libraries and PL 480." College and research libraries, 25 (1964), 472-74.

Statistical data on major Arabic collections in U.S.

2814. Minnesota, University, Middle East Library. Current accessions in the Middle East Library, University of Minnesota. Minneapolis, Jan. 1970- . no.1- . Quarterly.

2815. U.S. Dept. of the Army Library. Middle East: tricontinental hub, a strategic survey. Wash.: Govt. Print. Off., 1965-69. 2v. (DA pamphlet 550-2-1)

Based on publications located in Army Library.

2816. U.S. Library of Congress, American Libraries Book Procurement Center. Accessions lists: Israel. Tel-Aviv, Israel, April 1964- . no.1- . Monthly.

Materials acquired under Public Law 480 Program.

2817. ——— ———. Accessions list: Middle East. Cairo, Egypt, Jan. 1963- . no.1- . Monthly.

Materials acquired under Public Law 480 Program.

2818. ———, Near East Section. American doctoral dissertations on Arab world, 1883-1968, comp. by George Dimitri Selim. Wash., 1970. 103p.

2819. U.S. National Archives. Records of Department of State relating to internal affairs of Turkey, 1910-1929, prep. by Ralph E. Huss. Wash., 1969. 25p.

2820. ———. Records of Department of State relating to political relations between United States and Persia, 1921-29, and between Persia and other states, 1918-29, prep. by Frank S. Soriano. Wash., 1969. 9p.

2821. Utah, University, Middle East Center Library. Arabic collection, Aziz S. Atiya Library for Middle East Studies. Salt Lake City: Univ. of Utah Pr., 1968. 841p. (Middle East catalogue series, v.1)

A partial listing of Arabic monographic holdings.

2822. Washington University Libraries. Bibliography of materials concerning the Middle East and North Africa in the Washington University Libraries, by Andrew Carvely. St. Louis, 1970. Unpaged.

2823. Yamak, Labib Zuwiyya. "The Middle Eastern collections of the Harvard Library." Harvard Library bulletin, 16 (1968), 313-25.

History and description.

South and Southeast

2824. California, University, Center for South Asia Studies. Books on South Asia newly added to the General Library, University of California. Berkeley, 1955- . Bimonthly.

2825. Case, Margaret H. South Asian history, 1750-1950; a guide to periodicals, dissertations, and newspapers. Princeton, N.J.: Princeton Univ. Pr., 1968. 561p.

Holdings shown for 40 collections in U.S., England, India, Canada, and Sweden.

2826. Chicago, University, Committee on Southern Asian Studies. South Asian accessions list. Chicago, 1960 July-Aug. 1962. Irregular.

2827. ———, Library. South Asian materials in the University of Chicago Library, a guide to their location and use. Chicago, 1967-68. 6p.

2828. Harvard University Library. Southern Asia: Afghanistan, Bhutan, Burma, Cambodia, Ceylon, India, Laos, Malaya, Nepal, Pakistan, Sikkim, Singapore, Thailand, Vietnam. Cambridge, Mass., 1968. 543p. (Widener Library shelflist no.19)

Lists 10,292 titles.

2829. Johnson, Donald Clay. A guide to reference materials on Southeast Asia, based on the collections in the Yale and Cornell University Libraries. New Haven, Conn.: Yale Univ. Pr., 1970. 160p. (Yale Southeast Asia studies, no.6)

2830. Missouri, University, Library. Punjab bibliography of reference materials; emphasis on South Asia collection, University of Missouri. Columbia, 1969. 33*l.* (Univ. of Mo., South Asia Center, Research paper)

2831. ———. Ames Library of South Asia, founded by Charles Lesley Ames. Minneapolis, 1961. 4p.

Collection of 80,000 items, broad in scope, acquired by University of Minnesota Library.

2832. ———, Ames Library of South Asia. Bibliography of South Asian bibliographies in the Ames Library of South Asia; with a special section on Southeast Asia, comp. by Henry Scholberg. Minneapolis, 1970. 22p.

2833. Moid, Abdul. Urdu language collections in American libraries. 1964. 287*l.* (Ph.D. thesis, Graduate School of Library Science, Univ. of Ill.)

2834. Patterson, Maureen L. P. "South Asian area studies and the library." Library quarterly, 35 (1965), 223-59.

General review of status of U.S. library resources for South Asia.

2835. Puhvel, Jaan. "Sanskrit collection at UCLA." UCLA librarian, 16 (May 31, 1963), 115-16.

2836. U.S. Dept. of the Army Library. South Asia; a strategic survey. Wash.: 1966. 175p. (DA pamphlet 550-3)

2837. U.S. Library of Congress, Orientalia Division. Southeast Asia: an annotated bibliography of selected reference sources in Western languages, rev. ed., comp. by Cecil Hobbs. Wash., 1964. 180p.

Contains 535 entries, mainly for 1952-63 period.

India

2838. U.S. Library of Congress, American Libraries Book Procurement Center. Accessions list: India. New Delhi, July 1962- . no. 1- . Monthly.

Materials acquired under Public Law 480 Program.

2839. U.S. National Archives. Records of Department of State relating to internal affairs of India and Burma, 1910-29, prep. by Ralph E. Huss. Wash., 1970. 15p.

Indonesia

2840. California, University, Center for Southeast Asia Studies. University of California holdings on Indonesia in English, comp. by Betty Spry. Berkeley, 1968. 37*l.*

2841. Cornell University Libraries. A preliminary checklist of Indonesian imprints, 1945-1949, with Cornell University holdings, by John M. Echols. Ithaca, N.Y.: Modern Indonesia Project, Southeast Asia Program, Dept. of Asian Studies, Cornell Univ., 1965. 186p.

2842. U.S. Library of Congress, Library of Congress Office. Accessions list: Indonesia. Djakarta, Indonesia, July 1964- . no. 1- .

Materials acquired under Public Law 480 Program.

Pakistan

2843. U.S. Library of Congress, American Libraries Book Procurement Center. Accessions list: Pakistan. Karachi, Dacca, Pakistan, July 1962- . no. 1- . Monthly.

Materials acquired under Public Law 480 Program.

Thailand

2844. Cornell University, Dept. of Asian Studies, Thailand Project. Bibliography of materials relating to Thailand and project personnel. Ithaca, N.Y., 1967. 40p.

2845. Cornell University Libraries. Catalogue of Thai language holdings in the Cornell University Libraries through 1964, comp. by Frances A. Bernath. Ithaca, N.Y.: Cornell Univ. Pr., 1964. 236p. (Cornell Univ., Southeast Asia Program, Data paper, no.54)

2846. U.S. National Archives. Records of Department of State relating to internal affairs of Siam, 1910-1929, prep. by Frank S. Soriano. Wash., 1969. 8p.

2847. ———. Records of Department of State relating to political relations between United States and Siam, 1910-29, prep. by Frank S. Soriano. Wash., 1969. 11p.

Vietnam

2848. California, University, Center for Southeast Asia Studies. University of California Library holdings on Vietnam. Berkeley, 1968. 53*l.*

2849. Cornell University Library. A bibliography of North Vietnamese publications in the Cornell University Library, by Jane Godfrey Keyes. Ithaca, N.Y.: Cornell Univ. Pr., 1962. 116p. (Cornell Univ., Southeast Asia Program, Data paper, no.47)

2850. Florida, University, Libraries. Some keys to the Vietnam puzzle, comp. by Russell W. Ramsay. Gainesville, 1968. 55p. (Bibliographic series, no.7)

2851. Northwestern University Library. A selected list

of U.S. government publications on the Vietnam War. Evanston, Ill., 1969. 5p.

2852. Southern Illinois University, Center for Vietnamese Studies and Programs. Bibliography. Carbondale, 1969. 43p.

"Materials available at the Center as of July 31, 1969," including books, periodicals, and public documents.

Far East

2853. Association for Asian Studies, Committee on East Asian Libraries. Library resources on East Asia. Zug, Switzerland: Inter Documentation Company AG, 1968. 100p.

Survey and directory of East Asian collections in American libraries.

2854. California, University, East Asiatic Library, Berkeley. Author-title catalog; subject catalog. Boston: G. K. Hall, 1968. 19v.

2855. Chicago, University, Far Eastern Library. A brief guide to the use of the Far Eastern Library. Chicago, 1970. 6p.

2856. ——— ———. Recent acquisitions in Western languages, May 1953- . no. 1- . Irregular.

2857. Columbia University, East Asian Library. Recent acquisitions in the Western language collection. N.Y., Jan. 1970- . Quarterly.

2858. Cornell University Libraries. The Wason collection. Ithaca, N.Y., 1969. Unpaged. (Special collection, no.1)

Description of special collection on East and Southeast Asia, numbering about 250,000 volumes.

2859. East-West Center Library. Select list of recent acquisitions. Honolulu: Univ. of Hawaii, Aug. 1963-70. v.1-7.

2860. Harvard University Library. China, Japan, and Korea; classification schedule, classified listing by call number, alphabetical listing by author or title, chronological listing. Cambridge, Mass., 1968. 494p. (Widener Library shelflist, no.14)

Lists 11,400 titles in Western languages.

2861. Huang, C. K. "Building an East Asian library." University of Rochester Library bulletin, 21 (Winter 1966), 31-40.

Description of some significant works in University of Rochester's East Asian Library.

2862. Nunn, G. Raymond. East Asia; a bibliography of bibliographies. Honolulu: East-West Center Library, 1967. 92p. (East-West Center Library, Occasional papers, no.7)

Union list of bibliographies in Library of Congress, Harvard, Cornell, Berkeley, Hoover, and University of Hawaii.

2863. ———. "East-West Center research collections." Hawaii Library Association journal, 20 (Fall 1963), 9-11.

2864. Rochester, University, East Asian Library. Catalog of the East Asian collection, East Asian Library, East Asian Language and Area Center, University of Rochester. Rochester, N.Y., 1968. 592p. Supplement. 1970. 364p.

Subject and author lists of 20,000-volume collection, Chinese and Japanese.

2865. Tsien, Tsuen-hsuin. "East Asian collections in America." Library quarterly, 35 (1965), 260-82.

Includes statistical summaries of "present status of East Asian collections in America."

2866. ———. "Holdings of Far Eastern materials in American libraries." Newsletter of the Committee on East Asian Libraries, Association for Asian Studies, 29 (15 May 1969), 9.

Statistical summary of volumes held by about 60 libraries, by languages: Chinese, Japanese, Korean, and others.

2867. Tsuneishi, Warren M. "East Asian collections." Farmington Plan newsletter, no.3 (May 1970), 25-33.

Discusses "current status of East Asian collections in North American libraries"; Appendix I, "Holdings of Far Eastern materials in American libraries," reports number of volumes by languages in individual libraries.

2868. Yale University Library, East Asia Collection. Accessions list. New Haven, Conn., 1967- . v.1- .

Lists Chinese, Japanese, and Korean works, and Western-language works relating to East Asia.

China

2869. California, University, Library, Los Angeles. Chinese collection. Boston: G. K. Hall, 1963. 2v. (Dictionary catalog of the University Library, 1919-1962. v.127-128)

2870. Chicago, University, Far Eastern Library. Chinese local histories. Chicago, 1969. 139p. (Reference list, no.1)

2871. ——— ———. Selective list of recent Chinese acquisitions. Chicago, June 1953- . Frequency varies.

2872. ———. Institute for Far Eastern Librarianship. Chinese library resources, a syllabus, prep. by Tsuen-hsuin Tsien and Kuang-Tsing Wu. Chicago, 1969. 40*l.*

2873. ——— ———. A guide to reference and source materials for Chinese studies, by Tsuen-hsuin Tsien and Weiying Wan. Chicago, 1969. 114*l.*

2874. ———, Program on Contemporary China. Selective list of basic English-language research materials on Communist China. Chicago, 1969. 13p.

2875. Chiu, A. K'aiming. "Annotated catalogue of Ming (1368-1644) encyclopaedias and reference works in the Chinese-Japanese Library of the Harvard-Yenching Institute at Harvard University." Tsing Hua journal of Chinese studies, n.s. 2 (June 1961), 94-115. Reprinted.

In Chinese with English summary.

2876. Chung, E. W. H. Chinese collections in the United States. University, Miss., 1969. 68p. (M.L.S. thesis, Univ. of Miss.)

2877. [Claremont Colleges, Honnold Library, Claremont, Calif. Chinese collection] College & research libraries news, no.2 (Feb. 1970), 29.

Describes collection of 3,322 volumes of most important Chinese classics, history, philosophy, and literature received by Claremont.

2878. Columbia University, East Asian Library. Quarterly bibliography of new titles in Chinese. Oct. 1963- . v.1- . N.Y., 1963- .

2879. Cornell University Libraries. Chinese local gazetteers (Fang Chih) in the Wason collection, Cornell University Libraries, comp. by John T. Ma. Ithaca, N.Y., 1964. 11*l.*

2880. ———, Wason Collection. A select bibliography of recently cataloged Chinese reference books, comp. by John T. Ma. Ithaca, N.Y., 1963. 12*l.*

2881. Harvard University, Dept. of History, Committee on American Far Eastern Policy Studies. American-Chinese relations, 1784-1941; a survey of Chinese language materials at Harvard, by Robert L. Irick and others. Cambridge, Mass.: Harvard Univ. Pr., 1960. 296p.

2882. Krueger, John R. "Catalogue of the Laufer Mongolian collections in Chicago." Journal of the American Oriental Society, 86 (1966), 157-83.

Based on University of Chicago Library's holdings.

2883. Lovett, Robert W. "The Heard collection and its story." Business history review, 35 (1961), 567-73.

Description of extensive manuscript collection in Baker Library, Harvard Graduate School of Business Administration, relating to China trade of 19th century.

2884. Michigan, University, Asia Library. A checklist of Chinese local gazetteers in Asia Library. Ann Arbor, 1968. 53*l.*

2885. ——— ———. A checklist of Chinese materials on microfilm in Asia Library, comp. by Raymond N. Tang and Wei-yi Ma. Ann Arbor, 1968. 96*l.*

2886. Pittsburgh, University, Libraries. Chinese local history—a descriptive holding list. Pittsburgh: Univ. Book Center, 1969. 87*l.*

Describes holdings of university's East Asian Library in Chinese social studies.

2887. Princeton University, Gest Oriental Library. Chinese microfilms in Princeton University; a checklist of the Gest Oriental Library, comp. by Shih-kang Tung. Wash.: ARL Center for Chinese Research Materials, 1969. 57p.

Lists 361 items.

2888. Stanford University, Hoover Institution. The Chinese Communist movement, 1937-1949; an annotated bibliography of selected materials in the Chinese collection of the Hoover Institution on War, Revolution and Peace, by Chun-tu Hsüeh. Stanford, Calif., 1962. 312p. (Bibliographical series, no.11)

2889. ——— ———. Contemporary China: a research guide, by Peter Berton and Eugene Wu. Stanford, Calif., 1967. 695p. (Bibliographical series, no.31)

2890. U.S. Dept. of the Army Library. Communist China. Wash., 1966. 143p. (DA pamphlet 20-67)

2891. ———. Communist China: ruthless enemy or paper tiger? Wash., 1962. 137p. (DA pamphlet 20-61)

2892. U.S. National Archives. Records of Department

of State relating to internal affairs of China, 1910-29, prep. by Ralph E. Huss. Wash., 1967. 29p.

2893. ———. Records of Department of State relating to political relations between China and other states, 1910-29, prep. by Ralph E. Huss. Wash.: 1970. 6p.

2894. Virginia, University, Library. The Ellen Bayard Weedon Chinese collection at the University of Virginia; catalogue of the Makiam Library, by Ng Tung King, ed. by Roy Land. Charlottesville, 1965. 43, 17*l*.

Catalog of about 11,000 titles of Chinese literature. Text in Chinese.

2895. Washington University Libraries. Bibliography of new titles in Chinese and Japanese in the Washington University Library. St. Louis, 1964- . (In progress)

2896. Washington, University, Library, Seattle. A catalog of the official gazetteers of China in the University of Washington, by Joseph D. Lowe. Zug, Switzerland: Inter Documentation Co., 1966. 72p.

2897. Young, John. The research activities of the South Manchurian Railway Company, 1907-1945: a history and bibliography. N.Y.: East Asian Institute, Columbia Univ., 1966. 682p.

Lists 6,300 titles held by 10 institutions in the U.S. and 25 in Japan.

2898. Yüan, T'ung-li. Russian works on China, 1918-1960, in American libraries. New Haven, Conn.: Yale Univ., 1961. 162p.

Lists 1,348 books and periodicals; based primarily on Hoover Institution, Berkeley and UCLA Libraries, but lists no specific locations.

Japan

2899. California, University, Library, Los Angeles. Japanese collection A-Z. Armenian collection A-Z. Boston: G. K. Hall, 1963. 606p. (Dictionary catalog of the University Library, 1919-1962. v.129)

2900. Chicago, University, Institute for Far Eastern Librarianship. Japanese reference works, a syllabus, prep. by Yukihisa Suzuki. Chicago, 1969. 68*l*.

2901. East-West Center Library. Catalog of the Glenn Shaw collection at the East-West Center Library, by Hirotake Arai and Morio Gibu. Honolulu, 1967. 239p. (East-West Center Library, Occasional papers, no.8)

Relates to Japanese language, literature, and history.

2902. ———. Research resources on Hokkaido, Sakhalin, and the Kuriles at the East-West Center Library, comp. by Masato Matsui and Katsumi Shimanaka. Honolulu, 1967. 266p.

2903. Michigan, University, Library. List of Japanese bibliographies: the holdings of the Asia Library of the University of Michigan, by Hiroshi Mori. Ann Arbor, 1966. 95p. (Asia Library bibliographic series, no.3)

2904. ———. Local studies of Japan, Hoppo Chiiki: the holdings of the University of Michigan by Hiroshi Mori. Ann Arbor, 1965. 33p. (Asia Library bibliographic series, no.1)

2905. ———. Local studies of Japan, Tohoku district: the holdings of the University of Michigan, by Hiroshi Mori. Ann Arbor, 1966. 97p. (Asia Library bibliographic series, no.2)

2906. Stanford University, Hoover Institution. Catalog of the Japanese collection. Boston: G. K. Hall, 1969. 7v.

2907. Syracuse University Library. Catalog of the Ryukyu research collection: a special collection of books, articles, and manuscripts in relevant languages dealing with the Ryukyu Islands, as of March, 1969, comp. by Douglas G. Haring. Syracuse, N.Y., 1969. 157p.

Lists 1,979 items dealing with Ryukyu Islands, held by Syracuse University Library. Updates 1964 list.

2908. Washington, University, Far Eastern Library. A classified catalogue of modern Japanese literature (Meiji, Taisho, Showa) with periodical index in the Far Eastern Library, University of Washington, comp. by Masato Matsui and Hitoshi Inoue. Seattle: Univ. of Wash. Library, 1964. 39*l*.

Korea

2909. Chung, Yong Sun. Publications on Korea in the era of political revolutions, 1959-1963; a selected bibliography. Kalamazoo, Mich.: Korea Research and Publication, Inc. [1965] 117p.

Classified list of 967 titles in Korean, Chinese, Japanese, and Western languages. Most of the titles listed are in the Library of Congress' Korean unit.

2910. Harvard University, Harvard-Yenching Institute Library. A classified catalogue of Korean books in the Harvard-Yenching Institute Library at Harvard University. Cambridge, Mass., 1962. 194p.

Lists 3,160 Korean works. Supplement, v.2 (1966), lists books more recently acquired.

2911. Hawaii, University, Center for Cultural and Technical Interchange Between East and West. A guide to reference and research materials on Korean history; an annotated bibliography, comp. by William E. Henthorn. Honolulu, 1968. 152*l.*

Philippines

2912. California, University, Center for Southeast Asia Studies. University of California Library holdings on the Philippines, comp. by Betty Spry. Berkeley, 1967. 62*l.*

2913. Indiana University, Lilly Library. Catalogue of the Philippine manuscripts in the Lilly Library, by C. R. Boxer. Bloomington, 1968. 63p. (Indiana University, Asian Studies Research Institute, Occasional papers, no.2)

2914. Syracuse University Libraries. Syracuse University Filipiniana manuscript collection, by Howard L. Applegate. Syracuse, N.Y., n.d. 3p.

2915. U.S. National Archives. Philippine insurgent records, 1896-1901, with associated records of United States War Department, 1900-1906. Wash., 1967. 52p.

2916. ———. Preliminary inventory of the records of the U.S. High Commissioner to the Philippine Islands, comp. by Richard S. Maxwell. Wash., 1963. 24p. (Preliminary inventories, no.151)

Other Countries

2917. Cornell University, Southeast Asia Program. Checklist of holdings on Borneo in the Cornell University Libraries, comp. by Michael B. Leigh and John M. Echols. Ithaca, N.Y.: Southeast Asia Program, 1966. 62p. (Data paper, no.62)

2918. Poleman, Horace I. A survey of Tibetan xylographs and manuscripts in institutions and private collections in the United States and Canada. Ann Arbor, Mich., 1961? 19*l.*

2919. U.S. Library of Congress, American Libraries Book Procurement Center. Accessions list: Ceylon. New Delhi, India, March 1967- . no.1- . Quarterly.

Materials acquired under Public Law 480 Program.

2920. ——— ———. Accessions list: Nepal. New Delhi, India, 1966- . no.1- . Three times yearly.

Materials acquired under Public Law 480 Program.

2921. Washington, University, Far Eastern Library. Tibetan catalogue, by E. Gene Smith. Seattle, 1969. 2v.

AFRICAN

2922. Alexander, Helen P. A supplement to the catalog of the African collection in the Moorland Foundation of the Howard University Library. 1963. 106p. (Master's thesis, Dept. of Library Science, Catholic Univ. of America)

2923. "American library collections on Africa." African studies bulletin, 8 (April 1965), 59-68.

Describes collections at Harvard and Howard University Libraries.

2924. Atiyeh, George N. "Recent American works on Northwestern Africa." Quarterly journal of the Library of Congress, 27 (1970), 277-82.

Report on acquisitions, Library of Congress.

2925. Boston University Library. Africa and the United States; an exhibit of current publications relative to Africa. Boston, 1961. 20p.

2926. ———. Catalog of African government documents and African area index, 2d ed., comp. by Mary D. Herrick. Boston: G. K. Hall, 1964. 471p.

Arranged by Library of Congress schedule J 700-881 for African states; lists about 4,000 monographs and serials.

2927. ———. List of French doctoral dissertations on Africa, 1884-1961, comp. by Marion Dinstel. Boston: G. K. Hall, 1966. 334p.

2928. Brown University Libraries. Discovering Africa; source materials on the opening of a great continent, comp. by Norman Robert Bennett. An exhibition at the Chenery Library, October 1 thru October 30, 1961. Boston, 1961. 12p.

2929. California State College Library, Fresno. Afro– and Mexican–Americana; books and other materials in the Library of Fresno State College relating to the history, culture, and problems of Afro-Americans and Mexican Americans. Fresno, 1969. 109p.

2930. California State College Library, Los Angeles. A library guide to Afro-American studies. Los Angeles, 1969. 15p.

2931. Center for Research Libraries. Cameroun political ephemera; Rhodesia and Nyasaland political ephemera; Belgian Congo political ephemera: an inventory of the Herbert J. Weiss collection on the Belgian Congo available on microfilm. Chicago: Center for Research Libraries, 1965. Unpaged.

Originals in private collections.

2932. Chicago, University, Library. A checklist of bibliographies and serial publications for studies of Africa south-of-the-Sahara, by Jan Wepsiec. Chicago: Univ. of Chicago Pr., 1966. 60p.

"Includes publications in the University of Chicago libraries."

2933. Collins, Robert O., and Duignan, Peter. Americans in Africa; a preliminary guide to American missionary archives and library manuscript collections on Africa. Stanford, Calif.: Hoover Institution, 1963. 96p. (Hoover Inst. Bibliographical series, no.12)

A listing by institutions, with descriptions of holdings.

2934. De Benko, Eugene, and Wells, Margo A. "American library collections on Africa." African studies bulletin, 9 (Sept. 1966), 20-24.

Describes Michigan State University Library's collection.

2935. Duignan, Peter, and Crossey, J. D. M. "American library, art, and ethnographic collections on Africa." African studies bulletin, 9 (Sept. 1966), 12-20.

Describes collections at Yale, American Geographical Society, and in several museums.

2936. Duignan, Peter. "American library collections on Africa: Stanford University." African studies bulletin, 9 (Sept. 1968), 25-34.

Describes Hoover Institution's resources on Africa.

2937. ———. Handbook of American resources for African studies. Stanford, Calif.: Hoover Institution, 1967. 218p. (Hoover Institution bibliographical series, no.29)

Guide to the principal library and manuscript collections in U.S.

2938. Goff, Frederick R. "Early Africana in the Rare Book Division." Quarterly journal of the Library of Congress, 27 (1970), 267-76.

2939. Harvard University Library. Africa: classification schedule, classified listing by call number, alphabetical listing by author or title, chronological listing. Cambridge, Mass., 1965. 786p. (Widener Library shelflist, no.2)

Records 13,299 titles (15,370 volumes) devoted mainly to history, travel, and politics of Africa. All countries included.

2940. ———. African history and literatures. Cambridge, Mass., 1971. 500p. (Widener Library shelflist, no.34)

Lists 20,000 works for all areas of African continent, except ancient North Africa.

2941. Kaplan, Milton. "Africa through the eye of a camera." Quarterly journal of the Library of Congress, 27 (1970), 222-37.

Reproductions from Carpenter collection, Prints and Photographs Division, Library of Congress.

2942. Lee, Hwa-wei. "Africana, a special collection at Duquesne University." Catholic library world, 35 (1963), 209-11.

2943. Lehman, Robert L. Africa south of the Sahara: a selected and annotated bibliography of books in the Missionary Research Library on Africa and African countries south of the Sahara, 2d ed., ed. by Frank W. Price. N.Y., 1961. 70p.

Lists 748 books and periodicals.

2944. Lindfors, Bernth. "American university and research library holdings in African literature." African studies bulletin, 11 (1968), 286-311.

Union list of 1,182 titles recorded in Jahn's A bibliography of neo-African literature (1965); locations in numerous libraries.

2945. Michigan State University Library. Research sources for African studies; a checklist of relevant serial publications based on library collections at Michigan State University, by Eugene De Benko and Patricia L. Butts. East Lansing: African Studies Center, Mich. State Univ., 1969. 384p.

2946. Michigan, University, Library. Holdings on Algeria, August 1, 1967, prep. by D. Partington. Ann Arbor, 1967. 42*l.*

2947. ———. Holdings on Morocco, August 1, 1967, comp. by D. Partington. Ann Arbor, 1967. 59*l.*

2948. Northwestern University Library. Catalog of South Africa political ephemera collection. Evanston, Ill., 1964? 232*l.*

2949. ———. Catalog of the African collection of the Northwestern University Library. Boston: G. K. Hall, 1962. 2v.

Catalog of 21,500-volume collection, comprehensive in scope, but strongest for Africa south of the Sahara.

2950. ———. Joint acquisitions list of Africana. Evanston, Ill., 1962- . v.1- . Bimonthly.

Alphabetical list of Africana acquired by principal libraries of United States.

2951. ———. Program of African studies collection, new acquisitions. Evanston, Ill., Feb. 1957- . Quarterly.

2952. Panofsky, Hans E. "African studies in American libraries." Library quarterly, 35 (1965), 298-307.

General review of field, including brief discussion of African collections in U.S. libraries.

2953. Pinkett, Maude Moore. A bibliography of works on Africa in the Trevor Arnett Library of Atlanta University, published before 1900. 1962. 53p. (Master's thesis, School of Library Service, Atlanta Univ.)

2954. Price, Arnold H. "Recent German-language publications on Africa." Quarterly journal of the Library of Congress, 22 (1965), 149-56.

Report on acquisitions, Library of Congress.

2955. Princeton University Library. Ghana and the Gold Coast colony including British Togoland, comp. by Edgar W. Davy. Princeton, N.J., 1969. 25*l.* (African government documents holdings, no.1)

2956. ———. Nigeria, including British Cameroons and Biafra, comp. by Edgar W. Davy. Princeton, N.J., 1970. 196p. (African government documents holdings, no.2)

Lists Princeton's holdings as of 1970.

2957. Stanford University, Hoover Institution. Africa south of the Sahara; a select and annotated bibliography, 1958-1963, by Kenneth M. Glazier. Stanford, Calif., 1964. 65p. (Hoover Institution bibliographical series, no.16)

Lists 150 items.

2958. ——— ———. Africa south of the Sahara; a select and annotated bibliography, 1964-1968, by Kenneth M. Glazier. Stanford, Calif., 1969. 139p. (Bibliographical series, no.42)

Lists 222 titles.

2959. ——— ———. Belgian Congo political ephemera: an inventory of the Herbert J. Weiss collection on the Belgian Congo available on microfilm. Chicago: Center for Research Libraries, 1965. 19*l.*

Available in Center for Research Libraries, Chicago.

2960. ——— ———. Cameroun political ephemera; an inventory of miscellaneous short publications issued in Cameroun 1952-1961 available on microfilm, comp. by David Gardinier and Victor Levine. Chicago: Midwest Inter-Library Center, 1964. 9*l.*

2961. ——— ———. Emerging nationalism in Portuguese Africa: a bibliography of documentary ephemera through 1965, comp. by Ronald H. Chilcote. Stanford, Calif., 1969. 114p. (Bibliographical series, no.39)

Material on microfilm in Hoover Institution from Brazil, Portugal, and Africa.

2962. ——— ———. German Africa: a selected annotated bibliography, by Jon Bridgman and David E. Clarke. Stanford, Calif., 1965. 120p. (Bibliographical series, no.19)

2963. ——— ———. Handbook of American resources for African studies, by Peter Duignan. Stanford, Calif., 1967. 218p. (Bibliographical series, no.29)

Describes resources available in numerous libraries and archival agencies.

2964. ——— ———. List of microfilmed South African political ephemera, collected by Benjamin Pogrund. Stanford, Calif., 1967? Unpaged.

2965. ——— ———. Madagascar (the Malagasy Republic); a list of materials in the African collections of Stanford University and the Hoover Institution on War, Revolution, and Peace, by Peter Duignan. Stanford, Calif.: Hoover Institution, 1962. 25p. (Hoover Institution bibliographical series, no.9)

Lists 257 titles.

2966. ——— ———. Nigeria collection, comp. by Simon Ottenberg. Stanford, Calif., 1968. 17*l.*

2967. ——— ———. The treason trial in South Africa: a guide to the microfilm record of the trial, by Thomas Karis. Stanford, Calif., 1965. 124p. (Bibliographical series, no.23)

2968. ——— ———. United States and Canadian publications on Africa, ed. by Peter Duignan: 1961, 114p.; 1962, 104p.; 1963, 136p.; 1964, 180p.; 1965, 227p.; 1966, 200p. Stanford, Calif., 1963-68. 6v. (Bibliographical series, no.14, 15, 25, 34, 38).

2969. Stewart, Kate M. "Theodore Roosevelt, hunter-naturalist on safari." Quarterly journal of the Library of Congress, 27 (1970), 242-56.

Letters to and by Roosevelt about Africa in Library of Congress collections.

2970. Syracuse University Library. A list of Africana holdings in the Syracuse University Library. Part I: Books and monographs, prep. by the Program of Eastern African Studies. Syracuse, N.Y., n.d. 275p.

2971. U.S. Dept. of the Army Library. Africa, its problems and prospects. Wash.: The Library, 1962. 195p. (DA pamphlet 20-62)

2972. ———. Africa: its problems and prospects: a bibliographic survey. Wash.: Govt. Print. Off., 1967. 226p. (DA pamphlet 550-5)

Records more than 900 items relating to Africa's economic, political, and sociological prospects and problems; lists Army Library holdings.

2973. U.S. Library of Congress, African Section. Africa south of the Sahara: a guide to serials. Wash.: The Library, 1969. 409p.

2974. ——— ———. Africa south of the Sahara; an introductory list of bibliographies, comp. by Helen F. Conover. Wash.: The Library, 1961. 7p.

2975. ——— ———. Africa south of the Sahara; a selected, annotated list of writings, comp. by Helen F. Conover. Wash.: Govt. Print. Off., 1964. 354p.

Includes 2,173 items, with Library of Congress classification numbers.

2976. ——— ———. French-speaking West Africa; a guide to official publications, comp. by Julian W. Witherell. Wash.: The Library, 1967. 201p.

Lists published government records from mid-19th century on to date, with locations in the Library and other American libraries.

2977. ——— ———. Ghana; a guide to official publications, 1872-1968, comp. by Julian W. Witherell and Sharon B. Lockwood. Wash.: Govt. Print. Off., 1969. 110p.

Locates copies in 31 libraries; 1,283 entries.

2978. ——— ———. A list of American doctoral dissertations on Africa. Wash.: The Library, 1962. 69p.

Lists more than 700 dissertations, with Library of Congress card and book numbers.

2979. ——— ———. Madagascar and adjacent islands; a guide to official publications, comp. by Julian W. Witherell. Wash.: The Library, 1965. 58p.

Locates copies in 19 libraries.

2980. ——— ———. Nigeria; a guide to official publications, rev. ed., comp. by Sharon B. Lockwood. Wash.: The Library, 1966. 166p.

Covers 1861-1965 period; locations in Library of Congress and other American libraries.

2981. ——— ———. Official publications of British East Africa, Part II, Tanganyika, comp. by Audrey A. Walker. Wash.: The Library, 1962. 134p.

Locates copies in 30 libraries.

2982. ——— ———. Official publications of British East Africa, Part III, Kenya and Zanzibar, comp. by Audrey A. Walker. Wash.: The Library, 1962. 162p.

Copies located in 20 libraries.

2983. ——— ———. Official publications of British East Africa, Part IV, Uganda, comp. by Audrey A. Walker. Wash.: The Library, 1962. 100p.

Copies located in the Library of Congress and elsewhere.

2984. ——— ———. Official publications of French Equatorial Africa, French Cameroons, and Togo, 1946-1958, comp. by Julian W. Witherell. Wash.: Govt. Print. Off., 1964. 78p.

Locates copies in 10 libraries.

2985. ——— ———. Official publications of Sierra Leone and Gambia, comp. by Audrey A. Walker. Wash.: Govt. Print. Off., 1963. 92p.

Locates copies in 20 libraries of 700 titles.

2986. ——— ———. Portuguese Africa; a guide to official publications, ed. by Mary Jane Gibson. Wash.: The Library, 1967. 217p.

Covers documents from 1850 to 1964. Many items located in American libraries.

2987. ——— ———. The Rhodesias and Nyasaland; a guide to official publications, comp. by Audrey A. Walker. Wash.: The Library, 1965. 285p.

Covers 1889-1963 period; copies located in 20 libraries.

2988. ——— ———. Sub-Saharan Africa: a guide to serials. Wash.: The Library, 1970. 409p.

Entries for 4,700 titles, with locations in Library of Congress or 49 other libraries.

2989. ———, Library of Congress Office. Accessions list: Eastern Africa. Nairobi, Kenya, 1968- . v.1- . Quarterly.

Materials acquired under Library of Congress National Program for Acquisitions and Cataloging.

2990. U.S. National Archives. Records of Department of State relating to internal affairs of British Africa, 1910-29, prep. by James E. Primas. Wash., 1967. 18p.

2991. U.S. Library of Congress, General Reference and Bibliography Division. United States and Canadian publications on Africa in 1960. Wash.: The Library, 1962. 98p.

Lists books and pamphlets published in U.S. and Canada in 1960 relating to Africa south of the Sahara, except North African areas.

2992. U.S. National Archives. Records of Department of State relating to political relations between Liberia and other states including the United States, 1919-29, prep. by Frank S. Soriano. Wash., 1969. 5p.

2993. Wepsiec, Jan. A checklist of bibliographies and serial publications for studies of Africa south-of-the-Sahara. Chicago: Univ. of Chicago Pr., 1966. 60p.

"Includes publications in the University of Chicago libraries."

2994. Wisconsin, University, Library. Swahili materials in the Memorial Library of the University of Wisconsin: a preliminary checklist, by Michael J. Briggs. Madison, 1969. 7*l.*

2995. ———. Tanzanian publications received under an exchange agreement with the Library of University College, Dar es Salaam, January-March 1970. Madison, 1970. 3*l.*

2996. Witherell, Julian W. "Africana in the Library of Congress: the role of the African Section." Quarterly journal of the Library of Congress, 27 (1970), 184-96.

CANADIAN

2997. Harvard University Library. Canadian history and literature. Cambridge, Mass., 1968. 411p. (Widener Library shelflist, no.20)

More than 10,000 titles listed by classes, author and title, and chronologically.

2998. Jones, Joseph. "Canadiana at the University of Texas: a progress report." Library chronicle of the University of Texas, 8, no.3 (1967), 40-44.

Survey of Canadian literature in the University of Texas Library.

2999. Maine, University, Library. The Atlantic provinces of Canada; union lists of materials in the larger libraries of Maine, comp. by Alice R. Stewart. Orono: Univ. of Maine Pr., 1965. 85p. (Bulletin, v.68, no.23)

3000. Winks, Robin W. "Canadiana at Yale: a report." Yale University Library gazette, 36 (1962), 97-118.

Describes extensive holdings relating to Canada in Yale Library.

UNITED STATES–GENERAL

3001. Allen, Robert V. "Russian documents about the United States." Quarterly journal of the Library of Congress, 21 (1964), 217-23.

Report on acquisitions, Library of Congress.

3002. Brown University, John Carter Brown Library. Opportunities for research in the John Carter Brown Library. Providence, R.I.: Brown Univ., 1968. 88p.

3003. California, University, Libraries, Davis. Asians in America: a bibliography, by William Wong Lum. Davis, 1969. 48p.

Based on holdings of University of California Library, Davis, relating to Asian-Americans; includes book, periodical, and thesis references.

3004. California, University, Library. America's third world: a guide to bibliographic resources in the Library of the University of California, Berkeley, comp. by Philip Whitney. Berkeley, 1971. 89p.

Bibliography of bibliographies on blacks, Chinese, Japanese, Mexican, Indian, and other racial minorities, listing all types of material, 1866-1970.

3005. Carman, Harry J., and Thompson, Arthur W. A guide to the principal sources for American civilization, 1800-1900, in the City of New York: printed materials. N.Y.: Columbia Univ. Pr., 1962. 630p.

Locating guide for bibliographies, collected works, documents, correspondence, corporate records, and other sources.

3006. Cincinnati and Hamilton County Public Library, Rare Book Room. Catalog of the Inland Rivers Library, comp. by Clyde N. Bowden. Cincinnati, 1968. 156p.

Based on collection of the Sons and Daughters of

Pioneer Rivermen, in Cincinnati Public Library; includes books, pamphlets, periodicals, maps, charts, manuscripts, photographs, and phonorecords.

3007. Harvard University Library. American history. Cambridge, Mass., 1967. 5v. (Widener Library shelflist, no.9-13)

Classified, alphabetical, and chronological listing of 126,000 volumes and pamphlets.

3008. Hoskins, Janina W. "The image of America in accounts of Polish travelers of the 18th and 19th centuries." Quarterly journal of the Library of Congress, 22 (1965), 226-45.

Report on acquisitions, Library of Congress.

3009. Howes, Wright. U.S.iana (1650-1950); a selective bibliography in which are described 11,620 uncommon and significant books relating to the continental portion of the United States, 2d ed. N.Y.: R. R. Bowker for Newberry Library, 1962. 652p.

Locations of copies in American libraries frequently noted.

3010. Huntington Library. The Huntington Library as a research center for the study of American history, by James Thorpe. San Marino, Calif., 1968. 8p.

3011. Kent, George O. "A survey of German manuscripts relating to American history in the Library of Congress." Journal of American history, 56 (March 1970), 868-81.

3012. Kentucky, University, Libraries. Americana in a state university library. Lexington, 1963. 11p. (Library bulletin, no.23)

3013. Larson, Esther E. Swedish commentators on America, 1638-1865: an annotated list of selected manuscript and printed materials. N.Y.: New York Public Library, 1963. 139p.

Copies located in 17 American and 15 Swedish libraries.

3014. Massachusetts Historical Society. The catalog of manuscripts. Boston: G. K. Hall, 1969. 7v.

Approximately 247,000 cards reproduced for a collection rich in American history, including papers of numerous eminent Americans.

3015. Michigan, University, William L. Clements Library. Arbiters of taste for early America; a guide to an exhibition in the William L. Clements Library. Ann Arbor: Univ. of Mich. Pr., 1962. 20p. (Bulletin, no.69)

3016. ———. Author-title and chronological card catalogs of Americana, 1493-1860, in the William L. Clements Library, University of Michigan (Ann Arbor). Boston: G. K. Hall, 1970. 7v.

Reproduces 95,500 cards.

3017. Monaghan, Frank. French travellers in the United States, 1765-1932: a bibliography. N.Y.: Antiquarian Pr., 1961. 130p.

Lists 1,653 items, with locations of copies.

3018. New-York Historical Society Library. Treasures of Americana from the Library of the New-York Historical Society; a short-title list of rare and important books, broadsides, maps and manuscripts on exhibition, comp. by James Gregory. N.Y., 1969. 24p.

3019. New York Public Library. Dictionary catalog of the history of the Americas collection. Boston: G. K. Hall, 1961. 28v.

Contains 594,000 entries covering North and South America.

3020. Newberry Library. Dictionary catalog of the Edward E. Ayer collection of Americana and American Indians. Boston: G. K. Hall, 1961. 16v.

Catalog of 90,000-volume collection, outstanding for early American and Indian history, voyages and travels, early cartography, Hawaii, Philippines, and Oceania.

3021. O'Neill, James E. "Copies of French manuscripts for American history in the Library of Congress." Journal of American history, 51 (1965), 674-91.

3022. ———. "European sources for American history in the Library of Congress." Library of Congress quarterly journal of current acquisitions, 24 (1967), 152-57.

Reviews Library of Congress' program of microfilming manuscripts in European collections.

3023. Rice, Howard C., Jr. "Swedish Americana in the Princeton Library." Princeton University Library chronicle, 30 (Autumn 1968), 39-52.

3024. Riggs, John A. "American history in the Harvard College Library." Harvard Library bulletin, 15 (1967), 387-400.

Traces history of collections.

3025. Syracuse University Libraries. American history periodicals held in Syracuse University Libraries, comp. by Margery Ganz. Syracuse, N.Y., 1970. 17p.

3026. Thomas Gilcrease Institute of American History and Art Library. A guidebook to manuscripts in the Library of the Thomas Gilcrease Institute of American History and Art, prep. by Mrs. H. H. Keene. Tulsa, Okla., 1969. 101p.

American Indians

3027. American Philosophical Society Library. The American Indian: a conference in the American Philosophical Library. Philadelphia, 1968. 54p. (Library publication, no.2)

Conference on research in Indian languages and history, with special reference to American Philosophical Society's collection.

3028. ———. A guide to manuscripts relating to the American Indian in the Library of the American Philosophical Society, comp. by John F. Freeman and Murphy D. Smith. Philadelphia, 1966. 491p. (APS memoirs 65)

Detailed description of collections and index of individual manuscripts relating to history and languages of Indians of North and Middle America.

3029. Day, Gordon M. "Dartmouth Algonkian collection." Dartmouth College library bulletin, 5 (May 1962), 41-43.

Relates to Indians from northwestern New England who settled in Canadian mission village on St. Francis River; collection of tapes, manuscripts, etc. in Dartmouth Library.

3030. Freeman, John Finley. "The American Indian in manuscript; preparing a guide to holdings in the Library of the American Philosophical Society." Ethnohistory, 8 (Spring 1961), 156-78.

3031. ———. "Manuscript sources on Latin American Indians in the Library of the American Philosophical Society." Proceedings of the American Philosophical Society, 106 (Dec. 12, 1962), 530-40.

3032. Gibson, Charles. "The Ingham Indian collection." Books at Iowa, 4 (April 1966), 3-8.

Description and partial list of University of Iowa Library collection.

3033. Lundin, Dorothy. An inventory of manuscript materials in the National Archives, relating to the Indian land cessions, 1800-1805. Wash., 1961. 36p. (Master's thesis, Dept. of Library Science, Catholic Univ. of America)

3034. Michigan, University, William L. Clements Library. Pontiac's War, 1763-1764; an exhibition of source materials in the William L. Clements Library two hundred years later. Ann Arbor, 1963. 19p. (Bulletin, no.70)

3035. Minnesota Historical Society. Chippewa and Dakota Indians: a subject catalog of books, pamphlets, periodical articles, and manuscripts in the Minnesota Historical Society. St. Paul, 1969. Unpaged.

3036. Oregon State Library. Indians of Oregon; a bibliography of materials in the Oregon State Library, ed. by Leroy Hewlett. Salem, 1969. 125p.

3037. Princeton University Library. American Indian periodicals in the Princeton University Library, by Alfred L. Bush and Robert S. Fraser. Princeton, N.J., 1970. 78p.

Alphabetical list of 271 titles with holdings.

3038. Tennessee State Library and Archives, Manuscript Division. Cherokee collection. Nashville, 1966. 98*l.* (Register, no.11)

3039. U.S. Dept. of the Interior Library. Biographical and historical index of American Indians and persons involved in Indian affairs. Boston: G. K. Hall, 1966. 8v.

Reproduction of card file developed in Bureau of Indian Affairs and now in the Dept. of the Interior Library.

3040. U.S. Federal Records Center. Preliminary inventory of the records of the Bureau of Indian Affairs; Warm Springs Agency records, 1861-1925, comp. by Elmer W. Lingard. Seattle, 1968. 4p.

3041. U.S. National Archives. List of special reports and related records of the Irrigation Division, Bureau of Indian Affairs, 1891-1946, comp. by Choosri Satorn. Wash., 1964. 53p.

3042. ———. Preliminary inventory of the records of the Bureau of Indian Affairs, comp. by Edward E. Hill. Wash., 1965. 2v. (Preliminary inventories, no.163)

Describes 1,401 separate series; v.1, records of Secretary of War relating to Indian affairs, Office of Indian Trade, and of Bureau of Indian Affairs; v.2, field-office records of Indian agencies and superintendencies.

3043. ———. Preliminary inventory of the Sir Henry S. Wellcome papers in the Federal Records Center, Seattle,

Washington, comp. by Elmer W. Lingard. Wash., 1963. 13p. (Preliminary inventories, no.150)

Relate chiefly to Father William Duncan's Metlakahtla Indian Mission, Annette Island, Alaska.

3044. ———. Records of Arizona Superintendency of Indian Affairs, 1863-1873, prep. by Herman J. Viola. Wash., 1968. 7p.

Colonial Period

3045. Brown University, John Carter Brown Library. Bibliotheca Americana, Catalogue of the John Carter Brown Library in Brown University. Providence, R.I., 1919-31. 3v. Reprinted, N.Y.: Kraus, 1961. v.1-2.

Records early Americana through 1674.

3046. ———. A collection's progress: two retrospective exhibitions. Providence, R.I.: Associates of the John Carter Brown Library, 1968. 79p.

Exhibits of early Americana.

3047. ———. The great frontier; an exhibition illustrating the impact made by the discovery of America. Providence, R.I., 1962. 20*l.*

3048. ———. The new found land; English voyage to North America before the Jamestown settlement; an exhibition. Providence, R.I., 1964. 17*l.*

3049. ———. The Northwest Passage; an exhibition. Providence, R.I., 1966. 12*l.*

3050. Colonial Williamsburg. Guide to the manuscript collections of Colonial Williamsburg, 2d ed., comp. by Marylee G. McGregor. Williamsburg, Va.: Colonial Williamsburg, Inc., 1969. 74p.

A collection of 18th-century Tidewater Virginia manuscripts.

3051. Donahue, Jane. "Colonial shipwreck narratives: a theological study." Books at Brown, 23 (1969), 101-34.

Essay followed by bibliography listing original editions with locations in libraries.

3052. Kolbet, Richard M. "Narratives of North American exploration." Books at Iowa, 6 (April 1967), 3-12.

Late 17th- to early 19th-century editions of trans-Mississippi travel accounts in University of Iowa Libraries.

3053. Princeton University Library. Ancient America; five centuries of discovery; an exhibition in the Princeton University Library. Princeton, N.J., 1965. 6p.

Revolution and Confederation

3054. Boston Public Library. Manuscripts of the American Revolution in the Boston Public Library; a descriptive catalog. Boston: G. K. Hall, 1968. 157p.

Lists 1,238 items chronologically.

3055. Brown University, John Carter Brown Library. The decisive decade, 1790-1800; an exhibition. Providence, R.I., 1965. 15*l.*

3056. California, University, Library. Revolutionary War letters and documents from the collection presented to the University Library, Univ. of Calif., San Diego. San Diego, 1965. 8*l.*

3057. Gaines, Pierce W. "Political writings in the Young Republic." Proceedings of the American Antiquarian Society, 76 (1966), 261-92.

Discussion and listing of titles for 1789-1810 period, with some locations.

3058. Harvard University Library. Pamphlets of the American Revolution, 1750-1776, ed. by Bernard Bailyn. Cambridge, Mass.: Belknap Pr. of Harvard Univ. Pr., 1965. 772p. v.1, 1750-1765.

Locates copies.

3059. Houston, University, Libraries. The Shreve papers, 1776-1792, comp. by Mary A. Benjamin. Houston, Tex., 1967. 18p.

Catalog of a collection of American Revolutionary War letters in University of Houston Libraries.

3060. Leary copy of the first printing of the Declaration of Independence printed by John Dunlap at Philadelphia, July 4-5, 1776. Philadelphia: Samuel T. Freeman, 1969. 31p.

Auction catalog. Census of 16 surviving copies, p.4-5.

3061. Morristown National Historical Park. A guide to the manuscript collection, comp. by Bruce W. Stewart and Hans Mayer. Morristown, N.J., 1968. 142p.

An important Revolutionary War collection.

3062. Mugridge, Donald H. "In Roxbury Camp: an American orderly book of 1775." Library of Congress quarterly journal of current acquisitions, 19 (1962), 63-76.

Manuscript company book kept in Sixth Connecticut Regiment during summer months of 1775, acquired by Library of Congress.

3063. North Carolina State Dept. of Archives and

History. North Carolina's Revolutionary War pay records, by C. F. W. Coker and Donald R. Lennon. Raleigh, 1968. 8p. (Archives information circular, no.1)

3064. Stewart, Donald H. The opposition press of the Federalist period. Albany: State Univ. of N.Y. Pr., 1969. 957p.

"Annotated list of newspapers," p.867-93, locates files in 45 U.S. libraries.

3065. Union College, Schaffer Library. The W. Wright Hawkes collection of Revolutionary War documents; a catalogue. Schenectady, N.Y., 1968. 48p.

Detailed descriptions of 81 manuscript and printed documents in Union College Library, including 51 letters of George Washington.

3066. U.S. Library of Congress. The American Revolution: a selected reading list, prep. by Stefan M. Harrow. Wash.: Govt. Print. Off., 1968. 38p.

Includes Library of Congress call numbers.

3067. U.S. National Archives. Preliminary inventory of the War Department collection of Revolutionary War records, comp. by Mabel E. Deutrich. Wash., 1962. 40p. (Preliminary inventories, no.144)

3068. ———. Select picture list, Revolutionary War. Wash., 1969. 12p. (General information leaflet, no.12)

3069. Verner, Coolie. "Maps of the Yorktown Campaign 1780-81: a preliminary checklist of printed and manuscript maps prior to 1800." Map collectors' circle, no.18. 1965. 64p.

War of 1812

3070. Indiana University, Lilly Library. An exhibit to commemorate the one hundred fiftieth anniversary of the beginning of the War of 1812. Bloomington, 1962. 72p.

3071. Michigan, University, William L. Clements Library. "What so proudly we hail'd," an exhibition in the William L. Clements Library marking the sesquicentennial of the War of 1812. Ann Arbor, 1964. 50p. (Bulletin, no.71)

Civil War and Reconstruction

3072. Alabama, University, Library. Confederate imprints in the University of Alabama Library, comp. by Sara Elizabeth Mason and others. University, 1961. 156*l.*

Catalog of 755 titles not recorded by Harwell or Crandall.

3073. Black, Patti Carr, and Grimes, Maxyne Madden. "Civil War manuscripts in the Mississippi Department of Archives and History." Journal of Mississippi history, 23 (1961), 164-95.

3074. Bowman, Albert H. "Blue and Gray in books: the Hyde and Wilder Civil War collections of the University of Chattanooga." Tennessee librarian, 17 (Winter 1965), 47-51.

3075. California, University, Library. The Monitor and the Merrimac: a bibliography, by David R. Smith. Los Angeles, 1968. 35p. (UCLA occasional papers, no.15)

Based partly on UCLA Library's holdings.

3076. Calloway, Ina Elizabeth. An annotated bibliography of books in the Trevor Arnett Library Negro collection relating to the Civil War. Wash., 1963. 41p. (Master's thesis, School of Library Service, Atlanta Univ.)

3077. Carter, George E. "The Breyfogle papers." Dartmouth College Library bulletin, n.s. 9 (Nov. 1970), 40-46.

Inventory of collection of Civil War letters and journals.

3078. Cobb, Jessie E. "Publications in Alabama during the Confederacy located in the State Department of Archives and History." Alabama historical quarterly, 23 (Spring 1961), 73-137.

3079. Davis, O. L., Jr. "E. H. Cushing: textbooks in Confederate Texas." Library chronicle of the University of Texas, 8, no.2 (1966), 46-50.

Description of Cushing's textbooks, with list of University of Texas Library's holdings.

3080. Decker, Eugene D. "A selected, annotated bibliography of sources in the Kansas State Historical Society pertaining to Kansas in the Civil War." Emporia State research studies, 9, no.4 (June 1961), 7-95.

3081. Dornbusch, Charles E. Regimental publications and personal narratives of the Civil War; a checklist. N.Y.: New York Public Library, 1961-67. 2v.

Locates copies.

3082. Faust, Barbara Louise. A study of materials in the University of Texas Littlefield collection dealing with four American Civil War figures. 1960. 170p. (Master's thesis, Graduate School of Library Science, Univ. of Tex.)

3083. Georgia Archives and History Department. Civil War records in the Georgia Department of Archives and History. Atlanta, n.d. 9p.

3084. Georgia, University, Library. Confederate imprints in the University of Georgia Libraries, ed. by Richard B. Harwell. Athens: Univ. of Ga. Pr., 1964. 49p. (Univ. of Ga. Libraries miscellaneous publications, no.5)

Lists 103 previously unrecorded imprints, plus 2,000 others and 2,000 periodical issues.

3085. Illinois Civil War Centennial Commission. Descriptive bibliography of Civil War manuscripts in Illinois, by William L. Burton. Evanston, Ill.: Northwestern Univ. Pr., 1966. 393p.

Gives locations.

3086. Indiana Civil War Centennial Commission. Guide to Indiana Civil War manuscripts, by Ann Turner. Indianapolis, 1965. 402p.

3087. Maine State Library. Maine in the Civil War; a list of material in the Maine State Library. Augusta, 1961. 13p.

3088. Michigan Historical Commission. Records of the Michigan Department of the Grand Army of the Republic, 1861-1957. Lansing, 1966. 60p. (Finding aid, no.15)

3089. Mississippi Dept. of Archives and History. Guide to Civil War source material in the Department of Archives and History, State of Mississippi, comp. by Patti Carr Black and Maxyne Madden Grimes. Jackson, 1962. 71p.

Includes manuscripts, imprints and newspapers, and official papers or archives.

3090. Nevins, Allan, and others. Civil War books; a critical bibliography. Baton Rouge: Louisiana State Univ. Pr., 1967. 2v.

Critical bibliography of more than 6,000 works concerned with the Civil War; locations in Library of Congress and other libraries.

3091. North Carolina State Dept. of Archives and History. Civil War pictures, by D. L. Corbitt and Elizabeth W. Wilborn. Raleigh, 1964. 87*l*.

3092. ———. Guide to Civil War records in the North Carolina State archives. Raleigh, 1966. 128p.

3093. "Personal narratives of the Civil War in the collection of the Vermont Historical Society." Vermont history, 31 (April 1963), 117-21.

3094. Shetler, Charles. West Virginia Civil War literature: an annotated bibliography. Morgantown: W.Va. Univ. Library, 1963. 184p.

"Library symbols are not given for works held by the West Virginia University Library"; other items located in 21 libraries.

3095. Sinclair, Donald A. A bibliography: the Civil War and New Jersey. New Brunswick, N.J.: Friends of the Rutgers Univ. Library, 1968. 186p.

Records holdings of 50 libraries; 70 percent of items listed are in Rutgers University Library.

3096. Tennessee State Library and Archives. Index to Tennessee Confederate pension applications. Nashville, 1964. 323p.

3097. ———, Manuscript Section. Civil War collection, Confederate and Federal. Nashville, 1966. 78p. (Register, no.10)

3098. U.S. Civil War Centennial Commission. The Civil War Centennial: a report to the Congress. Wash.: Govt. Print. Off., 1968. 69p.

Includes a Centennial bibliography with Library of Congress classification symbols.

3099. U.S. Dept. of the Army Library. The Civil War; a catalog of books in the Army Library pertinent to the American Civil War. Wash., 1961. 51p. (Special list, no.1961-1)

3100. U.S. Library of Congress. The American Civil War; a centennial exhibition. Wash., 1961. 88p.

3101. ———, General Reference and Bibliography Division. Civil War in pictures, 1861-1961; a chronological list of selected pictorial works, comp. by Donald H. Mugridge. Wash.: The Library, 1961. 30p.

3102. ———, Map Division. Civil War maps; an annotated list of maps and atlases in map collections of the Library of Congress, comp. by Richard W. Stephenson. Wash.: Govt. Print. Off., 1961. 138p.

Lists 700 maps, including military, commercial, and political.

3103. ———, Prints and Photographs Division. Civil War photographs, 1861-1865, comp. by Hirst D. Milhollen and Donald H. Mugridge. Wash.: The Library, 1961. 74p.

Based on Mathew B. Brady collection in Library of Congress.

3104. ———, Stack and Reader Division. The Civil War in motion pictures; a bibliography of films produced in the United States since 1897, comp. by Paul C. Spehr. Wash: Govt. Print. Off., 1961. 109p.

3105. U.S. National Archives. Civil War maps in the National Archives, ed. by A. Philip Muntz. Wash., 1964. 127p.

Describes about 8,000 maps, charts, and plans included in the Cartographic Branch of the National Archives.

3106. ———. Guide to federal archives relating to the Civil War, by Kenneth W. Munden and Henry P. Beers. Wash.: National Archives, National Archives and Records Service, 1962. 721p. (National Archives Pub. no.63-1)

Record of material in National Archives, Federal Records Centers, and elsewhere.

3107. ———. Guide to the archives of the Government of the Confederate States of America, by Henry P. Beers. Wash., 1968. 536p.

Records of the Confederacy in National Archives, Library of Congress, and elsewhere.

3108. ———. Preliminary inventory of records relating to Civil War claims; United States and Great Britain, comp. by George S. Ulibarri and Daniel T. Goggin. Wash., 1962. 21p. (Preliminary inventories, no.135)

3109. ———. Preliminary inventory of the records of the Provost Marshal General's Bureau (Civil War), Part 1, comp. by Patricia Andrews. Wash., 1966. 47p.

3110. ———. Preliminary inventory of the records of the Provost Marshal General's Bureau (Civil War), Part 2, comp. by Patricia Andrews and Ellen Garrison. Wash., 1966. 107p.

3111. ———. Preliminary inventory of the records of the Provost Marshal General's Bureau (Civil War), Part 3, comp. by Patricia Andrews. Wash., 1966. 132p.

3112. ———. Preliminary inventory of the records of the Provost Marshal General's Bureau (Civil War), Part 4, comp. by Patricia Andrews and Ruth Johnson. Wash., 1967. 121p.

3113. ———. Preliminary inventory of the records of the Provost Marshal General's Bureau (Civil War), Part 5, comp. by Patricia Andrews and others. Wash., 1967. 96p.

3114. ———. Preliminary inventory of the records of the Provost Marshal General's Bureau (Civil War), Part 6, comp. by Patricia Andrews and Mark German. Wash., 1967. 109p.

3115. ———. Preliminary inventory of the records of the Provost Marshal General's Bureau (Civil War), Part 7, comp. by Patricia Andrews and others. Wash., 1967. 133p.

3116. ———. Preliminary inventory of the records of the Provost Marshal General's Bureau (Civil War), Part 8, comp. by Patricia Andrews and others. Wash., 1967. 46p.

3117. ———. Preliminary inventory of the records of the Treasury Department collection of Confederate records, comp. by Carmelita S. Ryan. Wash., 1967. 65p. (Preliminary inventories, no.169)

3118. ———. Records of Assistant Commissioner for Georgia, Bureau of Refugees, Freedmen, and Abandoned Lands, 1865-69, prep. by Elaine Everly. Wash., 1969. 10p.

3119. ———. Records of Superintendent of Education for State of Georgia Bureau of Refugees, Freedmen, and Abandoned Lands, 1865-1870, prep. by Elaine Everly. Wash., 1969. 8p.

3120. ———. Selected series of records issued by Commissioner of Bureau of Refugees, Freedmen, and Abandoned Lands, 1865-72, prep. by Elaine C. Everly. Wash., 1969. 8p.

3121. West Virginia University Library. West Virginia Civil War literature, an annotated bibliography, by Charles Shetler. Morgantown, 1963. 184p.

Contains 892 entries, citing institutional and private collections.

3122. Wisconsin, State Historical Society. Wisconsin's Civil War archives, by William G. Paul and others. Madison, 1965. 66p.

Describes various types of national, state, and local records in society's possession.

UNITED STATES—REGIONAL

New England

3123. Boston Public Library. Ships and the sea; a

catalog of an exhibition of books and manuscripts in tribute to Boston's maritime past July 1-September 30, 1966, in the Boston Public Library. Boston, 1966. 26*l.*

Lists 99 items from 15th to 20th century.

3124. ———, History Department. New England local histories, 1945-64. Boston, 1965. 9p.

Lists more than 100 titles, arranged by geographical area.

3125. Flaherty, David H. "A select guide to manuscript court records of Colonial New England." American journal of legal history, 11 (April 1967), 107-26.

3126. Sherman, Stuart C. The voice of the whaleman: with an account of the Nicholson whaling collection. Providence, R.I.: Providence Public Library, 1965. 210p.

Describes collection of whaling records in Providence Public Library.

3127. Schultz, Charles R. "Manuscript collections of the Marine Historical Association, Inc. (Mystic Seaport)." American Neptune, 25 (April 1965), 99-111.

In Mystic, Connecticut.

South and Southwest

3128. Dunn, Roy S. "The Southwest collection at Texas Tech." American archivist, 28 (1965), 413-19.

General description of collection of manuscripts and printed records relating mainly to West Texas.

3129. ———. "Southwest collection preserves flavor of region." Texas libraries, 30 (1968), 116-24.

Describes special collection on Southwestern history held by Texas Technological College, Lubbock.

3130. North Carolina, University, Library. The Southern historical collection; a guide to manuscripts, by Susan K. Blosser and Clyde N. Wilson, Jr. Chapel Hill, 1970. 48p.

3131. Wallace, Carolyn Andrews. "The Southern historical collection." American archivist, 28 (1965), 427-36.

Analyzes major collection in University of North Carolina Library of 3,600,000 items in 3,600 groups relating principally to Southern history.

3132. ———. "Southern historical collection." North Carolina libraries, 19 (Winter 1961), 16-21.

3133. West Virginia University Library. The Southern Appalachians; a bibliography and guide to studies, by Robert F. Munn. Morgantown, 1961. 106p.

3134. Woody, Robert H. "The George Washington Flowers memorial collection of Southern Americana." Gnomon (1970), 31-38. (Special number of Duke University Library's Library notes)

Describes Duke Library's holdings.

Midwest

3135. Beers, Henry P. The French and British in the old Northwest; a bibliographical guide to archive and manuscript sources. Detroit: Wayne State Univ. Pr., 1964. 297p.

Describes administrative, legal, national, land, and ecclesiastical records and where they have been preserved in manuscript collections and archives.

3136. Hubach, Robert R. Early Midwestern travel narratives: an annotated bibliography, 1634-1850. Detroit: Wayne State Univ. Pr., 1961. 149p.

Locations indicated for many manuscripts included.

West

3137. Billington, Ray A. "Books that won the West: the guidebooks of the forty-niners and fifty-niners." The American west, 4 (August 1967), 25-32, 72-75.

Based on Newberry Library collection.

3138. California, University, Bancroft Library. Catalog of printed books. Boston: G. K. Hall, 1964. 22v. Supplement. 1969. 6v.

Represents collection of 150,000 books, pamphlets, documents, periodicals, newspapers, etc., rich in history of Western U.S., Mexico, and Central America.

3139. ———. A guide to the manuscript collections, ed. by Dale L. Morgan and George P. Hammond. Berkeley: Univ. of Calif. Pr., 1963. 379p.

Covers Pacific and Western manuscripts, except California.

3140. California, University, Library. The West; from fact to myth; catalog of an exhibit in the UCLA Library, by Philip Durham and Everitt L. Jones. Los Angeles, 1967. 19p.

Rare books, magazines, and miscellaneous material dealing with the history of the American West.

3141. Cornell University, Collection of Regional History and University Archives. George Bancroft papers at Cornell University, 1811-1901, ed. by Herbert Finch. Ithaca, N.Y., 1965. 13p.

3142. Denver Public Library. Catalog of the Western History Department, Denver Public Library. Boston: G. K. Hall, 1970. 7v.

Reproduces 117,000 cards; collection outstanding for history of Rocky Mountain region.

3143. ———. Western history department, its beginning and growth, rev. ed., by Malcolm G. Wyer. Denver, 1965. 18p.

3144. Friend, Llerena. "Posses all over the place: publications of the Westerners." Library chronicle of the University of Texas, 8, no.4 (1968), 58-65.

Survey of publications of the Westerners Corrals, with listing of University of Texas Library's holdings.

3145. Goosman, Mildred. "Maximilian-Bodmer collection." Mountain plains library quarterly, 9 (Spring 1964), 16-20.

Collection of drawings, original documents, and early printed editions, relating to Prince Maximilian of Wied's expedition to America in 1832; the West and Indians. Collection held by Joslyn Art Museum, Omaha, Nebraska.

3146. Hanna, Archibald, Jr. "Manuscript resources in the Yale University Library for the study of Western travel." In McDermott, John F., ed., Travelers on the Western frontier. Urbana: Univ. of Ill. Pr., 1970. p.79-88.

A general description.

3147. ———. "The Yale collection of Western Americana and the Benjamin Franklin collection." Yale University Library gazette, 38 (1964), 160-66.

General description of two major collections in Yale Library.

3148. Michigan, University, William L. Clements Library. Frontier pages and pistols; a guide to an exhibition in the William L. Clements Library, by Albert T. Klyberg and Nathaniel N. Shipton. Ann Arbor, 1966. 19p. (Bulletin, no.72)

3149. Morgan, Dale L. "Western travels and travelers in the Bancroft Library." In McDermott, John F., Travelers on the Western frontier. Urbana: Univ. of Ill. Pr., 1970, p.100-11.

A general description.

3150. Nevada, University, Center for Western North American Studies. Summary of acquisitions deposited in the Nevada and the West collection, University Library, 1964-65. Reno. 43*l.* Annual.

3151. Newberry Library. Catalogue of an exhibition of Western materials selected from the Everett D. Graff collection. Chicago, 1965. 20p.

3152. ———. A catalogue of the Everett D. Graff collection of Western Americana, comp. by Colton Storm. Chicago: Univ. of Chicago Pr., 1968. 854p.

Collection comprises 10,000 books, pamphlets, maps, broadsides, and manuscripts relating to exploration, settlement, and development of trans-Mississippi West. Catalog of 4,801 items limited mainly to source materials.

3153. Parker, Thomas F. "Burbank Western history collection." California librarian, 26 (1965), 104-7.

Collection of 6,000 volumes in Burbank Public Library relating to California and Western history.

3154. Smith, Dwight L. "The westward traveler: unexploited manuscript resources of the Newberry Library." In McDermott, John F., ed., Travelers on the Western frontier. Urbana: Univ. of Ill. Pr., 1970, p.89-99.

A general description.

3155. U.S. National Archives. Federal exploration of the American West before 1880. Wash., 1963. 32p.

Catalog of exhibition.

3156. Weber, Francis J. "Estelle Doheny collection of Western Americana." California librarian, 29 (Jan. 1968), 41-45.

Collection in Doheny Memorial Library, Saint John's Seminary, Camarillo, California.

3157. Yale University Library. Catalog of the Yale collection of Western Americana. Boston: G. K. Hall, 1961. 4v.

Catalog of outstanding collection of rare books relating to American West, the William Robertson Coe collection.

3158. ———. Yale collection of Western Americana. A catalogue of the Frederick W. and Carrie S. Beinecke collection of Western Americana, comp. by Jeanne M. Goddard and Charles Kritzler. New Haven, Conn.: Yale Univ. Pr., 1965- . v.1- . In progress.

Stresses materials on Spanish Southwest and California from period of discovery to Mexican War and gold rush.

Pacific Northwest

3159. Harris, Phoebe M. "Northwest history collection in the Seattle Public Library." Library news bulletin (Washington State Library), 33 (1966), 175-79.

3160. Mills, Hazel Emery. "Pacific N.W. history collection of the Washington State Library." Library news bulletin (Washington State Library), 33 (1966), 187-97.
General description.

UNITED STATES–STATE AND LOCAL

Alabama

3161. U.S. Library of Congress. Alabama: the sesquicentennial of statehood; an exhibition in Library of Congress. Wash.: U.S. Govt. Print. Off., 1969. 74p.
Describes 112 documents, rare books, manuscripts, maps, and photographs included in exhibit.

Alaska

3162. Allen, Robert V. "Alaska before 1867 in Soviet literature." Quarterly journal of the Library of Congress, 23 (1966), 243-50.
Report on acquisitions, Library of Congress.

3163. Dorosh, John T. "The Alaskan Russian Church archives." Library of Congress quarterly journal of current acquisitions, 18 (1961), 193-203.
Archival materials in Library of Congress' Manuscript Division relating to Alaskan history, 1772-1933.

Arkansas

3164. Arkansas Library Commission. Arkansas books and materials; a compilation of Arkansas shelf lists of the public libraries of Arkansas, comp. by LaNell Compton and others. Little Rock, 1967. 224p.

3165. ———. Arkansiana for high schools, comp. by Anne Jackson. Little Rock, 1964. 54p.

California

3166. California Library Association. California local history: a bibliography and union list of library holdings, 2d ed., ed. by Margaret Miller Rocq. Stanford: Stanford Univ. Pr., 1970. 611p.
Lists more than 17,000 items with holdings in about 230 libraries.

3167. Stoughton, Gertrude K. Books of California; an introduction to the history and the heritage of this state as revealed in the collection in the Pasadena Public Library, assembled by Nellie May Russ. Los Angeles: Ward Ritchie Press, 1968. 213p.

Connecticut

3168. Turner, Sylvie J. "The Connecticut archives." Connecticut Historical Society bulletin, 33 (July 1968), 81-89.
Describes Connecticut State Library's "Connecticut Archives."

Delaware

3169. Delaware Public Archives Commission. Calendar of Sussex County, Delaware, probate records, 1680-1800, comp. by Leon deValinger, Jr. Dover, 1964. 310, 87p.

3170. ———. List of accessions, Dover, Oct. 1951- . v.1- . Quarterly.

3171. Reed, H. Clay, and Reed, Marion B. A bibliography of Delaware through 1960. Newark: Univ. of Del. Pr., 1966. 196p.
Compiled from holdings of Historical Society of Delaware (Wilmington), Wilmington Institute Free Library, University of Delaware, and Public Archives at Dover; some locations given.

Florida

3172. Humphrey, Sr. M. Kathleen Ann. The Floridiana collection of St. Leo Abbey; a descriptive survey. Wash., 1968. 155p. (Master's thesis, Dept. of Library Science, Catholic Univ. of America)
In St. Leo, Florida.

Georgia

3173. Pollard, William R. An analysis and evaluation with a chronological check list of the Georgia section of the Southern pamphlet collection, 1820-1919. 1965. 172p. (Thesis, Univ. of N.C.)
Collection in University of North Carolina Library.

Hawaii

3174. Hawaii State Library. Admiral Thomas papers; a special collection of important manuscripts and printed documents relating to Hawaii (1841-1877), Hawaiian historical collection. Honolulu, 1967. 15p.

3175. ———. The James Tice Phillips collection, presented to the Hawaii State Library historical collection. Honolulu: Office of Library Services, State of Hawaii, 1968. 50p.

Lists 1,705 books, pamphlets, and maps about Hawaii.

3176. Hawaii, University, Library. Dictionary catalog of the Hawaiian collection, Sinclair Library, University of Hawaii (Honolulu). Boston: G. K. Hall, 1963. 4v.

Catalog of 42,000 items of Hawaiiana.

3177. ———, Hawaiian and Pacific Collection. A selective reading list of Hawaiian books, comp. by Janet E. Bell. Honolulu, 1966. 11*l.* New edition. 1970. 17*l.*

3178. ——— ———. Current Hawaiiana. Honolulu, 1944- . Quarterly.

Idaho

3179. Idaho State Library. Idaho the Gem state; a bibliography of books about Idaho and by Idaho authors, selected by Mildred Selby and Rose Coventry. Boise, 1966. 30p.

Illinois

3180. Illinois State Historical Library. Manuscripts acquired during 1963, a descriptive inventory, by Robert L. Brubaker. Springfield, 1964. 32p.

3181. ———. Manuscripts acquired during 1964-1965; a descriptive inventory. Springfield, 1967. 44p.

3182. ———. "Microfilm collections of periodicals, manuscripts and miscellany in the Illinois State Historical Library." Illinois libraries, 47 (March 1965), 276-81.

3183. Illinois, University, Chicago Circle Library. Guide to the manuscript collections in the Department of Special Collections, the Library. Chicago, 1969. Unpaged.

Descriptions and listings of about 100 collections relating chiefly to Chicago organizations and individuals.

3184. Kaige, Richard H., and Vaughn, Evelyn L. "Illinois county histories; a checklist of Illinois county histories in the Illinois State Library." Illinois libraries, 50 (1968), 694-722.

Alphabetical by counties.

3185. McCree, Mary Lynn. "Illinois State Archives: guide to records holdings." Illinois libraries, 46 (1964), 319-63.

3186. Pease, Marguerite Jenison. "Archives in Randolph County; a revised inventory." Illinois libraries, 43 (1961), 433-48.

Randolph County, Illinois.

3187. Tingley, Donald F. "Manuscript materials relating to Illinois in California's Henry E. Huntington Library." Journal of the Illinois State Historical Society, 60 (Autumn 1967), 313-19.

3188. U.S. Library of Congress. Illinois; the sesquicentennial of statehood: an exhibition in the Library of Congress. Wash.: Govt. Print. Off., 1968. 58p.

Based primarily on Library of Congress' holdings with several items lent by National Archives.

Indiana

3189. Indiana University, Lilly Library. One hundred and fifty years; an exhibit commemorating the sesquicentennial of Indiana statehood, comp. by Cecil K. Byrd and Wilborn R. Cagle. Bloomington, 1966. 94p. (Lilly Library publication, no.3)

A catalog of the exhibit.

Iowa

3190. Swierenga, Robert P. "The Iowa land records collection." Books at Iowa, 13 (Nov. 1970), 25-30.

In University of Iowa Libraries.

Kansas

3191. Kansas State Historical Society. Guide to the microfilm edition of the New England Emigrant Aid Company papers 1854-1909 in the Kansas State Historical Society, ed. by Joseph W. Snell. Topeka, 1967. 22p.

Kentucky

3192. Western Kentucky State College Library. Supplement list of books and pamphlets in Kentucky Library. Bowling Green, 1965. 25*l.*

Louisiana

3193. Daniel, Katherine Dusenberry. The Southern pamphlet collection: an analysis and evaluation, with a chronological check list of the Louisiana portion, 1820-

1950. Wash., 1968. 109p. (Master's thesis, School of Library Science, Univ. of N.C.)

In University of North Carolina Library.

3194. Griffith, Connie G. "Summary of inventory: Louisiana Historical Association collection." Louisiana history, 9 (Fall 1968), 365-70.

In Tulane University Library; summary of a 230-page typewritten inventory.

3195. Louisiana Library Association. The Louisiana union catalog, pre-1968 index. Baton Rouge, 1968. 497p.; 1959-1962 supplement. 1963. 173p.; 1963-1967 supplement. 1968. 443p.; 1968-70 supplement and index. 1971. 600p.

Louisiana materials found in numerous Louisiana libraries.

3196. Louisiana State Archives and Records Commission. Calendar of Louisiana colonial documents, vol. 1, Avoyelles Parish, comp. by Winston Deville. Baton Rouge, 1961. 50p.

Maine

3197. Bangor Public Library. Bibliography of the state of Maine. Boston: G. K. Hall, 1962. 803p.

Author and dictionary catalogs of 11,000 entries relating to Maine.

3198. U.S. Library of Congress. Maine: the sesquicentennial of statehood. Wash.: Govt. Print. Off., 1970. 86p.

Catalog of exhibition in Library of Congress.

Maryland

3199. Maryland Hall of Records. Index holdings, May 1966. Annapolis, 1966. 16p. (Bulletin, no.13)

3200. Maryland Historical Society. The manuscript collections of the Maryland Historical Society, comp. by Avril J. M. Pedley. Baltimore, 1968. 390p.

Describes 1,724 collections, containing a total of a million items; extensive index.

3201. Maryland Historical Society Library, Baltimore. Catalog. Westport, Conn.: Greenwood, 1970. 10v.

Massachusetts

3202. Massachusetts Historical Society. Collecting for Clio; an exhibition of representative materials from the holdings of the Massachusetts Historical Society. Boston, 1969. 73p.

Michigan

3203. Dutch-American Historical Commission. Guide to the Dutch-American historical collections of Western Michigan, ed. by Herbert Brinks. Grand Rapids and Holland, Mich., 1967. 52p.

3204. Hathaway, Richard J. Directory of historical collections in Michigan. Lansing: Michigan Archivists Association, 1969. 74p.

3205. Michigan Bureau of Library Services. Michigan county histories; a bibliography. Lansing, 1970. 29p.

3206. ———. The people of Michigan; a history and selected bibliography of the races and nationalities who settled our state, by George P. Graff. Lansing, 1970. 77p.

3207. Michigan Historical Commission. Directory of major Michigan history research collections, comp. by Alan S. Brown. Lansing, 1961. 10p. (Information leaflets, no.99)

3208. ———. Permanent records of all units of Michigan government, 1796-1958. Lansing, 1966. 9p.

3209. ———. Subject index to manuscripts in the Michigan Historical Commission Archives. Lansing, 1966. 12p.

3210. Michigan State University Library. A guide to the historical collections of Michigan State University, comp. by Anthony Zito. East Lansing, 1969. 110p.

Includes archival and printed records relating to Michigan and regional history, Michigan State University, and the land-grant movement.

3211. Michigan, University, Michigan Historical Collections. Guide to manuscripts in the Michigan Historical Collections of the University of Michigan, comp. by Robert M. Warner and Ida C. Brown. Ann Arbor, 1963. 315p.

A collection of 3,255,000 bound manuscripts and 12,350 volumes, especially strong in Michigan history.

3212. ——— ———. The Michigan Historical Collections of the University of Michigan. Ann Arbor, 1964. 12p.

3213. Netherlands Museum. A guide to the archives of

the Netherlands Museum, Holland, Michigan. Holland, 1968. 36p.

Collection relating to Dutch heritage of Holland, Michigan.

3214. Western Michigan University Library. Guide to the regional history collections, comp. by Phyllis B. Burnham. Kalamazoo, 1964. 29p. Supplement, 1966. 30p.

Mississippi

3215. U.S. Library of Congress. Mississippi: the sesquicentennial of statehood; an exhibition in the Library of Congress. Wash., 1967. 61p.

Based mainly on Library of Congress collections, with several added items from National Archives.

Nebraska

3216. Nebraska State Historical Society. A guide to the archives and manuscripts of the Nebraska State Historical Society, comp. by William F. Schmidt and Harold E. Kemble, Jr. Lincoln, 1966. 93p. (Bulletin, no.2) A supplement. Lincoln, 1966. 218*l.*

3217. ———. A guide to the archives and manuscripts of the Nebraska State Historical Society, comp. by Douglas A. Bakken and others. Lincoln, 1967. 100p. (Bulletin, no.3)

Nevada

3218. Nevada Division of Archives. Your Nevada State archives, by Frederick C. Gale. Carson City, 1966. 7*l.*

3219. Nevada State Library. Nevada in print, 2d ed. Carson City, 1961. 32p.

3220. Nevada, University, Library. A preliminary union catalog of Nevada manuscripts, comp. by Robert D. Armstrong. Reno, 1967. 218p.

3221. U.S. Library of Congress. Nevada: the centennial of statehood; an exhibition in the Library of Congress. Wash., 1965. 66p.

Includes engravings, lithographs, photographs, maps, and manuscripts.

New Jersey

3222. New Jersey Archives and History Bureau. Guide to county archives in the Bureau of Archives and History, comp. by Kenneth W. Richards. Trenton, 1963. 8p.

3223. ———. Guide to municipal archives in the Bureau of Archives and History, comp. by Kenneth W. Richards. Trenton, The Bureau, 1963. 4p.

3224. New Jersey State College Library. This is New Jersey, a tercentenary bibliography, comp. by Doris M. Perry. Trenton, 1963. 53p.

3225. Rutgers University Library. A guide to the manuscript collection of the Rutgers University Library, comp. by Herbert F. Smith. New Brunswick, N.J.: Rutgers Univ. Pr., 1964. 179p.

Includes listing of 1,309 groups and collections, comprising about 500,000 items, relating principally to New Jersey.

New Mexico

3226. New Mexico State Records Center, Archives Division. Guide to the microfilm of the Spanish archives of New Mexico, 1621-1821, in the Archives Division of the State of New Mexico Records Center, ed. by Myra Ellen Jenkins. Santa Fe, 1967. 23p.

New York

3227. Cole, G. Glyndon. Historical materials relating to northern New York: a union catalog. Potsdam, N.Y.: State Univ. College, 1968. 307p.

Lists 2,700 titles in 92 libraries. Includes all known publications relating to or published in area of state north of Mohawk Valley prior to 1960.

3228. D'Innocenzo, Michael, and Turner, John. "The Peter Van Gaasbeek papers: a resource for early New York history, 1771-1797." New York history, 47 (April 1966), 153-59.

3229. Syracuse University Library. The Oneida Community collection in the Syracuse University Library. Syracuse, N.Y., 1961. 38p.

Manuscript and printed material relating to a 19th-century communitarian settlement near Oneida, New York.

3230. White, William C. "90 feet of Adirondackana in the Saranac Lake Free Library." Bookmark, New York State Library, 22 (May 1963), 223-25.

North Carolina

3231. "Archives and manuscripts in North Carolina." North Carolina libraries, 19, no.2 (Winter 1961), 40p. (Special issue)

3232. Martin, Carolyn Patricia. The North Carolina collection in the University of North Carolina Library. 1961. 59p. (Master's thesis, School of Library Science, Univ. of N.C.)

3233. North Carolina State Dept. of Archives and History. Guide to private manuscript collections in the North Carolina State Archives, prep. by Beth G. Crabtree. Raleigh, 1964. 492p.

3234. ———. Summary guide to research materials in the North Carolina State Archives; Section A: Records of State agencies. Raleigh, 1963. 86p.

3235. ———. Surry County records inventory. Raleigh, 1963. 57p.

3236. Powell, William S. "Carolina in the seventeenth century: an annotated bibliography of contemporary publications." North Carolina historical review, 41 (Winter 1964), 74-104.

Locates copies in major U.S. research libraries.

North Dakota

3237. North Dakota, University, Library. Orin G. Libby manuscript collection; guide to microfilm edition of the Dakota territorial records, ed. by Daniel Rylance. Grand Forks, 1969. 44p.

3238. Rose, Margaret. "Manuscript collections of the State Historical Society of North Dakota." North Dakota history, 30 (Jan. 1963), 17-61.

Ohio

3239. Colket, Meredith B., Jr. "Collections and exhibits: the Western Reserve Historical Society." Ohio history, 72 (April 1963), 140-49.

Enumerates fields of specialization, identifies special research resources, and includes partial checklist of manuscript holdings.

3240. Ohio State Library. The Buckeye State in books, comp. by Mary Jane Myrice. Napoleon, n.d. 24*l.*

Oregon

3241. Belknap, George N. "An Oregon miscellany." Papers of the Bibliographical Society of America, 57 (1963), 191-200.

Detailed descriptions and locations of 8 major titles of early Oregoniana.

3242. Oregon State Library, Division of State Archives. Guide to legislative records in the Oregon State Archives. Salem, 1968. 13p. (Bulletin, no.8)

3243. ——— ———. Guide to microfilms in the Oregon State Archives. Salem, 1968. 19p. (Publication, no.32).

Pennsylvania

3244. Harpster, John W. "The manuscript and miscellaneous collections of the Historical Society of Western Pennsylvania." Western Pennsylvania historical magazine, 49 (1966), 67-78, 345-58.

3245. Pennsylvania Historical and Museum Commission. Guide to the microfilm of the records of the Provincial Council, 1682-1776, in the Pennsylvania State Archives, ed. by George Dailey and George R. Beyer. Harrisburg, 1966. 130p.

3246. ———. Historical manuscript depositories in Pennsylvania, comp. by Irwin Richman. Harrisburg, 1965. 73p.

3247. ———. Summary guide to the Pennsylvania State Archives in the Division of Public Records, comp. by Frank B. Evans and Martha L. Simonetti. Harrisburg, 1963. 41p.

3248. ———, Bureau of Archives and History. Inventory of Canal Commissioners' maps in the Pennsylvania State Archives. Harrisburg, 1968. 91p.

South Carolina

3249. Kinken, Ann Daly. The Southern pamphlet collection: an evaluation and chronological check list of the South Carolina portion, 1820-1900. 1963. 145*l.* (Master's thesis, School of Library Science, Univ. of N.C.)

In University of North Carolina Library.

Tennessee

3250. North Carolina State Dept. of Archives and History. Records relating to Tennessee in the North Carolina State Archives, by C. F. W. Coker. Raleigh, 1968. 6p.

3251. Owsley, Harriet C. "The Rugby papers: a bibliographic note." Tennessee historical quarterly, 27 (Fall 1968), 225-28.

Originals at Rugby Colony; copies in Tennessee State Library and Archives Manuscript Section.

3252. Tennessee Historical Commission. Guide to the processed manuscripts of the Tennessee Historical Society, ed. by Harriet Chappell Owsley. Nashville, 1969. 70p.

3253. Tennessee State Library and Archives. Index to county records microfilm of Henry County, Paris, Tennessee. Nashville, 1969. 24*l.*

3254. ———. Land records in the Tennessee State Library and Archives. Nashville, n.d. 7p.

3255. ———. Tennessee diaries, memoirs and church records in the Manuscript Division. Nashville, 1965. 34p.

3256. ———. Writings on Tennessee counties available on interlibrary loan from the Tennessee State Library and Archives. Nashville, 1967. 33p.

Texas

3257. Day, James M. Handbook Texas archival and manuscript depositories. Austin: Tex. Library and Historical Commission, 1966. 76p.

Describes many collections.

3258. Friend, Llerena. "The Frank Kell collection." Library chronicle of the University of Texas, 7 (Fall 1961), 3-12.

Collection dealing with Texas and Mormon history in University of Texas Library.

3259. Holley, Edward G. "The William B. Bates collection of Texana and Western Americana." Extra, Univ. of Houston Alumni Federation (Feb. 1965), 2-3.

Describes University of Houston Library's collection of rare Texas and Southwestern material.

3260. Houston, University, Libraries. The William B. Bates collection of Texana and Western Americana, catalog of an exhibition, comp. by Lorene Pouncey. Houston, Tex., 1965. 24p.

Rare books and other outstanding items selected from collection in University of Houston libraries.

3261. Maxwell, Robert S. "Manuscript collections at Stephen F. Austin State College." American archivist, 28 (1965), 421-26.

Describes papers, diaries, and few rare books dealing with early Texas history, and business records.

3262. Perry, Carmen. "Daughters of the Republic of Texas library." Texas library journal, 39 (Spring 1963), 7-8.

3263. Sam Houston State College Library. The Thomason Room; special collections at Sam Houston State College. Huntsville, Tex., 1969. 14p.

Describes collections relating to Texas history, Sam Houston, Southwest history, and criminology.

3264. Santos, Richard G. "Spanish archives of Laredo." Texana, 4 (Spring 1966), 41-46.

Presently located in St. Mary's University, San Antonio, Texas.

3265. Stephens, Robert O. "The oral history of Texas oil pioneers." Library chronicle of the University of Texas, 7, no.1 (1961), 35-39.

Special collection in University of Texas Library, consisting of 200 reels of tape transcribed into 4,000 pages of typescript.

3266. Texas State Library. Handbook of Texas archival and manuscript depositories, comp. by James M. Day. Austin: Tex. Library and Historical Commission, 1966. 73p.

Guide to holdings of 85 Texas institutions.

3267. Texas, University, Humanities Research Center. Texana at the University of Texas: an exhibition of manuscripts, broadsides, books, photographs & miscellaneous items relating to Texas. Austin, 1962. 42p.

3268. ———, Library, Archives Collection. Guide to the microfilm edition of the Bexar archives, 1717-1803, ed. by Chester V. Kielman. Austin, 1967. 28p.

Collection of 250,000 pages of manuscript documentation and 4,000 pages of printed materials, in University of Texas Library; consists of colonial archives of Texas during Spanish and Mexican periods, 1717-1836.

3269. Thomas, Laura, and Foos, Donald D. Library resources in the Trans-Pecos region; an inventory and evaluation. El Paso, Texas, 1967. 91p.

3270. Whitney, Dorman H. "The Ashbel Smith papers." Library chronicle of the University of Texas, 7 (Fall 1961), 32-34.

Collection of 6,369 documents relating to Texas history from 1837 to 1880s.

Utah

3271. U.S. National Archives. Records relating to

appointment of Federal judges, attorneys, and marshals for Territory and State of Utah, 1853-1901, prep. by Norman D. Moore. Wash., 1967. 16p.

Vermont

3272. Wallace, Marlene, and Williams, John. "Vermont state papers: rich sources for the study of Vermont history." Vermont history, 38 (1970), 214-49.

Describes archives in Vermont Secretary of State's office.

Virginia

3273. Isaac, Oliver B. A selected, annotated bibliography of resources on the history of Franklin, Henry, and Patrick counties in Virginia. Wash., 1964. 122p. (Master's thesis, Dept. of Library Science, Catholic Univ. of America)

3274. Virginia, University, Library. Guide to the microfilm edition of the Virginia gazette day books 1750-1752 & 1764-1766, ed. by Paul P. Hoffman. Charlottesville, 1967. 55p. (Microfilm publications, no.5)

3275. William and Mary College Library. A guide to historical materials; a selected bibliography of reference books with emphasis on Virginia history. Williamsburg, Va., 1965. 39*l.*

3276. ———. A guide to historical materials compiled by and found in the College of William and Mary Library and the Research Dept., Colonial Williamsburg, Inc. Williamsburg, 1961. 30*l.*

Washington

3277. Washington, University, Libraries. Washington Territorial government papers, 1853-1875, at the University of Washington Libraries. n.p., n.d. 4p.

West Virginia

3278. U.S. Library of Congress. West Virginia, the centennial of statehood, 1863-1963; an exhibition in the Library of Congress. Wash.: Govt. Print. Off., 1964. 82p.

Annotated entries for manuscripts, broadsides, newspapers, rare books, maps, prints, drawings, and photographs.

3279. West Virginia University Library. Guide to manuscripts and archives in the West Virginia collection—Number II, 1958-1962, comp. by F. Gerald Ham. Morgantown, 1965. 147p.

Lists 437 collections of private papers, institutional archives, and business records; regional in scope.

Wisconsin

3280. Milwaukee County Historical Society. A preliminary survey of manuscript and archival collections of the Milwaukee County Historical Society. n.p., 1967. 20p.

3281. Smith, Alice E. "Wisconsin's history, written and unwritten." Wisconsin magazine of history, 44 (Winter 1960-61), 95-101.

Relates to resources for research in State Historical Society of Wisconsin.

3282. Wisconsin, State Historical Society, Library. Catalogs, arranged by subject and by author and title, including pamphlet, city directory, atlas, newspaper, and local labor papers catalogs. Westport, Conn.: Greenwood, 1971. 45v.

Library outstanding for U.S. history, with emphasis on Wisconsin and Midwest.

3283. ———. Checklist of archives and manuscripts holdings in the University of Wisconsin Milwaukee Area Research Center. Madison, 1969. 40*l.*

Lists private and governmental manuscripts and archives for 8 Wisconsin counties in Milwaukee area.

3284. ———. Checklist of archives and manuscripts holdings in the Wisconsin State University—Eau Claire Area Research Center. Madison, 1967. 16*l.*

Lists private and governmental manuscripts and archives for 11 Wisconsin counties in Eau Claire area.

3285. ———. Checklist of archives and manuscripts holdings in the Wisconsin State University—La Crosse Area Research Center. Madison, 1969. 27*l.*

Lists private and governmental manuscripts and archives for 8 Wisconsin counties in La Crosse area.

3286. ———. Checklist of archives and manuscripts holdings in the Wisconsin State University—Oshkosh Area Research Center. Madison, 1967. 30*l.*

Lists private and governmental manuscripts and archives for 11 Wisconsin counties in Oshkosh area.

3287. ———. Checklist of archives and manuscripts holdings in the Wisconsin State University—Platteville Southwestern Wisconsin Area Research Center. Madison, 1966. 7*l.*

Lists private and governmental manuscripts and archives for 5 counties in Platteville area.

3288. ———. Guide to the manuscripts of the State Historical Society of Wisconsin: supplement number two, by Josephine L. Harper. Madison, 1966. 275p.

Original work, 1944; supplement no.1, 1957.

3289. ———. Guide to the Wisconsin State archives, comp. by David J. Delgado. Madison, 1966. 262p.

Describes about 1,600 record series from 62 agencies, 1836 to date, a total of 20,000 cubic feet, in State Historical Society of Wisconsin.

3290. ———. A guide to theses on Wisconsin subjects, by Roger E. Wyman. Madison, 1964. 88p.

Material in society's library.

3291. ———. A guide to theses on Wisconsin subjects, supplement number one, by Jeanne Hunnicutt Chiswick. Madison, 1966. 33p.

Material in society's library.

AMERICAN ALMANACS

3292. Bear, James A., Jr., and Caperton, Mary. A checklist of Virginia almanacs, 1732-1850. Charlottesville: Bibliographical Society of the Univ. of Va., 1962. Unpaged.

Locates copies.

3293. Drake, Milton. Almanacs of the United States. N.Y.: Scarecrow, 1962. 2v.

Locates copies, in numerous libraries, of 14,385 titles by state, year, and alphabetically by title.

LATIN AMERICAN

General

3294. Auburn University Library. A selected checklist of works by Latin American authors, comp. by Raúl Santo-Tomás. Auburn, Ala., 1969. 43, 4*l.*

Record of Auburn Library's holdings.

3295. Coale, Robert P. "Evaluation of a research library collection: Latin American colonial history at the Newberry." Library quarterly, 35 (1965), 173-84.

Description of the Newberry Library's holdings based on sampling standard bibliographies.

3296. ———. An evaluation of the Newberry Library collections in the colonial history of Mexico, Peru, Chile, and the Colombia-Venezuela region. Chicago, 1964. 65*l.* (Master's thesis, Graduate Library School, Univ. of Chicago)

3297. Dillon, Richard H. "Sutro Library's resources in Latin Americana." Hispanic American historical review, 45 (1965), 267-74.

Branch of California State Library in San Francisco.

3298. Garner, Jane. "Significant acquisitions of Latin American material by U.S. libraries, 1966-67." In Acquisition of Latin American library materials [Seminar, 12th, 1967. Los Angeles]. Final report and working papers, v.1, p.183-218. Wash.: Pan American Union, 1968.

3299. Haro, Robert P. Latin Americana research in the United States and Canada: a guide and directory. Chicago: American Library Assoc., 1971. 111p.

"Latin American library collections," p.27-86, summarizes subject strengths and other data on 86 libraries.

3300. Harvard University Library. Latin American literature. Cambridge, Mass., 1969. 498p. (Widener Library shelflist, no.21)

Lists 16,300 titles in all literary forms.

3301. Hispanic Society of America. Catalogue of the Library. Boston: G. K. Hall, 1962. 10v.

3302. ———. Printed books, 1468-1700, in the Hispanic Society of America; a listing, by Clara Louisa Penney. N.Y., 1965. 614p.

Lists Latin American, Spanish, and other imprints relating to Latin America; combines 1929 and 1938 published bibliographies, plus more recent additions.

3303. Indiana University, Lilly Library. Manuscritos Latinoamericanos en la Biblioteca Lilly, Universidad de Indiana, by Elfrieda Lang. Bloomington, n.d. Various pagings.

3304. Kansas, University Libraries. Publications received by subscription and exchange from Latin American countries. Lawrence, 1964. 14*l.*

3305. Lamb, Ursula S. "Some books relating to colonial Latin America." Yale University Library gazette, 42 (1967), 8-20.

Rare books, 16th to 18th centuries, relating to Latin America in Yale Library.

3306. Louisiana State University, Dept. of Archives

and Manuscripts. A preliminary guide to uncataloged Hispanic American sources in the DeForest collection. [Baton Rouge] 1969. 8*l.* (Latin American Studies Institute bibliographical series, Dec. 1969)

3307. Macaulay, Neill. "Material on Latin America in the United States Marine Corps archives." Hispanic American historical review, 46 (1966), 179-81.

Located in the Marine Corps Historical Archives and Library, Arlington, Virginia.

3308. Michel, Julian G., and Becker, R. H. "Development of collections on Latin America and the Spanish Southwest at the University of California, Berkeley." In Acquisition of Latin American library materials [Seminar, 12th, 1967. Los Angeles] Final report and working papers, v.1, p.251-58. Wash.: Pan American Union, 1968.

3309. Montgomery, James. "Latin Americana in the Joint University Libraries." Tennessee librarian, 17 (Fall 1964), 16-19.

3310. Okinshevich, Leo. Latin America in Soviet writings: a bibliography. Baltimore: pub. for the Library of Congress by the Johns Hopkins Pr., 1966. 2v.

Covers 1917-64 period and includes 8,688 entries; items held by Library of Congress noted.

3311. Princeton University Library. Latin America: social sciences and humanities; serials (periodicals, monographs in series, documents) currently received in the Princeton University Library, comp. by Barbara H. Stein. Princeton, N.J., 1964. 41p.

3312. Southern Illinois University Library. Samuel Putnam, Latin Americanist; a bibliography, by C. Harvey Gardiner. Carbondale, 1970. 48p. (Bibliographic contribution, no.5)

Writings of Putnam, published and unpublished, on Latin America; in Southern Illinois University Library.

3313. Syracuse University Library. Organization and work; the Hispanic and Luso-Brazilian collection and the Slavic collection of the Area Studies Department, by André Preibish and Roger Beasley. Syracuse, N.Y., 1970. 23p.

3314. Texas, University, Library. Catalog of the Latin American collection of the University of Texas Library (Austin). Boston: G. K. Hall, 1969. 31v.

Records 160,000-volume collection.

3315. Tulane University Library. Catalog of the Latin American Library. Boston: G. K. Hall, 1971. 9v.

3316. U.S. Dept. of the Army Library. Latin America: hemispheric partner, a bibliographic survey. Wash., 1964. 128p. (DA pamphlet 550-1)

Based on publications in the Army Library.

3317. ———. Latin America and the Caribbean; analytical survey of literature. Wash.: U.S. Govt. Print. Office, 1969. 319p. (DA pamphlet 550-7)

3318. U.S. Library of Congress, Hispanic Foundation. Latin America: an annotated bibliography of paperback books, comp. by Georgette M. Dorn. Wash.: Govt. Print. Off., 1967. 77p.

List of 629 titles in humanities and social sciences.

3319. U.S. National Archives. Guide to materials on Latin America in the National Archives, by John P. Harrison. Wash., 1961. 246p.

3320. ———. Materials in National Archives relating to independence of Latin American nations, prep. by George S. Ulibarri. Wash., 1968. 20p.

3321. Washington University Libraries. A bibliographic guide to Olin Library's microform holdings in Ibero-American studies, comp. by David S. Zubatsky. St. Louis, 1970. 84p. (Washington University Library studies, no.7)

3322. ———. A list of Washington University theses and dissertations in the field of Ibero-American studies held by Olin Library, Washington University Libraries, by David S. Zubatsky. St. Louis, 1970. 14p.

3323. Watson, Alice Gayle Hudgens. A guide to reference materials of Colombia, Ecuador, and Venezuela useful in the social sciences and humanities. Austin, 1967. 179*l.* (Master's thesis, School of Library Science, Univ. of Tex.)

3324. Woods, William R. A program for cooperative Latin American serial acquisitions in major Southern California libraries. Los Angeles: Univ. of Southern Calif., 1965. 135p.

Covers policies and holdings of UCLA and USC libraries and Los Angeles Public Library.

3325. Workshop on Latin American Sources of Information. Bibliography of sources of information relative to Latin America, comp. by Francisco Chaves and others. Wash.: Pan American Union, 1967-68. 2 pts.

Locates some copies in University of Kansas Libraries, where workshop was held.

Argentina

3326. Texas, University, Library. Recent Argentine acquisitions of the Latin American collection of the University of Texas Library. Austin, 1962-64- . no.1- .

3327. U.S. National Archives. Records of Department of State relating to internal affairs of Argentina, 1910-1929, prep. by James E. Primas. Wash., 1968. 14p.

Bolivia

3328. Texas, University, Library. Recent Bolivian acquisitions of the Latin American collection. Austin: 1962- . no.1- .

3329. U.S. National Archives. Records of Department of State relating to political relations between Bolivia and other states, prep. by Ralph E. Huss. Wash., 1970. 6p.

Brazil

3330. [Arizona, University, Library. Brazilian collection] College & research libraries news, no.5 (May 1970), 145.

Important collection of Brazilian materials acquired by Arizona, including full runs of periodicals, 1,000 volumes on Brazilian folklore, and legal works.

3331. Gillett, Theresa, and McIntyre, Helen. Catalog of Luso-Brazilian material in the University of New Mexico Libraries. Metuchen, N.J.: Scarecrow, 1970. 961p.

Lists 10,000 monographic and serial publications, in Portuguese and other languages.

3332. Illinois, University, Library. Brazilian serial publications in the University of Illinois Library. Urbana, 1965. 38*l.*

Includes record of holdings.

3333. Jackson, William V. American library resources for Brazilian studies. Madison, Wis., 1963. 44p.

3334. ———. Library guide for Brazilian studies. Pittsburgh: Univ. Book Centers, 1964. 197p.

Describes resources for Brazilian studies in major U.S. research collections; includes "union list of selected Brazilian periodicals in the humanities and social sciences," with holdings for 63 U.S. libraries.

3335. Texas, University, Library. Recent Brazilian acquisitions of the Latin American collection of the University of Texas Library. Austin, 1968. 89*l.*

Covers acquisitions, May 1963-March 1967.

3336. U.S. National Archives. Records of Department of State relating to political relations between United States and Brazil, 1910-1929, and between Brazil and other states, 1910-1929, prep. by Ernestine Cognasso. Wash., 1969. 11p.

Caribbean

3337. Boston Public Library. Bibliotheca Barbadiensis; a catalog of materials relating to Barbados, 1650-1860, in the Boston Public Library. Boston, 1968. 27p.

3338. Brown University, John Carter Brown Library. The British West Indies; an exhibition of books, maps and prints. Providence, R.I., 1961. 16*l.*

3339. Florida, University, Libraries. Caribbean acquisitions; materials acquired by the University of Florida, 1957- . Gainesville, 1959- . Annual.

Books, pamphlets, periodicals, and newspapers listed from West Indies, Bermuda, Colombia, Venezuela, Guianas, Central America, and Mexico.

3340. ———. Caribbean serial titles microfilmed at source, comp. by Ada S. Carbeau. Gainesville, 1963. 17*l.*

Includes some books.

3341. New York Public Library. Puerto Rico. N.Y., 1963. 11p.

Bibliography of books in Spanish and English.

3342. Texas, University, Library. Recent acquisitions for the Caribbean Islands (excluding Cuba) and Guyana, French Guiana and Surinam of the Latin American collection of the University of Texas Library. Austin, 1962-67- . no.1- .

3343. U.S. National Archives. Preliminary inventory of the records of the Dominican Customs Receivership, comp. by Kenneth W. Munden. Wash., 1962. 36p. (Preliminary inventories, no.148)

3344. ———. Preliminary inventory of the records of the President's Commission for Study and Review of Conditions in Haiti, comp. by Kathryn M. Murphy. Wash., 1965. 4p.

3345. ———. Preliminary inventory of the records of

the Puerto Rico Reconstruction Administration, comp. by Mary Jane Schmittou and Mario D. Fenyo. Wash., 1963. 27p. (Preliminary inventories, no.152)

3346. ———. Preliminary inventory of the records of the United States-Puerto Rico Commission on the Status of Puerto Rico, comp. by Charles E. South. Wash., 1968. 8p.

3347. ———. Records of Department of State relating to internal affairs of Haiti, 1910-29, prep. by James E. Primas. Wash., 1970. 11p.

Central America

3348. Benson, Nettie Lee. "The Arturo Taracena Flores Library." Library chronicle of the University of Texas, 7, no.4 (1964), 37-39.

Description of Guatemalan materials added to University of Texas Library.

3349. Canal Zone Library-Museum. Subject catalog of the special Panama collection of the Canal Zone Library-Museum. Boston: G. K. Hall, 1964. 381p.

Relates mainly to the history of the Isthmus of Panama and interoceanic transportation.

3350. Hansen, Ralph W. Francis Butler Loomis and the Panama crisis. Stanford, Calif.: Stanford Univ. Pr., 1965. 8p.

Essay based on exhibition of Loomis papers in Stanford University Library; Loomis, 1861-1948, was American diplomat and foreign trade adviser.

3351. Texas, University, Library. Recent acquisitions of books, etc., from Central America by the Latin American collection. Austin, 1962- . no.1- .

3352. U.S. National Archives. Preliminary inventory of the textual records of the Panama Canal, comp. by Richard W. Giroux. Wash., 1963. 36p. (Preliminary inventories, no.153)

3353. ———. Records of Department of State relating to internal affairs of Costa Rica, 1910-29, prep. by James E. Primas. Wash., 1967. 10p.

3354. ———. Records of Department of State relating to internal affairs of El Salvador, 1910-29, prep. by Ralph E. Huss. Wash., 1968. 11p.

3355. ———. Records of Department of State relating to internal affairs of Guatemala, 1910-29, prep. by Thomas A. Devan and James E. Primas. Wash., 1967. 14p.

3356. ———. Records of Department of State relating to political relations between United States and Central America, 1910-29, prep. by Frank S. Soriano. Wash., 1969. 13p.

3357. ———. Records of Department of State relating to political relations between United States and El Salvador, 1910-1929, and between El Salvador and other states, 1910-1929, prep. by Ralph E. Huss. Wash., 1969. 11p.

3358. ———. Records of Department of State relating to political relations between United States and Guatemala, and between Guatemala and other states, 1910-29, prep. by Frank S. Soriano. Wash., 1970. 13p.

Chile

3359. Texas, University, Library. Recent Chilean acquisitions of the Latin American collection of the University of Texas Library. Austin: The Library, 1962-64- . no.1- .

Colombia

3360. Queens College Library. Colombia: 1958-1968; a selective bibliography. Flushing, N.Y., 1969. 14*l.*

3361. ———. Materials for the study of the Colombian economy: 1964-1969. Flushing, N.Y., 1969. 11*l.*

3362. Texas, University, Library. Recent Colombian acquisitions of the Latin American collection of the University of Texas Library, 1962/67- . no.1- .Austin,

Cuba

3363. Florida, University, Libraries. Bibliografía Cubana complementos: 1937-1961, comp. by Fermin Peraza. Gainesville, 1966. 233p.

3364. Fort, Gilberto V. The Cuban revolution of Fidel Castro viewed from abroad; an annotated bibliography. Lawrence: Univ. of Kans. Libraries, 1969. 140p. (Univ. of Kans. publications, library series, no.34)

3365. Pittsburgh, University, Libraries. Cuban periodicals in Hillman Library, comp. by Eduardo Lozano. Pittsburgh, June 1970- . Quarterly revision.

3366. Texas, University, Library. Recent acquisitions

for Cuba of the Latin American collection of the University of Texas Library, 1962/67- . no.1- . Austin, 1968.

3367. U.S. Library of Congress, Hispanic Foundation. Cuba: a select list of reference and research tools. Wash., 1966. 11p.

In 3 parts: bibliographies, journals, newspapers.

3368. U.S. National Archives. Preliminary inventory of the records of the military government of Cuba, comp. by Margareth Jorgensen. Wash., 1962. 65p. (Preliminary archives, no.145)

3369. ———. Preliminary inventory of the records of the Provisional Government of Cuba, comp. by Roland Rieder and Charlotte M. Ashby. Wash., 1962. 28p. (Preliminary inventories, no.146)

Ecuador

3370. Texas, University, Library. Recent Ecuadorian acquisitions. Austin, 1970. 36p.

Covers 1962-68 acquisitions.

Mexico

3371. Arizona Pioneers' Historical Society. The Aguiar collection in the Arizona Pioneers' Historical Society, by Paul and Greta Ezell. San Diego, Calif.: San Diego State College Pr., 1964. 100p. (Social science monograph series, v.1, no.1)

Relates to Mexican states of Sinaloa and Sonora.

3372. California State College Library, Long Beach. Chicano bibliography; a selected list of books on the culture, history, and socioeconomic conditions of the Mexican American. Long Beach, 1970. 45p.

3373. ———, Los Angeles. A library guide to Mexican-American studies. Los Angeles, 1969. 14p.

3374. California, University, Bancroft Library. Mexico: ancient and modern, by Lawton Kennedy. Berkeley: Friends of the Bancroft Library, 1962. 95p.

Catalog of an exhibit depicting Mexican history from pre-Columbian to modern times.

3375. California, University, Libraries. Chicano bibliography, by Ben Garza. Davis, 1969. 51p.

Compilation based on holdings of University of California Library, Davis; includes book, periodical, and document references.

3376. ———. Chicano library program, by Miriam Sue Dudley. Los Angeles, 1970. 85p. (UCLA Library occasional papers, no.17)

Introduction to main reference works, p.37-68.

3377. Clagett, Helen L. "Heroes or traitors." Quarterly journal of the Library of Congress, 23 (1966), 290-301.

Items in Library of Congress Law Library relating to Mexican history.

3378. Cortés, Vicenta, and Kiemen, M. C. "Manuscripts concerning Mexico and Central America in the Library of Congress, Washington, D.C." Américas, 18 (1962), 255-96.

3379. Grothey, Mina Jane. Seventeenth century Mexican news-sheets, precursors of the newspaper: a description of the García Icazbalceta collection. Austin, 1969. 102p. (Master's thesis, Graduate School of Library Science, Univ. of Tex.)

In University of Texas Library.

3380. Liebman, Seymour B. "The abecedario and a checklist of Mexican inquisition documents at the Henry E. Huntington Library." Hispanic American historical review, 44 (1964), 554-67.

Describes 46 volumes of Mexican inquisition documents.

3381. Texas, University, Library. Catálogo de los manuscritos del archivo de don Valentín Gómez Farías, prep. by Pablo Max Ynsfrán. Mexico: Editorial Jus, 1968. 566p.

In University of Texas Library's Latin American collection; consists of 4,600 items relating to political revolution in Mexico, 1770-1843.

3382. ———, Latin American Collection. El cinco de mayo; an exhibit commemorating the one hundredth anniversary of the victory over the French by the Mexican army led by Ignacio Zaragoza, May 5, 1862. Austin, 1962. 15p.

3383. ———. The Mariano Riva Palacio archives; a guide, by Jack Autrey Dabbs. Mexico: Editorial Jus, 1967-68. 2v.

Collection of 10,300 items dealing mainly with Mexican political history, 1716-1852; in Texas Library.

3384. ———. Recent Mexican acquisitions of the Latin American collection of the University of Texas Library. Austin, 1962-64- . no.1- .

3385. U.S. National Archives. Preliminary inventory of

records of United States and Mexican Claims Commissions, comp. by George S. Ulibarri. Wash., 1962. 51p. (Preliminary inventories, no.136)

3386. ———. Preliminary inventory of the records of the Military Government of Veracruz, comp. by Kenneth W. Munden. Wash., 1962. 51p. (Preliminary inventories, no.138)

3387. Washington State University Library. Three centuries of Mexican documents; a partial calendar of the Regla papers, by Jacquelyn M. Melcher Gaines. Pullman: Friends of the Wash. State Univ. Library, 1963. 124p. (Reprinted from Wash. State Univ. research studies, v.30, no.3-4; v.31, no.1-3)

Peru

3388. Indiana University, Lilly Library. Peruvian manuscripts in the Lilly Library, by Juan Friede. Bloomington, 1968. 38p. (Indiana University bookman, no.9, April 1968)

3389. Texas, University, Library. Recent Peruvian acquisitions of the Latin American collection of the University of Texas Library. Austin, 1962-64- . no.1- .

3390. U.S. National Archives. Records of Department of State relating to internal affairs of Peru, 1910-29, prep. by Frank S. Soriano. Wash., 1969. 10p.

3391. ———. Records of Department of State relating to political relations between Peru and other states, 1910-29, prep. by Frank S. Soriano. Wash., 1970. 7p.

Uruguay

3392. Texas, University, Library. Recent acquisitions for Uruguay of the Latin American collection of the University of Texas Library. Austin, 1962-67- . no.1- .

Venezuela

3393. Texas, University, Library. Recent Venezuelan acquisitions of the Latin American collection. Austin, 1962-64- .

OCEANIA AND POLAR REGIONS

3394. Bishop Museum Library. Dictionary catalog of the Library of the Bernice P. Bishop Museum (Honolulu). Boston: G. K. Hall, 1964. 9v. Supplements. 1967-69. 2v.

Library devoted entirely to study of Pacific region: archaeology, ethnology, linguistics, general and natural history.

3395. Brown University, John Carter Brown Library. The exploration of Antarctica: an exhibition of books and maps based on the Swan collection given to the John Carter Brown Library. Providence, R.I., 1967. 17*l.*

3396. Cammack, Floyd M., and Saito, Shiro. Pacific island bibliography. N.Y.: Scarecrow, 1962. 421p.

Lists 1,730 items in University of Hawaii Library's Pacific collection.

3397. Curvey, Mary F., and Johnson, Robert E. "A bibliography of Sir John Richardson (1787-1865)—printed books." Journal of the Society for the Bibliography of Natural History, 5 (1969), 202-17.

Locates works by and about Richardson, Arctic explorer, chiefly in University of Illinois Library.

3398. Dartmouth College Library. Dictionary catalog of the Stefansson collection on the Polar Regions in the Dartmouth College Library. Boston: G. K. Hall, 1967. 8v.

3399. Nef, Evelyn S. "Stefansson collection, Dartmouth College Library." Special Libraries Association, Geography and Map Division bulletin, no.56 (June 1964), 17-21.

3400. Pennsylvania State University Libraries. Australiana in the Pennsylvania State University Libraries, comp. by Bruce Sutherland. University Park, 1969. 391p. (Bibliographical series, no.1)

3401. U.S. Dept. of Defense. Arctic bibliography, ed. by Marie Tremaine. Wash.: Govt. Print. Off., 1953- . v.1- . Annual.

Locates copies in libraries.

3402. U.S. Dept. of State. Acquisitions list of Antarctic cartographic materials. Wash., March 1961- . no.1- .

Lists maps, charts, aerial photography, geodetic data, atlases and gazetteers found in Library of Congress and other federal agencies.

3403. U.S. Library of Congress, Science and Technology Division. Antarctic bibliography, ed. by George A. Doumani. Wash.: Govt. Print. Off., 1965- . v.1- .

Compiled from Library of Congress collections and other sources.

3404. U.S. National Archives. United States scientific

geographical exploration of the Pacific Basin, 1783-1899. Wash., 1961. 26p. (National Archives publication, no.62-2)

Catalog of an exhibition.

WORLD WAR I

3405. New York Public Library. Subject catalog of the World War I collection. Boston: G. K. Hall, 1961. 4v.

Comprehensive collection of various types of material, in many languages, and on all aspects of field.

3406. Newman, John. "The camp dodger: a military newspaper of the First World War." Books at Iowa, 10 (April 1969), 24-30.

Record of complete file in University of Iowa Libraries.

3407. U.S. National Archives. Preliminary inventory of records relating to United States claims against the Central Powers, comp. by George S. Ulibarri and Francis J. Heppner. Wash., 1962. 22p. (Preliminary inventories, no.143)

3408. ———. Preliminary inventory of the cartographic records of the American Expeditionary Forces, 1917-21, comp. by Franklin W. Burch. Wash., 1966. 70p. (Preliminary inventories, no. 165)

Contains 540 entries recording 24,000 maps.

3409. ———. Preliminary inventory of the records of the Committee on Public Information, 1917-19, comp. by Janet Weinert. Wash., 1962. 28p.

WORLD WAR II

3410. American Historical Association, Committee for the Study of War Documents. Guides to German records microfilmed at Alexandria, Va. Wash.: National Archives, National Archives and Records Service, 1958- . pt.1- . (In progress)

Microfilms are deposited in the National Archives; relate to all aspects of Nazi affairs.

3411. Arndt, Karl J. R. Microfilm guide and index to the Library of Congress collection of German prisoners of war camp papers published in the United States of North America from 1943 to 1946. Worcester? Mass., 1965. 63*l.*

3412. Gotlieb, Howard B. "Documenting the Third Reich: the Stutz collection of Nazi manuscripts." Yale University Library gazette, 37 (1963), 109-17.

In Yale Library.

3413. Michigan, University, Library. Checklist of selected German pamphlets and booklets of the Weimar and Nazi period in the University of Michigan Library, prep. by Herbert P. Rothfeder. Ann Arbor, 1961. 214*l.*

3414. Morris, Richard B. "A master spy's espionage collection." Columbia Library columns, 15 (Nov. 1965), 3-8.

Papers of Major General William H. ("Wild Bill") Donovan, of World War II fame, received by Columbia University Library.

3415. Stanford University, Hoover Institution. NSDAP Hauptarchiv: guide to the Hoover Institution microfilm collection, comp. by Grete Heinz and Agnes F. Peterson. Stanford, Calif.: 1964. 175p. (Bibliographical series, no.17)

Principally concerned with Nazi Party history and organization.

3416. U.S. Dept. of State, Historical Office. A catalog of files and microfilms of the German Foreign Ministry archives, 1920-1945, comp. by George O. Kent. Stanford, Calif.: Hoover Institution, 1962- . v.1- . (In progress)

Microcopies of listed items deposited in National Archives and Public Record Office, London.

3417. U.S. National Archives. Preliminary inventory of the field records of the Solid Fuels Administration for War, comp. by Forrest R. Holdcamper. Wash., 1966. 20p.

3418. ———. Preliminary inventory of the records of the American Commission for the Protection and Salvage of Artistic and Historic Movements in War Areas, comp. by H. Stephen Helton and Philip C. Brooks. Wash., 1965. 6p.

3419. ———. Preliminary inventory of the textual records of the United States Military Tribunals, Nuernberg, comp. by Aloha P. Broadwater. Wash., 1966. 38p.

3420. ———. Supplement to preliminary inventory No. 21, records of the United States Counsel for the Prosecution of Axis Criminality, comp. by Garry D. Ryan. Wash., 1966. 8p.

3421. Washington, University, Phonoarchive. History in sound; a descriptive listing of the KIRO-CBS collection of broadcasts of the World War II years and after, in the Phonoarchive of the University of Washington, by Milo Ryan. Seattle: Univ. of Wash. Pr., 1963. 617p.

Index